THE GREAT WAR'S SPORTING CASUALTIES

THE GREAT WAR'S SPORTING CASUALTIES

by

JAMES HOLDER

YOUCAXTON PUBLICATIONS
OXFORD & SHREWSBURY

Contents

Preface   xv
Introduction   xvii
Acknowledgements   xxiii

CHAPTER 1
England Footballers
1.1 James Conlin (1881-1917)   1
1.2 Edwin Latheron (1887-1917)   2
1.3 Evelyn Lintott (1883-1916)   3

CHAPTER 2
Scotland Footballers
2.1 Robert Christie (1865-1918)   6
2.3 James Speirs (1886-1917)   9

CHAPTER 3
Wales Footballers
3.1 Bobby Atherton (1876-1917)   11
3.2 Frederick Griffiths (1873-1917)   13
3.3 William Jones (1876-1918)   14
3.4 Leigh Roose (1877-1916)   15

CHAPTER 4
Ireland Footballers
4.1 Barney Donaghy (1882-1916)   18
4.2 Richard Moore (1867-1918)   19
4.3 Harold Sloan (1882-1917)   21
4.4 Edward Turner (1877-1917)   22

CHAPTER 5
England Cricketers
5.1 Colin Blythe (1879-1917)   24
5.2 Major Booth (1886-1916)   26
5.3 Kenneth Hutchings (1882-1916)   28
5.4 Leonard Moon (1878-1916)   30

CHAPTER 6
Australia Cricketer
6.1 Albert "Tibby" Cotter (1883-1917)   32

CHAPTER 7
South Africa Cricketers
7.1 Frederick Cook (1870-1915)   35
7.2 Reginald Hands (1888-1918)   36
7.3 Eric Balfour "Bill" Lundie (1888-1917)   38
7.4 Claude Newberry (1889-1916)   39
7.5 Arthur Edward Ochse (1870-1918)   40
7.6 Reggie Schwarz (1875-1918)   42
7.7 Gordon White (1882-1918)   45

CHAPTER 8
England Rugby Players

8.1 Harry Alexander (1879-1915)   47
8.2 Henry Berry (1883-1915)   48
8.3 Henry Brougham (1888-1923)   50
8.4 Arthur Dingle (1891-1915)   51
8.5 George Dobbs (1884-1917)   52
8.6 Leonard Haigh (1880-1916)   53
8.7 Reginald Hands (1888-1918)   55
8.8 Arthur Harrison (1886-1918)   56
8.9 Harold Hodges (1886-1918)   57
8.10 Rupert Inglis (1863-1916)   59
8.11 Percy "Toggie" Kendall (1878-1915)   61
8.12 John King (1883-1916)   62
8.13 Ronald Lagden (1889-1915)   63
8.14 Douglas "Danny" Lambert (1883-1915)   64
8.15 Alfred Maynard (1894-1916)   66
8.16 Edgar Mobbs (1882-1917)   68
8.17 William "Billy" Nanson (1880-1915)   70
8.18 Francis Oakeley (1891-1914)   71
8.19 Robert Pillman (1893-1916)   72
8.20 Ronald Poulter-Palmer (1889-1915)   73
8.21 John Raphael (1882-1917)   75
8.22 Reggie Schwarz (1875-1918)   77
8.23 Lancelot Andrew Noel Slocock (1886-1916)   79
8.24 Francis Tarr (1887-1915)   80
8.25 Alexander Todd (1873-1915)   81
8.26 James "Bungy" Watson (1890-1914)   83
8.27 Arthur Wilson (1886-1917)   85
8.28 Charles Wilson (1871-1914)   86

CHAPTER 9
Ireland Rugby Players

9.1 William Beatty (1888-1919)   88
9.2 Jasper Brett (1895-1917)   89
9.3 Robert Burgess (1890-1915)   90
9.4 Ernest Deane (1887-1915)   91
9.5 William Edwards (1887-1917)   92
9.6 William Hallaran (1861-1917)   93
9.7 Basil Maclear (1881-1915)   94
9.8 George McAllan (1879-1918)   96
9.9 Vincent McNamara (1891-1915)   97
9.10 Robertson Stewart " Robbie" Smyth (1879-1916)   98
9.11 Albert Stewart (1889-1917)   100
9.12 Alfred Taylor (1889-1917)   101

CHAPTER 10
Scotland Rugby Players

10.1 Cecil Abercrombie (1886-1916)   103
10.2 David Bain (1891-1915)   105
10.3 David Bedell-Sivright (1880-1915)   106
10.4 Patrick Blair (1891-1915)   109
10.5 John Argentine Campbell (1877-1917)   110
10.6 William "Bill" Campbell Church (1884-1915)   111

10.7 Walter Michael "Mike" Dickson (1884-1915)   112
10.8 John Henry "Harry" Dods (1875-1915)   114
10.9 Walter Forrest (1880-1917)   115
10.10 Rowland Fraser (1890-1916)   116
10.11 Roland Elphinstone Gordon (1893-1918)   117
10.12 James Young Henderson (1891-1917)   118
10.13 Dave Howie (1888-1916)   120
10.14 James Huggan (1888-1914)   121
10.15 William Hutchison (1889-1918)   122
10.16 George Lamond (1878-1918)   123
10.17 Eric Milroy (1887-1916)   125
10.18 Tommy Nelson (1876-1917)   126
10.19 James Pearson (1889-1915)   127
10.20 Lewis Robertson (1883-1914)   129
10.21 Andrew Ross (1879-1916)   130
10.22 James Ross (1880-1914)   132
10.23 Ronald Simson (1890-1914)   133
10.24 Stephen Steyn (1889-1917)   134
10.25 Walter "Wattie" Sutherland (1890-1918)   135
10.26 Fred Turner (1888-1915)   137
10.27 Albert Wade (1884-1917)   139
10.28 Willie Wallace (1892-1915)   140
10.29 George Will (1892-1917)   141
10.30 John Wilson (1884-1916)   142
10.31 Eric Young (1892-1915)   144

CHAPTER 11
Wales Rugby Players
11.1 Billy Geen (1891-1915)   145
11.2 Brinley "Bryn" Lewis (1891-1917)   146
11.3 Hopkin Maddock (1881-1921)   148
11.4 Fred Perrett (1891-1918)   149
11.5 Lou Phillips (1878-1916)   150
11.6 Charlie Pritchard (1882-1916)   152
11.7 Charles Taylor (1863-1915)   153
11.8 Edward John Richard "Dick" Thomas (1883-1916)   155
11.9 Horace Wyndham Thomas (1890-1916)   156
11.10 Phil Waller (1889-1917)   157
11.11 David Watts (1886-1916)   159
11.12 Dai Westacott (1882-1917)   160
11.13 John Lewis "Johnnie" Williams (1882-1916)   161
11.14 Richard Davies Garnons Williams (1856-1915)   163

CHAPTER 12
Lions Rugby Players
12.1 Charlie Adamson (1875-1918)   166
12.2 Sidney Crowther (1874-1914)   167
12.3 Ronald "Ron" Rogers (1883-1915)   168

CHAPTER 13
Australia Rugby Players
13.1 Harold George (1887-1915)   170
13.2 Bryan Hughes (1887-1918)   172
13.3 Hubert Jones (1888-1916)   173

13.4 Edward Larkin (1880-1915)   174
13.5 George Pugh (1890-1916)   175
13.6 Blair Swannell (1875-1915)   176
13.7 William Tasker (1891-1918)   178
13.8 Fred Thompson (1890-1915)   179
13.9 Arthur "Jack" Verge (1880-1915)   180
13.10 Clarrie Wallach (1889-1918)   181

CHAPTER 14
New Zealand Rugby Players

14.1 Jim Baird (1893-1917)   184
14.2 Bobby Black (1893-1916)   185
14.3 Henry Dewar (1883-1915)   186
14.4 Ernie Dodd (1880-1918)   187
14.5 Albert "Doolan" Downing (1886-1915)   188
14.6 David Gallaher (1873-1917)   190
14.7 Eric Harper (1877-1918)   192
14.8 Jim McNeece (1885-1917)   193
14.9 Alexander James "Jimmy" Ridland (1882-1918)   195
14.10 George Sellars (1886-1917)   196
14.11 Reg Taylor (1889-1917)   197
14.12 Hubert Turtill (1880-1918)   198

CHAPTER 15
South Africa Rugby Players

15.1 Adam Burdett (1882-1918)   201
15.2 Septimus "Sep" Heyns Ledger (1889-1917)   202
15.3 Tobias "Toby" Moll (1890-1916)   203
15.4 Jan "Jacky" Morkel (1890-1916)   204
15.5 Gerald Thompson (1886-1916)   205

CHAPTER 16
France Rugby Players

16.1 Joe Anduran (1882-1914)   207
16.2 Rene Boudreaux (1880-1915)   208
16.3 Maurice Boyau (1888-1918)   209
16.4 Marcel Burgun (1890-1916)   210
16.5 Albert Chatau (1893-1924)   212
16.6 Jean-Jacques Conilh de Beyssac (1890-1918)   212
16.7 Paul Decamps (1884-1915)   213
16.8 Julien Dufau (1888-1916)   214
16.9 Paul Dupre (1888-1916)   215
16.10 Albert Eutropius (1888-1915)   216
16.11 Marc Giacardy (1881-1917)   216
16.12 Pierre Guillemin (1887-1915)   217
16.13 Maurice Hedembaigt (1891-1918)   218
16.14 Emmanuel Iguiniz (1889-1914)   219
16.15 Daniel Ihingoue (1889-1917)   219
16.16 Henri Isaac (1883-1917)   220
16.17 Henri Lacassagne (1883-1918)   220

16.18 Gaston Lane (1883-1914)   222
16.19 Leon Larribau (1889-1916)   223
16.20 Marcel Legrain (1890-1915)   224
16.21 Albert Mayssonnie (1884-1914)   225
16.22 Francois Poeydebasque (1891-1914)   226

CHAPTER 17
USA Rugby Player
17.1 Frank Gard (1892-1918)   227

CHAPTER 18
British Olympians
18.1 Gordon Alexander (1885-1917)   229
18.2 Gerard Rupert Lawrence "Laurie" Anderson (1889-1914)   230
18.3 William Anderson (?-1915)   231
18.4 Henry Ashington (1891-1917)   232
18.5 Isaac Bentham (1886-1917)   233
18.6 Henry Brougham (1888-1923)   233
18.7 Edmond Bury (1884-1915)   234
18.8 George Butterfield (1879-1917)   235
18.9 Oswald Carver (1887-1915)   236
18.10 Ralph Chalmers (1891-1915)   238
18.11 Noel Chavasse (1884-1917)   238
18.12 Geoffrey Coles (1871-1916)   241
18.13 Percy Courtman (1888-1917)   241
18.14 Harry Crank (1889-1917)   243
18.15 Robert Davies (1876-1916)   244
18.16 Joseph Dines (1886-1918)   245
18.17 Hugh Durant (1877-1916)   246
18.18 George Fairbairn (1888-1915)   247
18.19 Alfred Flaxman (1879-1916)   248
18.20 Herbert Henry "Bert" Gayler (1881-1917)   249
18.21 Thomas Gillespie (1892-1914)   250
18.22 Henry Goldsmith (1885-1915)   251
18.23 Wyndham Halswelle (1882-1915)   252
18.24 George Hawkins (1883-1917)   254
18.25 Harold Hawkins (1886-1917)   255
18.26 George Hutson (1889-1914)   256
18.27 Frederick Kelly (1881-1916)   257
18.28 Paul Kenna (1862-1915)   259
18.29 Alister Kirby (1886-1917)   260
18.30 Frederick Kitching (1886-1918)   261
18.31 Ivan Laing (1885-1917)   262
18.32 Henry Leeke (1879-1915)   264
18.33 Henry Macintosh (1892-1918)   265
18.34 Duncan Mackinnon (1887-1917)   266
18.35 Gilchrist Maclagan (1879-1915)   267
18.36 Edward Nash (1888-1915)   268

18.37 Harcourt Ommundsen (1878-1915) — 270
18.38 Alan Patterson (1886-1916) — 271
18.39 William Philo (1882-1916) — 272
18.40 Kenneth Powell (1885-1915) — 273
18.41 Reggie Pridmore (1886-1918) — 274
18.42 Thomas Raddall (1876-1918) — 276
18.43 John Robinson (1885-1916) — 277
18.44 Patrick Roche (1886-1917) — 278
18.45 Ronald Sanderson (1876-1918) — 279
18.46 Robert Somers-Smith (1887-1916) — 280
18.47 Charles Vigurs (1888-1917) — 282
18.48 Arthur Wilde (1883-1916) — 283
18.49 Edward Williams (1888-1915) — 284
18.50 Arthur Wilson (1886-1917) — 285
18.51 Harold Wilson (1885-1916) — 285
18.52 Herbert Wilson (1875-1917) — 286
18.53 Richard Yorke (1885-1914) — 287

CHAPTER 19
Commonwealth Olympians

19.1 Australia — 289
19.1.1 Cecil Healy (1881-1918) — 289
19.1.2 Keith Heritage (1882-1916) — 291
19.1.3 Claude Ross (1893-1917) — 293
19.2 Canada — 294
19.2.1 Alex Decoteau (1887-1917) — 294
19.2.2 Jimmy Duffy (1890-1915) — 295
19.2.3 Percival Molson (1880-1917) — 296
19.2.4 Robert "Bobby" Powell (1881-1917) — 298
19.2.5 Geoffrey Taylor (1890-1915) — 299
19.3 New Zealand — 300
19.3.1 Albert Rowland (1885-1918) — 300
19.3.2 Anthony "Tony" Wilding (1883-1915) — 301
19.4 South Africa — 303
19.4.1 Ernest Keeley (1890-1918) — 303

CHAPTER 20
Other Olympians

20.1.1 Karl Braunsteiner (1891-1916) — 305
20.1.2 Adolf Kofler (1892-1915) — 306
20.1.3 Leopold Mayer (?-1914) — 306
20.1.4 Robert Merz (1887-1914) — 307
20.1.5 Rudolf Watzl (1882-1915) — 308
20.2 Belgium — 309
20.2.1 Herman Donners (1888-1915) — 309
20.2.2 Victor Willems (1877-1917 or 1918) — 310
20.3 Finland — 311
20.3.1 Juho Halme (1888-1918) — 311
20.4 France — 312
20.4.1 Louis Bach (1883-1914) — 312
20.4.2 Renon Boissiere (1882-1915) — 313
20.4.3 Henri Bonnefoy (1887-1914) — 313
20.4.4 Jean Bouin (1888-1914) — 314

20.4.5 Joseph Caulle (1885-1915) 316
20.4.6 Louis de Champsavin (1867-1916) 316
20.4.7 Georges de la Neziere (1878-1914) 317
20.4.8 Bertrand, Count de Lesseps (1875-1918) 318
20.4.9 Ismael de Lesseps (1871-1915) 319
20.4.10 Jean de Mas Latrie (1879-1914) 319
20.4.11 Felix Debax (1864-1914) 320
20.4.12 Charles Devendeville (1882-1914) 321
20.4.13 Rene Fenouilliere (1882-1916) 322
20.4.14 Leon Flameng (1877-1917) 323
20.4.15 Albert Jenicot (1885-1916) 324
20.4.16 Octave Lapize (1887-1917) 325
20.4.17 Georges Lutz (1884-1915) 326
20.4.18 Alphonse Meignant (1882-1914) 326
20.4.19 Alfred Motte (1887-1918) 327
20.4.20 Leon Ponscarme (1879-1916) 328
20.4.21 Joseph Racine (1891-1914) 328
20.4.22 Maurice Raoul-Duval (1866-1916) 329
20.4.23 Maurice Salomez (1880-1916) 330
20.4.24 Andre Six (?-1914) 331
20.4.25 Pierre Six (1888-1916) 332
20.4.26 Michel Soalhat (1875-1915) 332
20.4.27 Justin Vialaret (1883-1916) 333
20.4.28 Edmond Wallace (1876-1915) 334
20.5 Germany 335
20.5.1 Fritz Bartholomae (1886-1915) 335
20.5.2 Hermann Bosch (1891-1916) 335
20.5.3 Johannes "Hanns" Braun (1886-1918) 336
20.5.4 Kurt Bretting (1892-1918) 338
20.5.5 Wilhelm Brulle (1891-1917) 338
20.5.6 Heinrich Burkowitz (1892-1918) 339
20.5.7 Carl Heinrich Gossler (1885-1914) 340
20.5.8 Max Hermann (1885-1915) 341
20.5.9 Walther Jesinghaus (1887-1918) 342
20.5.10 Erich Lehmann (1890-1918) 343
20.5.11 Wilhelm Lutzow (1892-1916) 343
20.5.12 Georg Mickler (1892-1915) 344
20.5.13 Jakob "Jacques" Person (1889-1915) 345
20.5.14 Hermann Plaskuda (1879-1918) 346
20.5.15 Josef Rieder (1893-1916) 347
20.5.16 Heinrich Schneidereit (1884-1915) 347
20.5.17 Eberhard Sorge (1892-1918) 348
20.5.18 Alfred Staats (1891-1915) 349
20.5.19 Waldemar Tietgens (1879-1917) 350
20.5.20 Hermann von Bonninghausen (1888-1919) 350
20.5.21 Bernhard von Gaza (1881-1917) 351
20.5.22 Eduard von Lutcken (1882-1914) 352
20.5.23 Friedrich Carl, Prince of Prussia (1893-1917) 352
20.6 Haiti 354
20.6.1 Andre Corvington (1877-1918) 354
20.7 Hungary 355
20.7.1 Bela Bekassy (1875-1916) 355
20.7.2 Oszkar Demjan (1891-1914) 356
20.7.3 Lajos Gonczy (1881-1915) 356

20.7.4 Istvan Mudin (1881-1918)   357
20.7.5 Arpad Pedery (1891-1914)   358
20.7.6 Jeno Szantay (1881-1914)   359
20.7.7 Amon Ritter von Gregurich (1867-1915)   360
20.7.8 Bela von Las-Torres (1890-1915)   360
20.7.9 Bela Zulawszky (1869-1914)   361
20.8 Russia   362
20.8.1 Andrey Akimov (1888-1916)   362
20.8.2 Georg Baumann (1892-1915?)   363
20.8.3 Nikolay Kynin (1890-1916)   364
20.8.4 Feliks Leparsky (1875-1917)   364
20.8.5 Grigory Nikitin (1890-1917)   365
20.9 Serbia   366
20.9.1 Dragutin Tomasevic (1891-1915)   366
20.10 United States of America   367
20.10.1 William Lyshon (1887-1918)   367
20.10.2 Arthur Wear (1880-1918)   368

CHAPTER 21

Other Notable Sportsmen

21.1 Donald Bell (1890-1916)   369
21.2 Norman Callaway (1896-1917)   371
21.3 A. E. J. "James" Collins (1885-1914)   372
21.4 Francois Faber (1887-1915)   373
21.5 John "Jack" Harrison (1890-1917)   375
21.6 Frank McGee (1882-1916)   376
21.7 Walter Tull (1888-1918)   377
21.8 Sandy Turnbull (1884-1917)   379
21.9 Bernard Vann (1887-1918)   381

APPENDIX 1

A Summary of the Battles and Campaigns
at which the Casualties Occurred

The Battle of the Marne   385
First Battle of the Aisne   386
First Battle of Ypres   386
The Mesopotamia Campaign   387
Battle of Limanowa   388
Battle of Givenchy   389
Battle of Dogger Bank   390
The Sinai and Palestine Campaign   390
Battle of Neuve Chapelle   392
Second Battle of Ypres   393
The Gallipoli Campaign   394
Battle of Aubers Ridge   395
Battle of Loos   395
The Macedonian Front   396
The Battle of Verdun   397

Battle of Jutland   398
The Battle of the Somme   399
Battle of Arras   401
Battle of Vemy Ridge   402
Second Battle of Bullecourt   402
Battle of Messines   403
The Third Battle of Ypres   404
The Ludendorff Offensive   405
The Second Battle of the Marne   407
Battle of Amiens   408
The Second Battle of the Somme   408

APPENDIX 2
The Olympic Events Competed in
by the Olympians who died in the Great War
411

APPENDIX 3
The Football Internationals played in
by British and Irish Footballers who died in the Great War
427

APPENDIX 4
The Cricket Test Matches played in
by the Test Cricketers who died in the Great War
431

APPENDIX 5
The Rugby Internationals played in
by those who died in the Great War
439

APPENDIX 6
The dates on which the casualties occurred (where known)
465

BIBLIOGRAPHY
Archives and Databases   473
Articles and Newsapapers   473
Books   473
Websites   476

Preface

"There was a time for all things in the world. There was a time for games, there was a time for business and there was a time for domestic life. There was a time for everything, but there is only time for one thing now, and that thing is war. If the cricketer had a straight bat, let him look along the barrel of a rifle. If a footballer had a strength of limb, let them serve and march in the field of battle."

So wrote Sir Arthur Conan Doyle, the creator of Sherlock Holmes, on 6th September 1914, less than six weeks after the start of the Great War on 28th July 1914 and less than five weeks after Britain declared war on Germany on 4th August 1914; perhaps Conan Doyle had used cricket and football in his stirring words as he had played football as an amateur in goal for Portsmouth and a handful of games of first-class cricket for the MCC.

Over the four years, three months and fourteen days of the Great War, many a cricketer looked along the barrel of a rifle and many a footballer served and marched in the field of battle; and many lost their lives doing so.

Introduction

Towards the end of the 19th century, regular sporting fixtures between clubs and countries were taking place. In 1871, England and Scotland played against each other in the first ever rugby international and, a year later, in their first football match against each other. In 1877, England and Australia played the first cricket Test match and, by 1889, South Africa had joined the ranks of Test-playing countries. In 1883, England, Wales, Scotland and Ireland had their first Home Nations Championships at both rugby and football and, in 1910, the French rugby team joined the Home Nations to take part in the Five Nations Championship.

The first modern Olympics had also taken place before the end of the 19th century, in 1896 and, by the time war had been declared in 1914, six Olympic Games, including the Intercalated Games in 1906, had been staged.

When the Great War broke out, there were approximately 4,500 professional footballers in the United Kingdom and it is estimated that 2,000 of them had joined the military services by the end of the War. The Great War claimed the lives of 264 men who had played football for clubs playing in the English leagues or in the Scottish leagues and the lives of 12 who had represented either England, Scotland, Wales or Ireland in the Home Nations Championships; a 13th international footballer, who had played for Ireland in a friendly, also died in the War.

Of the many cricketers who lost their lives in the Great War, 242 had played first-class cricket and 11 were Test cricketers; a 12th Test cricketer, who was wounded in the War, died in France from the Spanish flu epidemic only seven days after the Armistice ending the War was signed on 11th November 1918.

By comparison, rugby was to suffer much worse – 89 international players from England, Wales, Scotland and Ireland, 22 from France and 27 from Australia, New Zealand and South Africa died in the War. Of the 1,010 rugby internationals who made their international debuts between the turn of the century and the outbreak of war, 125 died, whereas, in the case of cricket, of the 124 cricketers who made their Test debuts over the same period, only 10 died and, in the case of football, of the 418 footballers who made their debuts for England, Wales, Scotland or Ireland over the same period, only 10 died.

One explanation for rugby being affected more than football and cricket is that a significantly higher proportion of rugby internationals were privately educated and therefore more likely to serve as officers, who would have led from the front; however, this may explain the disparity between football and rugby but less so the disparity between rugby and cricket.

Olympians fared no better; 53 Olympians who had represented Great Britain in the Olympics died and another 87 Olympians from 14 other countries also lost their lives. With London having hosted the 1908 Olympics and with the 1912 Olympics having been hosted in neutral Sweden, it should not perhaps come as a surprise that Great Britain lost more Olympians in the War than any other country; however, had Rome hosted the 1908 Olympics as would have been the case but for the volcanic eruption at Vesuvius in 1906, it would undoubtedly have been a different story in terms of the number of British Olympians who died in the War.

Included as Olympians are those who competed in the Intercalated Games in 1906, commemorating the 10th anniversary of the first Modern Olympic Games. Although the International Olympic Committee no longer officially recognises the 1906

Games, they were, with 854 athletes from 20 countries taking part, better attended than the 1904 Games in St Louis where 651 athletes from 15 countries took part – of the 651 participants at the 1904 Games, 583 were representing North American countries; there was therefore a much more international flavour to the 1906 Games than there was to the 1904 Games.

Many of those who died in the Great War had played sport together or against each other. Three of those in the British boat which won the gold medal in the coxed eights at the 1908 Olympics died and two of the four in the coxless fours which won the gold medal for Great Britain at the same Olympics also died. All four Germans who ran in the 4 x 400 metres relay event at the 1912 Olympics were killed in the War. Ten of the Scottish XV who played in the Home Nations Championship match against Wales in 1913 and 14 out of the 30 who played in the game between Scotland and France that year died in the War. 26 of the rugby internationals who died in the War had been to Oxford or Cambridge University and, of those 26, nine took part in the Varsity match of 1911 and nine took part in the Varsity match of 1912.

A number of those who died in the War were, or had been, the best at their sport. 12 of those who died in the War had captained their countries at rugby and, amongst the Olympians who died are 61 who, between them, won 22 gold medals, 25 silver medals and 35 bronze medals; one of the Olympic medallists to be killed in the War was also one of the two winners of the Tour de France to be killed in the War and another Olympic medallist to be killed in the War was also a four-times Wimbledon champion.

The details of the war experiences of those who died vary. In the case of some of those who died, eyewitness accounts provide graphic details of the circumstances which led to the loss of life whilst, in other cases, it is merely recorded that they died or were killed in action; not surprisingly, with the Russian Revolution taking place as Russia ended its participation in the War, little is recorded about the Russian Olympians who lost their lives. The records are sufficient to show though that not only were they all talented sportsmen and able to put their skills as sportsmen to greater use but also courageous in war – three Victoria Crosses and 15 Military Crosses were awarded for deeds carried out in the War by international sportsmen who died in the War.

In the case of some of those listed, the cause of death was not as a direct result of enemy action; some died through illness whilst on active duty and two died from the Spanish flu epidemic, an epidemic that took between 50 million and 100 million lives in 1918 and 1919, making it much deadlier than the War itself, which claimed 17 million lives and 20 million wounded; in each such case though, the illness was picked up either during the War or whilst recovering from war wounds. It could be argued that, in such cases, those that died through illness should not be included in this book but they are because they contracted the illness which caused their deaths whilst on active service in the War. Others have not been included because the cause of death was not related to the War; by way of example, the Scottish athlete, Douglas McNicol, who was the AAA mile champion in 1911, died in October 1914 after having joined up but, because he died from pneumonia before he had been posted abroad, he is not included; nor too is Tom Gracie, who was joint top scorer in the Scottish league in the 1913/14 season, as he died from leukemia in Glasgow in October 1915, after having enlisted but before seeing action in the War.

There are also included the names of nine sportsmen who died after the War ended when the Armistice was signed; in each case though, the cause of death is attributable to wounds received during the War, hence their inclusion.

In total there are listed in this book over 300 sportsmen who represented their country at sport and who died in the Great War or died as a result of wounds suffered during the War; in addition there are nine other sportsmen who are listed and, although they did not represent their country at sport, they did achieve something extraordinary either in sport or in war.

All of them should be remembered for their achievements and the sacrifices they made.

Acknowledgements

Whilst discussing my first book, Sport's Great All-Rounders, with a journalist, I commented upon some of those included in the book having had not only distinguished sporting careers but also distinguished war careers; during a subsequent conversation with a good friend, who admitted to having less interest in sport than in history and wars, it was suggested to me that I combine the two.

It was these discussions that inspired me to produce this book, in recognition of the achievements of international sportsmen who also served, and lost their lives serving, their countries in the Great War. I am therefore indebted to, and take this opportunity to acknowledge and thank, Adam Care of the Cambridge News and Piers Marmion.

Lastly, this book could not have been written without the sacrifices made by the numerous sportsmen who fought for their countries in the Great War. It is to them and to the families they left behind, who suffered most their loss, that this book is dedicated.

CHAPTER 1
ENGLAND FOOTBALLERS

1.1 James Conlin (1881-1917)
born in Consett, County Durham

Conlin played on the left wing, playing his first games for the Scottish clubs Falkirk and Albion Rovers, before moving to Bradford City in 1904. Conlin spent two years with Bradford City for whom he played 61 games and scored five goals and whilst with Bradford, made his only appearance for England, in 1906, in a 2-1 defeat against Scotland.

Just a few months after his appearance for England, Manchester City paid £1,000 for Conlin, making him only the second footballer to be transferred for this sum. Conlin spent five years with Manchester City, playing 161 games and scoring 28 goals for them.

After his time at Manchester City, Conlin then spent one year with Birmingham City before moving to Airdrieonians and then on to Broxburn United.

Conlin retired from football just before the outbreak of the War; when war broke out, he enlisted with the Highland Light Infantry and was transferred to France in November 1915. Conlin served as a private and his battalion was involved in heavy fighting at the Battle of the Somme in 1916; after seeing further action in March and April 1917 during the German retreat to the Hindenburg Line, Conlin was transferred in June 1917 to Flanders to support the British offensive at the Third Battle of Ypres at Passchendaele.

Conlin was killed in action on 23rd June 1917, at the age of 35, 18 days before the commencement of the Third Battle of Ypres. His death is commemorated at the Nieuport Memorial in Belgium.

INTERNATIONAL APPEARANCE

7th April 1906 England v. Scotland at Hampden Park, Glasgow; Scotland won 2-1

1.2 Edwin Latheron (1887-1917)
born in Brotton, North Yorkshire

Latheron was an inside-forward who joined Blackburn Rovers in 1906 and over the next nine seasons, made 257 league appearances for them, in which he scored 94 goals and played in 25 F. A. Cup games for them, in which he scored 10 goals. He won the league title with them in the 1911/12 season and the 1913/14 season.

Latheron was selected to play for England in 1913 in their Home Championships match against Wales, a game in which he scored England's second goal in a 4-3 victory; his second and last game for England was a year later, a 3-0 defeat at the hands of Ireland.

Latheron signed up with the Royal Field Artillery in 1916, which allowed him to continue playing football for Blackburn in wartime friendlies up until March 1917, when he was posted overseas joining the 75th Battery, 5th Brigade of the Royal Field

Artillery on the Western Front. In October 1917, the Brigade was providing artillery support for the first assault on the village of Passchendaele; with British guns bogged down in the dire conditions and with ammunition running short, well-targeted battery fire from the Germans resulted in the British troops sustaining heavy losses, including the loss of Latheron who, along with another gunner, was killed on 14th October 1917 by splinters from a shell blast near to his dug-out.

Latheron was 29 when he died and he was buried at the Vlamertighe New Military Cemetery near Ypres in Belgium.

INTERNATIONAL APPEARANCES

17th March 1913 England v. Wales at Ashton Gate, Bristol; England won 4-3

14th February 1914 England v. Ireland at Ayresome Park, Middlesbrough; Ireland won 3-0

1.3 Evelyn Lintott (1883-1916)
born in Godalming, Surrey.

Lintott was a half-back who first played for Woking in the West Surrey League. Whilst at St Luke's College, Exeter training to be a teacher, he played two games for Plymouth Argyle in the Southern League before, in 1907, joining Queens Park Rangers, who were also playing in the Southern League. As a teacher, Lintott retained his amateur status and was picked five times to play for the England amateur team before he turned professional in 1908.

In February 1908, Lintott became the first QPR player to play for England when he made his debut against Ireland in the Home Championships, a game England won 3-1. Lintott kept his place in the team for the other two Home Championships matches in 1908, a 7-1 victory over Wales and a 1-1 draw against Scotland and again the following year in the 4-0 win over Ireland and the 2-0 win over Scotland. His sixth and seventh matches for England, which turned out to be his last two for them, were the two away friendly fixtures England played against Hungary in May 1909, matches England won 4-2 and 8-2.

In November 1908, Lintott joined First Division Bradford City, after having played 35 games for Queens Park Rangers in which he scored one goal and after winning the Southern League with them in the 1906/07 season. Whilst at Bradford, Lintott was elected chairman of the players' union, the PFA, a reflection of the respect his fellow footballers had for him. In June 1912, after 57 games for Bradford for whom he scored two goals, Lintott moved to Leeds in the Second Division, making 45 appearances and scoring one goal for them.

Lintott joined the 15th Battalion, the West Yorkshire Regiment (Prince of Wales's Own) soon after the outbreak of war and, by December 1914, had been promoted to lieutenant, making him the first professional footballer to gain a commission. His first overseas involvement in the War was when he was sent to Egypt in December 1914 to guard the Suez Canal; in March 1915, he was moved to France in preparation for the assault on the Somme.

Lintott was killed on 1st July 1916, the first day of the Battle of the Somme, at the age of 33. As was reported in the Yorkshire Post, "Lieutenant Lintott's end was particularly gallant. Tragically, he was killed leading his platoon of the 15th West Yorkshire Regiment, the Leeds Pals, over the top. He led his men with great dash and when hit the first time declined to take the count. Instead, he drew his revolver and called for further effort. Again he was hit but struggled on but a third shot finally bowled him over."

His body was never found and his death is commemorated, as one of the more than 72,000 British and Commonwealth troops who died at the Battle of the Somme and who have no known grave, on the Thiepval Memorial to the Missing, near Amiens in France.

INTERNATIONAL APPEARANCES

15th February 1908 England v. Ireland at Solitude, Belfast; England won 3-1

16th March 1908 England v. Wales at The Racecourse Ground, Wrexham; England won 7-1

4th April 1908 England v. Scotland at Hampden Park, Glasgow; match drawn 1-1

13th February 1909 England v. Ireland at Valley Parade, Bradford; England won 4-0

3rd March 1909 England v. Scotland at Crystal Palace, London; England won 2-0

29th May 1909 England v. Hungary at Budapest; England won 4-2

31st May 1909 England v. Hungary at Budapest; England won 8-2

Some records report that Frank Booth, who played one game for England in 1905, at outside-left against Ireland, died from war wounds sustained in the War. Other reports state that Booth served in the British Army during the War, being sent to France in March 1918 and that he survived the War, returning to England in February 1919; once back in England, he was diagnosed with a tumour on the heart (which might conceivably have been brought on because of his war experiences) and died in June 1919.

CHAPTER 2
Scotland Footballers

2.1 Robert Christie (1865-1918)
born in Dunblane, Scotland.

Whilst training as an architect in Glasgow in 1883, Christie joined Queen's Park and, within a year of joining them, had won the Scottish Cup, won an international cap and played in the F. A. Cup final. His international, which because of injury proved to be his only one, was playing on the left-wing in Scotland's 1-0 win over England in 1884.

In the F. A. Cup in 1884, Queen's Park reached the final after winning six matches in which they scored 42 goals and conceded only three; however, in the final, they were unable to overcome Blackburn Rovers who won 2-1; in scoring Queen's Park only goal in the final, Christie remains the only person to have scored a goal for a Scottish club in an F. A. Cup final and, at 18 years and 135 days old, was the youngest scorer of a goal in the F. A. Cup final, a record he held for exactly 100 years until Norman Whiteside scored for Manchester United in the 1984 F. A. Cup final.

A year later, Christie missed out, because of injury, on a second F. A. Cup final and on a further two internationals for which he had been selected but, in 1886, he won the Scottish Cup with Queen's Park for a second time, scoring a goal in their

3-1 victory over Renton. A recurrence of his injury brought a premature end to his football career.

After retiring from football, Christie represented Scotland at curling and was appointed President of the Scottish Football Association.

Prior to serving as a reservist in the Great War, Christie had seen active service in the Second Boer War in South Africa, commanding a Relief Company of the Black Watch. Considered too old for the front line in the Great War, Christie went with the Royal Scots Fusiliers to France and Salonika before being seconded to the Labour Corps in 1918, where he served as a major. Although engaged in a non-combat role carrying out essential work behind the scenes, the Company Christie was commanding was pounded by high-explosive shells spiked with mustard gas, whilst laying cables at Foncquevillers in the Somme valley on 11th May 1918. Christie died four days later from wounds and gas poisoning, at the age of 52, at a Red Cross hospital in Rouen. He is buried at the St Sever Cemetery in France.

Christie's younger brother, Alexander, also played football for Scotland, making the Christie brothers the first of two famous sets of brothers from Dunblane to represent their country, the other set being the tennis players, Andy and Jamie Murray.

INTERNATIONAL APPEARANCE

15th March 1884 Scotland v. England at Cathkin Park, Glasgow; Scotland won 1-0

2.2 Donald McLeod (1882-1917)

born in Laurieston, Scotland.

McLeod first played for Stenhousemuir before joining Celtic in 1902. Over the next six seasons, McLeod played 155 games for Celtic at right-back and, in 1905 and 1906, represented the Scottish Football League team in their fixtures against the English Football League. Although McLeod was on the losing side in both these matches, he had more success in his four international matches; his first was against Ireland in 1905, a match which Scotland won 4-0 and a year later McLeod played in all three of Scotland's Home Championships matches, winning against England and Ireland but losing to Wales, to share the Home Championships with England.

In October 1908, McLeod moved to Middlesbrough, for whom he played 148 games during his five seasons with them.

During the War, McLeod joined the Royal Field Artillery. Although the cause of his injuries is unknown, McLeod was wounded during the Battle of Passchendaele and died on 6th October 1917, at the age of 35. He was buried at the Dozinghem Military Cemetery in Belgium.

INTERNATIONAL APPEARANCES

18th March 1905 Scotland v. Ireland at Parkhead, Glasgow; Scotland won 4-0

3rd March 1906 Scotland v. Wales at Tynecastle Park, Edinburgh; Wales won 2-0

17th March 1906 Scotland v. Ireland at Dalymount Park, Dublin; Scotland won 1-0

7th April 1906 Scotland v. England at Hampden Park, Glasgow; Scotland won 2-1

2.3 James Speirs (1886-1917)

born in Glasgow

Speirs was an inside-forward and joined Rangers in 1905. In his three seasons with Rangers, Speirs played 62 league and Scottish Cup games for them, scoring 29 goals and in 1908, towards the end of his time with them, was selected to play for Scotland in their Home Championships fixture against Wales, a match Scotland won 2-1. Soon after his one and only appearance for Scotland, Speirs joined Clyde for one season, for whom he played 20 games and scored 10 goals before moving to Bradford City. Speirs spent three and a half seasons with Bradford City, playing in 96 league and F. A. Cup games and scoring 33 goals for them; his highlight was captaining them to their F. A. Cup success in 1911; in the final against Newcastle United, the first game was a goalless draw, but Bradford won the replay 1-0, with Speirs scoring the winning goal.

In December 1912, Speirs joined Leeds United and played 78 league and F. A. Cup games for them, in which he scored 32 goals, before signing up for the British Army and enlisting with the Queen's Own Cameron Highlanders in April 1915.

Whilst involved in heavy fighting in the Somme in September 1916, Speirs was wounded in his left elbow but returned to the action during the Battle of Arras in 1917, for which he was awarded the Military Medal. After home leave in June and early July 1917, Speirs returned to his unit where he served as a sergeant and, on 20th August 1917, moved into lines east of St Julien near Ypres, where the Cameron Highlanders prepared for an attack on a German stronghold. After leaving their trenches, the Cameron Highlanders came under heavy machine gun fire and it was reported that Speirs had been hit in the thigh. Following this attack, Speirs was reported as "missing presumed dead".

More than two years later, Speirs' wife received news that her husband's body had been found on the battlefield close to Iberian Farm from which the Germans had been firing; on the third anniversary of his death, the War Office informed Speirs' widow that he had been killed or died of wounds on or shortly after 20th August 1917 and a year later, more than four years after his death, informed her where he had been buried. Speirs was 31 when he died and was buried at Dochy Farm Cemetery near Zunnebeke in Belgium

INTERNATIONAL APPEARANCE

7th March 1908 Scotland v. Wales at Dens Park, Dundee; Scotland won 2-1

MILITARY HONOURS

Military Medal

CHAPTER 3
WALES FOOTBALLERS

3.1 Bobby Atherton (1876-1917)

born in Bethesda, North Wales

Although Welsh, Atherton was brought up in Scotland and after a brief spell with Hearts, joined Hibernian in 1897. Atherton played both in midfield and as a forward and, towards the end of his second season with Hibs, won his first cap for Wales, playing against Ireland in the 1898 Home Championships; although his second cap came a few weeks later in the fixture against England, it was another five years before he played for Wales again.

In 1902, Atherton captained Hibs when they won the Scottish Cup and a year later, when they won their first League Championship title. In 1903, Atherton played in all of Wales's Home Championships matches and again in 1904 but, after having played 97 games and having scored 26 goals for Hibs, was transferred to Middlesbrough in time for the 1903/04 season; in his second season there, Atherton was made captain, a position he relinquished to Alf Common after one year when Common was bought by Middlesbrough, making him the first player to be transferred for £1,000. Atherton also became Middlesbrough's first capped player when he played for Wales in their game against England in 1904.

In his three seasons with Middlesbrough, Atherton played 66 games for them and scored 13 goals before joining Chelsea in 1906; Atherton retired shortly after joining Chelsea and returned to Scotland, where he joined the Merchant Navy. By the time he retired, Atherton had played in nine matches for Wales and scored twice for them, one of his goals being in their 1-1 draw against Scotland in 1904 and the other in their 2-2 draw against Ireland in 1905 – the two games in which he scored were two of the three games which Atherton played for Wales which ended in draws, the other six all being lost.

Atherton lost his life whilst serving as a steward on the S/S Britannia, a steamship which had set off from Leith in October 1917; it is believed that the ship was torpedoed and sunk off Portland Head in the English Channel by a German U boat on 19th October 1917, with the lives of all 22 on board, including Atherton's, being lost.

Atherton was 41 at the time.

INTERNATIONAL APPEARANCES

19th February 1898 Wales v. Ireland at The Park, Llandudno; Ireland won 1-0

28th March 1898 Wales v. England at The Racecourse Ground, Wrexham; England won 3-0

2nd March 1903 Wales v. England at Fratton Park, Portsmouth; England won 2-1

9th March 1903 Wales v. Scotland at Cardiff Arms Park, Cardiff; Scotland won 1-0

28th March 1903 Wales v. Ireland at Solitude, Belfast; Ireland won 2-0

29th February 1904 Wales v. England at The Racecourse Ground, Wrexham; match drawn 2-2

12th March 1904 Wales v. Scotland at Dens Park, Dundee; match drawn 1-1

21st March 1904 Wales v. Ireland at Bangor; Ireland won 1-0

8th April 1905 Wales v. Ireland at Solitude, Belfast; match drawn 2-2

3.2 Frederick Griffiths (1873-1917)

born in Presteigne, Wales

Griffiths joined Blackpool in 1900 and, when selected to play in goal for Wales against Scotland in early 1900, he became the first Blackpool player to be capped. His first match ended in a 5-2 defeat with Griffiths reported to have had a disappointing game but his second match, a month later against England, was more successful, with Wales drawing 1-1 with England.

Griffiths was never selected again by Wales after the game against England but he continued to play for a number of clubs over the next six seasons, including Millwall, Preston North End and Spurs, but he had his longest spell at West Ham, for whom he played for two seasons. By 1906, Griffiths had joined Middlesbrough but never played for the first team. Not long after joining Middlesbrough, Griffiths retired from professional football and finished his playing days with Moore's Athletic in Shirebrook, in Derbyshire, where he worked as a coalminer.

During the War, Griffiths enlisted with the 15th Battalion, the Nottinghamshire and Derbyshire Regiment (the Sherwood Foresters) and spent the early part of 1917 in the Somme Valley, thereby avoiding the first months of the Flanders campaign. However, in October 1917, by which time he was a sergeant, his battalion was moved so that it could take part in the Passchendaele offensive. During a minor exchange of fire on 30th October 1917, Griffiths was killed along with three other members of his battalion. He was 44 when he died and was buried at the Dozinghem Military Cemetery in Belgium.

3rd February 1900 Wales v. Scotland at Pittodrie, Aberdeen; Scotland won 5-2

26th March 1900 Wales v. England at Cardiff Arms Park, Cardiff; match drawn 1-1

3.3 William Jones (1876-1918)
born in Penrhiwceiber, Wales

Jones was a half-back who was playing Aberdare Athletic in South Wales league football when he was first selected to play for Wales, in March 1901. His first international was against Scotland, a match drawn 1-1; later in the same month, he played his second game for Wales, a one-sided match which England won 6-0.

In September 1901, Jones joined Kettering but only stayed there three months before moving to West Ham United. Whilst at West Ham, Jones played two more matches for Wales, the first a 0-0 draw against England and the second a 5-1 defeat at the hands of Scotland.

Jones only spent a couple of seasons with West Ham for whom he played 15 matches before moving back to Wales and playing for Aberaman Athletic where, in his first season, he helped them become the first South Wales club to reach the final of the Welsh Cup, where they lost to 8-0 to Wrexham.

When War broke out, Jones joined the Royal Welch Fusiliers, serving as a private. Jones was killed in action in Macedonia in May 1918 and was buried at the Doiran Military Cemetery in North Greece. He was 41 when he died.

2nd March 1901 Wales v. Scotland at The Racecourse Ground, Wrexham; match drawn 1-1

18th March 1901 Wales v. England at St James Park, Newcastle; England won 6-0

3rd March 1902 Wales v. England at The Racecourse Ground, Wrexham; match drawn 0-0

15th March 1902 Wales v. Scotland at Cappielow Park, Greenock; Scotland won 5-1

3.4 Leigh Roose (1877-1916)
born in Holt, Wales

Roose spent his first five years as a footballer with Aberysthwyth Town, with whom he won the Welsh Cup in 1900. Whilst with Aberysthwyth, Roose also won his first cap for Wales, playing in goal in the Home Championships fixture against Ireland in 1900, keeping a clean sheet in a 2-0 victory.

In 1901, Roose moved to Stoke City, with whom he spent three seasons before moving to Everton. After a year with Everton, in which he played 18 games for them, Roose moved back to Stoke for another two seasons, before moving to Sunderland; during his two spells with Stoke, Roose played 147 games for them.

Roose's career at Sunderland came to an end after two seasons with them when he broke his wrist for a second time. Over the next couple of seasons, Roose played for a number of clubs, including Celtic, Port Vale, Aston Villa and Arsenal, before retiring from playing football in 1912.

Having played his first international match back in 1900, Roose continued to play for Wales up until 1911; he played a total of 24 games for Wales, all in the Home Championships. His record in his six matches against Ireland was five wins and one draw and his record against Scotland was four wins, two draws and three losses in his nine matches against them. Wales's record against England in the matches in which Roose played was poorer, with three draws and six defeats in the nine matches in which he played but the draw in 1907 was enough to secure for Wales their first Home Championships title.

During his playing days, Roose was one of greatest goalkeepers of his time and one of the country's best-known sportsmen, with a reputation as an entertainer and a playboy.

When war broke out, Roose joined the Royal Army Medical Corps and served in France and Gallipoli; due to a lack of information about his whereabouts, Roose's family believed that he had been killed at Gallipoli in 1915; however, he returned to England in 1916 and joined the Royal Fusiliers as a private, allowing him to fight rather than just provide medical care to those who were fighting.

On the first occasion he saw action, in August 1916, he was awarded the Military Medal for bravery, when he managed to get back along his trench whilst under attack from a new weapon deployed by the Germans, a flame-thrower; despite the fumes and his clothes being burnt, Roose, who used his goalkeeping skills to earn himself a reputation as a grenade thrower, continued to throw bombs for as long as he was physically able to, before resorting to his rifle.

Two months later, on 7th October 1916, during the Battle of the Somme, Roose was killed during an allied attack on the German defences known as Bayonet Trench, near the village of Gueudecourt in France; he was last seen charging in the direction of the German defences. His body, which was never found, was either blown up by a German shell or, if he had been shot by a bullet, would have sunk in the mud where he would have fallen. He was 38 when he died and is commemorated at the Thiepval Memorial to the Missing, in France.

INTERNATIONAL APPEARANCES

24th February 1900 Wales v. Ireland at The Park, Llandudno; Wales won 2-0

2nd March 1901 Wales v. Scotland at The Racecourse Ground, Wrexham; match drawn 1-1

18th March 1901 Wales v. England at St James Park, Newcastle; England won 6-0

23rd March 1901 Wales v. Ireland at Solitude, Belfast; Wales won 1-0

3rd March 1902 Wales v. England at The Racecourse Ground, Wrexham; match drawn 0-0

15th March 1902 Wales v. Scotland at Cappielow Park, Greenock; Scotland won 5-1

29th February 1904 Wales v. England at The Racecourse Ground, Wrexham; match drawn 2-2

6th March 1905 Wales v. Scotland at The Racecourse Ground, Wrexham; Wales won 3-1

27th March 1905 Wales v. England at Anfield, Liverpool; England won 3-1

8th April 1905 Wales v. Ireland at Solitude, Belfast; match drawn 2-2

3rd March 1906 Wales v. Scotland at Tynecastle Park, Edinburgh; Wales won 2-0

19th March 1906 Wales v. England at Cardiff Arms Park, Cardiff; England won 1-0

2nd April 1906 Wales v. Ireland at The Racecourse Ground, Wrexham; match drawn 4-4

23rd February 1907 Wales v. Ireland at Solitude, Belfast; Wales won 3-2

4th March 1907 Wales v. Scotland at The Racecourse Ground, Wrexham; Wales won 1-0

18th March 1907 Wales v. England at Craven Cottage, London; match drawn 1-1

7th March 1908 Wales v. Scotland at Dens Park, Dundee; Scotland won 2-1

16th March 1908 Wales v. England at The Racecourse Ground, Wrexham; England won 7-1

1st March 1909 Wales v. Scotland at The Racecourse Ground, Wrexham; Wales won 3-2

15th March 1909 Wales v. England at City Ground, Nottingham; England won 2-0

20th March 1909 Wales v. Ireland at Grosvenor Park, Belfast; Wales won 3-2

5th March 1910 Wales v. Scotland at Rugby Park, Kilmarnock; Scotland won 1-0

14th March 1910 Wales v. England at Cardiff Arms Park, Cardiff; England won 1-0

11th April 1910 Wales v. Ireland at The Racecourse Ground, Wrexham; Wales won 4-1

6th March 1911 Wales v. Scotland at Ninian Park, Cardiff; match drawn 2-2

MILITARY HONOURS

Military Medal

CHAPTER 4
IRELAND FOOTBALLERS

4.1 Barney Donaghy (1882-1916)
born in Derry

Donaghy was an inside-forward whose early playing days were with Derry Celtic and it was whilst he was with Derry Celtic that he made his one and only appearance for Ireland, in a friendly match in 1902 against Scotland, which Scotland won 3-0; it was only much later though that it was declared by FIFA to be an official international game. Earlier in the same year, Donaghy had also represented the Irish League in their fixture against the Scottish League, with the Scottish League also winning this game 3-0.

After spells with Glentoran and Hibernian, Donaghy was again selected, in 1905, to play for an Irish League representative team against the English League, a game won by the English 4-0. It was shortly after this game that Donaghy was transferred to Manchester United, for whom he only played three games before moving back to Derry. The 1907/08 season saw Donaghy play a few games for Burnley, before he retired. Although Donaghy did not score in any of his games for Manchester United, he did whilst at Hibernian, where he scored seven goals in his 15 games for them and at Burnley, where he scored twice in his five games for them.

At the outbreak of the War, Donaghy signed up with the Royal Inniskilling Fusiliers. He was posted to Gallipoli for the campaign there but suffered a head injury from a piece of flying shrapnel; he fared better though than the four soldiers beside him, all of whom were killed.

Following treatment to his head wound in a hospital in Egypt, Donaghy was posted with his battalion to France, to take part in the Battle of the Somme. On the first day of the battle, 1ˢᵗ July 1916, Donaghy's battalion was tasked with mounting attacks on both sides of the village of Beaumont-Havel; however, the wire in front of the German lines was almost uncut, making Private Donaghy and his colleagues easy targets for the German machine guns, as they tried to clamber through what gaps there were. Donaghy was just one of 568 members, including 20 officers, of the Royal Inniskilling Fusiliers who died that day.

Donaghy was 33 when he died; his body was never recovered and he is commemorated at the Thiepval Memorial to the Missing, in France.

INTERNATIONAL APPEARANCE

9ᵗʰ August 1902 Ireland v. Scotland at Grosvenor Park, Belfast; Scotland won 3-0

4.2 Richard Moore (1867-1918)

Richard Moore was born in 1867 and played as a half-back for Linfield from the 1890/91 season through to the 1896/97 season; in Moore's first three seasons, Linfield were the Irish league champions.

Moore made his debut for Ireland in the 1891 Home Championships; his first game, against Wales, was a resounding victory for the Irish, with Martin Stanfield scoring four of their goals in a 7-2 win. Moore kept his place for the next match against England but Ireland were overcome 6-1 despite England having to play their Home Championships match against Wales on the same day – England put out two different teams for the two fixtures. Moore's third and final international was Ireland's third match in the 1891 Home Championships, the game against Scotland which Scotland won 2-1.

Despite being in his 40s when war broke out, Moore served in the War and was in Greece in 1918. However, on 29th October 1918, less than a fortnight before the end of the War, Moore was killed, at the age of 50; some records report that he died as a result of an air attack but it is unknown whether this was the cause of death or whether the cause was Spanish flu – 75% of those who were buried at the Kirechkoi-Hortakoi Military Cemetery near Salonika in Greece, where Moore is buried, died from Spanish flu.

INTERNATIONAL APPEARANCES

7th February 1891 Ireland v. Wales at Ulsterville, Belfast; Ireland won 7-2

7th March 1891 Ireland v. England at Molineux, Wolverhampton; England won 6-1

28th March 1891 Ireland v. Scotland at Parkhead, Glasgow; Scotland won 2-1

4.3 Harold Sloan (1882-1917)

born in Castleknock, County Dublin

Sloan was a forward who played all his club football for
Bohemians, with whom he won the Leinster League title
three years in a row from the 1899/1900 season and, in 1908,
when he was captain, the Irish Cup.

Sloan played his first international for Ireland, in their 1903
Home Championships match against England, a game England
won 4-0. Sloan was next selected by Ireland for their 1904
fixture against Scotland and their 1905 fixture against England,
both games being drawn 1-1.

Sloan's fourth international, against Wales a year later, also
ended in a draw but this time Sloan got his name on the score
sheet when he scored a hat-trick in a 4-4 draw.

In 1907, Sloan played in two of Ireland's Home
Championships fixtures, the games against England (which
England won 1-0) and Wales (which Wales won 3-2, with
Sloan scoring one of Ireland's goals). Sloan played his last two
internationals in 1908, the first a 5-0 defeat at the hands of
the Scottish and the second against Wales when he scored the
winning goal in a 1-0 victory.

As an amateur, Sloan also played for the Ireland amateur
team in two fixtures against England; the first was in 1906 and
the second a year later, England winning both games. Sloan also
represented the Irish League on two occasions, in the fixture
against the English League in 1904 and the fixture against the
Scottish League in 1909.

Sloan ended his playing days at the end of the 1910/11
season. After enlisting in January 1916 and attending Cadet
School in August 1916, Sloan was commissioned in the 198th

Royal Artillery Garrison in October the same year, subsequently reaching the rank of second lieutenant. In November 1916, Sloan was sent to the Western Front and a month later transferred to the 49ᵗʰ Heavy Artillery Group, whose headquarters were at Combles in France. The exact circumstances of his death, on 21ˢᵗ January 1917 at the age of 34, are unknown; he is buried at the Guards Cemetery at Combles.

4.4 Edward Turner (1877-1917)

Little is recorded about Edward Turner's football career and his war service, but one record states he was born in 1877.

Turner was a striker who played for Cliftonville Belfast in the 1891/92 season, when they were runners-up in the Irish Cup; the following season he played for Linfield, returning to Cliftonville in 1894. The Irish football records have him listed as a Cliftonville player for the 1896/97 season and as a Cliftonville player when he made his sole appearance for Ireland in 1896, playing inside-right in the Home Championships fixture against England at Belfast, a game England won 2-0.

As with his football career, details of Turner's war career are vague but it is reported that he died on 2nd September 1917 "while serving in the Great War". He would have been 39 or 40 when he died.

INTERNATIONAL APPEARANCE

7th March 1896 Ireland v. England at Ballynafeigh, Belfast; England won 2-0

CHAPTER 5
ENGLAND CRICKETERS

5.1 Colin Blythe (1879-1917)
born in Deptford, Kent

Blythe was a slow left arm orthodox bowler, who made his first-class debut for Kent in 1899, taking a wicket with his first ball. Blythe continued playing for Kent until the outbreak of the War, during which time he played in 439 games of first-class cricket of which 381 were for Kent. In his 439 games, he took 2,503 wickets at an average of 16.81; as a batsman, he scored 4,443 runs at an average of 9.87, with a top score of 82 not out.

In 1904, Blythe was named as one of Wisden's five cricketers of the year and, in 1914, topped the bowling averages in English cricket, having taken 170 wickets at an average of 15.19. Blythe achieved his best bowling figures in 1907 when he took 10 wickets for 30 runs in Northamptonshire's first innings and 7 wickets for 18 runs in their second innings to give him match figures of 17 wickets for 48 runs; all 17 wickets were taken by him in one day, a record which has been matched twice since but never beaten and his match analysis of 17 for 48 has only been bettered once, by Jim Laker when he took 19 wickets for England in a Test match against Australia in 1956. Blythe's most successful season was in 1909, when he took 215 wickets in first-class matches, at a cost of 14.54 runs per wicket.

Blythe was first selected to play for England on their 1901/02 Ashes tour to Australia; he played in all five Tests on that tour but was not picked again by England until 1905, when he played in the third Test against Australia. The following year, Blythe was picked for England's tour to South Africa, where he played in all five Tests and, in 1907, he played in all three Tests when the South Africans toured England; it was in the second Test against South Africa in 1907 that he achieved his best bowling figures in Tests when he took 8 wickets for 59 runs in the first innings and 7 wickets for 40 runs in the second innings, to give him matches figures of 15 for 99 – this remains the eighth best bowling figures in Test cricket. For the Ashes series in Australia in 1907/08, Blythe only appeared in one of the five Tests and, when Australia came to England in 1909, in only two of the five Tests. Blythe's last Test appearances were on England's tour to South Africa in 1910, when he appeared in two of the five Tests. In his 19 Tests, Blythe took 100 wickets at an average of 18.63 and scored 183 runs at an average of 9.63, with a top score of 27.

Despite suffering from epilepsy, Blythe enlisted when war broke and joined the King's Own Yorkshire Light Infantry, eventually reaching the rank of sergeant. Blythe was killed on 8th November 1917 at the age of 38 when he was hit by random shell-fire on the military railway line between Pimmern and Forest Hall near Passchendaele.

He is buried at the Oxford Road Commonwealth War Graves Commission Cemetery near Ypres in Belgium.

TEST APPEARANCES

1901/02 England v. Australia, 1st Test at Sydney; England won by an innings and 124 runs

1901/02 England v. Australia, 2nd Test at Melbourne; Australia won by 229 runs

1901/02 England v. Australia, 3rd Test at Adelaide; Australia won by 4 wickets

1901/02 England v. Australia, 4th Test at Sydney; Australia won by 7 wickets

1901/02 England v. Australia, 5th Test at Melbourne; Australia won by 32 runs

1905 England v. Australia, 3rd Test at Leeds; match drawn

1905/06 England v. South Africa, 1st Test at Johannesburg; South Africa won by 1 wicket

1905/06 England v. South Africa, 2nd Test at Johannesburg; South Africa won by 9 wickets

1905/06 England v. South Africa, 3rd Test at Johannesburg; South Africa won by 243 runs

1905/06 England v. South Africa, 4th Test at Cape Town; England won by 4 wickets

1905/06 England v. South Africa, 5th Test at Cape Town; South Africa won by an innings and 16 runs

1907 England v. South Africa, 1st Test at Lord's; match drawn

1907 England v. South Africa, 2nd Test at Leeds; England won by 53 runs

1907 England v. South Africa, 3rd Test at the Oval; match drawn

1907/08 England v. Australia, 1st Test at Sydney; Australia won by 2 wickets

1909 England v. Australia, 1st Test at Birmingham; England won by 10 wickets

1909 England v. Australia 4th Test at Manchester; match drawn

1909/10 England v. South Africa, 4th Test at Cape Town; South Africa won by 4 wickets

1909/10 England v. South Africa, 5th Test at Cape Town; England won by 9 wickets

5.2 Major Booth (1886-1916)

born in Pudsey, Yorkshire

Major was his given name, not his military rank.

Booth was a right-handed batsman and a right-arm medium-fast bowler who first played for Yorkshire in 1908 but did not become a regular in the first team until 1910. Following his performances as an all-rounder in 1913, in which he took 158 wickets for Yorkshire and scored over 1,000 runs, Booth was selected by England for their tour of South Africa in 1913/14; Booth was also named as one of Wisden's cricketers of the year in 1914.

In a first-class career consisting of 162 games, of which 144 were for Yorkshire, Booth scored a total of 4,753 runs at an average of 23.29, with a top score of 210 and one other century to his name and took 603 wickets at an average of 19.82. On four occasions, he took eight wickets in an innings, his best return being his 8 for 47 against Middlesex in 1912 and his best match figures were the 14 for 160 he took against Essex in 1914. He also took two hat-tricks and, on three other occasions, took three wickets in four balls.

On England's tour to South Africa in 1913/14, Booth played in the first and last Tests of a five match series. In the first Test, which England won by an innings and 157 runs, Booth took 2 for 38 in South Africa's first innings and scored 14 runs in England's innings; he did not bowl in South Africa's second innings. In the fifth Test, which England won by 10 wickets, Booth scored 32 in the first innings but did not bat in the second innings and, with his bowling, took 1 for 43 in South Africa's first innings and 4 for 49 in their second innings. His performances in these two Tests gave him a batting average of 23 and a bowling average of 18.57.

In the War, Booth served in Egypt in December 1915, having received his commission as a second lieutenant in July that year. Booth was then moved to the Western Front and, whilst serving with the West Yorkshire Regiment (Prince of Wales's Own) was amongst those who went over the top near La Cigny on the first day of the Battle of the Somme on 1st July 1916. Shortly after being injured, Booth was joined in a shell hole by Abe Waddington, who went on to play cricket for Yorkshire and England after the War. Waddington stayed with Booth until Booth died from his wounds. Stretcher bearers were able to rescue Waddington later that day but

Booth's body was not recovered from the shell hole until the following spring.

Booth was 29 at the time of his death and was buried at the Serre Road No. 1 Cemetery, near Serre Les Prisieux in France.

TEST APPEARANCES

1913/14 England v. South Africa, 1ˢᵗ Test at Durban; England won by an innings and 157 runs

1913/14 England v. South Africa, 5ᵗʰ Test at Port Elizabeth; England won by 10 wickets

5.3 Kenneth Hutchings (1882-1916)
born in Southborough, Kent

Hutchings was a right-handed batsman and right-arm fast bowler who made his debut for Kent in 1902, just a month after leaving Tonbridge School. Although he only played one game for Kent in 1902, Hutchings was a first team regular from 1903 until his retirement at the end of the 1912 season. During Hutchings' time in the team, Kent won the County Championship title in 1906, 1909 and 1910 and, in 1907, Hutchings was one of Wisden's five cricketers of the year.

Hutchings was selected to tour Australia with England in 1907/08. Hutchings played in all five Tests on the tour but, after a promising start, his form tailed off towards the end of the tour – on his debut, he scored 42 in the first innings in a partnership in which he and George Gunn put on 117 runs and, in the second Test, he scored his one and only Test century, a score of 126. When Australia toured England the following summer, Hutchings played in the fourth and fifth Tests, scoring 59 in his last Test innings. In the 12 innings he played in his seven Tests, Hutchings scored 341 runs at an average of 28.41; his bowling was rarely used, but he did manage to take one wicket in the 15 overs he bowled, conceding 81 runs.

When he retired at the end of the 1912 season, Hutchings had played a total of 207 games of first-class cricket, 163 of them for Kent. In all first-class matches, he scored a total 10,054 runs at an average of 33.62, including 22 centuries and a top score of 176 and took 24 wickets at an average of 39.08.

Hutchings volunteered within days after war was declared, serving initially with the King's Liverpool Regiment. He was attached to the Royal Welch Fusiliers when he was sent to France in April 1915. Hutchings returned to England in December 1915 for a few days for an operation but was back in France later that month, back as a lieutenant with the King's Liverpool Regiment. On 3rd September 1916, during the Battle of the Somme, whilst leading his men in an attack at Ginchy, Hutchings was struck by a shell and died instantaneously. He was 33 years old and he is commemorated at the Thiepval Memorial to the Missing, in France. In his obituary, the Daily Telegraph wrote "by his death on the field of battle one of the greatest cricketers has been taken from us". Hutchings had three older brothers all of whom were seriously wounded in the War.

TEST APPEARANCES

1907/08 England v. Australia, 1st Test at Sydney; Australia won by 2 wickets

1907/08 England v. Australia, 2nd Test at Melbourne; England won by 1 wicket

1907/08 England v. Australia, 3rd Test at Adelaide; Australia won by 245 runs

1907/08 England v. Australia, 4th Test at Melbourne; Australia won by 308 runs

1907/08 England v. Australia, 5th Test at Sydney; Australia won by 49 runs

1909 England v. Australia, 4th Test at Manchester; match drawn

1909 England v. Australia, 5th Test at the Oval; match drawn

5.4 Leonard Moon (1878-1916)

born in Kensington, London

After attending Westminster School, Moon went to Cambridge University. He was a right-handed batsman and made his first-class debut in 1897 whilst at Cambridge; it was not until 1899 that he won his blue playing in the Varsity match against Oxford, the same year in which he both scored 138 for the university against the touring Australians and made his debut for Middlesex. Moon won a second blue the following year and, after graduating, continued to play for Middlesex until 1909.

Moon was picked to play for England on their tour to South Africa in 1905/06 and played in four of the Tests on that tour, missing out in the first Test. In five of the eight innings he played in his four Test matches, Moon scored 30 or more runs and in a sixth innings, scored 28, but his highest score was 36 and he was not picked by England again. In his four Tests, he scored 182 runs at an average of 22.75.

In his 13 years as a first-class cricketer, Moon played in 96 matches, 63 of which were for Middlesex and 19 for Cambridge University; he scored a total of 4,166 runs at an average of 26.87 and scored seven centuries, with a top score of 176.

Moon was also a useful footballer, winning a blue for this whilst at Cambridge, as well as playing for the leading amateur side, the Corinthians.

After retiring from cricket, Moon became a teacher but signed up during the War. Whilst serving as a lieutenant with the Devon Regiment, Moon died on 23rd November 2016; at the time, it was reported that he died from wounds whilst fighting near Karasouli, Salonika in Greece but it was subsequently reported that he took his own life by shooting himself, whilst suffering from depression or melancholia; he was 38 when he died and was buried at the Karasouli Military Cemetery in Greece.

Moon's older brother Billy also played two games of cricket for Middlesex and seven games of football for England.

TEST APPEARANCES

1905/06 England v. South Africa, 2nd Test at Johannesburg; South Africa won by 9 wickets

1905/06 England v. South Africa, 3rd Test at Johannesburg; South Africa won by 243 runs

1905/06 England v. South Africa, 4th Test at Cape Town; England won by 4 wickets

1905/06 England v. South Africa, 5th Test at Cape Town; South Africa won by an innings and 16 runs

CHAPTER 6
Australia Cricketer

6.1 Albert "Tibby" Cotter (1883-1917)

born in Sydney

Cotter was a right-arm fast bowler who made his debut for New South Wales in early 1902. Two years later, he made his debut for Australia in the fourth Test against England. He retained his place in the team for the final Test of England's Ashes tour, taking his best Test bowling figures, 7 for 148, in England's first innings.

Cotter toured New Zealand with the Australian team in 1904/05 and played in the two games against New Zealand, but as the home team had not yet been granted Test status, they were not Test matches. Instead, Cotter had to wait until the following summer when Australia toured England before playing Test cricket again, Cotter playing in three of the five Tests on that tour.

Cotter made his next two Test appearances when England toured Australia in 1907/08. Cotter was again picked to tour England in 1909 and played in all five Tests on that tour. 18 months later, Cotter was part of the Australian team which played in South Africa and again played in all five Tests. Cotter's last Tests came in 1911 when he played in the first four Tests against England. A year later, Cotter, along with five other

Australians, boycotted the Triangular Tournament in England featuring England, Australia and South Africa and was never picked again to play for his country.

In his 21 Tests, Cotter took 89 wickets at an average of 28.64, his best bowling analysis being the 7 for 148 in his second Test; with the bat, Cotter scored 457 runs at an average of 13.05, with a top score of 45.

Cotter's first-class cricket career came to an end in 1912, by which time he had played 113 games of first-class cricket. Of these 113 games, in addition to his 21 Tests, 53 were for Australia in other first-class games and the rest were for New South Wales; in these 113 games, Cotter took 442 wickets at an average of 24.27, with best bowling figures of 7 for 15, and scored 2,484 runs at an average of 16.89, with a best score of 82.

Cotter joined the Australian Imperial Forces in April 1915. Whilst serving with the 1st Light Horse Regiment, Cotter took part in the Gallipoli Campaign before being transferred to the 12th Light Horse Regiment; whilst with the 12th Light Horse Regiment, Cotter was involved in the second Battle of Gaza for which he was commended for his work under heavy fire.

On 31st October 1917, Cotter was serving as a trooper with the 4th Light Infantry which had captured Beersheba in Palestine, following a cavalry-style charge. Although one report suggests that Cotter was killed when he was hit in the head by a sniper's bullet as he peered over a trench parapet, other reports record that he was working as a stretcher-bearer and that, whilst he was carrying out such duties, was shot at close range by a Turk, as troops were dismounting to engage the enemy. One report states that, as a stretcher-bearer, Cotter was riding unarmed into the thick of the fighting to save wounded troops and that, whilst attempting to put out of action a retreating Turkish machine gun, he was killed when one of the Turks, who were throwing down their weapons as if to surrender, produced a concealed gun and shot Cotter in the back of the head. Cotter was 33 when he was killed and was buried near Beersheba.

TEST APPEARANCES

1903/04 Australia v. England, 4th Test at Sydney; England won by 157 runs

1903/04 Australia v. England, 5th Test at Melbourne; Australia won by 218 runs

1905 Australia v. England, 1st Test at Nottingham; England won by 213 runs

1905 Australia v. England, 4th Test at Manchester; England won by an innings and 80 runs

1905 Australia v. England, 5th Test at the Oval; match drawn

1907/08 Australia v. England, 1st Test at Sydney; Australia won by 2 wickets

1907/08 Australia v. England, 2nd Test at Melbourne; England won by 1 wicket

1909 Australia v. England, 1st Test at Birmingham; England won by 10 wickets

1909 Australia v. England, 2nd Test at Lord's; Australia won by 9 wickets

1909 Australia v. England, 3rd Test at Leeds; Australia won by 126 runs

1909 Australia v. England, 4th Test at Manchester; match drawn

1909 Australia v. England, 5th Test at the Oval; match drawn

1910/11 Australia v. South Africa, 1st Test at Sydney; Australia won by an innings and 114 runs

1910/11 Australia v. South Africa, 2nd Test at Melbourne; Australia won by 89 runs

1910/11 Australia v. South Africa, 3rd Test at Adelaide; South Africa won by 38 runs

1910/11 Australia v. South Africa, 4th Test at Melbourne; Australia won by 530 runs

1910/11 Australia v. South Africa, 5th Test at Sydney; Australia won by 7 wickets

1911/12 Australia v. England, 1st Test at Sydney; Australia won by 146 runs

1911/12 Australia v. England, 2nd Test at Melbourne; England won by 8 wickets

1911/12 Australia v. England, 3rd Test at Adelaide; England won by 7 wickets

1911/12 Australia v. England, 4th Test at Melbourne; England won by an innings and 225 runs

CHAPTER 7
South Africa Cricketers

94 cricketers had represented South Africa in the 40 Tests played by South Africa prior to the outbreak of the Great War, compared to 180 cricketers who had played for England in their 123 Tests and 105 cricketers who had played for Australia in their 105 Tests. Despite this, seven South African Test cricketers were killed in the War or died as a consequence of their involvement in the War, compared to only four England Test cricketers and one Australian.

7.1 Frederick Cook (1870-1915)
born in Java, the Dutch East Indies

Cook was a right-handed batsman whose cricketing career started in the 1893/94 season when he made two appearances in the Currie Cup for Eastern Province and ended in the 1904/05 season when he made his last appearance for Eastern Province. Despite a career spanning 12 seasons, Cook only played two other games for Eastern Province, both in the 1896/97 season and only played one other game of first-class cricket, the first Test match between England and South Africa when England toured in the 1895/96 season. In his one and only Test, Cook scored 7 in the first innings but failed to score in the second innings; his dismissal was George Lohmann's sixth of the innings and the first of a hat-trick in that innings, an innings in which South Africa were all out for 30 runs and in which Lohmann took 8 wickets for only 7 runs.

In his six games of first-class cricket, Cook scored 172 runs at an average of 17.2, with a highest score of 59.

When war broke out, Cook joined the Border Regiment. He went to Gallipoli in 1915, attached to the 1ˢᵗ Battalion of the Queen's Edinburgh Rifles (Royal Scots). Cook, who had been promoted to the rank of captain, was killed in action on 30ᵗʰ November 1915 during the Gallipoli Campaign at the age of 45 and was buried at the Pink Farm Cemetery in Helles on the Gallipoli Penisula.

TEST APPEARANCE

1895/96 South Africa v. England, 1ˢᵗ Test at Port Elizabeth; England won by 288 runs

7.2 Reginald Hands (1888-1918)
born in Cape Town

Hands won a Rhodes Scholarship to Oxford University in 1907, but did not play cricket for the university team. After being called to the Bar in 1911, Hands returned to South Africa in 1912 and, on 1ˢᵗ January 1913, made his first-class cricket debut for Western Province against Orange Free State. Hands played two more Currie Cup games for Western Province that season, against Natal and Eastern Province.

The MCC toured South Africa in the 1913/14 season and Hands appeared in the two games which Western Province played against the MCC and in the game Cape Province played against the MCC. Hands was also picked for the fifth Test against the England tourists, but only scored 0 and 7 in his two innings, being out stumped in both of them.

By the time the Great War had started, Hands had only played seven games of first-class cricket, in which he had scored 289 runs at an average of 28.90, with a top score of 79 not out; his six overs in first-class cricket had brought him no wickets and had cost 22 runs.

Hands did not play any more first-class cricket once war had broken out, but his younger brother Philip, who also played in the Test against England that Reginald had played in, went on to play seven more Tests for South Africa up until 1924; another younger brother, Kenneth, also played cricket for Western Province up until 1931.

Hands's cricketing career was less successful than his rugby career. Whilst at Oxford, he played in the Varsity matches against Cambridge in 1908 and 1909, his younger brothers following in his footsteps with Philip playing in the 1910 Varsity match and Kenneth in the 1912 Varsity match. As well as playing for the Barbarians and Blackheath, Hands played in a couple of trials, playing for the South of England following which he was picked to play for England as a forward in 1910 in their Five Nations fixtures against France and Scotland, both of which were won by England.

Hands enlisted shortly after the start of the War, serving initially with the Imperial Light House in German South West Africa, where he was principally involved in rounding up German settlers in Namibia. After transferring to the South African Heavy Artillery, Hands was posted to the Western Front, where his unit was seconded to the Royal Garrison Artillery.

On 21st March 1918, the Germans embarked on a final attempt to land a decisive blow before the arrival of significant numbers of US troops at the Western Front; although this offensive failed, Hands, who had achieved the rank of captain, was wounded in action whilst defending the line. Hands died from his wounds, after being gassed, on 20th April 1918, at the age of 29. He is buried in the Eastern Cemetery at Boulogne in France.

TEST APPEARANCE

1913/14 South Africa v. England, 5th Test at Port Elizabeth; England won by 10 wickets

7.3 Eric Balfour "Bill" Lundie (1888-1917)

born in Willowvale, Cape Province

Lundie was a right-arm fast bowler who made his first-class debut for Eastern Province in March 1909. He played two more games for Eastern Province that year and, in the following season, played first for Western Province and then for Eastern Province in their fixtures against the touring MCC team. In the 1910/11 season, Lundie made just one appearance, for Western Province against the South African team selected to tour Australia.

Lundie did not play again until the MCC were touring South Africa in 1913/14; he played in two games for Transvaal against the MCC, following which he was selected to play in the fifth Test against England. In England's first innings, Lundie bowled 46 overs, taking 4 wickets for 101 runs; Lundie bowled just 1.1 overs in the second innings, conceding six runs as England won by 10 wickets. With the bat, Lundie was 0 not out in South Africa's first innings but out for 1 in the second.

The one Test Lundie played proved to be his last game of first-class cricket; in a first-class cricket career spanning six seasons, he only played nine matches, in which he scored 126 runs at an average of 8.40 with a top score of 29 and took 26 wickets at an average of 25.34, with best bowling figures of 6 for 52.

During the War, Lundie served as a second lieutenant with the 4th Battalion, the Coldstream Guards; he was killed on 11th September 1917 at the Battle of Passchendaele at the age of 29 and is commemorated at the Tyne Cot Memorial, near Ypres in Belgium.

TEST APPEARANCE

1913/14 South Africa v. England, 5th Test at Port Elizabeth; England won by 10 wickets

7.4 Claude Newberry (1889-1916)
born in Port Elizabeth

Newberry bowled right-arm fast as well as leg-breaks and made his first-class debut for Transvaal in October 1910, in a match against the South African team selected to tour Australia; he played in six more games for Transvaal that season, all in the Currie Cup. The following two seasons saw him make only one more appearance for Transvaal but he was playing again in the 1913/14 season when the MCC toured South Africa. That season he played four games for Transvaal, three of them against the MCC and, after South Africa had suffered a heavy defeat in the first Test against England, Newberry was picked to bowl his leg-breaks for the remaining four Tests.

In his four Tests, Newberry took 11 wickets at an average of 24.36, with best figures of 4 for 72 and, with the bat, scored 62 runs at an average of 7.75, with a highest score of 16.

Newberry's final first-class match was the fifth Test of the tour; in all his 16 first-class games, Newberry took 49 wickets at an average of 24.75, with best figures of 6 for 28 and scored 251 runs at an average of 11.95, with a top score of 42.

In the War, Newberry served as a private with the South African Infantry. He died on 1st August 1916 during the Battle of the Somme at the age of 27 and was buried at the Delville Wood Cemetery, near Longueval in France.

TEST APPEARANCES

1913/14 South Africa v. England, 2nd Test at Johannesburg; England won
by an innings and 12 runs

1913/14 South Africa v. England, 3rd Test at Johannesburg; England won by 91 runs

1913/14 South Africa v. England, 4th Test at Durban; match drawn

1913/14 South Africa v. England, 5th Test at Port Elizabeth; England won by 10 wickets

7.5 Arthur Edward Ochse (1870-1918)
born in Graaff-Reinet, Cape Colony

A right-handed batsman, Ochse's first game of first-class cricket came when he was selected to play in South Africa's first ever Test match, against the England team touring South Africa in the 1888/89 season. With the first Test being played a day after Ochse's 19th birthday, Ochse was at the time South Africa's youngest Test cricketer.

Although Ochse, like a number of the South Africans, struggled against the more experienced England team, Ochse retained his place for the second Test but, after becoming the eighth victim bowled by Johnny Briggs in South Africa's second innings, Ochse lost his place in the team and was never re-selected. In his two Tests, Ochse did not bowl and only scored 16 runs at an average of 4.00, with a highest score of 8.

Ochse only played three more games of first-class cricket, when he played a game for Transvaal in 1891 and two more for them in 1895. Ochse enjoyed more success for Transvaal in these matches than he had in his two matches for South Africa, scoring 215 runs in his six innings with a top score of 99; although he had not bowled for South Africa, he did bowl in his other first-class matches, taking two wickets whilst conceding 145 runs.

Ochse served with the Rand Rifles during the Second Boer War, after which he served with the Witwatersrand Rifles and the Field Intelligence Department.

In the Great War, Ochse served as a corporal with the 2nd South African Infantry Regiment. He was killed in action on 11th April 1918 at Messines Ridge during the German Spring Offensive; his body was never found and he is commemorated at the Ypres (Menin Gate) Memorial, in Belgium. He was 48 when he died.

7.6 Reggie Schwarz (1875-1918)

born in London

Schwarz played his first two games of first-class cricket in 1901 and, by the time he emigrated to South Africa in time for the 1902/03 cricket season in South Africa, he had played 19 games of first-class cricket, 12 of which had been for Middlesex in 1902.

Schwarz returned to England in 1904 as part of the South African touring team and, although he played 21 games for the South Africans on the tour, he was not selected to play in any of the Test matches. It was however on this tour that he learnt from its inventor, Bernard Bosenquet, how to bowl the googly.

Schwarz made his Test debut in January 1906 in the first Test against the touring England team and kept his place in the Test team for the remainder of the series. Schwarz continued to play for South Africa for their next four Test series, which included two more tours to England and one to Australia; in his second tour to England, in 1907, Schwarz enjoyed considerable success, taking 137 wickets at an average of 11.70 and earning himself the nomination of one of Wisden's criceters of the year. Schwarz's Test career came to an end after the Triangular Tournament in England featuring the home team, South Africa and Australia, by which time he had played in 20 Tests for South Africa. In his 20 Tests, Schwarz had scored 374 runs with the bat, at an average of 13.85 with a top score of 61 and taken 55 wickets at an average of 25.76, with best bowling figures of 6 for 47 – his strike rate as a bowler in Tests was 47.8 balls per wicket, a feat only matched by two other South Africans who have played as many Tests as Schwarz.

By the time he retired from cricket in 1912 to pursue a career as a stockbroker, Schwarz had played 125 games of first-class cricket; in addition to his 20 Tests, Schwarz played in another 56 matches for the South Africans, as well as 20 games for Transvaal and 12 for Middlesex; he scored 3,798 runs at an average of 22.60 with one century to his name, a score of 102 and took 398 wickets at an average of 17.58, with best bowling figures of 8 for 55.

Before Schwarz had made a name for himself as a cricketer, he had made his name as a rugby player. After school, Schwarz went to Cambridge University, where he won his blue at rugby playing in the 1893 Varsity match against Oxford. Six years later, he made his debut at fly-half playing for England against Scotland. In 1901, two years after his debut, Schwarz was picked for England's games against Wales and Ireland, but as with his debut, ended up on the losing side.

During the War, Schwarz served in German West Africa before arriving on the Western Front in March 1916 and serving as deputy assistant quartermaster. After being awarded the Military Cross for his good work, Schwarz then served as a major in a number of posts commanding labour companies but, after suffering poor health, was transferred to the salvage corps in early 1918. Although he suffered two serious wounds during the War, he did survive the War, but was admitted to hospital on the day the Armistice was signed and died seven days later, on 18th November 1918, from the Spanish flu epidemic whilst still in France. He was 43 years old and was buried at the Etaples Military Cemetery in France.

In his obituary in The Times, it was recorded that "Schwarz was a man of exceptional charm. He had a great gift of absolute modesty and self-effacement. No one meeting him casually would ever have guessed the renown he had won in the world of sport".

TEST APPEARANCES

1905/06 South Africa v. England, 1ˢᵗ Test at Johannesburg; South Africa won by 1 wicket

1905/06 South Africa v. England, 2ⁿᵈ Test at Johannesburg; South Africa won by 9 wickets

1905/06 South Africa v. England, 3ʳᵈ Test at Johannesburg; South Africa won by 243 runs

1905/06 South Africa v. England, 4ᵗʰ Test at Cape Town; England won by 4 wickets

1905/06 South Africa v. England, 5ᵗʰ Test at Cape Town; South Africa won by an innings and 16 runs

1907 South Africa v. England, 1ˢᵗ Test at Lord's; match drawn

1907 South Africa v. England, 2ⁿᵈ Test at Leeds; England won by 53 runs

1907 South Africa v. England, 3ʳᵈ Test at the Oval; match drawn

1909/10 South Africa v. England, 1ˢᵗ Test at Johannesburg; South Africa won by 19 runs

1909/10 South Africa v. England, 2ⁿᵈ Test at Durban; South Africa won by 95 runs

1909/10 South Africa v. England, 4ᵗʰ Test at Cape Town; South Africa won by 4 wickets

1909/10 South Africa v. England, 5ᵗʰ Test at Cape Town; England won by 9 wickets

1910/11 South Africa v. Australia, 1ˢᵗ Test at Sydney; Australia won by an innings and 114 runs

1910/11 South Africa v. Australia, 2ⁿᵈ Test at Melbourne; Australia won by 89 runs

1910/11 South Africa v. Australia, 3ʳᵈ Test at Adelaide; South Africa won by 38 runs

1910/11 South Africa v. Australia, 4ᵗʰ Test at Melbourne; Australia won by 530 runs

1910/11 South Africa v. Australia, 5ᵗʰ Test at Sydney; Australia won by 7 wickets

1912 South Africa v. Australia, 1ˢᵗ Test at Manchester; Australia won by an innings and 88 runs

1912 South Africa v. England, 1ˢᵗ Test at Leeds; England won by 174 runs

1912 South Africa v. Australia, 2ⁿᵈ Test at Lord's; Australia won by 10 wickets

MİLİTARY HONOURS

Mentioned in despatches (twice)

Military Cross

7.7 Gordon White (1882-1918)

born in Port St Johns, Cape Province

White was a right-handed batsman and leg-break bowler who made his first-class debut for Transvaal in 1904. By the summer of 1904, he had been selected as a member of the South African party to tour England and, although he did not play in any of the Tests, played 22 games for the South Africans on that tour.

White made his Test debut for South Africa when England were on tour in 1905/06 and played in all five Tests. Another tour to England followed in 1907, when White played in three of the Tests and in another 23 games for the South Africans. When the MCC next toured South Africa, in the 1909/10 season, White played in four of the Tests against England. White made his third and final tour to England for the Triangular Tournament in 1912 and played in five of South Africa's Tests in that tournament, three against Australia and two against England, as well as 22 other first-class games for the South Africans.

By the time White retired from cricket in September 1912, he had played in 17 Tests, scoring 872 runs at an average of 30.06, with two centuries to his name and a top score of 147 and taking nine wickets at an average of 33.44, with best bowling figures of 4 for 47. In his 97 games of first-class cricket, of which 84 were either Tests for South Africa or other first-class tour matches for the South Africans, White scored 3,740 runs at an average of 27.70, including four centuries and a top score of 162 not out and took 155 wickets at an average of 20.05, with best figures of 7 for 33.

During the War, White joined the South African Army and served at Morogoro during the East African Campaign in

1916/17. In March 1918, White, who was a lieutenant at the time, was sent with his unit to Egypt to join the 160th (Wales) Brigade. During a bayonet charge against Turkish troops on 20th September 1918 at Khan Jibeit, near Jerusalem, as part of the Battle of Megiddo, White was wounded; he died in hospital four weeks later on 17th October 1918, at the age of 36; he was buried at the Gaza War Cemetery in Palestine.

TEST APPEARANCES

1905/06 South Africa v. England, 1st Test at Johannesburg; South Africa won by 1 wicket

1905/06 South Africa v. England, 2nd Test at Johannesburg; South Africa won by 9 wickets

1905/06 South Africa v. England, 3rd Test at Johannesburg; South Africa won by 243 runs

1905/06 South Africa v. England, 4th Test at Cape Town; England won by 4 wickets

1905/06 South Africa v. England, 5th Test at Cape Town; South Africa won by an innings and 16 runs

1907 South Africa v. England, 1st Test at Lord's; match drawn

1907 South Africa v. England, 2nd Test at Leeds; England won by 53 runs

1907 South Africa v. England, 3rd Test at the Oval; match drawn

1909/10 South Africa v. England, 1st Test at Johannesburg; South Africa won by 19 runs

1909/10 South Africa v. England, 2nd Test at Durban; South Africa won by 95 runs

1909/10 South Africa v. England, 3rd Test at Johannesburg; England won by 3 wickets

1909/10 South Africa v. England, 4th Test at Cape Town; South Africa won by 4 wickets

1912 South Africa v. Australia, 1st Test at Manchester; Australia won by an innings and 88 runs

1912 South Africa v. England, 1st Test at Leeds; England won by 174 runs

1912 South Africa v. Australia, 2nd Test at Lord's; Australia won by 10 wickets

1912 South Africa v. Australia, 3rd Test at Nottingham; match drawn

1912 South Africa v. England, 2nd Test at the Oval; England won by 10 wickets

CHAPTER 8
ENGLAND RUGBY PLAYERS

8.1 Harry Alexander (1879-1915)
born in Birkenhead, Cheshire

After attending Uppingham School, Alexander went to Oxford University and played as a forward in the rugby Varsity matches against Cambridge in 1897 and 1898. After graduating, Alexander worked first as a teacher before becoming a professional singer; he played his rugby for Birkenhead Park and, in 1900, was picked for his first game for England. A victory over Ireland in his first match was followed by a draw the same year against Scotland but 1901 was less successful as Alexander played in, and lost, all three of England's matches in the Home Nations Championship.

Alexander played his last two games for England in 1902; in the first, he captained the team in a narrow defeat at the hands of the Welsh and, in the second, recorded only his second win in an England shirt.

After writing "How to Play Rugby. The Theory and Practice of the Game", Alexander joined Richmond and captained them in the 1905/06 season, including in the 17-0 defeat at the hands of the All Blacks on their first tour to England. His season as captain of Richmond proved to be his last one as a player.

As well as being an international rugby player, Alexander played fives, cricket and hockey for his school and went on to play county hockey; he also was an excellent ice-skater and a scratch handicap golfer.

In the War, Alexander served as a second lieutenant with the Grenadier Guards. He was sent to the Western Front with his battalion in early 1915; 13 days after arriving at the Front, Alexander's battalion was taking part in an assault on Hohenzollern towards the end of the Battle of Loos when he was hit by a shell at Hulluch. Alexander was just one of 400 soldiers from his battalion to die during the assault in a three hour period on 17th October 1915.

Alexander was 36 years old when he died and was buried at the Arras Road Cemetery in Pas de Calais in France.

INTERNATIONAL APPEARANCES

3rd February 1900 England v. Ireland at Richmond; England won 15-4

10th March 1900 England v. Scotland at Inverleith; match drawn 0-0

5th January 1901 England v. Wales at the National Stadium, Cardiff; Wales won 13-0

9th February 1901 England v. Ireland at Lansdowne Road, Dublin; Ireland won 10-6

9th March 1901 England v. Scotland at Blackheath; Scotland won 18-3

11th January 1902 England v. Wales at Blackheath; Wales won 9-8

8th February 1901 England v. Ireland at Leicester; England won 6-3

8.2 Henry Berry (1883-1915)
born in Gloucester

After leaving school, Berry joined the 4th Battalion of the Gloucestershire Regiment at the age of 16, at the outbreak of the Second Boer War but was too young for active service in South Africa; instead, he was sent to St Helena in 1900 to guard prisoners-of-war.

His time in St Helena allowed him time to play rugby, as did his subsequent posting to India. Whilst in Ceylon in 1909, Berry contracted malaria and was sent home. Back in England, Berry started playing rugby for Gloucester, first as a back and then as a wing forward. In 1910, the year in which he played for Gloucestershire in their county championship winning side, Berry was also picked to play for England in all four of their Five Nations fixtures; a draw against Ireland in the second match denied England the Grand Slam but not the Five Nations Championship.

Berry scored a try in the games against France and Scotland but, despite his success with England in 1910 and being described as a fast and clever loose forward, Berry was not picked to play for England again.

Whilst an Army reservist, Berry was called up in August 1914 and sent to the Western Front in February 1915. In May 1915, Berry took part in the Battle of Aubers Ridge; on 9th May 1915, Berry's battalion went over the top, only to be cut down by German machine gun fire during the attack. The Gloucestershire Regiment gained no ground but lost 262 men, including Berry whose body was never recovered. Berry was 32 when he died and is commemorated on the Le Touret Memorial in Pas de Calais, France

8.3 Henry Brougham (1888-1923)

born at Wellington College, Berkshire

Brougham was also educated at Wellington College and, after leaving school, went to Oxford University and, although he represented both his school and university at cricket and rackets, he did not represent them at rugby.

It was not until after Brougham had graduated and was playing rugby on the wing for Harlequins in the 1911/12 season that his performances as a rugby player were first noticed and he was picked to play in all four of England's Five Nations Championship matches in 1912. Brougham scored a try on his debut against Wales and in the games against Ireland and France, but failed to score in England's one defeat that season, against Scotland. Despite scoring in three of England's matches in 1912, Brougham was not picked to play for them again.

Brougham also represented Great Britain at the Olympics in the singles rackets event (see Chapter 18.6). He also played cricket for Oxford University in the Varsity match against Cambridge in 1909 and for Berkshire from 1905 until 1914, including in their fixture against the touring South African team in 1912.

In the War, Brougham served as a major in the Royal Artillery. In 1917, he was caught in a German gas attack; after being invalided home, he contracted tuberculosis whilst commanding a battery in Northern Ireland. Brougham never properly recovered from the gassing he had suffered and died five years later, on 18th February 1923, in St Croix-Valmer in France, at the age 34.

20th January 1912 England v. Wales at Twickenham; England won 8-0

10th February 1912 England v. Ireland at Twickenham; England won 15-0

16th March 1912 England v. Scotland at Inverleith; Scotland won 8-3

8th April 1912 England v. France at Parc des Princes, Paris; England won 18-8

8.4 Arthur Dingle (1891-1915)

born in Helton le Hole, County Durham

After leaving school, Dingle went to Oxford University and won his blue at rugby playing on the wing in the 1911 Varsity match, a match Oxford won 19-0 and in which Dingle scored one of their three tries. Dingle was not selected for the Varsity match the following year, but, despite this, was selected by England in early 1913 to play against Ireland.

Dingle did not play again for England until England's last two matches in 1914, the first against Scotland and the second against France. Although The Times was critical of his performances in all three matches, Dingle was on the winning side in all of them.

As well as appearing for Oxford, Dingle also played for Richmond and, on his return to Durham to teach after graduating, for Hartlepool Rovers and Durham County.

During the War, Dingle served as a captain with the 6th Battalion, the East Yorkshire Regiment and, on 6th August 1915, took part in the landing at Sulva Bay in the Gallipoli Campaign. On 21st August 1915, Dingle's battalion was ordered to re-take Scimitar Hill, a position they had previously taken but been forced to withdraw from for tactical reasons.

The second assault on Scimitar Hill proved to be a disaster for the British troops and Dingle was killed defending a trench on 22nd August 1915. He was 23 at the time and his body was never recovered; he is commemorated at the Helles Memorial in Turkey.

INTERNATIONAL APPEARANCES

8th February 1913 England v. Ireland at Lansdowne Road, Dublin; England won 15-4

21st March 1914 England v. Scotland at Inverleith; England won 16-15

13th April 1914 England v. France at Colombes; England won 39-13

8.5 George Dobbs (1884-1917)
born in Castlecomer in County Kilkenny

Dobbs went on a maths scholarship to Shrewsbury School, where he captained the school football team. After leaving school, Dobbs attended the Royal Military Academy, where he switched football codes and took up rugby.

Playing club rugby for Plymouth Albion, Devonport Albion and Llanelli, Dobbs's versatility as a flanker was noticed by the England selectors and he was picked for the match against Wales in 1906. Despite losing 16-3, Dobbs retained his place for England's next match against Ireland but a 16-6 defeat proved to be his last game in an England shirt.

At the outbreak of war, Dobbs was sent to France and, following the retreat from Mons, was awarded the Legion of Honour by the French.

Whilst serving with the Royal Engineers Signal Service, Dobbs was mentioned three times in despatches. On 17th June

1917, by which time he had been promoted to lieutenant colonel, Dobbs was killed during a brief lull between the Battle of Messines Ridge and the Third Battle of Ypres when he was hit by a shell whilst surveying a new cable trench on the front line near Poperinghe in Belgium; he was 32 when he died and was buried at the Lijssenthoek Military Cemetery near Ypres.

INTERNATIONAL APPEARANCES

13th January 1906 England v. Wales at Richmond; Wales won 16-3

10th February 1906 England v. Ireland at Leicester; Ireland won 16-6

MILITARY HONOURS

Legion of Honour

Mentioned in despatches (three times)

8.6 Leonard Haigh (1880-1916)
born in Prestwick, Manchester

At school, Haigh played cricket and football and it was not until later in life that he took up rugby. Haigh was a forward who played his club rugby for Manchester Rugby Club and his performances for them resulted in him being selected to play for Lancashire on 18 occasions.

Towards the end of 1909, Haigh was picked to play in the England trial match for the Rest against England and the success of the Rest team resulted in Haigh being picked for England's game against Wales in January 1910, England's first game at Twickenham. After winning 11-6 against Wales, Haigh was picked for England's next game against Ireland which was drawn 0-0 and, after missing the game against France, the game against Scotland, which England won 14-5 and, with it the Five Nations Championship.

The following year, Haigh played in all four of England's Five Nations Championship games, but England were unable to repeat their success of the previous year, losing the games against Wales and Ireland.

Haigh was also picked the same year to join the Barbarians on their Easter tour to Wales.

During the War, Haigh joined the Army Service Corps. Being a motorbike enthusiast, Haigh's knowledge of motorised vehicles meant that he could not be spared on the front line; whilst serving at Woolwich, he contracted double pneumonia whilst on a training exercise and died on 6th August 1916 at the age of 35. He was buried at St Christopher's Church in the village of Pott Shrigley in Cheshire.

INTERNATIONAL APPEARANCES

15th January 1910 England v. Wales at Twickenham; England won 11-6

12th February 1910 England v. Ireland at Twickenham; match drawn 0-0

19th March 1910 England v. Scotland at Inverleith; England won 14-5

21st January 1911 England v. Wales at Swansea; Wales won 15-11

28th January 1911 England v. France at Twickenham; England won 37-0

11th February 1911 England v. Ireland at Lansdowne Road, Dublin; Ireland won 3-0

18th March 1911 England v. Scotland at Twickenham; England won 13-8

8.7 Reginald Hands (1888-1918)

born in Cape Town

As well as being a rugby international, Hands also played cricket for South Africa (see Chapter 7.2).

Hands attended Oxford University on a Rhodes Scholarship and played rugby for the university in the matches against Cambridge in 1908 and 1909, both matches being won by Oxford; his younger brothers Philip and Kenneth also played for Oxford in the Varsity match, Philip in 1910 and Kenneth in 1912.

After university, Hands played for Blackfriars and the Barbarians; after playing for the South of England in a couple of trial matches, Hands was picked to play for England as a forward in 1910 in their Five Nations Championship matches against France and Scotland; England won both matches on their way to winning the Five Nations Championship that year.

Soon after the outbreak of war, Hands enlisted. He initially served in Namibia with the Imperial Light House where he was involved in rounding up German settlers. Hands was subsequently transferred to the South African Heavy Artillery and posted to the Western Front.

On 21st March 1918, the Germans embarked on a final attempt to land a decisive blow before significant numbers of US troops arrived on the Western Front. During this offensive, Hands was wounded and gassed; he died on 20th April 1918 at the age of 29 and is buried at the Eastern Cemetery at Boulogne.

INTERNATIONAL APPEARANCES

3rd March 1910 England v. France at Parc des Princes, Paris; England won 11-3

19th March 1910 England v. Scotland at Inverleith; England won 14-5

8.8 Arthur Harrison (1886-1918)

born in Torquay

After attending Dover College, Harrison embarked on a naval career in 1902. In the Navy, Harrison was able to play rugby and after playing a couple of seasons for Hampshire as a forward, he was selected to play for England, making his debut against Ireland in 1914. Success against Ireland led to Harrison being picked for the game against France; victory over France secured for England their second successive Grand Slam.

As a serving naval officer, Harrison was engaged in a number of key naval battles in the War, including the battles of Heliogoland Bight in 1914, Dogger Bank in 1915 and Jutland in 1916 for which he was mentioned in despatches.

Following a plan devised in 1917, Harrison took part in the raid in Zeebrugge on 23rd April 1918, designed to prevent the Germans use of the port there for their submarines. With unexpected winds affecting the raid, Harrison was hit by a shell whilst on board HMS Vindictive, the shell breaking his jaw and knocking him unconscious. After regaining consciousness, Harrison went on shore to command those charged with disabling the German shore batteries. All of Harrison's party were either killed or wounded and the raid was only a partial success with the port only being blocked for a few days. Harrison died in the attack, at the age of 32 and his body was never recovered; he is commemorated on the Zeebrugge Memorial in Belgium.

Following his death, Harrison was awarded the Victoria Cross, the citation for which reads as follows.

"On 22/23 April 1918 at Zeebrugge, Belgium, Lieutenant-Commander Harrison was in command of the naval storming parties, but immediately before coming alongside the Mole he was struck on the head by a fragment of a shell which broke his jaw and knocked him senseless. Regaining consciousness, he resumed command, leading his men in the attack on the seaward batteries, but was killed at once. Although in great pain he had continued to press his attack, knowing that any delay in silencing the enemy guns might jeopardise the main object of the expedition."

INTERNATIONAL APPEARANCES

14ᵗʰ February 1914 England v. Ireland at Twickenham; England won 17-12

13ᵗʰ April 1914 England v. France at Colombes; England won 39-13

MILITARY HONOURS

Mentioned in despatches

Victoria Cross

8.9 Harold Hodges (1886-1918)
born in Mansfield Woodhouse, Nottinghamshire

Hodges went to Sedbergh School, captaining their rugby team for two years and their cricket team for three. After leaving school, Hodges went to Oxford University in 1905 and was chosen in his freshman year for the rugby Varsity match, playing as a prop against one of his brothers who was at Cambridge.

In 1906, Hodges was selected to play in two matches for England but, after two defeats at the hands of the Welsh and the Irish, he was not selected again. He continued playing rugby for Oxford and, by the time he graduated, had played in four

Varsity matches, including as captain in 1908 and, as captain, against the touring Australian team.

Whilst at Oxford, Hodges also represented the university at lacrosse.

After graduating, Hodges spent some time in Paris before returning to England to teach at Tonbridge School. His teaching allowed him to continue playing rugby for Nottingham and to play cricket for Nottinghamshire; he played three county championship games of cricket for Nottinghamshire, one against Derbyshire in 1911 and two in 1912, against Surrey and Middlesex; in his three games, he scored a total of 141 runs at an average of 47; his 62 on his debut was not only his top score but Nottinghamshire's highest score in the match.

In the War, Hodges first served with the 3rd Battalion, the Monmouthshire Regiment. He was seriously wounded by shellfire at Ypres in May 1915. By July 1916, Hodges had been transferred to the 11th Battalion of the South Lancashire Regiment. For his services in 1916, Hodges was mentioned in despatches; he received a second mention in 1917, which is believed to be for saving a man's life when he carried a wounded soldier across more than a mile of no man's land.

In March 1918, Hodges was involved in the last major offensive of the War which was launched by the Germans before the arrival of US troops; on 24th March 1918, three days after the offensive had started, Hodges was stationed at Ham and tasked with trying to regain contact with a battalion which was reported to be in a small factory on the road from Ham to Eppeville. On arriving at the factory, Hodges expected to see a British battalion only to find that it was occupied by the advancing German troops. Hodges drew his gun and opened fire but was shot and killed. He was 32 and is buried at the Roye New British Cemetery in France.

8.10 Rupert Inglis (1863-1916)

born in London

Inglis attended Rugby School before going up to Oxford University, where he played rugby as a forward in the 1883 and 1884 Varsity matches. After graduating, Inglis continued playing rugby for Blackheath and, in 1886, was selected for England's match against Wales; Inglis retained his place for England's matches against Ireland and Scotland that season but, after the game against Scotland, did not play again for England.

After attending the Ely Theological College, Inglis was ordained as a deacon in 1889 and served as a curate at Helmsley and Basingstoke before becoming the Rector of Frittenden in Kent.

In 1915, Inglis signed up as a volunteer at the age of 51, to encourage younger men to sign up; in a letter to his parishioners from France in July 1915, Inglis wrote "I think most of you will understand how I have come to be writing from France. I have felt that in this great crisis of our nation's history, everyone ought to do what he can to help. I have said this both publicly and privately, and it has been hard to tell people that they ought to leave their homes to go into strange and new surroundings to endure discomforts and danger – perhaps to face death – it has been hard to tell people that this is their duty and then remain comfortably at home myself. So that is why I have left you for an indefinite period."

During the War, Inglis spent time at Vlamertinghe, Calais, Etaples and Ypres, before being stationed at Ginchy during the Battle of the Somme. On 18th September 1916, Inglis was struck by a fragment of shell when searching for the wounded to enable stretcher-bearers to bring them back from no man's land. Whilst receiving treatment for his wound, Inglis was killed when hit by another shell.

Inglis was aged 53 when he died; his body was never recovered and he is commemorated on the Thiepval Memorial to the Missing, near Amiens in France. After his death, one of the tributes sent by one of his fellow officers to his widow reads "He died nobly, doing his duty and setting a striking example to others".

INTERNATIONAL APPEARANCES

2nd January 1886 England v. Wales at Blackheath; England won by one goal and two unconverted tries to one goal and no tries

6th February 1886 England v. Ireland at Lansdowne Road, Dublin; match drawn 0-0

13th March 1886 England v. Scotland at Raeburn Place, Edinburgh; match drawn 0-0

8.11 Percy "Toggie" Kendall (1878-1915)

born in Prescot, Lancashire

Kendall went to Tonbridge School and Cambridge University but, whilst at Cambridge, did not play in a Varsity match. He did however play as scrum-half for Blackheath and the Barbarians and, whilst working as a solicitor in Birkenhead after graduation, for Birkenhead Park.

Kendall made his debut for England against Scotland in 1901, with Scotland winning easily to take the Home Nations Championship and leaving England with the wooden spoon. Kendall played his second game for England a year later, against Wales; the match was much closer than Kendall's previous international but he still ended up on the losing side.

Despite criticism of his performances, Kendall was picked to captain the England team against Scotland a year later and, although he put in a better performance, England still lost the game and Kendall was not picked by England again. He did however play for, and captain, the combined Cheshire, Lancashire and Cumberland team that took on the touring New Zealand team in 1905.

In the War, Kendall served as a lieutenant with the 10th Battalion, the King's Liverpool Regiment. He was posted to France on 1st November 1914; Kendall died when he was shot by a sniper on 25th January 1915. He was 36 when he was killed and was buried at the Kemmel churchyard in Huevelland in Belgium.

INTERNATIONAL APPEARANCES

9th March 1901 England v. Scotland at Blackheath; Scotland won 18-3

11th January 1902 England v. Wales at Blackheath; Wales won 9-8

21st March 1903 England v. Scotland at Richmond; Scotland won 10-6

8.12 John King (1883-1916)

born in Leeds

After leaving Giggleswick School, King went to live in South Africa, before moving back to England and working as a farmer in Yorkshire where he played rugby for Headingley.

For three years from 1911, King was the regular number 8 in the England team, missing only the game against France in 1912 over this period. After losing the first game of 1913 to South Africa, the next four matches which King played in 1913 were all won by England and secured for them their first Grand Slam.

In August 1914, King joined the Yorkshire Hussars, later transferring to the Liverpool Scottish Regiment serving as a lance corporal. On 9th August 1916, King was involved in the attack on Waterlot Farm in Guillemont during the Battle of the Somme; King was killed during one of the attacks that day, along with Lance Slocock (see Chapter 8.23) who was leading the attack.

King was 32 years old when he died. His body was never recovered and he is commemorated at the Thiepval Memorial to the Missing, at Amiens.

INTERNATIONAL APPEARANCES

21st January 1911 England v. Wales at Swansea; Wales won 15-11

28th January 1911 England v. France at Twickenham; England won 37-0

11th February 1911 England v. Ireland at Lansdowne Road, Dublin; Ireland won 3-0

18th March 1911 England v. Scotland at Twickenham; England won 13-3

20th January 1912 England v. Wales at Twickenham; England won 8-0

10th February 1912 England v. Ireland at Twickenham; England won 15-0

16th March 1912 England v. Scotland at Inverleith; Scotland won 8-3

4th January 1913 England v. South Africa at Twickenham; South Africa won 9-3

18th January 1913 England v. Wales at the National Stadium, Cardiff; England won 12-0

25th January 1913 England v. France at Twickenham; England won 20-0

8th February 1913 England v. Ireland at Lansdowne Road, Dublin; England won 15-4

15th March 1913 England v. Scotland at Twickenham; England won 3-0

8.13 Ronald Lagden (1889-1915)

born in Maseru in what was Basutoland and is now Lesotho.

After attending Marlborough College, Lagden went to Oxford University. A talented all-round sportsman, Lagden played in 10 Varsity matches against Cambridge, four at cricket, three at rugby, two at hockey and one at rackets.

By the time he had graduated, Lagden had played 30 games of first-class cricket for Oxford University and one for a combined Oxford and Cambridge team. His games included one against the touring Australians in 1909, one against the touring Indians in 1911 and one against the touring South Africans in 1912. His last game of first-class cricket was the Varsity match in 1912, a match in which he dismissed his brother Reginald who was playing for Cambridge. In his 31 games of first-class cricket, Lagden scored 1,197 runs batting right-handed at an average of 25.46, with a highest score of 99 not out and, with his fast right-arm bowling, took 56 wickets at an average of 25.10, with best figures of 6 for 57.

Whilst playing rugby at Oxford, Lagden was picked to play in his one and only game for England, as a forward against Scotland; a win, with Lagden kicking two conversions, was not enough though for him to retain his place, although there was speculation that he had damaged his knee.

After graduating, Lagden took up a teaching post at Harrow School, which allowed him to continue his rugby, with Richmond.

Lagden enlisted on the first day of the War, joining the King's Royal Rifle Corps. In early 1915, he travelled to France for active duty and was based in the St Eloi sector north of Neuve Chapelle. On 3rd March 1915, Lagden led the men he was commanding over the top, never to return; one of the survivors of the attack reported that Lagden was "well away in front and the first to fall".

Lagden was 25 when he died and is commemorated at the Ypres (Menin Gate) Memorial.

INTERNATIONAL APPEARANCE

18th March 1911 England v. Scotland at Twickenham; England won 13-8

8.14 Douglas "Danny" Lambert (1883-1915)
born in Cranbrook, Kent

Lambert went to St Edward's School, Oxford before moving to Eastbourne College. He played rugby for Harlequins, making his debut on the wing in 1905. A year later Lambert was invited to join the Barbarians on their tour to Wales and, in 1907, was selected to play his first game for England, when the original choice pulled out. Lambert's first game for England was against France and, in England's winning score of 41-13, Lambert scored five tries.

Despite such an impressive performance on debut, Lambert was not picked by England again until the following year. His second game for England was again against France and Lambert scored another try in England's 19-0 win; Lambert played in two more of England's games in the 1908 season, against Wales and Scotland, but was on the losing side in both.

It was another three years before Lambert was picked by England again. A loss against the Welsh was followed by Lambert's third game against the French; in England's 37-0 victory, Lambert scored two tries and kicked five conversions and two penalties, which accounted for 22 of England's points. Lambert's final match for England was against Ireland, a game Ireland won 3-0.

Lambert's three wins for England were all against France and his record of 22 points against them in 1911 was the most points scored by an England player in an international until beaten by Simon Hodgkinson in 1990; his eight tries in his three games against France was also a record, although it has since been matched by New Zealand's Joe Rokocoko (who played 10 games against France between 2003 and 2009) and by Ireland's Brian O'Driscoll (who played 15 games against France between 2002 and 2014).

In the War, Lambert served as a second lieutenant with the 6th Battalion, the Buffs (East Kent Regiment). After being posted to France in December 1914, Lambert took part in the Battle of Loos in September 1915. On 13th October 1915, whilst attempting to break through German lines, the Buffs lost 400 men in a matter of minutes, including Lambert. He was 32 at the time and his body was never recovered; he is commemorated at the Loos Memorial.

5th January 1907 England v. France at Richmond; England won 41-13

1st January 1908 England v. France at Colombes; England won 19-0

18th January 1908 England v. Wales at Ashton Gate, Bristol; Wales won 28-18

21st March 1908 England v. Scotland at Inverleith; Scotland won 16-10

21st January 1911 England v. Wales at Swansea; Wales won 15-11

28th January 1911 England v. France at Twickenham; England won 37-0

11th February 1911 England v. Ireland at Lansdowne Road, Dublin; Ireland won 3-0

8.15 Alfred Maynard (1894-1916)
born in Anerly, Kent

Maynard went to Durham School and, as well as playing rugby for them, also played for Durham City and the Durham county team. After leaving Durham School, for whom he captained the school cricket, fives and gymnastics teams, Maynard went to Cambridge University; he was picked to play second row in the 1912 Varsity match and Cambridge's win over Oxford that year was their first since 1903. The following year Maynard again played for Cambridge against Oxford, scoring a try running almost unimpeded from close to the half-way line on their way to a second successive victory. Maynard also played for Harlequins whilst at university.

In early 1914, a month after his second Varsity match, Maynard was making his debut as hooker for England in their match against Wales; a 10-9 victory saw him retain his place for the next international against Ireland, a game England won 17-12 and the following one against Scotland, which England, as had been the case in the game against Wales, won by just one point. The three victories secured for England the Triple Crown on their way to a second successive Grand Slam.

At the outbreak of war, Maynard joined the Royal Navy and was thrown into active service early on, when despatched in October 1914 to Belgium to defend the port of Antwerp. Due to having to withdraw, Maynard returned to England before being posted to Egypt to defend the Suez Canal. Maynard next saw action when he was sent to the Dardenelles to take part in the Gallipoli campaign but, after being shot in the leg in May 1915, he was evacuated to Alexandria.

After recovering from his wound, Maynard was sent to France and his division was transferred to the Front Line to prepare for the Battle of Ancre, the final act in the Somme offensive which had started in July 1916. Maynard's division was tasked with attacking the east side of the river Ancre and, although the attacks were successful, Maynard was killed on 13th November 1916, the first day of the attack, between Beaumont Hamel and Beaumont sur l'Ancre.

Maynard was just 22 at the time and his body was never recovered; he is commemorated at the Thiepval Memorial to the Missing at Amiens.

Maynard's father was an international footballer, who had played in goal for England in their first international against Scotland in 1872.

INTERNATIONAL APPEARANCES

17th January 1914 England v. Wales at Twickenham; England won 10-9

14th February 1914 England v. Ireland at Twickenham; England won 17-12

21st March 1914 England v. Scotland at Inverleith; England won 16-15

8.16 Edgar Mobbs (1882-1917)

born in Northampton

Mobbs played on the wing for Northampton, captaining them from 1907 up until his retirement in 1913. In December 1908, Mobbs captained the combined Midlands/East Midlands team which inflicted against Australia their only defeat on their 1908/09 tour; a month later, Mobbs was picked by England to play against Australia and, although he scored a try on his debut, he was unable to record a second win against the tourists. Mobbs played in all of England's Home Nations Championship fixtures in 1909, scoring tries against France, Ireland and Scotland; in 1910, he played in two more of England's Home Nations Championship matches, captaining them in the game against France, a game which proved to be his last for England.

Mobbs continued playing rugby for Northampton, East Midlands and the Barbarians up until his retirement in 1913. By the time he had retired, Mobbs had played 234 games for Northampton and scored 177 tries for them, including on two occasions scoring six tries in a match. As well as playing rugby, Mobbs also played cricket for Buckinghamshire.

When war broke out, Mobbs tried to enlist but was initially turned down because of his age; he therefore decided to raise his own company of fellow sportsmen for the Northampton Regiment, which became known as Mobbs' Own.

Mobbs went with his battalion to France in September 1915 and took part in the Battle of Loos. By March 1916, he had been promoted to major and was subsequently promoted to lieutenant colonel. In August 1916, Mobbs was wounded by shrapnel during an attack on Guillemont during the Battle of the Somme. He was twice mentioned in despatches and, in

December 1916, awarded the Distinguished Service Order for his work as a battalion commander.

In June 1917, Mobbs was wounded for the second time whilst at Messines but back with his battalion by the end of the month. On 31st July 1917, whilst taking part in the Third Battle of Ypres at Zillebeke, Mobbs was killed in action; records differ as to how he died, with one report stating he was killed when he was hit whilst marshalling his troops whilst other reports record that he was killed when he was leading his battalion from the front in an attack on a machine gun post that had trapped a detachment of his battalion.

Mobbs was 35 years old when he died; his body was never recovered and he is commemorated at the Ypres (Menin Gate) Memorial.

Also commemorating Mobbs, there has been played since 1921 the Mobbs Memorial match; initially the match was between the Barbarians and East Midlands but in more recent years has been between the Army and, in alternate years, Northampton and Bedford.

INTERNATIONAL APPEARANCES

9th January 1909 England v. Australia at Blackheath; Australia won 9-3

16th January 1909 England v. Wales at the National Stadium, Cardiff; Wales won 8-0

30th January 1909 England v. France at Leicester; England won 22-0

13th February 1909 England v. Ireland at Lansdowne Road, Dublin; England won 11-5

20th March 1909 England v. Scotland at Richmond; Scotland won 18-8

12th February 1910 England v. Ireland at Twickenham; match drawn 0-0

3rd March 1910 England v. France at Parc des Princes, Paris; England won 11-3

MILITARY HONOURS

Mentioned in despatches (twice)

Distinguished Service Order

8.17 William "Billy" Nanson (1880-1915)
born in Carlisle

Having joined the Border Regiment at the age of 19, Nanson was sent to South Africa to fight in the Second Boer War but invalided home after becoming ill. Nanson returned to South Africa once he had recovered, only to return to England again at the end of the Boer War.

On his return, Nanson played his club rugby as a forward for Carlisle and, in 1907, was chosen to represent England against France, a game won easily by England with Nanson scoring one of their nine tries – five of England's tries were scored by Danny Lambert (see Chapter 8.14). Nanson retained his place for England's game against Wales but, with Wales winning a one-sided match, Nanson was not picked again.

In June 1908, Nanson switched codes when he joined Oldham Rugby League Club, for whom he played for four seasons, before joining the newly-formed Coventry Rugby Club.

Nanson was called up in August 1914, joining the 1/10th Battalion, the Manchester Regiment. Nanson was sent with the battalion to Egypt on its way to Gallipoli, taking part in the Gallipoli landings in April 1915.

On 4th June 1915, Nanson took part in the Third Battle of Krithia; Nanson's battalion suffered heavy losses and he was last seen with his rifle and bayonet moving along a Turkish trench, in an attempt to clear it. He was not seen again and was reported missing in action, although it was another 13 months before he was declared presumed dead.

Nanson was 34 years old when he died; his body was never recovered and he is commemorated at the Helles Memorial in Turkey.

5th January 1907 England v. France at Richmond; England won 41-13

12th January 1907 England v. Wales at Swansea; Wales won 22-0

8.18 Francis Oakeley (1891-1914)
born in Hereford

After attending Hereford Cathedral School, Oakeley went at the age of 13 to the Royal Naval College at Osbourne on the Isle of Wight, before finishing his naval training at Dartmouth.

Oakeley played scrum-half for the Navy, playing in four of their matches against the Army. In October 1912, Oakeley was selected to play for the Combined Army and Navy team against the touring South Africans and, following the Navy's win over the Army in March 1913, for England against Scotland.

The following year, Oakeley played in three of England's games in the Five Nations Championship, on their way to the Grand Slam.

Having joined the Navy's submarine service in 1913, Oakeley was assigned to the submarine HMS D2 in 1914 and took part in the Battle of Heligoland Bight on 28th August 1914, a battle which saw the German Navy lose three of its light cruisers with the British Navy suffering no losses.

On 25th November 1914, two days after losing its commanding officer when he was swept overboard in poor weather, HMS D2 was sent out on patrol again, never to return. It is believed that the submarine was rammed on 1st December 1914 by a German patrol boat off Borkum close to the border between Germany and The Netherlands; all those on board the submarine lost their lives.

Oakeley was 23 years old when he died; he is commemorated at the Portsmouth Naval Memorial.

INTERNATIONAL APPEARANCES

15th March 1913 England v. Scotland at Twickenham; England won 3-0

14th February 1914 England v. Ireland at Twickenham; England won 17-12

21st March 1914 England v. Scotland at Inverleith; England won 16-15

13th April 1914 England v. France at Colombes; England won 39-13

8.19 Robert Pillman (1893-1916)
born in Sidcup

After attending Rugby School, Pillman played his club rugby as a flanker for Blackheath; in 1912, he was selected to represent the London Counties XV in their fixture against the touring South Africans, one of only two matches the visitors lost on their tour.

Pillman's older brother Cherry also played for Blackheath and 18 times for England and it was as a result of his brother breaking his leg in the game against Scotland that Pillman was picked for England's last match before the War, the away match against the French; England's win secured for them their second successive Grand Slam.

Pillman was also a scratch golfer and, after qualifying as a solicitor, won the London Solicitors Golfing Society's gold medal.

At the outbreak of war, Pillman enlisted with the 10th Battalion, the Royal West Kent Regiment; after being promoted to captain, Pillman was sent to the Western Front in May 1916, where he served as a bombing officer. Leading his men through barbed wire defences into enemy trenches on a night raid on 9th July 1916 as part on the Somme offensive near Armentieres, Pillman was shot in the thigh and, although he made it back to his own trenches, he died shortly afterwards. Pillman was 23 years old when he died and was buried at the Calvaire (Essex) Military Cemetery in Hainaut in Belgium.

INTERNATIONAL APPEARANCE

13th April 1914 England v. France at Colombes; England won 39-13

8.20 Ronald Poulter-Palmer (1889-1915)
born in Oxford

Although he was born Ronald Poulter, he changed his name in 1914 following the death in October 1913 of his uncle, the Right Honourable George Palmer, whose family had co-founded the biscuit manufacturers Huntley & Palmer; it was a condition of his inheritance that he did so and, although he did change his name to Ronald Palmer, he is best known by the name Ronald Poulton-Palmer.

Before attending Rugby School, Poulton-Palmer had shown his potential as a rugby player when scoring 15 tries in one match for his prep school. After school, Poulton-Plamer went to Oxford University and, although he had already played for Harlequins, was not selected for the Varsity match against Cambridge in his fresher year; notwithstanding this omission, he was selected to play for England against France only six weeks later.

In his second year at university, Poulton-Palmer did win his blue, scoring five of Oxford's nine tries in their 35-3 victory; a year later, Poulter-Palmer was to score two more tries and, in 1911, one more try, in Oxford's wins over Cambridge. Despite his rugby commitments whilst at university, Poulter-Palmer also represented Oxford University at hockey.

After graduating, Poulter-Palmer worked in Liverpool, playing his club rugby Liverpool, before returning south following the death of his uncle.

Following his first game for England in January 1909, Poulter-Palmer was not a regular in the England team until the end of the 1911 season but over the next three years up to the outbreak of war only missed one of England's 13 matches. He scored his first try for England in their match against Ireland in 1912 and scored his second try in the defeat against South Africa in January 1913. Poulter-Palmer scored two more tries in the 1913 Five Nations Championship when England won the Grand Slam and the following year captained England to their second successive Grand Slam, scoring one try in England's win over Scotland and four tries in their win over France. Ireland's captain, Dickie Lloyd, who had played with him at Liverpool, considered Poulton-Palmer to be the greatest player he came in contact with whilst others considered him to have been the greatest-ever attacking three-quarter.

Before war had broken out, Poulter-Palmer had been commissioned into the 1st/4th Battalion, Princess Charlotte of Wales's (Royal Berkshire Regiment) (Territorial Force). In March 1915, Poulter-Palmer left with his battalion for France. In the early hours of 5th May 1915, whilst directing a working party carrying out repairs to a trench near Ploegsteert Wood in Belgium, Poulter-Palmer was shot and killed by an enemy sniper; he was 25 years old when he died and was buried at the Hyde Park Corner (Royal Berks) Cemetery near Ypres in Belgium.

INTERNATIONAL APPEARANCES

30th January 1909 England v. France at Leicester; England won 22-0

13th February 1909 England v. Ireland at Lansdowne Road, Dublin; England won 11-5

20th March 1909 England v. Scotland at Richmond; Scotland won 18-8

15th January 1910 England v. Wales at Twickenham; England won 11-6

18th March 1911 England v. Scotland at Twickenham; England won 13-8

20th January 1912 England v. Wales at Twickenham; England won 8-0

10th February 1912 England v. Ireland at Twickenham; England won 15-0

16th March 1912 England v. Scotland at Inverleith; Scotland won 8-3

4th January 1913 England v. South Africa at Twickenham; South Africa won 9-3

18th January 1913 England v. Wales at the National Stadium, Cardiff; England won 12-0

25th January 1913 England v. France at Twickenham; England won 20-0

8th February 1913 England v. Ireland at Lansdowne Road, Dublin; England won 15-4

15th March 1913 England v. Scotland at Twickenham; England won 3-0

17th January 1914 England v. Wales at Twickenham; England won 10-9

14th February 1914 England v. Ireland at Twickenham; England won 17-12

21st March 1914 England v. Scotland at Inverleith; England won 16-15

13th April 1914 England v. France at Colombes: England won 39-13

8.21 John Raphael (1882-1917)
born in Brussels

After attending Merchant Taylors School, Raphael went up to Oxford University in 1901. Raphael played as a three-quarter and played in four Varsity matches for Oxford against Cambridge; only weeks after playing in his first Varsity match,

Raphael was picked to play for England, playing in all three of their Home Nations Championship fixtures in 1902.

Raphael missed out on the 1903 and 1904 Home Nations Championships but played against Wales and Scotland in 1905. Later that same year, Raphael played in England's first match against New Zealand and in two of England's games in the 1906 Home Nations Championship, as well as in the friendly against France, who were at that stage not competing in what became the Five Nations Championship. Raphael's only try in an England shirt came in their 9-3 win over Scotland in 1906.

In 1910, Raphael captained the Great Britain team on their tour to Argentina and, in Argentina's first Test, Raphael scored one of the tourists' five tries and kicked one of their three conversions in their 28-3 victory; although caps were awarded to the Argentine players for this fixture, they were not awarded to the British team.

Raphael was also a cricketer and had played his first game of first-class cricket by the time he went up to Oxford. He appeared in three cricket Varsity matches, scoring 130 runs in the first innings of his first Varsity match and being bowled out for 99 in the first innings of his final Varsity match. He continued playing for Surrey after graduating and by the time he retired from first-class cricket in 1913, he had played a total of 77 games of first-class cricket, in which he had scored 3,717 runs at an average of 30.97 and five centuries. His score of 201 for Oxford against Yorkshire in 1904 was his highest and his final game in 1913 was playing for an England XI against Yorkshire.

In addition to representing his university at rugby and cricket, Raphael was also president of the Oxford University Swimming

Club and played for Oxford against Cambridge in two water polo Varsity matches.

In the War, Raphael served as a lieutenant with the King's Royal Rifle Corps, after having enlisted into the Honourable Artillery Company at the outbreak of war. Raphael died at Remy on 11th June 1917 at the age of 35 after he had been wounded when a shell burst in front of him during the Battle of Messines. He was buried at Lijssenthoek Military Cemetery near Poperinghe in Belgium.

INTERNATIONAL APPEARANCES

11th January 1902 England v. Wales at Blackheath; Wales won 9-8

8th February 1902 England v. Ireland at Leicester; England won 6-3

15th March 1902 England v. Scotland at Inverleith; England won 6-3

14th January 1905 England v. Wales at the National Stadium, Cardiff; Wales won 25-0

18th March 1905 England v. Scotland at Richmond; Scotland won 8-0

2nd December 1905 England v. New Zealand at Crystal Palace; New Zealand won 15-0

13th January 1906 England v. Wales at Richmond; Wales won 16-3

17th March 1906 England v. Scotland at Inverleith; England won 9-3

22nd March 1906 England v. France at Parc des Princes, Paris; England won 35-0

8.22 Reggie Schwarz (1875-1918)
born in London

Not only was Schwarz an international at rugby, but he also played cricket for South Africa (see Chapter 7.6).

After school, Schwarz went to Cambridge University where he won a blue at rugby, playing in the 1893 Varsity match. Six years later he was making his debut for England, playing fly-half against Scotland. Schwarz was next picked for England in 1901, when he played against Wales and Scotland.

After these matches, which were Schwarz's last two games of rugby for England, he continued playing cricket for Middlesex but, after two more seasons with them, emigrated to South Africa, where he played for Transvaal. In 1905, Schwarz made his debut as a Test cricketer and, over the next eight years played 20 Tests for them, his principal role being a leg-spin bowler who could also bowl a googly.

Schwarz retired from cricket in 1912 to pursue a career as a stockbroker.

During the War, Schwarz served as a major in the King's Royal Rifle; he served in German West Africa (now Namibia) for which he was mentioned in despatches, before joining the King's Royal Rifle Corps on the Western Front. During his time in France, Schwarz was mentioned in despatches a second time and also awarded the Military Cross. Although he suffered two serious wounds, Schwarz survived the War but died from the Spanish flu epidemic whilst still in France, just seven days after the Armistice was signed. Schwarz was 43 when he died and was buried at the Etaples Military Cemetery.

INTERNATIONAL APPEARANCES

11th March 1899 England v. Scotland at Blackheath; Scotland won 5-0

5th January 1901 England v. Wales at the National Stadium, Cardiff; Wales won 13-0

9th February 1901 England v. Ireland at Lansdowne Road, Dublin; Ireland won 10-6

MILITARY HONOURS

Mentioned in despatches (twice)

Military Cross

8.23 Lancelot Andrew Noel Slocock (1886-1916)

born in Wootton Warren, Warwickshire

After attending Marlborough College, Slocock played his club rugby for Liverpool. His reputation as a line-out jumper resulted in him being picked to play for England against the touring South Africans in late 1906 but a clerical error denied him the opportunity to play against South Africa, his place being taken by Arnold Alcock.

It was not long though after the England game against South Africa that Slocock made his debut, the game against France in early 1907. After scoring a try on his debut, Slocock played in all of England's other Home Nations Championship games in 1907, scoring a second try against Ireland and being praised by The Times for his performance in the defeat against Wales.

Slocock kept his place for England's games in 1908; Slocock captained the team in the last game of the season, against Scotland and, although he scored his third try for England in this game, he ended up on the losing side.

Business commitments in the cotton trade put an end to his international rugby career and, by 1914, Slocock had moved with his family to the USA. Not long after moving to the USA, Slocock returned to England to take part in the War. He was commissioned as a second lieutenant in the 1/10th Battalion, the King's Regiment (Liverpool) and, by January 1916, had been sent to France. In early August 1916, Slocock was taking part in the Somme offensive and, on 9th August, whilst leading his men in one of the attacks aimed at capturing the village of Guillemont, was killed in action.

Slocock was 29 years old when he died and is commemorated at the Thiepval Memorial, near Amiens in France.

5th January 1907 England v. France at Richmond; England won 41-13

12th January 1907 England v. Wales at Swansea; Wales won 22-0

9th February 1907 England v. Ireland at Lansdowne Road, Dublin; Ireland won 17-9

16th March 1907 England v. Scotland at Blackheath; Scotland won 8-3

1st January 1908 England v. France at Colombes; England won 19-0

18th January 1908 England v. Wales at Ashton Gate, Bristol; Wales won 28-18

8th February 1908 England v. Ireland at Richmond; England won 13-3

21st March 1908 England v. Scotland at Inverleith; Scotland won 16-10

8.24 Francis Tarr (1887-1915)

born near Belper, Derbyshire

After attending Uppingham School, Tarr went up to Oxford University in 1906 and played in the 1907, 1908 and 1909 Varsity matches against Cambridge.

In January 1909, whilst still at university, Tarr made his England debut at centre, against the touring Australian team; although England lost the match 9-3, the try scored by Edgar Mobbs (see Chapter 8.16) was described as one of the very best ever scored "being perfect in execution from the moment Tarr first received the ball to the moment Mobbs touched down for a try".

Tarr won his second cap a week later against Wales and his third cap a fortnight later against France; in the game against France, Tarr scored two tries but was dropped from the England side after the game.

It was another four years before England called upon Tarr's services again, for the final fixture of the 1913 season, against Scotland; a narrow victory secured for England their first Grand Slam.

As well as representing Oxford and England, Tarr played 94 games for Leicester, as well as games for Headingley and Richmond.

After graduating, Tarr qualified as a solicitor; when war was declared, he enlisted, serving as machine gun officer with the Leicestershire Regiment. Tarr was sent with his battalion to France in March 1915. On 18th July 1915, after the Second Battle of Ypres, Tarr went to the dugouts of the 5th Battalion of the Lincolnshire Regiment near Zillebeke to liaise with their adjutant. Tarr was killed when a splinter from a shell struck him in the face – he was hit when he put his head above the parapet of a dugout as he was telling some of the men to keep under cover.

Tarr was 27 years old when he died and was buried at the Railway Dugouts Burial Ground at West Vlaanderen in Belgium.

INTERNATIONAL APPEARANCES

9th January 1909 England v. Australia at Blackheath; Australia won 9-3

16th January 1909 England v. Wales at the National Stadium, Cardiff; Wales won 8-0

30th January 1909 England v. France at Leicester; England won 22-0

15th March 1913 England v. Scotland at Twickenham; England won 3-0

8.25 Alexander Todd (1873-1915)

born in Lewisham, London

After attending Mill Hill School, where he had been captain of football and rugby, Todd went to Cambridge

University and won his blue at rugby in 1893, 1894 and 1895. After graduating, Todd continued playing club rugby for Blackheath and, in 1896, was picked as a member of the Great Britain team to tour South Africa. Todd played as a forward in all four of the tourists' matches, scoring his only international try in the second game, which Great Britain won 17-8.

Despite having been picked to play for Great Britain in 1896, Todd had to wait more than three years before being selected to play for England. His England debut came after England, with 13 new caps, lost to Wales in the opening game of the 1900 Home Nations Championship, Todd playing in England's final two games of those championships.

Todd joined the British Army after university and, in 1900, he returned to South Africa to serve as squadron commander in the Second Boer War with Roberts' Horse and Carrington's Horse; during the Battle of Diamond Hill in June 1900, Todd was wounded.

Todd was also a competent cricketer; he played four games for London County in 1896 and kept wicket for Berkshire from 1910 until 1913, playing in 23 Minor County Championship matches for them.

At the outbreak of war, Todd joined the Reserve Battalion, the Norfolk Regiment and, by the time he was sent to France, had reached the rank of captain. On 18th April 1915, Todd was taking part in the British assault on Hill 60 at Ypres Salient, days before the start of the Second Battle of Ypres, when he was shot in the neck whilst in the trenches; he died three days later at the age of 41 and was buried at the Poperinghe Old Military Cemetery, in Belgium.

30ᵗʰ July 1896 Great Britain v. South Africa at Port Elizabeth; Great Britain won 8-0

22ⁿᵈ August 1896 Great Britain v. South Africa at Johannesburg; Great Britain won 17-8

29ᵗʰ August 1896 Great Britain v. South Africa at Kimberley; Great Britain won 9-3

5ᵗʰ September 1896 Great Britain v. South Africa at Cape Town; South Africa won 5-0

3ʳᵈ February 1900 England v. Ireland at Richmond; England won 17-4

10ᵗʰ March 1900 England v. Scotland at Inverleith; match drawn 0-0

8.26 James "Bungy" Watson (1890-1914)
born in Southsea

Watson was educated at King's School Canterbury, before he finished his schooldays at the Edinburgh Academy. After school, Watson went to Edinburgh University to study medicine.

Watson played centre for the university team and was also the university's middleweight boxing champion. During his time in Edinburgh, Watson also played rugby for Edinburgh Academicals, whom he captained in 1912/13 and for the Barbarians before returning to London after completing his medical studies, to work at the London Hospital.

Back in London, Watson joined Blackheath and, in 1914, made his debut for England against Wales at Twickenham – in 1913, he had been picked as reserve centre for Scotland but was never capped by them; an injury caused Watson to miss England's next game against Ireland but he was fit again in time to play in the matches against Scotland and France. After the narrowest of victories over Wales and Scotland, England won more comfortably against the French, with Watson scoring one of their tries on their way to their second successive Grand Slam.

In addition to being an international at rugby and a university champion at boxing, Watson was also an international athlete, having represented Scotland against Ireland in the long jump in 1912; Watson won his event with a jump of 22 feet 9.5 inches.

At the start of the War, Watson was appointed surgeon on the HMS Hawke. On 15th October 1914, Watson was on board HMS Hawke as she was patrolling the North Sea with HMS Theseus, 60 miles off the coast near Aberdeen, when she was struck by a torpedo launched by the German submarine U-9; the torpedo was intended for HMS Theseus but missed and struck HMS Hawke. After two large explosions caused by the ship's magazine being detonated, HMS Hawke sunk within eight minutes of being hit; HMS Hawke only had time to launch one safety boat and, although 49 on board were picked up three hours later by a Norwegian steamer, 525 lives were lost, including Watson's.

Watson was 24 years old when he died and is commemorated at the Chatham Naval Memorial at Twickenham.

INTERNATIONAL APPEARANCES

17th January 1914 England v. Wales at Twickenham; England won 10-9

21st March 1914 England v. Scotland at Inverleith; England won 16-15

13th April 1914 England v. France at Colombes; England won 39-13

8.27 Arthur Wilson (1886-1917)

born in Newcastle-upon-Tyne

After attending Glenalmond School, Wilson moved to Cornwall following his decision to become a mining engineer and attended the Camborne School of Mines. He played as a forward for Camborne and was picked for the Cornish county team, making 23 appearances for them, including when they won the County Championship title in 1908.

As a result of winning the County Championship title, the Cornish team were selected to represent Great Britain at the 1908 Olympics; with only two teams competing and with the other team being an Australian team consisting of international players rather than county standard players, the Great Britain team, with Wilson its youngest player and playing as a forward, came off second best to win the silver medal.

Less than four months later, Wilson was picked to play in his only international for England, the game against Ireland in Dublin, which England won.

After finishing his studies at the Camborne School of Mines, Wilson worked overseas, first as an engineer in South Africa and then as a tea planter in India before returning to England to fight in the War. He enlisted as a private with the Royal Fusiliers and was killed on 1st July 1917 at the age of 30 at the Third Battle of Ypres. His resting place remains unknown but he is commemorated at the Ypres (Menin Gate) Memorial in Belgium.

INTERNATIONAL APPEARANCE

13th February 1909 England v. Ireland at Lansdowne Road, Dublin; England won 11-5

8.28 Charles Wilson (1871-1914)

born in Fernoy, County Cork

After attending Dover College, Wilson went to the Royal Military Academy at Sandhurst and, on graduation, was commissioned as a lieutenant with the Queen's (Royal West Surrey) Regiment. Whilst at Sandhurst, Wilson played rugby for the Army and Blackheath, a club he continued to play for after his graduation. In 1898, Wilson was called up to play for England against Ireland in the Home Nations Championship and, although the score was close with Ireland wining 9-6, Ireland dominated the game and Wilson, who was one of four forwards making his debut for England that day, was not picked by England again.

Wilson's Army career saw him serving in the Second Boer War, taking part in the Relief of Ladysmith, the Battle of Scion Kop and the Battle of Tugela Heights. In August 1901, Wilson was promoted to captain and, in April 1902, was appointed a staff officer, as an Adjutant-Provost Marshall in South Africa. For his services in South Africa, Wilson was mentioned in despatches and awarded the Queen's Medal with two clasps and the King's Medal with two clasps. After returning home, Wilson was posted to India.

During the Great War, Wilson served as adjutant of the 1st Battalion, Queen's (Royal West Surrey) Regiment. He served on the Western Front and was awarded the Legion d'Honneur but was killed in action on 17th September 1914 at the age of 43 on the River Aisne, during the Battle of the Aisne. He was buried at the Paissy Churchyard in Aisne, France.

INTERNATIONAL APPEARANCE

5th February 1898 England v. Ireland at Richmond; Ireland won 9-6

MİLİTARY HONOURS

Mentioned in despatches

Queen's Medal with two clasps

King's Medal with two clasps

Legion d'Honneur

CHAPTER 9
IRELAND RUGBY PLAYERS

9.1 William Beatty (1888-1919)
born in Belfast

Beatty was a prop forward who played his club rugby for Sydenham, Ulster and Richmond; he also played for the Barbarians. He made his debut for Ireland in 1910, in the away fixture against France. Beatty next played for Ireland in the corresponding fixture two years later and in the game against Wales that year but, after three wins out of three, was not selected again.

In the War, Beatty served as a major with the Army Service Corps and was attached to Fourth Army heavy artillery division. He was mentioned in despatches in 1917 but later was seriously wounded in action, following which he was evacuated to the 20th Casualty Clearing Station at Charleroi, where he died from pneumonia on 10th February 1919, three months after the War ended. Beatty was 30 years old when he died and was buried at the Charleroi Community Cemetery, in Belgium; he was posthumously awarded the OBE.

INTERNATIONAL APPEARANCES

28th March 1910 Ireland v. France at Parc des Princes, Paris; Ireland won 8-3

1st January 1912 Ireland v. France at Parc des Princes, Paris; Ireland won 11-6

9th March 1912 Ireland v. Wales at Balmoral Showgrounds, Belfast; Ireland won 12-5

MILITARY HONOURS

Mentioned in despatches

9.2 Jasper Brett (1895-1917)

born in Kingstown, County Dublin

At school, Brett showed his all-round talent as a sportsman, captaining his school's cricket and rugby teams, as well as holding long jump and high jump records; he was also a low handicap golfer.

After leaving school, Brett took articles with his father's firm of solicitors and played his club rugby as centre for Monkstown. In March 1914, not long after his 19th birthday, Brett was picked for Ireland against Wales; although he was also picked as a reserve for Ireland's following match against France, Brett did not get on to the pitch in this match and the defeat against Wales proved to be his only international.

In the War, Brett joined as a second lieutenant in the 7th Battalion, the Royal Dublin Fusiliers. On 7th August 1915, Brett landed with his battalion at Sulva Bay in Gallipoli and, within days of landing, was taking part in the battle of Chocolate Hill and the fighting at Kizlar Dagh Ridge. By the end of October 1915, the battalion had moved to Salonika where it was based whilst taking part in operations in Macedonia.

In June 1916, Brett was admitted to hospital suffering from severe shell shock; after being released from a military hospital in Richmond in January 1917, Brett returned to Dublin. On 4th February 1917, Brett left his home to go for a walk in the evening; he then took his own life, his body being found in a railway tunnel after having been hit by a train.

Brett was 21 years old when he died and was buried at the Deansgrange Cemetery in County Dublin.

INTERNATIONAL APPEARANCE

14th March 1914 Ireland v. Wales at Balmoral Showgrounds, Belfast; Wales won 11-3

9.3 Robert Burgess (1890-1915)

born in London on Christmas Day

Burgess attended Trinity College, Dublin and played his club rugby as a forward for the Dublin University Football Club. He was selected to represent Ireland in their match against the touring South African team in 1912; after suffering a heavy defeat at the hands of the tourists, Burgess was not picked again by the Irish selectors. As well as playing rugby, Burgess also excelled as a huntsman, fisherman and shot.

After graduating, Burgess was called to the Bar, working on the North East circuit in England, but the outbreak of war came soon after he was called; he therefore had very limited opportunities to practise as a barrister before he returned to Dublin once war broke out to help out in a casualty depot. By January 1915, Burgess had been promoted to the rank of captain, serving with the Royal Engineers in the inland water transport unit.

On 9th December 1915, Burgess was hit by a shell whilst cycling down a street in Armentieres; he was taken to a casualty clearing station, where he died. He was 24 years old when he died and was buried at the Bailleul Communal Cemetery, in France.

INTERNATIONAL APPEARANCE

30th November 1912 Ireland v. South Africa at Lansdowne Road, Dublin; South Africa won 38-0

9.4 Ernest Deane (1887-1915)

born in Limerick

Deane studied medicine at the Royal College of Surgeons in Ireland and graduated in 1909, the same year he played his one and only game of rugby for Ireland, on the wing against England in Dublin. Later that year, Deane broke his leg playing for Monkstown against Oxford University, bringing a premature end to his rugby career.

A talented sportsman, Deane was also a useful shot and horseman, as well as a competent tennis player and golfer.

In 1911, Deane was commissioned in to the Royal Army Medical Corps and posted to India, where he was serving when war broke out. Deane was sent back to France, arriving in Marseille in September 1914 before being sent to the Western Front. After serving with the 20th Field Ambulance, Deane was then posted as a medical officer with the 2nd Battalion of the Leicestershire Regiment.

On 22nd August 1915, Deane's gallantry earned him the Military Cross when, after a standing patrol 120 yards in front of the lines near Fauquissant had been bombed and without any knowledge of the enemy's strength, he ran out over the parapet under machine gun and rifle fire to find four wounded soldiers, returning with stretchers and getting them back to safety.

Just over a month later, Deane was taking part in the Battle of Loos at Neuve Chappelle when, on 25th September 1915, he was shot dead after going to help some injured men, for which he was posthumously mentioned in despatches. Deane was 28 years old when he died and was buried at the Rue-du-Bacquerot No 1 Military Cemetery at Laventie in

Pas de Calais. Following his death, Deane's colonel wrote to his father to tell him that "everyone knew Deane as one of the bravest of the brave" and that his award of the Military Cross was "one of the best deserved and gallantry won honours".

INTERNATIONAL APPEARANCE

13th February 1909 Ireland v. England at Lansdowne Road, Dublin; England won 11-5

MILITARY HONOURS

Military Cross

Mentioned in despatches

9.5 William Edwards (1887-1917)
born in Belfast

Edwards attended Campbell College in Belfast before going to Queen's University, Belfast. He played rugby as a forward for Malone RFC and, after a few games for Ulster, was picked to play in Ireland's two away fixtures in the 1912 Five Nations Championship.

Edwards was also the Irish swimming champion over 220 yards and a water polo champion and said to have been the first person to swim Belfast Lough.

An accountant by profession, Edwards initially served in the War with the 6th Battalion, East Belfast of the Ulster Volunteer Force. From May 1915, he served with the expeditionary forces in France and Flanders.

On 9th September 1916, Edwards was wounded at the capture of Ginchy when a bullet hit him in the head, causing him to suffer from dizziness and insomnia; prior to being wounded in the head, Edwards had already appeared on the casualty lists after having been gassed.

In September 1917, Edwards was sent to Egypt and took part in the Battle of Gaza during the first week of September 1917. The following month, Edwards took part in the capture of Jerusalem and the defence of the city following its capture.

On 29th December 1917, Edwards was killed in action near Deir Ibzia in Palestine, just three days after he had assumed command of D Company, 7th Battalion of the Royal Dublin Fusiliers. Edwards was 30 years old when he died and after having been initially buried near Deir Ibzia, was finally buried at the Jerusalem War Cemetery near the village of Deis Ibsis.

INTERNATIONAL APPEARANCES

1st January 1912 Ireland v. France at Parc des Princes, Paris; Ireland won 11-6

10th February 1912 Ireland v. England at Twickenham; England won 15-0

9.6 William Hallaran (1861-1917)

William Hallaran was born in 1861; his place of birth is unknown but, with his father having been the Archdeacon of Ardfelt, it is likely that he was born there.

Hallaran attended Dublin University and played half-back at rugby for the university team. He also represented Leinster and, in 1884, made his only appearance for Ireland against Wales, playing as one of Ireland's two half-backs in the match. Hallaran's one international was Ireland's second ever fixture against Wales and, with the scoring system being what it was at the time, Wales won the match by one goal to nil, even though Wales scored one goal and two tries to Ireland's two touch-downs and one touch in goal. Because he did not want his father to know he was playing in the match, Hallaran played under the name R. O. N. Hall.

After graduating, Hallaran qualified as a doctor and joined the Royal Army Medical Corps, becoming Surgeon General in July 1887. He served in Burma from 1887 to 1889 and in India in 1899 and 1900 before being sent to South Africa where he took part in the relief of Kimberley in the Second Boer War. After the Second Boer War, Hallaran returned to India, becoming Director of Medical Studies in Jabalpur, where he died, at the age of 55, on 23rd January 1917. Hallaran is commemorated on the Kirkee 1914-1918 Memorial in India.

INTERNATIONAL APPEARANCE

12th April 1884 Ireland v. Wales at the National Stadium, Cardiff;

Wales won by one goal to nil

9.7 Basil Maclear (1881-1915)
born in Portsmouth

Maclear attended Bedford School moving going to the Royal Military Academy, Sandhurst; as well as representing Sandhurst at rugby, cricket, athletics and shooting, Maclear also received the Sword of Honour.

After leaving Sandhurst, Maclear served with the Royal Dublin Fusiliers in the Second Boer War from 1900 to 1902, receiving the Queen's Medal with five clasps and being mentioned in despatches; in 1903, Maclear served in Aden before returning home. Maclear played his club rugby for a number of clubs, including Blackheath, Monkstown and the Barbarians and, in 1905, captained Munster against the touring New Zealand team.

Despite being recommended for a trial with England, the English selectors ignored him and instead Maclear played for Ireland, making his debut in early 1905 playing as a three-quarter. On his debut against the country which had overlooked him, Maclear created two tries, scored one and kicked a conversion; a year later, he scored another try and kicked another conversion against England, a country he played against three times and always ended up on the winning side against. Maclear also scored a try in the games against Wales and South Africa in 1906 and kicked a conversion in his second international, the game against Scotland in 1905.

In the War, Maclear served with the 2nd Battalion of the Royal Dublin Fusiliers, with whom he was sent to the Western Front in March 1915.

In the early hours of 25th May 1915, Maclear's battalion came under attack from gas whilst bunkering up at Mouse Trap Farm not far from Ypres. The gas attack was followed by an infantry attack and, later that morning, Maclear launched a grenade attack on the trenches taken by the Germans; during the attack, Maclear was shot in the throat and killed; he was 34 years old.

Maclear's body was never recovered and he is commemorated at the Ypres (Menin Gate) Memorial. Maclear was mentioned in despatches for his actions.

11th February 1905 Ireland v. England at Cork; Ireland won 17-3

25th February 1905 Ireland v. Scotland at Inverleith; Ireland won 11-5

1st March 1905 Ireland v. Wales at Swansea; Wales won 10-3

25th November 1905 Ireland v. New Zealand at Lansdowne Road, Dublin; New Zealand won 15-0

10th February 1906 Ireland v. England at Leicester; Ireland won 8-6

24th February 1906 Ireland v. Scotland at Lansdowne Road, Dublin; Scotland won 13-6

10th March 1906 Ireland v. Wales at Balmoral Showgrounds, Belfast; Ireland won 11-6

24th November 1906 Ireland v. South Africa at Balmoral Showgrounds, Belfast; South Africa won 15-12

9th February 1907 Ireland v. England at Lansdowne Road, Dublin; Ireland won 17-9

23rd February 1907 Ireland v. Scotland at Inverleith; Scotland won 15-3

9th March 1907 Ireland v. Wales at the National Stadium, Cardiff; Wales won 29-0

MILITARY HONOURS

Queen's medal with five clasps

Mentioned in despatches twice

9.8 George McAllan (1879-1918)

born in Belfast in 1879,

although some records suggest he was born a year later.

Whilst still at school at Royal School Dungannon, McAllan became the first schoolboy to be picked for Ireland when he played at full-back against Scotland in 1896, shortly after his 18th birthday. A month later, he played his second and final game for Ireland, against Wales.

After leaving school, McAllan first worked as a schoolteacher before moving to London to work for the Hong Kong and Shanghai Bank. In February 1901, he emigrated to South Africa and, on his arrival there, joined the South African Constabulary; whilst with them, he was injured in the Second Boer War.

When the Great War broke out, McAllan volunteered for active service and, in February 1915, was gazetted second lieutenant with the Royal Flying Corps. After being initially stationed in England, McAllan was then transferred to German East Africa. After being badly injured in an air crash, McAllan was transferred to the South African Medical Corps, as lieutenant and quartermaster.

McAllan died in the Roberts' Heights Hospital in December 1918 as a result of the injuries he sustained whilst with the Royal Air Force; some reports state his death was on 1st December 1918 and others on 14th December 1918, but his tombstone states it was on 4th December 1918. McAllan was 39 years old when he died and was buried at the Thaba Tshwane Cemetery in Gauteng, South Africa.

INTERNATIONAL APPEARANCES

15th February 1896 Ireland v. Scotland at Lansdowne Road, Dublin; match drawn 0-0

14th March 1896 Ireland v. Wales at Lansdowne Road, Dublin; Ireland won 8-4

9.9 Vincent McNamara (1891-1915)
born in Blackrock, County Cork

After leaving the Christian Brother's College in Cork, McNamara studied engineering at University College Cork. McNamara played scrum-half for his university team and, after being chosen to play for Munster, was selected to play for Ireland in 1914. After a defeat against England's Grand

Slam winning team, McNamara played in Ireland's next match against Scotland and scored one of Ireland's two tries in their 6-0 victory. McNamara's third cap came in Ireland's final game before the War, the game against Wales which was recorded as one of the most violent games between the two countries. When war broke out, McNamara was commissioned as second lieutenant with the Royal Engineers. He was serving in the Gallipoli Campaign in 1915 when, on 29th November 1915, he went to investigate after he had detonated a charge under mines which the Turkish forces were using to deploy tear gas. Unfortunately the gas had not dispersed and, overcome by the gas, McNamara died. He was 24 years old and buried at the Lancashire Landing Cemetery at Gallipoli.

INTERNATIONAL APPEARANCES

14th February 1914 Ireland v. England at Twickenham; England won 17-12

28th February 1914 Ireland v. Scotland at Lansdowne Road, Dublin; Ireland won 6-0

14th March 1914 Ireland v. Wales at Balmoral Showgrounds, Belfast; Wales won 11-3

9.10 Robertson Stewart " Robbie" Smyth (1879-1916)
born in Banbridge, County Down

Whilst at Trinity College Dublin where he was studying medicine, Smyth played as a forward for the university team, captaining it in the 1902/03 season. During his year as captain, Smyth was picked to play for Ireland in their fixtures against England and Scotland in the 1903 Home Nations

Championship. Later that year, Smyth was selected to join the Great Britain team touring South Africa and played in all three of the games against South Africa.

The following season Smyth was picked again by Ireland but only played in the game against England and was not picked again.

In 1902, Smyth had played in two matches for the Barbarians and, after leaving Dublin University, played for Wanderers, with whom he won the Leinster Senior Cup in 1906.

Smyth obtained his doctorate in 1906 and joined the Royal Army Medical Corps, serving in India from 1907 to 1912.

Soon after the outbreak of war, Smyth was sent to the Western Front, arriving there in September 1914. He continued to serve there until December 1915 by which time he had reached the rank of major but he was invalided out because he was suffering from gas poisoning. Smyth returned to the action by the end of the month but was invalided out a second time in early January 1916, returning to London. Smyth received a mention in despatches in January 1916 for gallantry and distinguished services in the field.

Smyth retired a month later and was recuperating in a nursing home in London when he died two months later, on 5th April 1916, from the effects of exposure to gas poisoning. Smyth was 36 years old when he died and was buried at the Banbridge Municipal Cemetery.

INTERNATIONAL APPEARANCES

14th February 1903 Ireland v. England at Lansdowne Road, Dublin; Ireland won 6-0

28th February 1903 Ireland v. Scotland at Inverleith; Scotland won 3-0

26th August 1903 Great Britain v. South Africa at Johannesburg; match drawn 10-10

5th September 1903 Great Britain v. South Africa at Kimberley; match drawn 0-0

12th September 1903 Great Britain v. South Africa at Cape Town; South Africa won 8-0

13th February 1904 Ireland v. England at Blackheath; England won 19-0

9.11 Albert Stewart (1889-1917)

born in Belfast

Stewart attended the Royal Belfast Academical Institution, where he excelled at rugby, cricket, athletics and swimming; after leaving school, Stewart played club rugby as a centre for North of Ireland Football Club from 1907 until 1914, captaining them in his last season and winning the Ulster Senior League in 1909. Stewart also played a number of games for Ulster.

Stewart was selected to play for Ireland against Wales in 1913, scoring a try on his debut but ending up on the losing side. Stewart played in Ireland's last game in the 1913 Five Nations Championship, against France and the first one the following year, also against France but was not picked again.

Having been with the Ulster Volunteer Force, Stewart applied for a commission with the Royal Irish Rifles in September 1914. In October 1915, Stewart left England for the Western Front with his battalion; by December 1915, he had transferred to the Machine Gun Corps and was involved in the fighting over the winter of 1915/16.

On 1st July 1916, Stewart took part in the Battle of the Somme; his actions in the battle that day led to him being recommended for the Victoria Cross but it was turned down. 15 months later, on 4th October 1917, Stewart was taking part in the Third Battle of Ypres when he was killed in action at the Battle of Broodseinde; he had been fighting in the Glencorse Wood, trying to seize ground from the Germans. Stewart was 28 years old when he was killed and was buried at the Hooge Crater Cemetery in Belgium.

After his death, Stewart was awarded the Distinguished Service Order for "distinguished service in the field", to add to the two mentions in despatches he received in 1916 and 1917.

INTERNATIONAL APPEARANCES

8th March 1913 Ireland v. Wales at Swansea; Wales won 16-13

24th March 1913 Ireland v. France at Cork; Ireland won 24-0

1st January 1914 Ireland v. France at Parc des Princes, Paris; Ireland won 8-6

MILITARY HONOURS

Mentioned in despatches (twice)

Distinguished Service Order

9.12 Alfred Taylor (1889-1917)
born in Belfast

Taylor was educated at Campbell College before attending Belfast University and Edinburgh University, where he studied medicine. Whilst at Edinburgh, Taylor was president of the university union and captain of the university rugby team.

By the time he was captain of the Edinburgh University rugby team, Taylor had already played for Ulster and three games for Ireland at centre, having made his debut in 1910. Taylor played in three of Ireland's Five Nations Championship games in 1910 but only ended up on the winning side in his fourth and last international, against France in 1912, when he scored one of Ireland's three tries in their 11-6 victory.

When war broke out, Taylor took a temporary commission in the Royal Army Medical Corps. After being invalided home from Mesopotamia, Taylor returned to France, having taken a permanent commission in January 1917.

On 31st July 1917, during the first day of the Third Battle of Ypres, Taylor was killed when a shell burst near him whilst he was dressing the wound of a fellow officer.

Taylor was 28 years old when he died and was buried in the Ypres Town Cemetery Extension.

INTERNATIONAL APPEARANCES

12th February 1910 Ireland v. England at Twickenham; match drawn 0-0

26th February 1910 Ireland v. Scotland at Balmoral Showgrounds, Belfast; Scotland won 14-0

12th March 1910 Ireland v. Wales at Lansdowne Road, Dublin; Wales won 19-3

1st January 1912 Ireland v. France at Parc des Princes, Paris; Ireland won 11-6

CHAPTER 10
Scotland Rugby Players

10.1 Cecil Abercrombie (1886-1916)
born in Mozufferpore, India

After attending Berkhamstead School, Abercrombie went to the Royal Naval College at Dartmouth where he trained to be a naval officer.

In 1902, Abercrombie served on board the HMS Hyacinch during the capture of Mullah Hassan's stronghold in Somaliland and, for his time in Africa, was awarded the African General Service Medal. Back home, Abercrombie played rugby as a forward for the United Services team. In 1910, he made his debut for Scotland against Ireland and the following year scored his only try for Scotland in the game against France but ended up on the losing side as France recorded their first international win, a 16-15 victory. It would have been a different story though had Abercrombie touched the ball down as he crossed the French try line with the Scots behind 16-15; instead, Abercrombie tried to touch down nearer the posts, crossed back over the try line and was tackled.

Abercrombie was also a first-class cricketer, making his debut for the combined Army & Navy team in their 1910 fixture against a combined Oxford & Cambridge Universities team; after playing for the Navy in their fixtures against the Army in

1912 and 1913, Abercrombie made his debut for Hampshire in 1913, scoring 126 in the first innings. Abercrombie played in 12 of Hampshire's County Championship matches in 1913, after which he retired; in his 16 first-class matches, Abercrombie scored a total of 1,126 runs, at an average of 40.21 and with a highest score of 165 and, with his right-arm medium pace bowling, took eight wickets at an average of 41.12.

When war broke out, Abercrombie was serving in the Mediterranean but returned to England in early 1915. On 31st May 1916, Abercrombie was on board HMS Defence during the Battle of Jutland; after being fired upon by a number of enemy ships away from the main battle fleet, HMS Defence's magazines were hit and exploded, causing the ship to sink with the loss of all lives on board. Abercrombie was 30 years old when he died and is commemorated at the Plymouth Naval Memorial.

INTERNATIONAL APPEARANCES

26th February 1910 Scotland v. Ireland at Balmoral Showgrounds, Belfast; Scotland won 14-0

19th March 1910 Scotland v. England at Inverleith; England won 14-5

2nd January 1911 Scotland v. France at Colombes; France won 16-15

4th February 1911 Scotland v. Wales at Inverleith; Wales won 32-10

1st January 1913 Scotland v. France at Parc des Princes, Paris; Scotland won 21-8

1st February 1913 Scotland v. Wales at Inverleith; Wales won 8-0

MILITARY HONOURS

African General Service Medal

10.2 David Bain (1891-1915)

born in Edinburgh

Bain went to Edinburgh Academy, where he was captain of the school rugby and fives teams and in the shooting team. After school, Bain went to Oxford University and, as well as playing football, cricket and golf for his college, played in four rugby Varsity matches for the university team against Cambridge, including as captain in 1913. By the time he graduated, Bain had also been President of the Vincent's Club, in 1913/14.

Whilst still at school, Bain was picked as reserve for the Scotland team to play in the 1910 Calcutta Cup match against England but he had to wait a year before making his debut for Scotland, as a prop in the game against England in 1911. In 1912 and 1913, Bain played in all but one of Scotland's international matches and, for the game against Wales in 1914, was made captain; however, a heavy defeat saw the captaincy taken away from him after just the one game and, after that, Bain only played one more game for Scotland.

When war broke out, Bain had applied to join the Egyptian Civil Service but joined the Army instead, serving with the Gordon Highlanders. He was sent to the Western Front in December 1914; after being wounded at Neuve Chapelle in March 1915, Bain returned to the Front on 20th May 1915, having been promoted to captain. Just two weeks after he returned, Bain was killed when, on 3rd June 1915, a shell struck his dug-out at Festubert. Bain was 23 when he was killed and was buried at the Brown's Road Military Cemetery in Festubert in France.

18th March 1911 Scotland v. England at Twickenham; England won 13-8

20th January 1912 Scotland v. France at Inverleith; Scotland won 31-3

3rd February 1912 Scotland v. Wales at Swansea; Wales won 21-6

16th March 1912 Scotland v. England at Inverleith; Scotland won 8-3

23rd November 1912 Scotland v. South Africa at Inverleith; South Africa won 16-0

1st January 1913 Scotland v. France at Parc des Princes, Paris; Scotland won 21-3

1st February 1913 Scotland v. Wales at Inverleith; Wales won 8-0

22nd February 1913 Scotland v. Ireland at Inverleith; Scotland won 29-14

15th March 1913 Scotland v. England at Twickenham; England won 3-0

7th February 1914 Scotland v. Wales at the National Stadium, Cardiff; Wales won 24-5

28th February 1914 Scotland v. Ireland at Lansdowne Road, Dublin; Ireland won 6-0

10.3 David Bedell-Sivright (1880-1915)
born in Edinburgh

After attending Fettes College, Bedell-Sivright went to Cambridge University and played as a forward in four Varsity matches for them against Oxford from 1899; he was captain of the university team in 1901 and 1902 and joined in the team by his brother John, in his last three years.

Bedell-Sivright made his debut for Scotland against Wales in 1900, whilst still in his first year at university. The following year, Bedell-Sivright played in all three of Scotland's games in the Home Nations Championship as they won the Triple Crown. In 1902, Bedell-Sivright again played in all of Scotland's Home Nations Championship games and was joined in the game against Wales by his brother. In 1903, Scotland won the

Triple Crown again, with Bedell-Sivright playing in two of their wins, following which he was selected for the Great Britain team to tour South Africa; after playing in the first 12 matches on tour, Bedell-Sivright missed out on the Test matches against South Africa due to injury.

After playing in all of Scotland's Home Nations Championship matches in 1904, Bedell-Sivright was chosen as captain of the Great Britain team to tour Australia and New Zealand. Bedell-Sivright was only able to play in one of the international games on the tour, missing out on second and third Tests against Australia due to injury and the Test against New Zealand after breaking his leg in the first tour match in New Zealand. Before arriving in New Zealand, Bedell-Sivright had already gained notoriety when, in one of the tour games in Australia in which he was not playing, he took the British team off the field after one of their players was sent off, in the opinion of Bedell-Sivright, unfairly.

Following the tour to Australia and New Zealand, Bedell-Sivright settled in Australia briefly, working as a jackeroo. After a year in Australia, Bedell-Sivright returned to Scotland to study medicine. By the end of 1905, he was back wearing the Scotland rugby shirt, captaining them in their match against the visiting All Blacks. Bedell-Sivright continued playing for Scotland up until 1908, winning a third Triple Crown in 1907. By the time he retired from international rugby, Bedell-Sivright had played 22 games for Scotland and one for Great Britain; his three tries for Scotland all came against Ireland in Dublin, two in the game in 1904 and one in the game two years later.

After retiring from international rugby, by which time he had earned the reputation of being one of Scotland's greatest and hardest forwards, Bedell-Sivright continued playing club rugby for Edinburgh University, captaining them for two seasons and had also taken up boxing; in 1909, Bedell-Sivright became Scotland's heavyweight boxing champion.

By the time war broke out, Bedell-Sivright had become a surgeon; he joined the Royal Navy and, in May 1915, was posted to the Hawke Battalion of the Royal Naval Division stationed in Gallipoli. After spending some time in the trenches while serving at an advanced dressing station, Bedell-Sivright was bitten by an insect; the bite turned septic and Bedell-Sivright complained of feeling fatigued, following which he was transferred to the hospital ship, the Dunluce Castle. Two days later, on 5th September 1915, Bedell-Sivright died of septicaemia and was buried at sea off Cape Helles. Bedell-Sivright was 34 years old when he died.

INTERNATIONAL APPEARANCES

27th January 1900 Scotland v. Wales at Swansea; Wales won 12-3

9th February 1901 Scotland v. Wales at Inverleith; Scotland won 18-8

23rd February 1901 Scotland v. Ireland at Inverleith; Scotland won 9-5

9th March 1901 Scotland v. England at Blackheath; Scotland won 18-3

1st February 1902 Scotland v. Wales at the National Stadium, Cardiff; Wales won 14-5

22nd February 1902 Scotland v. Ireland at Balmoral Showgrounds, Belfast; Ireland won 5-0

15th March 1902 Scotland v. England at Inverleith; England won 6-3

7th February 1903 Scotland v. Wales at Inverleith; Scotland won 6-0

28th February 1903 Scotland v. Ireland at Inverleith; Scotland won 3-0

6th February 1904 Scotland v. Wales at Swansea; Wales won 21-3

27th February 1904 Scotland v. Ireland at Lansdowne Road, Dublin; Scotland won 19-3

19th March 1904 Scotland v. England at Inverleith; Scotland won 6-3

2nd July 1904 Great Britain v. Australia at Sydney; Great Britain won 17-0

18th November 1905 Scotland v. New Zealand at Inverleith; New Zealand won 12-7

3rd February 1906 Scotland v. Wales at the National Stadium, Cardiff; Wales won 9-3

24th February 1906 Scotland v. Ireland at Lansdowne Road, Dublin; Scotland won 13-6

17th March 1906 Scotland v. England at Inverleith; England won 9-3

17th November 1906 Scotland v. South Africa at Glasgow; Scotland won 6-0

2nd February 1907 Scotland v. Wales at Inverleith; Scotland won 6-3

23rd February 1907 Scotland v. Ireland at Inverleith; Scotland won 15-3

16th March 1907 Scotland v. England at Blackheath; Scotland won 8-3

1st February 1908 Scotland v. Wales at Swansea; Wales won 6-5

29th February 1908 Scotland v. Ireland at Lansdowne Road, Dublin; Ireland won 16-11

10.4 Patrick Blair (1891-1915)
born in Wanlockhead, Dumfriesshire

Blair went to Fettes College and then to Cambridge University where he played in four Varsity matches against Oxford, as a prop forward.

Whilst still at university, Blair made his debut for Scotland. During the South African tour to Britain in 1912, Blair played against the South Africans twice, once for Cambridge University and once when making his debut for Scotland. Blair then played in all four of Scotland's Five Nations Championship matches in 1913 but only ended up on the winning side in the game against France.

After graduating, Blair worked in the finance department for the Egyptian Civil Service but returned home in January 1915 to serve in the War.

Blair was posted to the Western Front with the 5th Battalion, the Rifle Brigade in June 1915. On 6th July 1915, Blair was killed by a shell whilst he was scaling a German parapet at Boesinghe near Ypres; he was 23 years old when he was killed. Although he was buried, the exact location of his grave could not be found after the War and, as a consequence, he is commemorated on a special memorial at the Talana Farm Cemetery, near Ypres in Belgium.

INTERNATIONAL APPEARANCES

23rd February 1912 Scotland v. South Africa at Inverleith; South Africa won 16-0

1st January 1913 Scotland v. France at Parc des Princes, Paris; Scotland won 21-3

1st February 1913 Scotland v. Wales at Inverleith; Wales won 8-0

22nd February 1913 Scotland v. Ireland at Inverleith; Ireland won 29-14

15th March 1913 Scotland v. England at Twickenham; England won 3-0

10.5 John Argentine Campbell (1877-1917)
born in Buenos Aires

Despite living in Argentina, Campbell was educated in Britain, attending Fettes College before going up to Cambridge University. At university, Campbell played as a forward in three rugby Varsity matches against Oxford, from 1897 to 1899, captaining the team in his third year; Campbell also won a blue in athletics in 1898.

After graduating, Campbell played rugby for West of Scotland FC and, in 1900, was picked to play for Scotland against Ireland; a scoreless draw proved to be his only international.

Campbell returned to Argentina to live, working as a teacher and a rancher. Back in Argentina, Campbell played cricket, including in one game of first-class cricket, for

Argentina against the MCC in 1912. Picked for his batting, Campbell only managed to score 4 in one innings and a duck in the other.

After war broke out, Campbell returned to Europe and was sent to France in 1916, serving as a lieutenant with the 6th Dragoons (Inniskilling). On 1st December 1917, Campbell was reported missing; a colleague informed Campbell's family that he had carried Campbell to a German dressing station after Campbell had been badly wounded and, in January 1918, Campbell's family received news from a German officer that Campbell had died from his wounds.

Campbell was 40 years old when he died and he was buried in the Honnechy British Cemetery in France.

INTERNATIONAL APPEARANCE

24th February 1900 Scotland v. Ireland at Lansdowne Road, Dublin; match drawn 0-0

10.6 William "Bill" Campbell Church (1884-1915)
born in Glasgow

After attending Glasgow Academy, Church spent his last year at school in Switzerland before going to Glasgow University in 1904. Whilst at university, Church played on the wing for Glasgow Academicals and, with them, won the Scottish Club Championship in the 1904/05 season.

Church was first selected to play for Scotland in their first ever Test against New Zealand, in November 1905 but he declined to play in the game. Instead, he made his debut less than three months later against Wales in Cardiff; after losing a match which Scotland were expected to win because of their stronger scrum, Church was not picked again.

On 16th May 1913, Church was commissioned as a second lieutenant with the 8th Battalion, the Cameronians; by December 1913, he had been promoted to lieutenant and, by the start of the War, to captain. In 1915, Church's battalion was mobilised and embarked for Gallipoli, landing there on 14th June 1915. Two weeks after arriving at Gallipoli, Church took part in the attack on Gully Ravine on 28th June 1915 but was killed when shot down by machine gun fire whilst leading his men towards enemy trenches; another Scottish rugby international, Eric Young (see Chapter 10.31) suffered the same fate that day in the same attack.

Church was shot down just ten yards short of the enemy trenches and his body was never recovered; he was 30 years old when he died and is commemorated on the Helles Memorial at Gallipoli.

INTERNATIONAL APPEARANCE

3rd February 1906 Scotland v. Wales at the National Stadium, Cardiff; Wales won 9-3

10.7 Walter Michael "Mike" Dickson (1884-1915)
born in South Africa

After attending Rondebosch College in Cape Town, Dickson won a Rhodes Scholarship to Oxford University, which he represented at full-back in the 1912 Varsity Match.

Only two weeks before winning his blue, Dickson was playing for Scotland against the country of his birth, South

Africa, on their tour in 1912. The game against South Africa was Dickson's fourth game for Scotland, after having made his debut in January 1912 against France. A year later in the return fixture against France, Dickson had to be encouraged to leave the ground after the game as, due to his deafness, he failed to recognise that the home crowd was turning violent after Scotland had inflicted a heavy defeat on the home team.

Dickson played in three of Scotland's Five Nations Championship games in both 1912 and 1913 before returning to South Africa to work as a surveyor; before leaving, Dickson had taken part in motor racing at the Brooklands racing circuit which had opened in 1907.

After the War broke out, Dickson returned to Britain and served as a lieutenant with the 11th Battalion, the Argyll and Sutherland Highlanders. After arriving in France in July 1915, Dickson was killed in action less than three months later, on 26th September 1915, during the Battle of Loos. Dickson was 30 years old when he died; his body was never recovered and he is commemorated at the Loos Memorial in Pas de Calais.

INTERNATIONAL APPEARANCES

20th January 1912 Scotland v. France at Inverleith; Scotland won 31-3

3rd February 1912 Scotland v. Wales at Swansea; Wales won 21-6

16th March 1912 Scotland v. England at Inverleith; Scotland won 8-3

23rd November 1912 Scotland v. South Africa at Inverleith; South Africa won 16-0

1st January 1913 Scotland v. France at Parc des Princes, Paris; Scotland won 21-3

1st February 1913 Scotland v. Wales at Inverleith; Wales won 8-0

22nd February 1913 Scotland v. Ireland at Inverleith; Scotland won 29-14

10.8 John Henry "Harry" Dods (1875-1915)
born in Glasgow

Dods played his club rugby as a forward for Edinburgh Academicals and made his debut for Scotland in 1895. Dods played in all of Scotland's Home Nations Championship matches in 1895 when Scotland won the Triple Crown and in 1896; the following year, he played in his last two games for Scotland. Dods's younger brother, Francis, also played rugby for Scotland.

Dods worked as a civilian contractor for the Royal Navy. On 30th December 1915, Dods was invited on board HMS Natal, as a guest, along with his wife and three children, whilst the ship was anchored up in Cromarty Firth, near Inverness. Whilst Dods was on board, the ship, which was part of the Second Cruiser Squad of the Grand Fleet, capsized following a series of explosions, the cause of which was never explained. Over 400 lives were lost, including that of Dods and his family.

Dods was 40 years old when he died and is commemorated on the Maxton War Memorial, in the South of Scotland.

INTERNATIONAL APPEARANCES

26th January 1895 Scotland v. Wales at Raeburn Place, Edinburgh; Scotland won 5-4

2nd March 1895 Scotland v. Ireland at Raeburn Place, Edinburgh; Scotland won 6-0

9th March 1895 Scotland v. England at Richmond; Scotland won 6-3

25th January 1896 Scotland v. Wales at the National Stadium, Cardiff; Wales won 6-0

15th February 1896 Scotland v. Ireland at Lansdowne Road, Dublin; match drawn 0-0

14th March 1896 Scotland v. England at Glasgow; Scotland won 11-0

20th February 1897 Scotland v. Ireland at Powderhall, Edinburgh; Scotland won 8-3

13th March 1897 Scotland v. England at Manchester; England won 12-3

10.9 Walter Forrest (1880-1917)

born in Kelso

A talented all-round sportsman who played football, cricket and golf, Forrest concentrated on his rugby, playing full back for Hawick RFC. Forrest made his debut for Scotland in 1903 and played in all of Scotland's Home Nations Championship games in 1903 and 1904. Forrest also played in Scotland's first two games the following year but missed the final game of the season against England, after breaking his collar bone in a club match for Hawick only a few days earlier. The injury put an end to Forrest's international career.

In the War, Forrest served with the King's Own Scottish Borderers. Although his battalion suffered terrible casualties during the Gallipoli Campaign, Forrest survived and was then sent to Palestine.

As well as being mentioned in despatches, Forrest was awarded the Military Cross for conspicuous gallantry in action, in recognition of the daring reconnaissance work he carried out, to obtain information.

Forrest's battalion had been held in reserve during the Second Battle of Gaza but, on 19th April 1917, they were ordered to retake the Turkish redoubt positioned on Outpost Hill. After rushing up the hill, Forrest was mortally wounded when he was shot on the parapet of the enemy trench. Forrest was 36 years old when he died and was buried in the Gaza War Cemetery.

INTERNATIONAL APPEARANCES

7th February 1903 Scotland v. Wales at Inverleith; Scotland won 6-0

28th February 1903 Scotland v. Ireland at Inverleith; Scotland won 3-0

21st March 1903 Scotland v. England at Richmond; Scotland won 10-6

6th February 1904 Scotland v. Wales at Swansea; Wales won 21-3

27th February 1904 Scotland v. Ireland at Lansdowne Road, Dublin; Scotland won 19-3

19th March 1904 Scotland v. England at Inverleith; Scotland won 6-3

4th February 1905 Scotland v. Wales at Inverleith; Wales won 6-3

25th February 1905 Scotland v. Ireland at Inverleith; Ireland won 11-5

10.10 Rowland Fraser (1890-1916)
born in Perth

After attending Merchiston School, Fraser went to Cambridge University and, in 1908, 1909 and 1910, played for Cambridge in the Varsity matches against Oxford, captaining the team in 1910.

After graduating from Cambridge, Fraser went to Edinburgh University after which he worked as a lawyer in Edinburgh.

In 1911, Fraser was picked to play as a forward in all four of Scotland's Five Nations Championship games; a defeat in his first game against France, which was France's first ever win, was followed by three more defeats as Scotland took the wooden spoon. Fraser was not picked again.

Fraser was also a keen cricketer and played for Perthshire.

In the War, Fraser was commissioned into the Rifle Brigade. He crossed over the English Channel to France in January 1915 and, by November 1915, had been promoted to captain.

On 20th June 1916, Fraser married whilst on four days' leave, returning to France the day after his wedding.

10 days after returning, on 1st July 1916, Fraser was involved in the action on the first day of the Battle of the

Somme. Whilst leading his company on an assault on a German position on Ridge Redoubt south of Serre, Fraser was hit by a machine gun bullet within a few yards of a German trench; although his orderly got him into a shell hole and dressed his wound, Fraser was then struck by shrapnel – he died six hours later with his orderly still by his side. Fraser was 26 years old when he died.

Fraser's body was never found and he is commemorated at the Thiepval Memorial to the Missing.

INTERNATIONAL APPEARANCES

2nd January 1911 Scotland v. France at Colombes; France won 16-15

4th February 1911 Scotland v. Wales at Inverleith; Wales won 32-10

25th February 1911 Scotland v. Ireland at Inverleith; Ireland won 16-10

18th March 1911 Scotland v. England at Twickenham; England won 12-8

10.11 Roland Elphinstone Gordon (1893-1918)
born in Selangor, Malaya

Gordon was educated at King's School Canterbury, where he was in the cricket, rugby and fives teams for three years. After leaving school, Gordon went to the Royal Military Academy at Woolwich and, during his time there, represented the Army at rugby. In January 1913, Gordon made his debut for Scotland three weeks before he was commissioned in the Royal Artillery, playing at centre against France and scoring two tries in Scotland's win. Gordon played in two more of Scotland's games that season before being posted to India with the Royal Field Artillery in May 1913.

After war broke out, Gordon was posted to Mesopotamia; in September 1915, Gordon was badly wounded when hit in the chest whilst involved in a major attack at Chahela and was evacuated back to England. After recovering, Gordon returned to the Western Front and was awarded the Military Cross in June 1917. Gordon was wounded for the second time in November 1917 and a third time in May 1918. In June 1918, Gordon was awarded a bar to his Military Cross; he was also mentioned in despatches.

In August 1918, Gordon was wounded for the fourth time, following which he was sent to a casualty clearing station, where, on 30th August 1918, he died from his wounds. Gordon was 25 years old when he died and was buried at the Daours Communal Cemetery Extension near Amiens.

INTERNATIONAL APPEARANCES

1st January 1913 Scotland v. France at Parc des Princes, Paris; Scotland won 21-3

1st February 1913 Scotland v. Wales at Inverleith; Wales won 8-0

22nd February 1913 Scotland v. Ireland at Inverleith; Scotland won 29-14

MILITARY HONOURS

Military Cross (twice)

Mentioned in despatches

10.12 James Young Henderson (1891-1917)
born in Edinburgh

Henderson attended Watson's College; he was an all-round sportsman who was good at cricket, hockey, badminton and billiards and a junior East of Scotland swimming champion but it was at rugby that he excelled.

In 1911, Henderson was picked to play scrum-half in Scotland's first Calcutta Cup match at Twickenham; a promising international career lay ahead but, after the game against England, Henderson went to work in India, where he played rugby for Madras.

By the time war broke out, Henderson had returned to England and was working as a works manager for McVitie and Price in London.

During the War, Henderson served with the Highland Light Infantry and was mentioned in despatches. After seeing action during the Battle of Loos in September 1915, Henderson's battalion prepared for the Third Battle of Ypres; on 31st July 1917, the first day of the battle, Henderson's brigade attacked Frezenburg Village before a party from King's Own Scottish Borderers outflanked the enemy position. After taking Low Farm, enemy fire from Pommerm Castle and Hill 35 halted the advance by Henderson and his comrades and he was killed.

Henderson's body was never recovered and he is commemorated at the Ypres (Menin Gate) Memorial. Henderson was 26 years old when he was killed; only five days before his death, in his last letter home, he had written "if I have to go, I will be quite happy, as I will go out doing my duty."

INTERNATIONAL APPEARANCE

18th March 1911 Scotland v. England at Twickenham; England won 13-8

MILITARY HONOURS

Mentioned in despatches

10.13 Dave Howie (1888-1916)

born in Rosebery Temple, Midlothian

Howie went to Kirkcaldy High School where, as well as playing rugby for the school team for three years, he was also the athletics champion. After leaving school, Howie played his club rugby as a forward for Kirkcaldy RFC and, in 1912, became the first player from the club to be selected to play for Scotland.

Howie played in all four of Scotland's Five Nations Championship games in 1912 and the fixture against the touring South Africans later in the year. In 1913, Howie played in Scotland's first two games before losing his place; the home defeat against Wales in the second game proved to be his last game for Scotland.

Howie worked with his family on a farm and, when war broke out, he enlisted as a trooper with the Fife and Forfar Yeomanry. In April 1915, Howie was commissioned into the 1st Highland Brigade, Royal Field Artillery.

In April 1915, Howie left with his brigade for Gallipoli. During the evacuation from Anzac Cove in December 1915, Howie contracted pneumonia and, on arrival in Cairo, put into a hospital. On 19th January 1916, Howie died when he shot himself while "in a state of unsound mind, due to the delirium of pneumonia".

Howie was 27 years old when he died and was buried at the Cairo War Memorial Cemetery.

Howie's younger brother, Bob, also played rugby for Scotland and for Great Britain on their tour to South Africa in 1924.

INTERNATIONAL APPEARANCES

20th January 1912 Scotland v. France at Inverleith; Scotland won 31-3

3rd February 1912 Scotland v. Wales at Swansea; Wales won 21-6

24th February 1912 Scotland v. Ireland at Lansdowne Road, Dublin; Ireland won 10-8

16th March 1912 Scotland v. England at Inverleith; Scotland won 8-3

23rd November 1912 Scotland v. South Africa at Inverleith; South Africa won 16-0

1st January 1913 Scotland v. France at Parc des Princes, Paris; Scotland won 21-3

1st February 1913 Scotland v. Wales at Inverleith; Wales won 8-0

10.14 James Huggan (1888-1914)
born in Jedburgh

After attending Watson's College and Darlington Grammar School, Huggan studied medicine at Edinburgh University, which he represented at football and athletics, as well as rugby.

After graduating, Huggan was gazetted to the Royal Army Medical Corps and played rugby on the wing for London Scottish and the Army. In 1914, Huggan was picked to play in Scotland's Calcutta Cup match against England in 1914; Huggan scored one of Scotland's three tries in the game but Scotland still ended up losing the match 16-15 in what proved to be Scotland's final match before the War.

When war broke out, Huggan was due to go to India. Instead, he was sent to France with the first part of the Expeditionary Force on 13th August 1914.

Although records suggest he was killed in action during the First Battle of the Aisne on 16th September 1914, his obituary in The British Medical Journal suggests it was two days later on 18th September. His obituary recounts that, on 16th September 1914, during the retreat from the Aisne, the Guards Brigade were ordered to retreat from their position at Soupir Farm, temporarily leaving behind a barn which had been used as a hospital and which was occupied by approximately 60 German prisoners; in spite of this, it was shelled by the Germans and caught fire. With shot and shell falling all around him, Huggan called for volunteers to help save the German prisoners. After saving them, Huggan moved many of the wounded men into a cave or an old quarry at the rear. On 18th September, after moving one of the Prussian officers to whom Huggan was attending to the entrance of a cave to get better sight of the officer's severe haemorrhaging, a shell landed and killed Huggan and the Prussian.

For his actions, Huggan was recommended for the Victoria Cross but, perhaps because his actions involved saving Germans, it was not taken any further; instead, he was mentioned in despatches.

Huggan was 25 years old when he died and he is commemorated at La Ferte-sous-Jouarre Memorial in the Seine-et-Marne region in France.

INTERNATIONAL APPEARANCE

21st March 1914 Scotland v. England at Inverleith; England won 16-15

MILITARY HONOURS

Mentioned in despatches

10.15 William Hutchison (1889-1918)
born in Glasgow

Hutchison attended Glasgow High School and, after leaving school in 1905, continued to play rugby up until 1911 for his school's Former Pupils' team.

Starting off as a half-back, Hutchison had by 1911 changed position and played lock. The change in position saw him selected in 1911 for Glasgow for their inter-city match against Edinburgh and for Scotland's Calcutta Cup match that same year at Twickenham. Hutchison then moved to Canada to work, bringing to an end his international rugby career.

When war broke out, Hutchison was on holiday in Scotland and, by September 1914, he had joined the 17th Battalion, the Highland Light Infantry. After training, Hutchison was commissioned in to the Royal Scots Fusiliers.

Hutchison's first overseas posting was to France; he was then posted to Salonika where he was wounded. After recovering from his wounds, Hutchison was sent back to Arras in France.

On 22nd March 1918, on the second day of the German Ludendorff offensive, Hutchison was killed when hit by machine gun fire whilst he and part of his company were forming a strong post whilst the others in his company were digging a line of defence.

Hutchison was 29 years old when he was killed and is commemorated on the Arras Memorial.

INTERNATIONAL APPEARANCE

18th March 1911 Scotland v. England at Twickenham; England won 13-8

10.16 George Lamond (1878-1918)
born in Glasgow

Lamond was educated at Kelvinside Academy and played centre for Kelvinside Academicals.

In 1899, Lamond was picked to play for Scotland in their matches against Wales and England but it was another six years before he made his third and final appearance for Scotland. In between his appearances in 1899 and 1905, Lamond had moved to England where he worked as a civil engineer and played rugby for Bristol; whilst working in Bristol, Lamond worked on the construction of the King Edward Dock in Avonmouth.

After his last game for Scotland, Lamond worked in Egypt on three of the Nile barrages.

Lamond returned to Britain when war broke out and joined the Royal Engineers, working in the inland water transport division. After spending time in France involved in engineering work and fighting, Lamond was sent to Mesopotamia in 1917 where he was put in charge of a major construction project for which he received a mention in despatches.

Whilst in Mesopotamia, Lamond contracted a fever and was invalided to Ceylon (now Sri Lanka); Lamond did not recover from the fever and died on 25th February 1918 at the age of 39; he was buried in the Colombo (Kanatte) General Cemetery.

INTERNATIONAL APPEARANCES

4th March 1899 Scotland v. Wales at Inverleith; Scotland won 21-10

11th March 1899 Scotland v. England at Blackheath; Scotland won 5-0

18th March 1905 Scotland v. England at Richmond; Scotland won 8-0

MILITARY HONOURS

Mentioned in despatches

10.17 Eric Milroy (1887-1916)

born in Edinburgh

Milroy went to Watson's College before going to Edinburgh University where he studied mathematics. Whilst at university, Milroy played for his school's old boys' team, Watsonians, rather than the university team and, during his playing days with Watsonians from 1908 until 1914, Watsonians won the Scottish club championship five times, including in 1909/10 when they went the season undefeated.

After graduating, Milroy qualified as a chartered accountant.

In 1910, Milroy played his first game for Scotland, as scrum-half against Wales; later that year, he was selected for the Great Britain team that toured South Africa but, after three matches on tour, was unwell and missed the three Test matches against South Africa.

In 1912, Milroy played in three of Scotland's Five Nations Championship matches, scoring his only try for Scotland in the game against Wales; he also played in the match later that year against South Africa. The following year, Milroy played in all of Scotland's Five Nations Championship games; in 1914, there was no fixture between Scotland and France and Milroy missed the game against Wales but played in Scotland's other two matches, including as captain in the game against England, which was Scotland's last international before the War.

In the War, Milroy served as a gun officer with the 8th Battalion, Black Watch (the Royal Highland Regiment). Milroy was posted to France in October 1915 and promoted to lieutenant in June 1916. On 18th July 1916, during the Battle of the Somme, Milroy was reported missing at Longueval, near Delville Wood; it is thought that he was killed in action.

Milroy was 28 years old at the time and his body was not found; he is commemorated at the Thiepval Memorial to the Missing near Amiens.

5th February 1910 Scotland v. Wales at the National Stadium, Cardiff; Wales won 14-0

18th March 1911 Scotland v. England at Twickenham; England won 13-8

3rd February 1912 Scotland v. Wales at Swansea; Wales won 21-6

24th February 1912 Scotland v. Ireland at Lansdowne Road, Dublin; Ireland won 10-8

16th March 1912 Scotland v. England at Inverleith; Scotland won 8-3

23rd November 1912 Scotland v. South Africa at Inverleith; South Africa won 16-0

1st January 1913 Scotland v. France at Parc des Princes, Paris; Scotland won 21-3

1st February 1913 Scotland v. Wales at Inverleith; Wales won 8-0

22nd February 1913 Scotland v. Ireland at Inverleith; Scotland won 29-14

15th March 1913 Scotland v. England at Twickenham; England won 3-0

28th February 1914 Scotland v. Ireland at Lansdowne Road, Dublin; Ireland won 6-0

21st March 1914 Scotland v. England at Inverleith; England won 16-15

10.18 Tommy Nelson (1876-1917)
born in Edinburgh

Nelson was educated at the Edinburgh Academy from 1887 until 1895 before spending four years at Oxford University, where he won a blue for rugby in 1897 and 1898. In between his two Varsity matches against Cambridge, Nelson played in his one and only international for Scotland, as centre in the Calcutta Cup match against England in 1898. After graduating, Nelson went into his family's publishing business; John Buchan, who worked as a literary advisor to the publishers Thomas Nelson & Sons, dedicated his book Thirty-Nine Steps to Nelson.

When war broke out, Nelson re-joined the 1st Lothian and Border Horse regiment and was posted to France in September 1915. 18 months later, whilst attached to the machine gun corps, Nelson was killed in action on 9th April 1917 when a shell burst as he was working as an observation officer for the tanks. His actions on the day of his death led to him being mentioned in despatches for the third time.

Nelson was 40 years old when he died and was buried at the Faubourg d'Amiens Cemetery.

INTERNATIONAL APPEARANCE

12th March 1898 Scotland v. England at Powderhall, Edinburgh; match drawn 3-3

MILITARY HONOURS

Mentioned in despatches (three times)

10.19 James Pearson (1889-1915)
born in Dalkeith

Pearson went to Watson's College where he excelled at cricket and athletics as well as rugby. After leaving school, Pearson continued playing cricket and rugby for Watsonians up until the War and, in his five years playing at centre for the club, scored 103 tries for them as they won the Scottish club championship in four of the five years. Pearson also played golf to a good standard, as well as tennis, badminton and fives.

Pearson made his debut for Scotland in 1909 and, over the next four years, played another 11 games for Scotland. In 1911, he scored a drop goal against France but it was not enough to prevent France recording their first international victory; a year later, he scored another drop goal, from a penalty and a try against France as they extracted revenge for their defeat a year earlier. With Pearson winning six of his 12 internationals, he did not enjoy the same success as he had at club level but this would have been partially down to his weighing no more than nine stone.

In the War, Pearson joined the 9th Battalion, the Royal Scots; he left for the Western Front on 24th February 1915, his 26th birthday. On 22nd May 1915, Pearson was killed when he was shot by a sniper at Hooge in Belgium, as he was making his way along the back of a trench to fetch water during fighting at Sanctuary Wood.

Pearson was 26 years old when he was killed; he was buried at Sanctuary Wood Cemetery at Ypres.

INTERNATIONAL APPEARANCES

27th February 1909 Scotland v. Ireland at Inverleith; Scotland won 9-3

20th March 1909 Scotland v. England at Richmond; Scotland won 18-8

22nd January 1910 Scotland v. France at Inverleith; Scotland won 27-0

5th February 1910 Scotland v. Wales at the National Stadium, Cardiff; Wales won 14-0

26th February 1910 Scotland v. Ireland at Balmoral Showgrounds, Belfast; Scotland won 14-0

19th March 1910 Scotland v. England at Inverleith; England won 14-5

2nd January 1911 Scotland v. France at Colombes; France won 16-15

20th January 1912 Scotland v. France at Inverleith; Scotland won 31-3

3rd February 1912 Scotland v. Wales at Swansea; Wales won 21-6

23rd November 1912 Scotland v. South Africa at Inverleith; South Africa won 16-0

22nd February 1913 Scotland v. Ireland at Inverleith; Scotland won 29-14

15th March 1913 Scotland v. England at Twickenham; England won 3-0

10.20 Lewis Robertson (1883-1914)

born in Edinburgh

After attending Fettes College, Robertson went to the Royal Military College at Sandhurst in December 1901 before joining the 1st Battalion, Cameron Highlanders in May 1903. In 1905, Robertson was transferred to Dublin where he played rugby for Monkstown but most of his club rugby was played for the Army team, including when he captained them, in 1914, in their last game against the Navy before the War.

Robertson made his debut for Scotland against England in 1908 playing as a forward, but it was another three years before he was selected again – he was selected after France beat Scotland to record their first ever victory, in the first game of the 1911 Five Nations Championship. It was another year before Robertson won his third cap for Scotland but, after playing in the second of Scotland's Five Nations Championship matches that year, he retained his place for their remaining Championship matches and the game later that year against South Africa.

In 1913, Robertson played his final two games for Scotland, the final game being a low scoring game which saw England win the Calcutta Cup and the Grand Slam.

After war broke out, Robertson was posted to France in September 1914 and took part in the Battle of the Aisne. On 2nd November 1914, Robertson was wounded during the First Battle of Ypres when he was shot through the shoulder; once the wound was dressed, he returned to the fighting only to be wounded again; the following day, Robertson died from the wounds he had sustained.

Robertson was 31 years old when he died; due to the cemetery in Ypres being shelled by the Germans, Robertson was buried in the garden of the Convent of the Blessed Virgin in Ypres; later, his body was moved and buried at the Ypres Reservoir Cemetery.

INTERNATIONAL APPEARANCES

21st March 1908 Scotland v. England at Inverleith; Scotland won 16-10

4th February 1911 Scotland v. Wales at Inverleith; Wales won 32-10

3rd February 1912 Scotland v. Wales at Swansea; Wales won 21-6

24th February 1912 Scotland v. Ireland at Lansdowne Road, Dublin; Ireland won 10-8

16th March 1912 Scotland v. England at Inverleith; Scotland won 8-3

23rd November 1912 Scotland v. South Africa at Inverleith; South Africa won 16-0

1st February 1913 Scotland v. Wales at Inverleith; Wales won 3-0

22nd February 1913 Scotland v. Ireland at Inverleith; Scotland won 29-14

15th March 1913 Scotland v. England at Twickenham; England won 3-0

10.21 Andrew Ross (1879-1916)
born in Edinburgh

Ross attended the Royal High School in Edinburgh where he excelled at swimming and, due to a yearning to be at sea, left school at 16 and was apprenticed on board the Glenfyne on its journey from Dundee around Cape Horn to Iquique in Chile. On his return, Ross went back to school for a year before starting his apprenticeship with an engineering firm.

After leaving school, Ross played rugby as a forward for his school's former pupils' team and, in 1899, Ross was picked to play for Edinburgh in their inter-city fixture against Glasgow but, after serving his apprenticeship, became a marine engineer and did not return to Scotland until 1904. The following year

Ross played again for Edinburgh against Glasgow and his performance earned a place in the Cities team playing against the Rest, following which he was selected to play for Scotland.

Ross's first two games for Scotland in the 1905 Home Nations Championship were lost but the final game that season was against England and a win for Scotland meant they retained the Calcutta Cup; early in the game against England, Ross had two ribs cracked and another broken but he finished the game; however, his injuries put him out of action for a while and it was another four years before Ross played for Scotland again, when he was picked to play in two of Scotland's games in 1909.

When war broke out, Ross was working in Vancouver. Ross joined the 29th Battalion, the Canadian Regiment and arrived at the Western Front in September 1915. Ross spent Christmas in 1915 in hospital following a gas attack. At the end of January 1916, Ross's battalion raided the German position at the Spanbroekmolen salient where they encountered little resistance, it taking them less than five minutes to take three prisoners, bomb the dugouts and return to their own trenches.

On 3rd and 4th April 1916, the Canadian Corps relieved the British 5th Corps which had been attacking the St Eloi Craters; for the next two days, the Canadians were under constant bombardment. On the night of 5th April, the 27th Battalion, which had suffered particularly badly, were being relieved by Ross's battalion but they were held up by the mud, the additional equipment and the congestion of troops. On 6th April 1916, despite being wounded himself, Ross was attending, under heavy artillery fire, to wounded men when he was hit; he died instantly, falling over the man he was dressing.

Ross was 37 years old when he died and was buried at the Ridge Wood Military Cemetery in Belgium.

4th February 1905 Scotland v. Wales at Inverleith; Wales won 6-3

25th February 1905 Scotland v. Ireland at Inverleith; Ireland won 11-5

18th March 1905 Scotland v. England at Richmond; Scotland won 8-0

6th February 1909 Scotland v. Wales at Inverleith; Wales won 5-3

27th February 1909 Scotland v. Ireland at Inverleith; Scotland won 9-3

10.22 James Ross (1880-1914)

born in Roxburgh

After leaving Fettes College in 1899, Ross worked at the Stock Exchange in London, where he played rugby for London Scottish, captaining them in the 1901/02 and 1904/05 seasons.

In 1901, days before his 21st birthday, Ross was picked to play his first game for Scotland, playing as a forward against Wales. Ross retained his place for Scotland's other two fixtures in 1901 and in two of their games the following year. Ross did not play again for Scotland after the 1902 Home Nations Championship but his younger brother Edward played one game for Scotland in 1904.

When war broke out, Ross enlisted with the 14th Battalion, London Regiment (London Scottish) which was the first British regiment to be involved in the fighting in the War when, in October 1914, they were tasked with reinforcing the Allied line at Messines Ridge. After two German attacks had been held back by Ross's regiment, the Germans were able to break through at the third attempt but the actions of Ross's regiment stopped the Germans reaching Ypres; in doing so, Ross's regiment suffered heavy losses, with 394 officers losing their lives.

Ross was one of the many who never returned from the fighting and, after going missing on 31ˢᵗ October 1914, was presumed dead. Ross was 34 years old when he died and is commemorated at the Ypres (Menin Gate) Memorial.

10.23 Ronald Simson (1890-1914)

born in Edinburgh

After attending the Edinburgh Academy, Simson went to the Royal Military Academy at Woolwich.

Simson played as a centre and played his club rugby for London Scottish as well as for the Woolwich Academy team; after representing the Army and Navy team, Simson was selected to play in Scotland's Calcutta Cup match against England in 1911; Simson scored one of Scotland's two tries in the match but ended up on the losing side as England retained the Calcutta Cup.

Four months after his one and only international, Simson joined the Royal Field Artillery. When war broke out, Simson was sent to France in August 1914; during the First Battle of the Aisne, Simson was killed, along with his horse, when a shell exploded underneath the horse he was riding as he was looking to find a position for his battery.

Simson was killed on 14ᵗʰ September 1914 and was the first of Britain's rugby internationals to be killed in the War. Simson was 24 years old when he died and was buried in the Moulins New Communal Cemetery in Aisne.

10.24 Stephen Steyn (1889-1917)

After attending the Diocesan College in Rondebosch, Cape Town, Steyn went to Oxford University as a Rhodes Scholar in 1909. Steyn played on the wing for Oxford in the Varsity matches against Cambridge in 1911 and 1912; Steyn also played two games for the Barbarians in 1911.

By the time he had played in his first Varsity match, Steyn had already been picked to play for Scotland, Steyn making his debut for Scotland against England in 1911, in Scotland's first match at Twickenham. Steyn played his second and last game for Scotland a year later, against Ireland.

After leaving Oxford in 1913, Steyn went to Guy's Hospital to study medicine.

When war broke out, Steyn joined the King Edward's Horse as a private before being granted a commission in the Royal Field Artillery in November 1914.

Steyn was sent to France in September 1915 before being posted a few months later to Salonika, where he contracted typhoid fever. After recovering from his illness, Steyn was sent to Egypt. On 8th December 1917, Steyn was killed in action in Palestine, the day before General Allenby's forces took Jerusalem. Steyn was 28 years old when he was killed; he was initially buried in a temporary grave before his body was exhumed in 1920 and re-buried in the Jerusalem War Cemetery.

10.25 Walter "Wattie" Sutherland (1890-1918)
born in Hawick

Sutherland was a wing three-quarter who played his club rugby for Hawick RFC.

Sutherland was first picked to play for Scotland in 1910, when still only 19 years old; over the next four years, Sutherland played a further 12 games for Scotland at a time when the Scottish selectors seemed to favour those who played for the Former Pupils and Academicals teams based in Glasgow and Edinburgh or were Oxford or Cambridge Blues, rather than the likes of Sutherland who played for a club in the Borders region; he was however regarded as Scotland's best three-quarter of his day.

In his 13 internationals, Sutherland scored four tries for Scotland, one against England in 1911, two against France in 1912 and a second against England in 1912.

Sutherland also represented Scotland against Ireland in athletics from 1911 to 1913.

When war broke out, Sutherland enlisted with the Lothians and Border Horse in August 1914, before joining the Argyll and Sutherland Highlanders in July 1915 and finally the Seaforth Highlanders. Sutherland was involved in the fighting at Buzancy during the Third Battle of the Aisne and was one of only four of the 18 officers in his division to survive.

Sutherland was killed on 4th October 1918 at the age of 27, when he was hit by a stray shell whilst his battalion was being relieved from the front line near Hulloch in France. Sutherland was buried in the Houchin British Military Cemetery near Bethune in France.

As well as being one of Scotland's finest wings, one of the tributes to him was that "he was made of the stamp of which heroes are made".

INTERNATIONAL APPEARANCES

5th February 1910 Scotland v. Wales at the National Stadium, Cardiff; Wales won 14-0

19th March 1910 Scotland v. England at Inverleith; England won 14-5

2nd January 1911 Scotland v. France at Colombes; France won 16-15

18th March 1911 Scotland v. England at Twickenham; England won 13-8

20th January 1912 Scotland v. France at Inverleith; Scotland won 31-3

3rd February 1912 Scotland v. Wales at Swansea; Wales won 21-6

16th March 1912 Scotland v. England at Inverleith; Scotland won 8-3

23rd November 1912 Scotland v. South Africa at Inverleith; South Africa won 16-0

1st January 1913 Scotland v. France at Parc des Princes, Paris; Scotland won 21-3

1st February 1913 Scotland v. Wales at Inverleith; Wales won 8-0

22nd February 1913 Scotland v. Ireland at Inverleith; Scotland won 29-14

15th March 1913 Scotland v. England at Twickenham; England won 3-0

7th February 1914 Scotland v. Wales at the National Stadium, Cardiff; Wales won 24-5

10.26 Fred Turner (1888-1915)

born in Liverpool

After attending Sedbergh School, Turner went to Oxford University in 1907. In his second year at university, Turner played as a back row forward for the university team against the touring Australian team and, not long after this match, won his blue playing against Cambridge in the Varsity match. Turner played against Cambridge again in 1909 and in 1910 when he captained the team.

Turner also played cricket for the Oxford University team, appearing in five first-class games for them in 1909, but did not feature in a Varsity cricket match; in his five first-class matches, Turner scored a total of 67 runs at an average of 9.57, with a top score of 44 and took 17 wickets at an average of 16.

Whilst still in his last year at university, Turner played in all four of Scotland's Five Nations Championship games; his international career got off to a poor start when, on his debut, Scotland allowed France to record their first international win. This defeat was followed by two more at the hands of Wales and Ireland before a win at Twickenham over England in the last game of the 1911 Championship provided some consolation.

Turner played in all Scotland's matches not only in 1911 but also in 1912 and 1913. By 1914, Turner had been made captain of the Scottish team but only played in two of their games that year. In his 15 games for Scotland, Turner scored three tries and kicked 14 conversions; one of his tries and five of his conversions were in Scotland's game against France in 1912.

After leaving university, Turner worked for his father's printing business in Liverpool.

At the outbreak of war, Turner joined the King's Liverpool Regiment. Turner went to the Western Front on 2nd November 1914. On 10th January 1915, Turner was killed when overseeing the organisation of a barbed wire entanglement. One of those who witnessed Turner being shot recalled how Turner had been putting some barbed wire out in front of the trenches; after breakfast, he went to have a look at the position and, when he looked up, he was shot at twice. Turner then went to a place where the parapet was rather low and a shot from a sniper lying in no man's land went between him and his sergeant. Turner then went a bit lower and had a look at the wire when he was shot through the middle of his forehead, the bullet killing him instantly as it came out of the back of his head.

Turner was 26 years old when he was killed and was buried in Kemmel Churchyard, in Belgium.

INTERNATIONAL APPEARANCES

2nd January 1911 Scotland v. France at Colombes; France won 16-15

4th February 1911 Scotland v. Wales at Inverleith; Wales won 32-10

25th February 1911 Scotland v. Ireland at Inverleith; Ireland won 16-10

18th March 1911 Scotland v. England at Twickenham; England won 13-8

20th January 1912 Scotland v. France at Inverleith; Scotland won 31-3

3rd February 1912 Scotland v. Wales at Swansea; Wales won 21-6

24th February 1912 Scotland v. Ireland at Lansdowne Road, Dublin; Ireland won 10-8

16th March 1912 Scotland v. England at Inverleith; Scotland won 8-3

23rd March 1912 Scotland v. South Africa at Inverleith; South Africa won 16-0

1st January 1913 Scotland v. France at Parc des Princes, Paris; Scotland won 21-3

1st February 1913 Scotland v. Wales at Inverleith; Wales won 8-0

22nd February 1913 Scotland v. Ireland at Inverleith; Scotland won 29-14

15th March 1913 Scotland v. England at Twickenham; England won 3-0

10.27 Albert Wade (1884-1917)

born in Glasgow

Wade went to Dulwich College where he was the school captain at rugby. After leaving school, Wade played for the London Scottish until 1908 and after that for the Old Alleynians; he also, on three occasions, played for the Barbarians.

In 1908, after Scotland had lost their first two games in the Home Nations Championship, Wade was picked to play at scrum-half in Scotland's final game of the Home Nations Championship that year, the Calcutta Cup match against England. Despite being on the winning side, Wade was not picked again to play for Scotland.

At the outbreak of war, Wade joined the 13th Kensingtons before being given a commission, in November 1914, in the 17th Battalion, Middlesex Regiment. In September 1915, Wade was sent to France and, in December 1916, was attached on a temporary basis with the trench mortar battery.

On 28th April 1917, Wade was killed at Oppy Wood, Arras when the Germans counter-attacked after Wade's mortar battery had penetrated the German's third line of defences; his body was never recovered. Wade was 32 years old when he died and is commemorated at the Arras Memorial.

INTERNATIONAL APPEARANCE

21st March 1908 Scotland v. England at Inverleith; Scotland won 16-10

10.28 Willie Wallace (1892-1915)
born in Edinburgh

Wallace attended Edinburgh Academy where he excelled at cricket, athletics, gymnastics and fives, as well as rugby. After leaving school, Wallace went to Cambridge University in 1912 and played in the Varsity match against Oxford in his first term; he also played in the Varsity match a year later. Whilst still a freshman, Wallace played his first game for Scotland, their final match of the 1913 Five Nations Championship. In 1914, Wallace played in all three of Scotland's Five Nations Championship matches, the match against France not having been played that year. Although Wallace was on the losing side in all four games he played for Scotland, he was considered by the rugby author E. H. D. Sewell to be, in 1913 and 1914, the best full-back in Britain.

Whilst still an undergraduate, Wallace was gazetted to the Rifle Brigade on 15th August 1914 and left for France on 30th August 1914. After having been present at the Battle of Aisne at Frelinghien and Ploegsteert Wood, Wallace became an observer in the Royal Flying Corps. Wallace fought at Neuve Chapelle, Aubers, rue d'Ouvert and saw a number of other actions in the Armentieres-La Bassee area.

By July 1915, Wallace had become a senior observer in his squadron and had been promoted to lieutenant. On 22nd August 1915, Wallace died when carrying out photographic reconnaissance; his plane was shot down by anti-aircraft gunfire at Sainghin, near Lille. Wallace was 22 years old when he was killed and was buried at the Cabaret-Rouge British Cemetery at Souchez.

15th March 1913 Scotland v. England at Twickenham; England won 3-0

7th February 1914 Scotland v. Wales at the National Stadium, Cardiff; Wales won 24-5

28th February 1914 Scotland v. Ireland at Lansdowne Road, Dublin; Ireland won 6-0

21st March 1914 Scotland v. England at Inverleith; England won 16-15

10.29 George Will (1892-1917)
born in Croydon

Will went to Merchant Taylors School before going up to Cambridge University in 1911. Will played rugby on the wing and played in three Varsity matches for Cambridge against Oxford, from 1911 to 1913.

Whilst still in his first year at university, Will was picked to play for Scotland; Will played in all four of Scotland's Five Nations Championship games in 1912 and scored a try in each of his first three internationals. Will missed the 1913 Five Nations Championship games but played in Scotland's three fixtures in 1914, scoring two tries in the defeat to England.

In the War, Will joined the Honourable Artillery Company; he went to France in September 1914. The following March, Will took a commission with the Worcester Regiment and, after being wounded near Hooge in August 1915, transferred to the Leinster Regiment. In November 1915, Will joined the Royal Flying Corps.

After training, Will returned to France as a fighter pilot in February 1917, with the 29th Squadron. On 25th March 1917, after Will took off from Le Hameau aerodrome near Nieuport on an escort mission, another pilot had to return to the aerodrome due to revolution counter problems; after changing planes the other pilot returned to the front but was unable to find Will. It is thought that Will was killed in an air battle over Arras; although the claim was disallowed, it is possible that Will was shot down by Lother von Richthofen, the brother of the Red Baron, Manfred von Richthofen, who had shot down one of the other planes that had taken off with Will that day.

Will was 24 years old when he died and is commemorated on the Arras Flying Services Memorial.

INTERNATIONAL APPEARANCES

20th January 1912 Scotland v. France at Inverleith; Scotland won 31-3

3rd February 1912 Scotland v. Wales at Swansea; Wales won 21-6

24th February 1912 Scotland v. Ireland at Lansdowne Road, Dublin; Ireland won 10-8

16th March 1912 Scotland v. England at Inverleith; Scotland won 8-3

7th February 1914 Scotland v. Wales at the National Stadium, Cardiff; Wales won 24-5

28th February 1914 Scotland v. Ireland at Lansdowne Road, Dublin; Ireland won 6-0

21st March 1914 Scotland v. England at Inverleith; England won 16-15

10.30 John Wilson (1884-1916)
born in Trinidad

At the age of 14, Wilson signed up as a navy officer cadet at the Britannia Royal Naval College and, by 1900, was working on board ships. Leading up to the War, Wilson served on board a number of ships and spent time in submarines as well as undertaking specialist torpedo training.

Serving in the Navy, Wilson played rugby as a forward for the United Services RFC, which he captained in 1908 and

1909 and for the Navy in their fixtures against the Army in 1907, 1908 and 1913.

Wilson made his debut for Scotland in 1908, playing in the away fixture against Ireland. A year later, he played his second game for Scotland, the home fixture against Wales but, after losing both matches, Wilson was not picked again.

As well as being an international rugby player, Wilson excelled at rowing and sailing.

By 1913, Wilson was serving on board HMS Indefatigable and was on board this ship serving as a lieutenant commander when it was engaged in the Battle of Jutland on 31st May 1916. In the opening minutes of the engagement, HMS Indefatigable was destroyed and sunk after coming under fire from the German battlecruiser SMS von der Tann; all but two of the 1,057 officers and men on board HMS Indefatigable, including Wilson, were killed.

Wilson was 32 years old when he died and is commemorated at the Plymouth Naval Memorial.

INTERNATIONAL APPEARANCES

29th February 1908 Scotland v. Ireland at Lansdowne Road, Dublin; Ireland won 16-11

6th February 1909 Scotland v. Wales at Inverleith; Wales won 5-0

10.31 Eric Young (1892-1915)

After attending Fettes College, Young went to Oxford University from 1910 to 1913 and, although he played rugby for the university team, he was never selected for the Varsity match against Cambridge.

After graduating, Young played for Glasgow Academicals and, in 1914, was called up to play as flanker for Scotland in their match against England. It proved to be Scotland's last international before the War and, as a consequence, Young's only international appearance.

Having joined the Territorial Force in 1911, Young had been promoted to captain by August 1914. In 1915, Young was sent to Gallipoli with the 8th Battalion, the Cameronians, arriving in June 1915. Two weeks after arriving in Gallipoli, on 28th June 1915, Young took part in the attack at Gully Ravine; Young's battalion lost 349 men in the attack, including that of Young who was reported missing and presumed dead.

Young was 23 years old when he died and his body was never recovered. Young is commemorated on the Helles Memorial in Turkey after having been mistakenly commemorated on the Le Touret Memorial in France along with the men of the 6th Battalion of the Cameronians who were killed in France in the War.

INTERNATIONAL APPEARANCE

21st March 1914 Scotland v. England at Inverleith; England won 16-15

CHAPTER 11
WALES RUGBY PLAYERS

11.1 Billy Geen (1891-1915)

born in Newport

After attending Haileybury College, Geen went to Oxford University where he played on the wing for the university rugby team in three Varsity matches. In his first Varsity match, Geen scored two tries and would have had a hat-trick of tries had he not dropped the ball after crossing the Cambridge line whilst trying to touch down nearer the posts, an error he was to repeat in both of his other matches for Oxford against Cambridge.

His performances in 1910 were enough for Geen to win trials for England but, after failing to make the England team, Wales selected him as a reserve against England in 1911. An injury playing for the Barbarians in December 1911 made him unavailable for the 1912 Five Nations Championship and it was not until December 1912 that Geen was fit enough to make his debut for Wales, against the touring South Africans; Geen was not able to add a second win against South Africa to the one he had when playing for Newport a few weeks earlier.

Geen played in two of Wales's Five Nations Championship matches in 1913 and was picked again in 1914 to play against England but withdrew following medical advice.

In addition to playing for Oxford University, Newport, the Barbarians and Wales, Geen also made a few appearances for Blackheath and Bridgend, as well playing cricket for Monmouthshire in the Minor Counties Championship.

At the outbreak of war, Geen joined the 9th Battalion, King's Royal Rifle Corps; after being sent to the Western Front in May 1915, Geen's battalion was assigned to the 14th (Light) Division, taking part in the Second Battle of Ypres. After six weeks of fighting, the battalion was allowed rest but, after only two days off, returned to the front at Hooge in Belgium to provide reinforcements for the 41st Brigade, to join in the counter-attack on the Germans who, following their first use of liquid fire, had captured a number of British trenches. Geen was last seen on 31st July 1915, leading his men in hand-to-hand fighting as they advanced towards ruined village buildings to take out enemy machine guns.

Geen was 24 years old when he was killed; his body was never recovered and he is commemorated at the Ypres (Menin Gate) Memorial.

INTERNATIONAL APPEARANCES

14th December 1912 Wales v. South Africa at the National Stadium, Cardiff; South Africa won 3-0

18th January 1913 Wales v. England at the National Stadium, Cardiff; England won 12-0

8th March 1913 Wales v. Ireland at Swansea; Wales won 16-13

11.2 Brinley "Bryn" Lewis (1891-1917)
born in Pontardawe, Glamorganshire

Lewis attended Swansea Grammar School and played for Welsh Schoolboys before going up to Cambridge University in 1909. Lewis played in three Varsity matches for Cambridge against Oxford, from 1909 to 1911 and not long after winning his third blue and whilst still an undergraduate, made his debut for Wales on the wing against Ireland.

It was another year before Lewis made his second appearance for Wales, again against Ireland and although he scored two tries in Wales's win, Lewis did not play for Wales again and had to settle for playing for Swansea and a couple of games for the Barbarians.

After war was declared, Lewis joined the Glamorgan Yeomanry. In April 1916, Lewis was mentioned in despatches for outstanding and brave conduct and, by November 1916, Lewis had been promoted to the rank of major with the 122nd Brigade of the 38th (Welsh) Infantry.

On 2nd April 1917, Lewis was killed when a high velocity enemy shell aimed at a battery about 300 yards behind the mess where Lewis was situated hit Lewis's mess, killing him instantly. Lewis was 26 years old when he was killed and was buried at the Ferme-Olivier Cemetery near Ypres.

INTERNATIONAL APPEARANCES

9th March 1912 Wales v. Ireland at Balmoral Showgrounds, Belfast; Ireland won 12-5

8th March 1913 Wales v. Ireland at Swansea; Wales won 16-13

MILITARY HONOURS

Mentioned in despatches

11.3 Hopkin Maddock (1881-1921)

born in Pontycymer, near Bridgend

Maddock went to school at Christ College, Brecon and, after leaving school, he played his first club rugby for Pontycymer RFC; after moving to London in 1900, Maddock joined London Welsh, playing on the wing and, in his 13 years with London Welsh, scored 170 tries including, on two occasions, five tries in a match.

Maddock's performances for London Welsh earned him international recognition in 1906 when he played in all of Wales's Home Nations Championship matches. After wins against England and Scotland, with Maddock scoring a try in both games, Wales were denied the Triple Crown when they lost their last match to Ireland.

After being dropped for the game against South Africa in December 1906, Maddock regained his place for Wales's Home Nations Championship game against England in 1907, a game in which Maddock scored two more tries. However a defeat at the hands of Scotland in the following match led to Maddock being dropped by the Welsh selectors.

After missing out on the Home Nations Championships in 1908 and 1909, Maddock was recalled one last time for the fixture against France in 1910 in what was France's first appearance in the Five Nations Championship. Maddock scored two of Wales's 10 tries in their 49-14 victory.

At the outbreak of war, Maddock joined the Royal Fusiliers. In July 1916, Maddock was injured during the Battle of the Somme, an injury from which he never properly recovered. Despite his injury, Maddock was commissioned into the Machine Gun Corps in September 1916 and, in 1918, was awarded the Military Cross for gallantry when, whilst almost surrounded, he continued firing until all his men had crossed a bridge, leaving him the last man to return to safety as his unit was retreating from Les Mesnil.

Although Maddock survived the War, the injury he sustained at the Battle of the Somme in 1916 eventually led to his death in Cardiff on 15th December 1921. Maddock was 40 years old when he died.

INTERNATIONAL APPEARANCES

13th January 1906 Wales v. England at Richmond; Wales won 16-3

3rd February 1906 Wales v. Scotland at the National Stadium, Cardiff; Wales won 9-3

10th March 1906 Wales v. Ireland at Balmoral Showgrounds, Belfast; Ireland won 11-6

12th January 1907 Wales v. England at Swansea; Wales won 22-0

2nd February 1907 Wales v. Scotland at Inverleith; Scotland won 6-3

1st January 1910 Wales v. France at Swansea; Wales won 49-14

MILITARY HONOURS

Military Cross

11.4 Fred Perrett (1891-1918)
born in Briton Ferry, South Wales

After playing for his local team, Perrett joined Neath and, towards the end of 1912, made his debut for Wales playing at prop against the touring South Africans. For the following Five Nations Championship, Perrett was one of only two to play for Wales in all four of their matches. After losing the first match against England, Wales won their other three matches to finish second in the Championship.

After the 1913 Five Nations Championship, Perrett turned professional, playing rugby league for Leeds before moving to Hull.

At the outbreak of war, Perrett joined the Welsh Guards, serving in France from February 1916. In June 1917, Perrett transferred to the Royal Welsh Fusiliers. Towards the end of the War, Perrett was seriously injured and died from his wounds in a casualty clearing station in Boulogne on 1st December 1918, three weeks after the Armistice had been signed.

Perrett was 27 years old when he died and was buried at the Terlincthun British Cemetery at Wimille in France.

INTERNATIONAL APPEARANCES

14th December 1912 Wales v. South Africa at the National Stadium, Cardiff; South Africa won 3-0

18th January 1913 Wales v. England at the National Stadium, Cardiff; England won 12-0

1st February 1913 Wales v. Scotland at Inverleith; Wales won 8-0

27th February 1913 Wales v. France at Parc des Princes, Paris; Wales won 11-8

8th March 1913 Wales v. Ireland at Swansea; Wales won 16-13

11.5 Lou Phillips (1878-1916)
born in Newport

After leaving Monmouth Grammar School, Phillips qualified as an architect and played his club rugby, as a half-back, for Newport, for whom he played 90 games between 1897 and 1901 before being forced to retire due to injuries.

Phillips made his debut for Wales in 1900 and played in all of Wales's Home Nations Championship matches that year as Wales won the Triple Crown. The following year, Phillips missed the opening game against England due to injury but played in the following match against Scotland; however, he had not properly recovered from his injury and, after aggravating his injury early in the game against Scotland, retired from rugby after the game.

Phillips was also a golfer, winning the Welsh Amateur Championship in 1907 and 1912; in 1913, he was runner-up in the Irish Amateur Championship and, in 1914, reached the sixth round of the British Amateur Championship, at a time when it was regarded as one of the four major golf tournaments.

In the War, Phillips enlisted with the 20th (Service) Battalion, Royal Fusiliers and was sent to the Western Front in November 1915.

During the night of 14th March 1916, Phillips went out on a "wiring party", near Cambrin in France, to repair damaged wire defences and sabotage the enemy's wire defences; while out wiring, Phillips was shot in the chest and killed. He was 38 years old when he died and was buried in the Cambrin Churchyard Extension.

INTERNATIONAL APPEARANCES

6th January 1900 Wales v. England at Gloucester; Wales won 13-3

27th January 1900 Wales v. Scotland at Swansea; Wales won 12-3

17th March 1900 Wales v. Ireland at Balmoral Showgrounds, Belfast; Wales won 3-0

9th February 1901 Wales v. Scotland at Inverleith; Scotland won 18-8

11.6 Charlie Pritchard (1882-1916)
born in Newport

Pritchard went to Long Ashton School in Bristol and, after leaving school, played his club rugby as a back row forward for Newport.

Pritchard made his first appearance for Wales in their last game of the 1904 Home Nations Championship. The following year he played in Wales's matches against England and Scotland and, later in the year, in their win over New Zealand in the first fixture between the two countries. In 1906 and 1907, Pritchard played in all of Wales's fixtures but the following year suffered a serious injury and it was not until 1910, when he played his last two games for Wales, that he was fit enough to be picked again.

In the War, Pritchard was commissioned into the 12th Battalion, South Wales Borderers. By November 1915, he had been promoted to captain and, in June 1916, went to the Western Front with his battalion.

On the night of 12th August 1916, Pritchard led a trench raid near Loos to capture a German prisoner; Pritchard led the raid into the enemy trenches and took the prisoner; although the raid was successful in terms of capturing the prisoner, Pritchard was wounded twice during the raid, the second time seriously. Pritchard was then taken to No.1 Casualty Clearing Station a few miles behind the front at Chocques in France but died of his wounds on 14th August 1916; he was 35 years old when he died and was buried at the Chocques Military Cemetery.

For his role in the raid, Pritchard was recommended for a Military Cross which was turned down and instead received a mention in despatches.

12th March 1904 Wales v. Ireland at Balmoral Showgrounds, Belfast; Ireland won 14-12

14th January 1905 Wales v. England at the National Stadium, Cardiff; Wales won 25-0

4th February 1905 Wales v. Scotland at Inverleith; Wales won 6-3

16th December 1905 Wales v. New Zealand at the National Stadium, Cardiff; Wales won 3-0

13th January 1906 Wales v. England at Richmond; Wales won 16-3

3rd February 1906 Wales v. Scotland at the National Stadium, Cardiff; Wales won 9-3

10th March 1906 Wales v. Ireland at Balmoral Showgrounds, Belfast; Ireland won 11-6

1st December 1906 Wales v. South Africa at Swansea; South Africa won 11-0

12th January 1907 Wales v. England at Swansea; Wales won 22-0

2nd February 1907 Wales v. Scotland at Inverleith; match drawn 6-6

9th March 1907 Wales v. Ireland at the National Stadium, Cardiff; Wales won 29-0

18th January 1908 Wales v. England at Ashton Gate, Bristol; Wales won 28-18

1st January 1910 Wales v. France at Swansea; Wales won 49-14

15th January 1910 Wales v. England at Twickenham; England won 11-6

MILITARY HONOURS

Mentioned in despatches

11.7 Charles Taylor (1863-1915)
born in Ruabon, near Wrexham

Taylor left home at the age of 16 and enrolled as a naval engineering student at HMS Marlborough in Portsmouth; whilst in Portsmouth, Taylor converted from being a footballer to a rugby player, playing as a three-quarter.

Taylor made his debut for Wales in 1884, whilst playing his club rugby for the HMS Marlborough rugby club. On his debut against England, Taylor very nearly won the game for

Wales with a drop goal which, according to the English full-back, was good but the officials were not as well placed as him to judge and disallowed it.

Taylor played in all of Wales's fixtures in 1884 and, in the following year, in which he joined the Royal Navy, he played in two more of Wales's fixtures. In 1885, whilst he was spending more of his time in London, Taylor and a number of other Welshmen living in London formed London Welsh Rugby Club.

1886 saw Taylor play two more matches for Wales; in the drawn match against England, Taylor converted the try scored by Wales but, because of the scoring system at the time, only the try-scorer was credited with scoring in the match. Taylor played his final two games for Wales in 1887.

Taylor was also an accomplished athlete and, in 1884, was runner-up in the pole vault at the AAA Championships.

By 1912, Taylor had been promoted to engineer captain. When war broke out, Taylor was posted to the battle cruiser HMS Queen Mary and, in November 1914, transferred to HMS Tiger. On 24th January 1915, Taylor was on board HMS Tiger when it was engaged in the Battle of Dogger Bank; although no British ships were lost during the battle, HMS Tiger suffered most of the British casualties when a shell launched by the German cruiser SMS Bluchen struck a compartment below the conning tower. Taylor was caught in the blast and killed instantly; he was 51 years old when he died and was buried at Tavistock New Cemetery.

INTERNATIONAL APPEARANCES

5th January 1884 Wales v. England at Cardigan Fields, Leeds; England won on tries scored

12th January 1884 Wales v. Scotland at Rodney Parade, Newport; Scotland won by one goal to nil

12th April 1884 Wales v. Ireland at the National Stadium, Cardiff; Wales won by one goal to nil

3rd January 1885 Wales v. England at Swansea; match drawn, one goal each

10th January 1885 Wales v. Scotland at Hamilton Crescent, Glasgow; match drawn 0-0

2nd January 1886 Wales v. England at Blackheath; England won by one goal and two unconverted tries

to one goal and no tries

9th January 1886 Wales v. Scotland at the National Stadium, Cardiff; Scotland won by two goals to nil

8th January 1887 Wales v. England at Llanelli Cricket Ground; match drawn 0-0

12th March 1887 Wales v. Ireland at Birkenhead; Wales won by one goal to nil

11.8 Edward John Richard "Dick" Thomas (1883-1916)
born in Ferndale, Rhonnda

After leaving school, Thomas joined the police force and served with the Glamorganshire Constabulary from 1904 until 1915. Thomas was a forward who played club rugby for Mountain Ash and Bridgend. He played his first game for Glamorgan in 1904 and, over an 11 year period, played 20 games for the county, including the game against the touring South Africans in October 1906. Just over a month later, Thomas made his debut for Wales against South Africa.

Due to having appendicitis, Thomas missed out on rugby in 1907 and it was not until Wales's last two games of the 1908 Home Nations Championship that Thomas was fit enough to play again. Thomas played one more game for Wales the following season before his international career came to an end.

Thomas was also a boxer and was the Glamorgan Police heavyweight boxing champion.

After war broke out, it was not until January 1915 that Thomas was relieved from his policing duties and able to enlist;

he joined the 16th Battalion, Welsh Regiment and was sent to the Western Front in December 1915.

Thomas was killed in action on 7th July 1916 when he was shot through the head during the Battle of the Somme, during the taking of Mametz Wood. Thomas was 32 years old when he was killed and he is commemorated at the Thiepval Memorial to the Missing.

INTERNATIONAL APPEARANCES

1st December 1906 Wales v. South Africa at Swansea; South Africa won 11-0

2nd March 1908 Wales v. France at the National Stadium, Cardiff; Wales won 36-4

14th March 1908 Wales v. Ireland at Balmoral Showgrounds, Belfast; Wales won 11-5

6th February 1909 Wales v. Scotland at Inverleith; Wales won 5-3

11.9 Horace Wyndham Thomas (1890-1916)
born in Bridgend

After attending Monmouth School, Thomas won a choral scholarship to Cambridge University; at university, Thomas played cricket for the 2nd XI and represented the university at both athletics and rugby. Only four days after winning a blue in rugby, Thomas made his debut for Wales as fly-half in the match against the touring South Africans.

Thomas played in Wales's next game, against England in the 1913 Five Nations Championship, after which he emigrated to India to work for the Mercantile Service in Calcutta, working in the Calcutta harbour defence force. During his time in Calcutta, Thomas captained the Calcutta Football Club, the club which was to provide the silver for the Calcutta Cup when the club was dissolved in 1920.

In 1916, Thomas returned to Britain to serve in the War with the Rifle Brigade. On 3ʳᵈ September 1916, Thomas was killed in action at Guillemont; in his last letter home before his death, Thomas had written "without wanting to be dramatic or boastful, I can say, truthfully that I am not afraid of death, my life has been a happy one."

Thomas was 26 years old when he was killed; his body was never recovered and he is commemorated at the Thiepval Memorial to the Missing.

INTERNATIONAL APPEARANCES

14ᵗʰ December 1912 Wales v. South Africa at the National Stadium, Cardiff; South Africa won 3-0

18ᵗʰ January 1913 Wales v. England at the National Stadium, Cardiff; England won 12-0

11.10 Phil Waller (1889-1917)

born in Bath, Somerset

Waller played rugby as a forward, playing for Newport from 1906 until 1910; he also represented both Somerset and Monmouthshire in county championship matches.

Waller made his debut for Wales in their win over Australia in 1908; a week after his debut, he was playing the tourists a second time in their match against Newport. The following season, Waller played in all three of Wales's Home Nations Championship matches as they won the Triple Crown and in their win over France but, as France were only added to the Home Nations Championship a year later, Wales were denied what would have been the first ever Grand Slam and had to settle instead for an unofficial one.

The following year, Waller only played one game for Wales and that proved to be his last one, leaving him with a record of six wins out of six for Wales. In the summer of 1910 though, Waller was picked as a member of the Great Britain team to tour South Africa; Waller played in all three Tests in a series won 2-1 by South Africa.

At the end of the tour to South Africa, Waller decided to stay there and worked as an engineer in Johannesburg; he continued to play club rugby though, playing for Johannesburg Golden Lions.

When war broke out, Waller enlisted with the South Africa Artillery Regiment, serving as a gunner. By February 1916, he had been sent to the Western Front and, in May 1917, received a field commission for distinguished conduct.

On 14th December 1917, Waller was killed by shellfire at Arras; he was 28 years old when he was killed and was buried at the Red Cross Corner Cemetery at Beugny in France.

INTERNATIONAL APPEARANCES

12th December 1908 Wales v. Australia at the National Stadium, Cardiff; Wales won 9-6

16th January 1909 Wales v. England at the National Stadium, Cardiff; Wales won 8-0

6th February 1909 Wales v. Scotland at Inverleith; Wales won 5-3

23rd February 1909 Wales v. France at Colombes; Wales won 47-5

13th March 1909 Wales v. Ireland at Swansea; Wales won 18-5

1st January 1910 Wales v. France at Swansea; Wales won 49-14

6th August 1910 Great Britain v. South Africa at Johannesburg; South Africa won 14-10

27th August 1910 Great Britain v. South Africa at Port Elizabeth; Great Britain won 8-3

3rd September 1910 Great Britain v. South Africa at Cape Town; South Africa won 21-5

MILITARY HONOURS

Field commission

11.11 David Watts (1886-1916)

born in Maesteg

Born into a coal mining family, Watts worked in the mines near Maesteg from his early teenage years. He played rugby as a lock for Maesteg and was a member of the team which won the Glamorgan Challenge Cup in 1912.

Two years later, Watts played his first game for Wales. A narrow defeat to England away was followed by three wins, as Wales came second in the Five Nations Championship. In 1915, Watts played one more game for Wales, a game against the Barbarians arranged to encourage recruitment in to the Welsh Guard; as a result of the match, 177 men enlisted.

In the War, Watts joined the Shropshire Light Infantry, rising to the rank of corporal. He was posted to France in October 1915 and after seeing action at the Ypres salient in 1915 and 1916, moved south to prepare for the Somme offensive.

During the early hours of 14th July 1916, Watts's battalion was ordered to advance towards German trenches at Bazentin Ridge but they were unable to advance beyond the two rows of wire defending the trenches. Although it is not known during which part of the day he was killed, Watts was one of over 150 men killed during the attacks.

Watts was 30 years old when he was killed; his body was never recovered and he is commemorated at the Thiepval Memorial to the Missing.

INTERNATIONAL APPEARANCES

17th January 1914 Wales v. England at Twickenham; England won 10-9

7th February 1914 Wales v. Scotland at the National Stadium, Cardiff; Wales won 24-5

11.12 Dai Westacott (1882-1917)
born in Cardiff.

After leaving school, Westacott worked as a docker and played rugby as a forward for Cardiff. Over a seven year period, Westacott played 120 games for Cardiff, including in their game against the touring Australians in 1908, a game which Cardiff won 24-8 to inflict upon the tourists the heaviest defeat of their tour – one of Westacott's contributions to Cardiff's success in the game was to be on the receiving end of a kick whilst on the ground from one of the Australian locks which led to the lock being sent off.

In 1905, Westacott played for Glamorgan against the first New Zealand team to tour Britain. A year later, Westacott was selected to play for Wales in their final game of the Home Nations Championship; having already beaten Scotland and England, a win over Ireland would have secured the Triple Crown for Wales but they ended up on the losing side, despite Ireland ending the game with only 13 players on the pitch as a result of injuries. Westacott's game against Ireland was his only international.

In the War, Westacott joined the Army and was posted to the Gloucestershire Regiment. He was sent to France in February 1915; in August 1916, Westacott was sent back to England after being wounded and it was another eight months before he returned to the front.

On 27th August 1917, during the Third Battle of Ypres, Westacott was with the 144th Brigade taking part in the advance on German positions at Springfield Farm, near Wieljte; after taking the bunker positions around the farm, Westacott was killed the next day when he was hit by a random shell.

Westacott was 34 years old when he was killed; his body was never recovered and he is commemorated at the Tyne Cot Memorial at Zonnebeke in Belgium.

INTERNATIONAL APPEARANCE

10th March 1906 Wales v. Ireland at Balmoral Showgrounds, Belfast; Ireland won 11-6

11.13 John Lewis "Johnnie" Williams (1882-1916)
born in Whitchurch, Glamorgan

After leaving Cowbridge Grammar School where he played football, Williams played rugby for his village team and was invited, in 1899, to play for Newport on the wing. After four seasons with Newport, Williams joined Cardiff RFC when his work as a coal exporter took him to Cardiff. Over 12 seasons with Cardiff, Williams made 199 appearances for them, in which he scored 150 tries and captained them in the 1909/10 season. His games for Cardiff included their 17-0 win in 1906 over the touring South African team in which Williams scored a memorable try just a month after he had made his debut for Wales against the tourists; he also played for Cardiff in their 24-8 win over the touring Australians in 1908, a game in which Williams scored two tries.

Williams made his debut for Wales towards the end of 1906, against South Africa. A defeat was followed by a victory over England and a defeat at the hands of Scotland but his remaining 14 games for Wales were all victories. In his 17 internationals for Wales, Williams scored a total of 17 tries and, on three occasions, Williams was a member of a Welsh team winning the Triple Crown; he also had the honour of captaining his country in the game against France in 1911, in part due to the fact he could speak French.

In 1908, Williams was also a member of the Anglo-Welsh team to tour New Zealand and played in two of the three Test matches on the tour.

In the War, Williams joined the Royal Fusiliers in September 1914; he was commissioned into the 16th Battalion, Welsh Regiment in December 1914 and his regiment was deployed to the Western Front a year later. During the Battle of the Somme, Williams's regiment was brought into the action on 5th July 1916 to the south of Mamtez Wood; on 7th July 1916, Williams was leading one of the attacks on the German positions in the wood which they were expected to capture within a matter of hours but they were beaten back by machine gun fire and shelling; during the fighting, Williams was wounded and evacuated but died five days later in No. 5 Casualty Clearing Station.

Williams was 34 years old when he died and was buried in the Corbie Communal Cemetery Extension near Amiens.

INTERNATIONAL APPEARANCES

1st December 1906 Wales v. South Africa at Swansea; South Africa won 11-0

12th January 1907 Wales v. England at Swansea; Wales won 22-0

2nd February 1907 Wales v. Scotland at Inverleith; Scotland won 3-0

9th March 1907 Wales v. Ireland at the National Stadium, Cardiff; Wales won 29-0

18th January 1908 Wales v. England at Ashton Gate, Bristol; Wales won 28-18

1st February 1908 Wales v. Scotland at Swansea; Wales won 6-5

14th March 1908 Wales v. Ireland at Balmoral Showgrounds, Belfast; Wales won 11-5

6th June 1908 Anglo-Welsh v. New Zealand at Dunedin; New Zealand won 32-5

27th June 1908 Anglo-Welsh v. New Zealand at Wellington; match drawn 3-3

12th December 1908 Wales v. Australia at the National Stadium, Cardiff; Wales won 9-6

16th January 1909 Wales v. England at the National Stadium, Cardiff; Wales won 8-0

6th February 1909 Wales v. Scotland at Inverleith; Wales won 5-3

23rd February 1909 Wales v. France at Colombes; Wales won 47-5

13th March 1909 Wales v. Ireland at Swansea; Wales won 18-5

12th March 1910 Wales v. Ireland at Lansdowne Road, Dublin; Wales won 19-3

21st January 1911 Wales v. England at Swansea; Wales won 15-11

4th February 1911 Wales v. Scotland at Inverleith; Wales won 32-10

28th February 1911 Wales v. France at Parc des Princes, Paris; Wales won 15-0

11th March 1911 Wales v. Ireland at the National Stadium, Cardiff; Wales won 16-0

11.14 Richard Davies Garnons Williams (1856-1915)
born in Llowes, Radnorshire

After attending Magdalen College School in Oxford, Williams went up to Cambridge University and, although he represented the university at rugby, he did not play in a Varsity match against Oxford.

After graduating, Williams went to the Royal Military College at Sandhurst, completing his officer training in 1876.

As well as playing rugby for Sandhurst, Williams played three games for Newport in 1880 before being selected, in 1881, to play as a forward in Wales's first ever rugby international, against England at Blackheath. After a heavy defeat, by eight goals to nil, Williams was not selected to play for Wales again.

After having served with the Army in Egypt and Gibraltar, Williams retired from regular service with the Army in 1892, although he continued to serve in a voluntary capacity up until 1906.

At the outbreak of war, Williams re-joined his regiment, the 12th Battalion, Royal Fusiliers in September 1914. According to official records, Williams was killed on 25th September 1915 when leading his battalion at the Battle of Loos; however, a soldier under his command reported that Williams was killed on 27th September 1915 when he was shot in the head; according to the report, the shot had been fired from a house nearby after Williams had ordered a retreat, because the flanks were exposed during an attack on German trenches; the order to retreat came after the battalion had captured a trench occupied by the Germans but further occupation of the trench became untenable and, as Williams gave orders to retreat and to the machine-gun section to fire over the trench to keep back the Germans, he was shot.

Williams was 59 years old when he died and he is commemorated at the Loos Memorial to the Missing.

INTERNATIONAL APPEARANCE

19th February 1881 Wales v. England at Blackheath; England won by 8 goals to nil

CHAPTER 12

Lions Rugby Players

Prior to the outbreak of war, Great Britain had made nine rugby tours overseas, four to South Africa, three combined tours to Australia and New Zealand, one to Australia and one, for which no international caps were awarded, to Argentina.

Alexander Todd (see Chapter 8.25) toured with the Great Britain team to South Africa in 1896; Blair Swannell (see Chapter 13.6) toured with the team to Australia in 1899 and to Australia and New Zealand in 1904 and, after emigrating, represented Australia; Robertson Smyth (see Chapter 9.10) toured with the team to South Africa in 1903; David Bedell-Sivright (see Chapter 10.3) captained the team which toured Australia and New Zealand in 1904; Phil Waller (see Chapter 11.10) toured with the team to South Africa in 1910; and John Raphael (see Chapter 8.21) toured with the team to Argentina in 1910.

In addition to the above, all of whom also played for their country, the following three also played for Great Britain in Test matches but never for their home country. A fourth, Noel Forbes Humphreys, was a member of the Great Britain team which toured South Africa in 1910 but never played in any of the Test matches against South Africa; Humphreys was killed in action during the War on 27th March 1918.

12.1 Charlie Adamson (1875-1918)
born in Durham

After attending Durham School, Adamson played rugby as a half-back for Durham and, after playing for the Barbarians on their 1899 Easter tour, was selected to play for the Great Britain team touring Australia in the summer of 1899.

Adamson played in all 20 of the games on tour, including the four Tests against Australia. For the first Test, Adamson played out of position at centre to accommodate the captain but, after the first game was lost, Adamson played in his normal position at fly-half. Great Britain's fortunes changed after Adamson's positional move, with Great Britain winning the last three Tests. Adamson was the top points scorer for Great Britain on the tour as well as in the Tests, in which he scored two tries and kicked four conversions and a penalty goal.

After the tour was over, Adamson stayed on in Australia and, in 1899, played in his only game of first-class cricket, for Queensland against New South Wales; in the match, he scored a duck in the first innings and 10 in the second and, with his bowling, failed to take a wicket in his 12 overs.

Whilst in Australia, Adamson enrolled with the Imperial Bushman (Mounted Infantry) which resulted in him having to serve in the Second Boer War but, after he was demobilised, he returned to England and continued to play rugby for Bristol and cricket for Durham; having played in Durham's first Minor Counties Championship game in 1895, Adamson continued playing for them right up until the outbreak of war, his last game being for them on 10th August 1914, two weeks after war had been declared. As well as playing in 78 Minor Counties Championship matches for Durham, Adamson also played for them against the touring South Africans in

1908 and captained the Durham team against the touring Australians in 1908.

In the War, Adamson served as a captain with the 6th Battalion, the Royal Scots Fusiliers; he was posted to Salonika and, on 17th September 1918, less than two months before the end of the War, he was killed during an attack by his battalion on Bulgarian trenches in northern Greece.

Adamson was 43 years old when he was killed and was buried at the Karasouli Military Cemetery in Salonika.

INTERNATIONAL APPEARANCES

24th June 1899 Great Britain v. Australia at Sydney; Australia won 13-3

22nd July 1899 Great Britain v. Australia at Brisbane; Great Britain won 11-0

5th August 1899 Great Britain v. Australia at Sydney; Great Britain won 11-10

12th August 1899 Great Britain v. Australia at Sydney; Great Britain won 13-0

12.2 Sidney Crowther (1874-1914)

born in Keston, Kent

After attending Warwick School, Crowther trained to be a doctor at Westminster Hospital; during his time at the hospital, he played rugby as a forward for the hospital team and for Lennox FC.

In 1904, Crowther was selected to join the Great Britain team touring Australia and New Zealand. He played in all four of the Tests on tour, three against Australia and one against New Zealand, Great Britain winning the games against Australia but losing the game against New Zealand. After the tour, Crowther stayed on in Australia but returned after a while to work in asylums.

When war broke out, Crowther enlisted as a motor cyclist dispatch rider and was assigned to the 2nd Signal Troop of the Royal Engineers. He was killed in action on 18th October 1914, at the age of 39, at L'Epinette near Armentieres and is commemorated at the Le Touret War Memorial.

12.3 Ronald "Ron" Rogers (1883-1915)

born in Weston-super-Mare

Rogers went to Blundells School and, after leaving school, played rugby for Bath and Somerset. In 1904, he was selected to join the Great Britain tour to Australia and New Zealand as one of the front row forwards. Although Rogers missed out on the three Tests against Australia, he was picked to play in the last Test of the tour, against New Zealand. The game against New Zealand, which the tourists lost 9-3, was Rogers' only international appearance.

In January 1901, before he went on the tour to Australia and New Zealand, Rogers was commissioned as a second lieutenant in the 4th Battalion, Royal Dublin Fusiliers. By the time he was transferred to the 14th Battalion, Rifle Brigade in March 1915, Rogers had been promoted to captain.

Rogers was sent to Turkey to take part in the Gallipoli Campaign, where he was killed in action on 28th June 1915. Rogers was 31 years old when he was killed and is commemorated at the Helles Memorial.

INTERNATIONAL APPEARANCE

13th August 1904 Great Britain v. New Zealand at Wellington; New Zealand won 9-3

CHAPTER 13
AUSTRALIA RUGBY PLAYERS

Australia's first international rugby match was against Great Britain on 24th June 1899 and, by the outbreak of war, Australia had played 24 rugby Test matches. 37 of the 147 men who had played rugby in internationals for Australia up to the War served in the War; of those 37, 12 were killed in the War and, of those 12, four were killed at Gallipoli.

13.1 Harold George (1887-1915)

Harold George was born in Sydney; the exact date of his birth is not known and although some reports state his birth as being circa 1885, other reports state it as being in 1887.

George was a front row forward who played for Eastern Suburbs RUFC from 1907; he played a total of 95 games for them and made 20 appearances for New South Wales.

George made his first appearances for Australia in the three-match series against New Zealand in 1910. He also toured with Australia to the USA in 1912 and, in each of the two three-match series against New Zealand in 1913 and 1914, played in two of the games. Although George was on the losing side in five of the seven games he played against New Zealand, he was on the winning side in both of Australia's wins over New Zealand before the War.

George enlisted in January 1915 with the 13th (New South Wales) Infantry Battalion, Australian Imperial Force. He left Sydney for Gallipoli in February 1915 and took part in the landing at Anzac Cove on 25th April 1915.

Fighting against entrenched Turkish forces at Gallipoli, George was wounded by sniper fire at Pope's Post; Rusty Richards, who played in the Australian team with George, reported that George "got the axe for a very brave action; it appears he was one of five to go midday and attempt to locate a machine gun and Turkish trenches. The sergeant got a rough time and was finally shot. Harold, after a while, found the corner too hot and taking the sergeant's body he made it back under heavy fire to the trenches. When he was preparing to get down into the trench himself a bullet passed through his body low down."

George died from his wounds on 10th May 1915 on board ship after being evacuated; he would have been in his late 20s when he died and is commemorated at the Lone Pine Memorial on the Gallipoli Peninsula.

INTERNATIONAL APPEARANCES

25th June 1910 Australia v. New Zealand at Sydney; New Zealand won 6-0

27th June 1910 Australia v. New Zealand at Sydney; Australia won 11-0

2nd July 1910 Australia v. New Zealand at Sydney; New Zealand won 28-13

16th November 1912 Australia v. USA at Berkeley; Australia won 12-8

6th September 1913 Australia v. New Zealand at Wellington; New Zealand won 30-5

20th September 1913 Australia v. New Zealand at Christchurch; Australia won 16-5

18th July 1914 Australia v. New Zealand at Sydney; New Zealand won 5-0

15th August 1914 Australia v. New Zealand at Sydney; New Zealand won 22-7

13.2 Bryan Hughes (1887-1918)

born in Sydney

After attending Saint Ignatius' College in Sydney, Hughes worked as a clerk and played rugby as a flanker for New South Wales. In 1913, Hughes followed in his brother's footsteps when he was picked to play for the last two games in the three-match Test series against New Zealand. After losing the first two games of the series, Australia restored some pride by winning the third game to inflict on New Zealand their first ever home defeat; Hughes converted two of the four tries scored by Australia in their 16-5 victory.

In the War, Hughes served as a second lieutenant with the 8th Battalion, 48 Brigade of the 16th Irish Division. In 1916, Hughes received the Military Cross for conspicuous gallantry and devotion to duty when "though severely wounded, he organised the battalion bombers and led them against the enemy, who had penetrated a portion of the front line. It was largely owing to his personal example and good leadership that the enemy was driven out."

In 1917, Hughes was wounded again but returned to the front in 1918; not long after returning to the front, Hughes was killed in action on 6th August 1918; he would have been 30 or 31 years old when he was killed and was buried at the British Cemetery in Borre, in northern France.

INTERNATIONAL APPEARANCES

13th September 1913 Australia v. New Zealand at Dunedin; New Zealand won 25-13

20th September 1913 Australia v. New Zealand at Christchurch; Australia won 16-5

MILITARY HONOURS

Military Cross

13.3 Hubert Jones (1888-1916)

born in Newcastle, New South Wales

There are conflicting stories about Jones's life and when he died and also, to a lesser extent, about his rugby career. Some reports suggest he was a coal trimmer who worked in the docks in Carrington and others that he studied medicine.

With regard to his rugby career, he was a centre three-quarter who played for New South Wales from 1911 until 1914; some reports state he played 16 games for New South Wales and others 21 games for them; whichever is correct, he did play for them against New Zealand in 1914, having also played for a New England team against the All Blacks.

In 1912, Jones toured with the Australian team to Canada and the USA and, although he did not play in the one Test on the tour, he played in seven of the other tour matches, scoring six tries. Jones made his debut for Australia the following year, on their tour to New Zealand, playing in all three Tests. In the second match against New Zealand at Dunedin, Jones scored two of Australia's three tries in their defeat and, in the final game against New Zealand at Christchurch, scored one of Australia's four tries in their victory.

With regard to his war record, one report suggests that he enlisted in December 1916 and left Australia in February 1917 and that he was killed in action on 9th July 1918 and buried in the Crucifix Corner Cemetery at Villers-Bretonneux in the Somme region. Another record states that he died in 1919 as a result of wounds received in action. However, the more reliable records state that he was killed in action by shell fire during the Battle of the Somme on 4th November 1916 at the age of 28 and that he was buried at the Australian Imperial Forces Burial Ground at Grass Lane in Flers in France.

6th September 1913 Australia v. New Zealand at Wellington; New Zealand won 30-5

13th September 1913 Australia v. New Zealand at Dunedin; New Zealand won 25-13

20th September 1913 Australia v. New Zealand at Christchurch; Australia won 16-5

13.4 Edward Larkin (1880-1915)
born in North Lambton, New South Wales

After leaving St Joseph's College, Larkin worked in journalism before joining the Metropolitan Police Force in 1903. He played his club rugby as hooker for Endeavour Rugby Club and, in 1903, was picked to play for New South Wales, in their games against Queensland and the touring New Zealand team. Larkin was then selected to play for Australia against New Zealand in what was the one and only Test between the two countries on the tour and New Zealand's first ever international match. Following New Zealand's win, Larkin was not selected again to play for Australia.

Larkin left the police force in 1909 to become the first full-time secretary of the New South Wales Rugby League. In December 1913, Larkin stood as the Labor Party candidate for Willoughby in the New South Wales Legislative Assembly, winning the seat.

Within days after the declaration of war, Larkin enlisted with the 1st Battalion, 1st Brigade (New South Wales) of the First Australian Imperial Force's 1st Division; in his final address to the New South Wales Parliament, he said that "I cannot engage in the work of recruiting and urge others to enlist unless I do so myself".

Larkin left Australia in October 1914 and arrived in Egypt in December 1914, en route to Gallipoli. After landing at Anzac Bay on 25th April 1915, Larkin took part with his battalion in the battle to control the hill known as Baby 700. After winning control of the hill, the Turks counter-attacked and, during the afternoon, Larkin was wounded in the chest from machine gun fire; after turning away stretcher bearers to attend to those who he thought would be suffering more than him, Larkin died from his chest wounds. Larkin was 34 years old when he died.

Larkin's brother, Martin, also lost his life on the heights above Anzac Bay on the same day as Edward Larkin died. Neither brother's body was recovered and they are both commemorated on the Lone Pine Memorial in Galipoli.

INTERNATIONAL APPEARANCE

15th August 1903 Australia v. New Zealand at Sydney; New Zealand won 22-3

13.5 George Pugh (1890-1916)

born in Glebe, New South Wales

Pugh played club rugby for Newtown as a lock and, in the 1910 season, Newtown, with Pugh in the team, were unbeaten. The following year Pugh represented New South Wales in six of their matches and his performances for New South Wales led to him being selected for the Australian team touring Canada and the USA in 1912.

Pugh played in the one Test on the tour, the game against the USA, which the Australians narrowly won after trailing 6-8 with only five minutes to go.

Pugh was also a leading member of the Sydney Swimming Club and, in 1908, a member of the winning team in the Roth Challenge Shield for life-saving.

Pugh enlisted with the 4th Battalion in July 1915 and left Sydney for France in October 1915. After arriving in France, Pugh took part in two charges at Pozieres and was promoted to second lieutenant.

On 5th September 1916, Pugh was killed by a mortar shell while fighting in Belgium – the Sydney weekly magazine The Referee reported that he had been killed in France but researchers have established that he was killed in Belgium.

Pugh was 26 years old when he was killed.

INTERNATIONAL APPEARANCE

16th November 1912 Australia v. USA at Berkeley; Australia won 12-8

13.6 Blair Swannell (1875-1915)

born in Weston Underwood, Buckinghamshire

After attending Repton School, Swannell qualified as a second mate at the Thames Nautical Training College. He made his first trip to Australia working as a mate on a schooner in 1897.

Swannell played his club rugby as a forward for Northampton and two years after his first trip to Australia was selected as a member of the Great Britain team to tour Australia. Swannell did not play in the first Test on the tour which the British team lost, but played in the next three games, all of which the British team won.

On returning to England, Swannell joined the British Army, serving with the Buckinghamshire Imperial Yeomanry during the Second Boer War.

Despite never being picked to play for England, Swannell was picked for the Great Britain team for their tour to Australia and New Zealand in 1904. Swannell played in all four Tests on the tour, scoring his only international try in the third game against Australia and, at the end of the tour, decided to settle in Australia. Swannell continued to play rugby for Northern Suburbs and on seven occasions for New South Wales; he was also selected to play for Australia, despite having already played six matches against them, when Australia made their first overseas tour, to New Zealand in 1905.

Throughout his playing days, Swannell was known for his violent play and this, along with his reputation for poor personal hygiene, made him unpopular with his team-mates, particularly those in Australia who had been on the receiving end when he had been playing for Great Britain.

After his playing days were over, Swannell coached junior teams and refereed matches.

When war broke out, Swannell enlisted with the Australian Imperial Force and, after being posted to Egypt, was sent to Gallipoli. After landing at Anzac Bay on 25th April 1915, Swannell was immediately involved in the heavy fighting; in the build-up to the assault on the hill known as Baby 700, Swannell and his men were pinned down by the heavy fire from the Turkish forces and, whilst showing his men how best to aim their rifles, was shot in the head and killed.

Swannell was 39 years old when he was killed and is commemorated at the Baby 700 Cemetery at Gallipoli.

INTERNATIONAL APPEARANCES

22nd July 1899 Great Britain v. Australia at Brisbane; Great Britain won 11-0

5th August 1899 Great Britain v. Australia at Sydney; Great Britain won 11-10

12th August 1899 Great Britain v. Australia at Sydney; Great Britain won 13-0

2nd July 1904 Great Britain v. Australia at Sydney; Great Britain won 17-0

23rd July 1904 Great Britain v. Australia at Brisbane; Great Britain won 17-3

30th July 1904 Great Britain v. Australia at Sydney; Great Britain won 16-0

13th August 1904 Great Britain v. New Zealand at Dunedin; New Zealand won 9-3

2nd September 1905 Australia v. New Zealand at Dunedin; New Zealand won 14-3

13.7 William Tasker (1891-1918)
born in Condobolin, New South Wales

After leaving school, Tasker worked as a bank clerk and played his club rugby for Newtown. His performances for Newtown earned him selection as fly-half for New South Wales and, in 1912, on Australia's tour in 1912 to Canada and the USA. Tasker missed out on the one Test on the tour but, on a tour during which the Australians let themselves down both on and off the pitch, Tasker had the dubious distinction in one of the tour games of being the first Australian to be sent off on the tour, for rough play.

The following year saw Tasker make his international debut for Australia on their tour to New Zealand; although the first two games were lost, Australia won the third game with Tasker having a hand in all four of Australia's tries. Tasker was also picked for all three of Australia's matches against New Zealand in 1914, but ended up on the losing side in all of them.

In January 1915, Tasker enlisted as a gunner in the 12th Field Artillery Brigade, 13th Battalion (Australia). On 25th April 1915, Tasker took part in the landings at Anzac Bay in Gallipoli but, following severe wounding to his legs and ankle from shell fragments at Quinn's Post, was invalided back to Australia.

Tasker re-enlisted in 1916 with the 116th Howitzer Battery and, on returning to France, saw further action on the Western Front. After being wounded on two more occasions and gassed, Tasker died from further shrapnel wounds he sustained at Harbonieres, on 9th August 1918 during the second day of the Battle of Amiens.

Tasker was 26 years old when he died and was buried at the Villers-Bretonneux Military Cemetery in northern France.

INTERNATIONAL APPEARANCES

6th September 1913 Australia v. New Zealand at Wellington; New Zealand won 30-5

13th September 1913 Australia v. New Zealand at Dunedin; New Zealand won 25-13

20th September 1913 Australia v. New Zealand at Christchurch; Australia won 16-5

18th July 1914 Australia v. New Zealand at Sydney; New Zealand won 5-0

1st August 1914 Australia v. New Zealand at Brisbane; New Zealand won 17-0

15th August 1914 Australia v. New Zealand at Sydney; New Zealand won 22-7

13.8 Fred Thompson (1890-1915)
born in Maroubra, New South Wales

Thompson played at number 8 for Eastern Suburbs RUFC and was picked to play for Australia on their tour to New Zealand in 1913. Thompson played in all three Tests on the tour and, in Australia's win in the third game, scored one of their four tries.

Thompson retained his place in the Australia team for the return tour by New Zealand in 1914, but was on the losing side in all three matches.

A carpenter by profession, Thompson signed up for war service in January 1915, serving as a private with the 13th Battalion. In February 1915, Thompson left Sydney bound for Gallipoli.

Thompson had only been in Gallipoli a little more than a month when he was killed in action on 29th May 1915. Thompson was 24 years old when he was killed and was buried at the Shrapnel Valley Cemetery in Gallipoli.

INTERNATIONAL APPEARANCES

6th September 1913 Australia v. New Zealand at Wellington; New Zealand won 30-5

13th September 1913 Australia v. New Zealand at Dunedin; New Zealand won 25-13

20th September 1913 Australia v. New Zealand at Christchurch; Australia won 16-5

18th July 1914 Australia v. New Zealand at Sydney; New Zealand won 5-0

1st August 1914 Australia v. New Zealand at Brisbane; New Zealand won 17-0

15th August 1914 Australia v. New Zealand at Sydney; New Zealand won 22-7

13.9 Arthur "Jack" Verge (1880-1915)
born in Kempsey, New South Wales

After attending King's School, Parramatta, Verge went in 1900 to Sydney University to study medicine. As well as playing cricket for the university, Verge also played full-back at rugby for the university. Performances for the university earned him selection to play for New South Wales and, after representing New South Wales in their two matches against the touring Great Britain team in 1904, Verge was picked to play for Australia against Great Britain. Verge played in the first two Tests against Great Britain but after losing both matches, Verge was not picked for the third and final Test of the tour.

Having practised as a dermatologist after graduating, Verge won a fellowship in 1907 at the Royal College of Surgeons in Edinburgh. Whilst in Edinburgh, Verge played rugby for the university team but gave up playing competitive rugby when he returned to Sydney in 1910 to work as a doctor.

In October 1914, Verge was commissioned as a captain in the Australian Army Medical Corps and attached as medical officer to the 6th Light Horse Regiment. Verge left Australia in December 1914 for Alexandra in Egypt. In May 1915, Verge was sent to Gallipoli but, after landing, contracted dysentery.

Verge was then evacuated back to Egypt but died from his illness in Alexandra on 8th September 1915. Verge was 35 years old when he died and was buried at the Chatby War Memorial Cemetery in Alexandra.

INTERNATIONAL APPEARANCES

2nd July 1904 Australia v. Great Britain at Sydney; Great Britain won 17-0

23rd July 1904 Australia v. Great Britain at Brisbane; Great Britain won 17-3

13.10 Clarrie Wallach (1889-1918)
born in Sydney

Wallach played rugby as a lock for Eastern Suburbs RUFC from 1910 until 1914 and his performances for Eastern Suburbs led to him being selected to play for New South Wales and Australia in 1913 and 1914. He played a total of eight games for New South Wales and five for Australia, two on the tour to New Zealand in 1913 and three when New Zealand toured Australia the following year.

During the War, Wallach was commissioned as a lieutenant with the 19th Battalion, 5th Brigade and set off for Gallipoli in July 1915; after landing at Anzac Bay on 21st August 1915, Wallach took part in the attack on Hill 60.

Unlike his team-mates Harold George (see Chapter 13.1) and Fred Thompson (see Chapter 13.8) Wallach survived the Gallipoli Campaign and, by February 1916, was serving in France.

During the night of 25th and 26th June 1916, Wallach took part in a trench raid for which he was mentioned in despatches.

In August 1916, Wallach was on the Western Front taking part in the Battle of Pozieres where his actions led to him being awarded the Military Cross for conspicuous gallantry during operations when "under a very heavy bombardment which lasted 48 hours, after his company commander had been killed, and his company had suffered severely, he took command and steadied his men by his fine example and cool courage".

In 1917, Wallach was promoted to captain and, in 1918, was involved with his battalion in repelling the German Spring Offensive. On 7th April 1918, Wallach took part in the attack on Hangard Wood; Wallach's front in the attack, which was launched in the early hours, was supposed to have been supported by a barrage ahead of them but the barrage never materialised and, as a consequence, Wallach had to lead his men across 400 yards of open country towards the wood. By the time, they reached the wood, Wallach had been hit in both knees by German machine gun fire; after suffering a compound fracture on his left leg, gangrene set in and Wallach's left leg had to be amputated. A blood transfusion failed to save his other leg and that too was amputated.

Weakening from his wounds and amputations and suffering from shock, Wallach died on 22nd April 1918 at the age of 28; he was buried at the Etretat Churchyard Extension in France.

INTERNATIONAL APPEARANCES

6th September 1913 Australia v. New Zealand at Wellington; New Zealand won 30-5

20th September 1913 Australia v. New Zealand at Christchurch; Australia won 16-5

19th July 1914 Australia v. New Zealand at Sydney; New Zealand won 5-0

1st August 1914 Australia v. New Zealand at Brisbane; New Zealand won 17-0

15th August 1914 Australia v. New Zealand at Sydney; New Zealand won 22-7

MILITARY HONOURS

Military Cross

Mentioned in despatches

CHAPTER 14
New Zealand Rugby Players

New Zealand played their first international rugby match on 15th August 1903 against Australia. By the time New Zealand went to war, 112 All Blacks had represented New Zealand in the 24 rugby Test matches they had played; of the 112, the following 12 were killed in the War.

14.1 Jim Baird (1893-1917)
born in Dunedin

After leaving Caversham School, Baird worked as a machinist and played rugby as a centre for Otago. After only two games for Otago, Baird was picked as a late replacement for New Zealand's second Test in the three-match home series against Australia in 1913 but, due to an injury, was unable to play in the third Test.

Due to illness, Baird was unable to play the following year and missed out on the New Zealand tour to Australia; due to the outbreak of war, the game he played against Australia in 1913 proved to be his only international.

In the War, Baird served as a private with the 1st Battalion, Otago Infantry. Baird left New Zealand in October 1916 and, after training in England, was posted to France in February 1917. On 7th June 1917, Baird's regiment was taking part in the Battle of Messines Ridge when he was hit in the hands and abdomen by artillery fire. Baird was transferred to the 1st Australian Casualty Clearing Station at Bailleul in France but died from his wounds that day. Baird was 23 years old when he died and was buried at the Bailleul Communal Cemetery Extension.

INTERNATIONAL APPEARANCE

13th September 1913 New Zealand v. Australia at Dunedin; New Zealand won 25-13

14.2 Bobby Black (1893-1916)

born in Arrowtown

After leaving school, Black worked as a bank clerk and played club rugby as fly-half for Dunedin Pirates. His performances for Dunedin led to selection for Otago in 1911 and a couple of games for South Island in 1912 and 1914, following which he was selected for the New Zealand team touring Australia in 1914.

Black played in six of the games on the tour in which he scored three tries but his only Test match was the first one against Australia, which New Zealand won 5-0.

In November 1915, Black enlisted in the Otago Mounted Rifles before transferring to the Canterbury Regiment whilst on his way to Egypt. Black took part with his regiment in the Battle of the Somme but was killed in action on 21st September 1916 when he went over the top in an attack on the town of Flers. Black was 23 years old when he was killed and his body was never recovered; he is commemorated, along with 1,200 New Zealand soldiers who died in the Battle of the Somme and whose bodies were never recovered, at the Caterpillar Valley (New Zealand) Memorial at Longueval in Picardie.

INTERNATIONAL APPEARANCE

18th July 1914 New Zealand v. Australia at Sydney; New Zealand won 5-0

14.3 Henry Dewar (1883-1915)

born in Foxton

Dewar played as a number 8 and after playing for the Melrose Club in Wellington and for the Wellington provincial team, moved to Taramata, where he worked as an iron moulder and played for Taramata.

In 1913, Dewar was a member of the Taramata team that won the Ranfurly Shield and, after representing North Island, was selected to play for New Zealand against Australia in the first Test of the 1913 series between the two countries. Dewar also went on the New Zealand tour to North America in 1913 and played for the All Blacks in the game against the USA; although Dewar ended up playing in only two Tests for New Zealand, he made a total of 16 appearances for them. As well as being an international rugby player, Dewar was also an excellent boxer and useful cricketer.

Before the conclusion of the Ranfurly Shield in 1914, Dewar joined the New Zealand Expeditionary Force and, in September 1914, went to German Samoa to take possession of the island, which the Expeditionary Force was able to do as it came across no opposition.

On his return from Samoa, Dewar joined the 9th Wellington Mounted Rifles as a machine gunner. Dewar left New Zealand in October 1914 bound for Egypt en route to Gallipoli. Dewar landed with his regiment at Anzac Bay on 8th August 1915 but was killed the next day whilst taking part in the assault on Chunuk Bair; Dewar's team-mate, Doolan Downing (see Chapter 14.5) was also killed in the same assault.

Dewar was 31 years old when he was killed and he is commemorated at Chunuk Bair (New Zealand) Memorial at Gallipoli.

INTERNATIONAL APPEARANCES

6th September 1913 New Zealand v. Australia at Wellington; New Zealand won 30-5

15th November 1913 New Zealand v. USA at Berkeley; New Zealand won 51-3

14.4 Ernie Dodd (1880-1918)
born in Dunedin

After leaving Wellington College in Wellington, Dodd worked as a clerk for the New Zealand Shipping Company in Wellington. Between 1901 and 1905, he played 45 games as hooker for Wellington and, in 1901, made his first two appearances for New Zealand, the first in a match against Wellington which was a warm-up match for the game four days later against the touring New South Wales team; his second appearance for New Zealand was the game against New South Wales.

In 1902, Dodd represented North Island and, in 1904, played for Wellington in the first Ranfurly Shield Challenge, when they beat Auckland. A year later, Dodd made his only appearance for New Zealand in an international, against Australia.

In the War, Dodd enlisted in February 1917 in the New Zealand Expeditionary Force; he set off for Liverpool in July 1917 and, after being hospitalised during the journey, arrived in September 1917.

In June 1918, Dodd was hospitalised again when a bullet from a German machine gun grazed his scalp; two months later he was back in hospital having contracted scabies.

In September 1918, serving as a lance-sergeant with the New Zealand Rifle Brigade, 2nd Battalion, Dodd took part in the assault from Havrincourt Wood on Trescault Spur, the last position before the Hindenburg Line. After taking "Dead Man's Corner", Dodd's regiment was driven out by a German counter-attack and, during the course of the fighting, Dodd was shot through the throat by a sniper's bullet; he died from his wounds on 11th September 1918, only two months before the end of the War.

Dodd was 38 years old when he died and was buried at the Metz-en-Couture Communal Cemetery British Extension.

INTERNATIONAL APPEARANCE

2nd September 1905 New Zealand v. Australia at Dunedin; New Zealand won 14-3

14.5 Albert "Doolan" Downing (1886-1915)
born in Napier

Downing was a lock forward who played for Napier Marist, Hawke's Bay, Auckland Marist and North Island before making his debut for New Zealand against Australia in September 1913.

A month later, Downing toured with the New Zealand to North America and played in 14 of the matches on tour, including the game against the USA. The following year, Downing toured again with the New Zealand team, this time to Australia and played in 10 of the 11 matches on tour, including in the three games against Australia.

By the time the tour to Australia had finished, war had been declared and, on the ship back to New Zealand at the end of the tour, Downing decided to volunteer for military service. He enlisted with the 5th Reinforcements (Wellington Battalion) in February 1915; in June 1915, Downing left New Zealand, arriving in Egypt in July 1915, before heading off to the Gallipoli Peninsula.

On arriving at Gallipoli, Downing was involved in the Battle of Chunuk Bair. On 6th August 1915, three New Zealand regiments led the attack on Chunuk Bair; Downing's battalion was ordered to continue the attack and, early in the morning of 8th August, occupied the Turkish trench on the crest of Chunuk Bair and dug a supply trench behind but a Turkish counter-attack at dawn forced Downing's unit to retreat. After Downing had distinguished himself in a bayonet charge, his unit lost ground on the slopes leading down to the sea during the 12 hour battle and Downing was, according to a witness, blown to pieces.

Downing was the first of the All Blacks to be killed in the War, a day before Henry Dewar (see Chapter 14.3). Downing was 29 years old when he died and is commemorated at New Zealand Memorial to the Missing at Chunuk Bair.

INTERNATIONAL APPEARANCES

6th September 1913 New Zealand v. Australia at Wellington; New Zealand won 30-5

15th November 1913 New Zealand v. USA at Berkeley; New Zealand won 51-3

18th July 1914 New Zealand v. Australia at Sydney; New Zealand won 5-0

1st August 1914 New Zealand v. Australia at Brisbane; New Zealand won 17-0

15th August 1914 New Zealand v. Australia at Sydney; New Zealand won 22-7

14.6 David Gallaher (1873-1917)
born as David Gallagher in Ramelton, County Donegal

Gallaher's family emigrated to New Zealand when he was four years old and, not long after arriving, the family name was changed to Gallaher.

Due to family hardships, Gallaher left school at the age of 13 and worked for a local stock and station agent in Katikati, where he first played rugby. After moving to Auckland later in his teens to work as a labourer, Gallaher made his debut for Auckland in 1896, as hooker, against the touring Queensland team.

In January 1901, Gallaher joined the New Zealand contingent of Mounted Rifles and served in the Second Boer War, returning to New Zealand in August 1902.

In 1903, Gallaher was selected as a member of the New Zealand team to tour Australia; Gallaher played in eight of the 11 games on the tour, initially as hooker and then as wing-forward, including in the one game against Australia which was New Zealand's first ever Test.

A year later, Gallaher played in New Zealand's first home Test against the Great Britain team which had just completed the Australian leg of their tour; after winning their three Tests against Australia, the Great Britain team were unable to finish the tour with a win over New Zealand, losing the match 9-3.

Towards the end of 1904, Gallaher was suspended from playing following a dispute over expenses but, after the dispute was settled, Gallaher was chosen to captain the New Zealand team, the first to be known as the All Blacks, on their tour to Europe and North America. New Zealand played 36 matches on the tour and their only defeat was at the hands of Wales. Gallaher played in the games against Scotland, England, Wales and France but missed out on the game against Ireland, the country of his birth, due to injury.

Gallaher retired from playing rugby after the tour but continued involvement in the game as a coach and selector. By the time of his retirement, Gallaher had played a total of 36 games for New Zealand, including six internationals and, although he did not score any tries in his six international appearances, he scored six tries in his other 30 appearances for New Zealand.

Despite being exempt from conscription because of his age, Gallaher enlisted in May 1916 and left New Zealand for Europe in February 1917. Serving with the 2nd Battalion, Auckland Regiment, Gallaher's unit fought at the Battle of Messines after which they prepared for the Passchendaele offensive. On 4th October 1917, during the attack on Gravenstafel Spur during the Battle of Broodseinde, which was one of the battles in the Third Battle of Ypres, a piece of shrapnel penetrated Gallaher's helmet as he was leaving his trench; Gallaher died from his wounds later that day at the 3rd Australian Casualty Clearing Station at Gravenstafel Spur.

Gallaher was 43 years old when he died and was buried at the Nine Elms British Cemetery near Poperinge in Belgium.

15th August 1903 New Zealand v. Australia at Sydney; New Zealand won 22-3

13th August 1904 New Zealand v. Great Britain at Wellington; New Zealand won 9-3

18th November 1905 New Zealand v. Scotland at Inverleith; New Zealand won 12-7

2nd December 1905 New Zealand v. England at Crystal Palace; New Zealand won 15-0

16th December 1905 New Zealand v. Wales at the National Stadium, Cardiff; Wales won 3-0

1st January 1906 New Zealand v. France at Parc des Princes, Paris; New Zealand won 38-8

14.7 Eric Harper (1877-1918)

born in Christchurch

After leaving school, Harper qualified and practised as a solicitor. He played centre for Christchurch and the Canterbury provincial team and, after playing for a combined Canterbury and West Coast team against the touring Great Britain team in 1904, was picked one week later to play for New Zealand against Great Britain.

Harper missed out on New Zealand's tour to Australia in 1905 but was included in the Originals All Blacks party which toured Europe towards the end of 1905. Harper only played in four of the games on the tour to Britain due to injury but was picked to play in the match against France on 1st January 1906; Harper scored two of New Zealand's 10 tries in their 38-8 victory.

As well as being an international rugby player, Harper was also a national hurdles champion, winning the 440 yards hurdles title in 1901 and the 880 yards hurdles title in 1902; he also played cricket for Canterbury and was a keen mountaineer.

On his return from the tour to Europe, Harper retired from playing rugby and concentrated on his legal practice.

After war was declared, Harper enlisted in October 1916 with the New Zealand Expeditionary Force and served as a sergeant-major with the Canterbury Mounted Rifles. Harper left Wellington in May 1917, bound for Palestine via Egypt. On 30th April 1918, the Allied forces were attacking the strongly fortified Shunet Nimrin position held by the Turks when Harper was killed during an artillery bombardment whilst trying to keep the horses quiet.

Harper was 40 years old when he was killed. He was buried in the desert and is commemorated on the Jerusalem Memorial.

14.8 Jim McNeece (1885-1917)
born in Invercargill

After leaving school, McNeece worked as farmer and played rugby as a lock forward for his local club Waikiwi, Southland and South Island.

After playing with his brother, Alex, in Southland's win over Australia in 1913, McNeece was selected to play for New Zealand in the last two Tests of Australia's tour. McNeece was not included in the New Zealand party touring to North America at the end of 1913, his non-selection being, in the views of some, due to bias in favour of North Islanders but he was included in the tour to Australia in 1914. In the first game against Australia, New Zealand won 5-0 with McNeece scoring the only try of the game.

McNeece played for New Zealand in the other two games against Australia on the tour and, in addition to his five internationals, represented New Zealand in six other games.

In the War, McNeece joined the 2nd Battalion, Otago Infantry Regiment. He left Wellington in September 1916 and, after training in England, was sent to France in January 1917. McNeece's battalion was heavily involved in the Battle of Messines and, on 8th June 1917, McNeece suffered gunshot wounds to his shoulder and back; he was transferred to a hospital in Rouen for treatment but died from his wounds in hospital on 21st June 1917.

McNeece was 31 years old when he died and was buried in the St Sever Cemetery Extension in Rouen.

INTERNATIONAL APPEARANCES

13th September 1913 New Zealand v. Australia at Dunedin; New Zealand won 25-13

20th September 1913 New Zealand v. Australia at Christchurch; Australia won 16-5

18th July 1914 New Zealand v. Australia at Sydney; New Zealand won 5-0

1st August 1914 New Zealand v. Australia at Brisbane; New Zealand won 17-0

15th August 1914 New Zealand v. Australia at Sydney; New Zealand won 22-7

14.9 Alexander James "Jimmy" Ridland (1882-1918)
born in Invercargill

Ridland was a blacksmith by profession and, between 1907 and 1913, Ridland played 22 games for Southland; after appearing for South Island in 1909 and 1910, Ridland was picked as hooker for New Zealand's tour to Australia in 1910; Ridland played in all three Test matches against Australia on the tour and in three of New Zealand's other matches but, after his return home, did not play for New Zealand again.

Ridland enlisted with the New Zealand Expeditionary Force in October 1917; he was posted to France in September 1918 and served as a rifleman with the 1st Battalion, 3rd New Zealand Rifle Brigade. On 4th November 1918, less than two months after arriving in France, Ridland along with other New Zealanders took part in the storming of the walls of the ancient town of Le Quesnoy; the town was liberated by the New Zealanders after they had used 30-foot long ladders to scale the walls. During the attack, Ridland sustained a gunshot wound to the head and died the following day, only six days before the end of the War.

Ridland was 36 years old when he died and was buried at the Caudry British Cemetery near Cambrai.

INTERNATIONAL APPEARANCES

25th June 1910 New Zealand v. Australia at Sydney; New Zealand won 6-0

27th June 1910 New Zealand v. Australia at Sydney; Australia won 11-0

2nd July 1910 New Zealand v. Australia at Sydney; New Zealand won 28-3

14.10 George Sellars (1886-1917)

born in Auckland

Sellars worked as a shipwright up until when he enlisted in 1916. He played club rugby as a hooker for Ponsonby from 1906 and for Auckland from 1909 until 1915; in 1910, he played for the first officially recognised Maori All Black team and, in 1912, was selected to play for North Island.

Sellars made his debut for New Zealand in the first game of Australia's tour to New Zealand in 1913 and, although he missed out on the other two games of the tour against Australia, he was a member of the New Zealand team that toured North America at the end of 1913. Sellars played in 14 games on the tour to North America, including in the Test against the USA.

During the War, Sellars enlisted with the 1st Battalion, Auckland Infantry Regiment and, after leaving New Zealand in September 1916, undertook further training in England before being posted to France in March 1917.

On 2nd June 1917, Sellars' battalion was preparing to advance on the German-held town of Messines in Belgium; five days later, on 7th June 1917, Sellars was killed whilst he was carrying a wounded comrade back to safety.

Sellars was 31 years old when he was killed; although it was recorded on his casualty form that he had been buried, his body was apparently never recovered and he is commemorated on the Messines Ridge (NZ) Memorial at Mesen in Belgium.

INTERNATIONAL APPEARANCES

6th September 1913 New Zealand v. Australia at Wellington; New Zealand won 30-5

15th November 1913 New Zealand v. USA at Berkeley; New Zealand won 51-3

14.11 Reg Taylor (1889-1917)

born in Taranaki

Taylor played as a flanker for Taranaki, Clifton and North Island and, in 1913, won the Ranfurly Shield with Taranaki. Taylor made his debut for New Zealand in the second Test against Australia on their tour of 1913, scoring a try in New Zealand's 25-13 victory; after the first Test of the series, an All Black team had left for their tour of North America and, as a consequence, the New Zealand team selected to play the last two Tests against Australia was made up of those not selected for the North America tour.

Taylor retained his place for the final Test of the series but was not selected the following year for the return tour by New Zealand to Australia.

In the War, Taylor enlisted with the 1st Battalion, Wellington Regiment in 1915. He left New Zealand in 1915 and, after training in Egypt, was posted to Gallipoli towards the end of the campaign.

After surviving in Gallipoli, Taylor was then posted to the Somme battlefields in 1916 before joining up with other New Zealand divisions as they prepared to attack Messines in Belgium.

At 3:00 a.m. on 7th June 1917, 19 mines which had been laid beneath the German lines were detonated – it is estimated that 10,000 German lives were lost as a result. Fierce fighting continued and, on 20th June 1917, Taylor was killed in action during one of the counter-attacks by the Germans as the Allied troops fought to retain control of the German positions at Messines that they had captured.

Taylor was 28 years old when he was killed and was buried at the Underhill Farm Cemetery at Ploegsteert in Belgium.

13th September 1913 New Zealand v. Australia at Dunedin; New Zealand won 25-13

20th September 1913 New Zealand v. Australia at Christchurch; Australia won 16-5

14.12 Hubert Turtill (1880-1918)

born in London 1880

emigrated with his family to New Zealand in 1884.

Turtill worked for a hardware merchant and played full-back at rugby for Christchurch, Canterbury and South Island. In 1905, Turtill was selected to play for New Zealand in their first match at home against Australia, a match New Zealand won 14-3.

By 1907, Turtill had turned professional and was picked to tour with the New Zealand rugby league team to England in 1907/08. Turtill played in 33 of New Zealand's 35 games on the tour, including in the games against Wales and England and in the three games against the Northern Union team representing Great Britain. Losses to Wales and England were followed by a loss in the first game against the Great Britain team, a game in which Turtill scored a try but New Zealand won the last two games against Great Britain to claim a 2-1 series win.

On the return trip to New Zealand, Turtill captained the New Zealand team in their first ever rugby league fixture against Australia and scored a decisive goal in New Zealand's 11-10 victory.

By 1909, Turtill had moved back to live in England where he worked as a pub landlord and played rugby league for St Helens up until 1915.

In the War, Turtill served as a sergeant with the Royal Engineers. By October 1915, he had been posted to France and, after seeing action at Hellencourt and Bretencourt, was transferred to Ypres in 1917. After serving in the battles of Pilkem Ridge and Menin Road Ridge, Turtill was transferred to the Cambrai area where the British troops were subjected to a massive tank attack by the Germans.

In March 1918, Turtill was seeing action on the front line at Givenchy and Festubert. The battle of Estaires and the defence of Festubert began on 9th April 1918 and, during the first day of the defence of Festubert, Turtill was killed when he was struck by shrapnel from a shell burst.

Turtill was 38 years old when he was killed and he was buried at the Brown's Road Military Cemetery at Festubert.

INTERNATIONAL APPEARANCE (RUGBY UNION)

2nd September 1905 New Zealand v. Australia at Dunedin; New Zealand won 14-3

INTERNATIONAL APPEARANCES (RUGBY LEAGUE)

1st January 1908 New Zealand v. Wales at Aberdare; Wales won 9-8

11th January 1908 New Zealand v. England at Wigan; England won 18-16

25th January 1908 New Zealand v. Great Britain at Leeds; Great Britain won 14-6

8th February 1908 New Zealand v. Great Britain at London; New Zealand won 18-6

15th February 1908 New Zealand v. Great Britain at Cheltenham; New Zealand won 8-5

9th May 1908 New Zealand v. Australia at Sydney; New Zealand won 11-10

Frank Wilson was selected for the New Zealand team to tour Australia in 1910. He played for New Zealand in a pre-tour match against Wellington and in New Zealand's first game of the tour, against New South Wales, but received an injury in the game against New South Wales and was never picked to play for New Zealand again. Wilson was wounded in action on 17th September 1916 during the Battle of the Somme and died from his wounds two days later.

Autini Pitara Kaipara played for the New Zealand Maori team in 1910 and 1911 but not for New Zealand; he was killed by a piece of shell on 3rd August 1917 whilst wiring posts near La Basseville.

CHAPTER 15
South Africa Rugby Players

South Africa's first rugby international was against Great Britain on 30ᵗʰ July 1891. By the start of the Great War, South Africa had played 23 rugby Test matches; of the 138 who represented South Africa at rugby before the War, the following five were to lose their lives in the War.

15.1 Adam Burdett (1882-1918)
born in Oudtshoorn, Cape Colony

Burdett attended Diocesan College in Rondebosch, which he captained at rugby and, after leaving school, played rugby as a forward for Western Province.

In 1906, Burdett was a member of the first South African team to tour Britain and played in the games against Scotland and Ireland; a defeat at the hands of Scotland was followed by a win over Ireland.

At the outbreak of war, Burdett joined the South Africa Service Corps and served in Tanganyika, in the campaign against the Germans in German East Africa. After contracting malaria, Burdett was sent home to recuperate but died on 4ᵗʰ November 1918, just seven days before the end of the War. Burdett was 36 years old when he died and was buried at the Thaba Tshwane (No 1) Military Cemetery in Pretoria.

17th November 1906 South Africa v. Scotland at Hampden Park, Glasgow; Scotland won 6-0

24th November 1906 South Africa v. Ireland at Balmoral Showgrounds, Belfast; South Africa won 15-9

15.2 Septimus "Sep" Heyns Ledger (1889-1917)
born in Kimberley

Ledger played as a forward for Griqualand West and was selected to join the tour to Britain, Ireland and France in 1912 and 1913. Ledger played in 15 matches in the tour, including in four of the five international matches, only missing out on the game against Wales. South Africa were victorious in all five Tests and, in his fourth and final Test against France, Ledger scored his only try for South Africa.

After the outbreak of war, Ledger joined the 2nd Natal Orange Free State Battalion and, by July 1916, had arrived in France. In April 1917, Ledger was involved in the attacks which, if successful, would allow the South Africans to advance on the village of Rouex. Ledger was amongst those who were killed during the attacks which were not a success as the barrage and artillery missed their targets, leaving the South Africans with too much open ground to cover.

Records differ as to the date of Ledger's death but it was either 12th or 13th April 1917. Ledger would have been 27 years old when he was killed and is commemorated at the Arras Memorial.

23rd November 1912 South Africa v. Scotland at Inverleith; South Africa won 16-0

30th November 1912 South Africa v. Ireland at Lansdowne Road, Dublin; South Africa won 38-0

15.3 Tobias "Toby" Moll (1890-1916)

born in Cape Town

Moll was educated at South Africa College and, after leaving school, played rugby as a forward for Transvaal from 1908 to 1910 and for Western Province from 1910 until 1914.

In 1910, Moll was picked to play for South Africa in the second Test match against the touring team from Great Britain; after losing the Test, Moll was not picked for the third match, which South Africa won to win the series 2-1.

At the outbreak of war, Moll served in the South West Africa campaign fighting the Germans in Namibia. At the conclusion of this campaign in July 1915, Moll travelled to England and joined the 9th Battalion, Leicestershire Regiment.

In July 1916, Moll took part in the Battle of Bazentin Ridge, which was part of the Battle of the Somme, with the objective of taking Bazentin-le-Petit village and wood. On 14th July 1916, the first day of the battle, Moll was wounded after the village had been taken when he was hit by shrapnel; he was evacuated but died from his wounds the next day.

Moll was five days short of his 26th birthday when he was killed; he was buried in the Mericourt-l'Abbe Communal Cemetery Extension in France.

INTERNATIONAL APPEARANCE

27th August 1910 South Africa v. Great Britain at Port Elizabeth; Great Britain won 8-3

15.4 Jan "Jacky" Morkel (1890-1916)

born in Somerset West

Morkel was born into a rugby-playing family and was just one of eight brothers and cousins to play rugby for South Africa.

Morkel played at centre and played club rugby for Somerset West and provincial rugby for Western Province from 1911 to 1912. Towards the end of 1912, Morkel was selected as a member of the South African team to tour Britain, Ireland and France that winter. On the tour, Morkel played in 27 matches, including in the five international matches against Scotland, Ireland, Wales, England and France. With his brother Gerhard and his cousins Dougie and Boy also playing in all five Test matches, South Africa won all five matches, with Jacky scoring two tries in the win over Ireland, South Africa's only try in their win over England and a fourth try, which he converted, in the game against France.

Morkel was also a cricketer and, in the 1912/12 and 1913/14 seasons, played five first-class games for Transvaal; he also played for a Transvaal XI in 1914 against the touring MCC team and, in his six first-class matches, scored 175 runs at an average of 17.50 with a highest score of 84.

When war broke out, Morkel served with the 1st South African Mounted Brigade. In early April 1916, whilst serving in German East Africa, Morkel's brigade began to advance southwards and, after taking Ufiome on 13th April, followed the enemy until they reached Ssalanga four days later. By this time though, the rainy season had set in and Morkel's brigade was cut off and unable to progress any further.

Living off limited local supplies, their health deteriorated and Morkel was just one of many to suffer. After contracting dysentery, Morkel died on 15ᵗʰ May 1916 at Unifami in German East Africa.

Morkel was 25 years old when he died and was buried at the Dar-es-Salaam War Cemetery.

INTERNATIONAL APPEARANCES

23ʳᵈ November 1912 South Africa v. Scotland at Inverleith; South Africa won 16-0

30ᵗʰ November 1912 South Africa v. Ireland at Lansdowne Road, Dublin; South Africa won 38-0

14ᵗʰ December 1912 South Africa v. Wales at the National Stadium, Cardiff; South Africa won 3-0

4ᵗʰ January 1913 South Africa v. England at Twickenham; South Africa won 9-3

11ᵗʰ January 1913 South Africa v. France at Bordeaux; South Africa won 38-5

15.5 Gerald Thompson (1886-1916)
born in Carnavon, Cape Colony

Thompson went to Rondebosch Boys' School and, after leaving school, played club rugby for Somerset West. In 1912, he played for the Western Province provincial team, following which he was selected to tour the British Isles and France in the winter of 1912/13.

Thompson played in 15 of the matches on the tour including in the three internationals against Scotland, Ireland and Wales, all of which South Africa won. Thompson's performance against Ireland led the rugby journalist and author E. H. D. Sewell to write of Thompson that he had never seen a better individual performance than Thompson's on the frost-bound pitch and only a few that he had seen to equal Thompson's all-round display.

In the War, Thompson served with the 5ᵗʰ South African Infantry. He was first posted to South West Africa (now

Namibia) and, when that campaign was over, in South East Africa (now Tanzania). In April 1916, Thompson was confined to hospital having contracted malaria; two months later, on 19ᵗʰ June 1916, he went with his regiment in pursuit of German forces to occupy Kangata. The following day, Thompson was killed in action in Kangata when a bullet pierced his neck.

Thompson was 29 years old when he died and was buried at the Dar-es-Salaam War Cemetery.

INTERNATIONAL APPEARANCES

23rd November 1912 South Africa v. Scotland at Inverleith; South Africa won 16-0

30th November 1912 South Africa v. Ireland at Lansdowne Road, Dublin; South Africa won 38-0

14th December 1912 South Africa v. Wales at the National Stadium, Cardiff; Cardiff won 3-0

CHAPTER 16
FRANCE RUGBY PLAYERS

France played their first game of international rugby, against New Zealand on 1st January 1906. They played their first Five Nations Championship match, against Wales on 1st January 1910 and by the time war had been declared on 28th July 1914, France had played 29 international matches. In those 29 matches, 112 players had been used and only one win had been recorded, the 16-15 victory over Scotland in 1911. Of the 122 to have played rugby for France before the War, the following 22 were killed in the War.

16.1 Joe Anduran (1882-1914)
born in Bayonne

Anduran played as hooker for Sporting Club Universitaire de France; on 31st December 1909, the day before France were due to play Wales in their first ever Five Nations match, only 14 of the team had gathered together for the trip to Wales and, as a consequence, the French team's manager added Andurin to the team to ensure they had a full team the next day for the fixture. Andurin played the next day against Wales, the French losing the match 49-14. It was Andurin's only match for France.

In the War, Andurin served as a private soldier with the 226th Infantry Regiment. He was killed on 2nd October 1914 at Bois-Bernard in the Pas-de-Calais region, when he was shot in the heart; he was 32 when he was killed.

16.2 Rene Boudreaux (1880-1915)

born in Paris

Boudreaux was a prop forward who played for Sporting Club Universitaire de France from 1907 to 1910 and for Racing Club de France from 1910 to 1912. Boudreaux was also a fencer and he continued with fencing after retiring from rugby.

Boudreaux was picked to play in France's first two games in the Five Nations, the first against Wales on 1st January 1910 and the second against Scotland three weeks later. Both games were lost by France, with Wales winning 49-14 and Scotland winning 27-0. After the game against Scotland, Boudreaux was not picked to play for France again.

In the War, Boudreaux was recalled to serve in the French Army, serving as a lieutenant in the 103rd Infantry Regiment. He was killed in action on 8th September 1915 at the age of 34, at Auberive-sur-Suippe, in the Marne region in France.

16.3 Maurice Boyau (1888-1918)
born in Mustapha, Algeria

Boyau played as a flanker for US Dax (whose stadium is named after him), Stade Bordelais and Racing Club de France.

Boyau played in all four of France's games in the Five Nations in 1912 and two in 1913, captaining the French team in his last game; with France relatively new to the Five Nations, having joined in 1910, success was hard to come by at first and France lost all six of the matches in which Boyau played.

During the War, Boyau first joined the Army Service Corps as a driver before being accepted for pilot training with the French Air Service. Boyau obtained his pilot's licence in November 1915 and became one of France's most successful balloon busters, bringing down enemy observation balloons which were usually heavily protected by anti-aircraft artillery and patrol flights. After downing an observation balloon on 5th June 1917, Boyau was awarded the Medaille Militaire when he was forced to land in enemy territory and after repairing his plane, flew back at an altitude of 200 metres under enemy fire. In July 1918, after reporting his 27th victory, after having downed 16 balloons and 11 enemy planes, Boyau was awarded the Legion d'Honneur; the citation for his award reads "pilot of remarkable bravery whose marvellous physical qualities are put to use by his most arduous spirit and fights at great heights. Magnificent officer with an admirable spirit of self-sacrifice, facing each day with the same smiling desire for new exploits. He excels in all branches of aviation; reconnaissance, photography in single-seaters, bombardments at low altitudes, attacks on ground troops and is classed among the best pursuit pilots."

After his 35th victory, made up of 21 balloons and 14 enemy aircraft, Boyau was killed when he was shot down by enemy fighters on 16th September 1918 at Mars-la-Tour in the Meurthe-et-Moselle region in France; he was 30 years old when he was killed; his 35 victories made him the fifth-highest ranking of French aces in the War.

INTERNATIONAL APPEARANCES

1st January 1912 France v. Ireland at Parc des Princes, Paris; Ireland won 11-6

20th January 1912 France v. Scotland at Inverleith; Scotland won 31-3

25th March 1912 France v. Wales at Newport; Wales won 14-8

6th April 1912 France v. England at Parc des Princes, Paris; England won 18-8

27th February 1913 France v. Wales at Parc des Princes, Paris; Wales won 11-8

24th March 1913 France v. Ireland at Cork; Ireland won 24-0

MILITARY HONOURS

Medaille Militaire

Legion d'Honneur

16.4 Marcel Burgun (1890-1916)
born in St Petersburg, Russia

Burgun played at centre for Racing Club de France and Castries Olympique. He was first picked to play for France in a friendly against Ireland in 1909; his second cap was a year later when he played in France's first Five Nations match and he continued playing for France in the Five Nations up until their last Five Nations match before the outbreak of war. In total, Burgun played 11 matches for France, his only victory coming when

France beat Scotland 16-15 in 1911 to record their first victory in the Five Nations Championship; in his 11 matches, Burgun failed to score any points.

Burgun joined the French artillery in 1914 and the newly formed French air force in 1915. Burgun first flew as an observer pinpointing targets for the French artillery but later became a fighter pilot. He was killed in combat when shot down by a German escort fighter whilst attacking a German aircraft on 2nd September 1916; he was 26 years old when he died. In addition to receiving three decorations for bravery, he also received a posthumous Croix de Guerre.

Burgun was buried at the Mont Frenet Cemetery at La Cheppe in the Marne region.

INTERNATIONAL APPEARANCES

20th March 1909 France v. Ireland at Lansdowne Road, Dublin; Ireland won 19-8

1st January 1910 France v. Wales at Swansea; Wales won 49-14

22nd January 1910 France v. Scotland at Inverleith; Scotland won 27-0

28th March 1910 France v. Ireland at Parc des Princes, Paris; Ireland won 8-3

2nd January 1911 France v. Scotland at Colombes; France won 16-15

28th January 1911 France v. England at Twickenham; England won 37-0

1st January 1912 France v. Ireland at Parc des Princes, Paris; Ireland won 11-6

20th January 1912 France v. Scotland at Inverleith; Scotland won 31-3

1st January 1913 France v. Scotland at Parc des Princes, Paris; Scotland won 21-3

25th January 1913 France v. England at Twickenham; England won 20-0

13th April 1914 France v. England at Colombes; England won 39-13

MILITARY HONOURS

Three citations for bravery

Croix de Guerre

16.5 Albert Chatau (1893-1924)

born in Urrugne, Pyrenees-Atlantiques region

Chatau played for Aviron Bayonnais and was picked to play fly-half for France at the age of 19 in their match against South Africa in 1913, a match which the South Africans won 38-5; it was Chatau's only game for France.

Although Chatau survived the War, he died from wounds suffered in the War, dying in Bayonne on 15th July 1924 at the age of 31.

INTERNATIONAL APPEARANCE

11th January 1913 France v. South Africa at Bordeaux; South Africa won 38-5

16.6 Jean-Jacques Conilh de Beyssac (1890-1918)

born in Bordeaux

De Beyssac played most of his rugby for Bordeaux but, whilst in England in 1910, joined Rosslyn Park. In 1912, he was picked to play as prop for France in two of the their Five Nations matches, the games against Ireland and Scotland; his next internationals were in 1914 when he played in three of France's four Five Nations matches, the games against Ireland and Wales in which he played as prop and the game against England, which proved to be the last game before the War, in which he played at number 8. All five internationals in which de Beyssac played were lost by the French team.

In 1917, de Beyssac also played in a wartime match for the French military team against a combined Australia/New

Zealand forces team, which the team from "Down Under" won 40-0.

At the outbreak of war, de Beyssac served as a lieutenant with the 81st Artillery Division. In October 1917, he joined the 501st Tank Regiment and first saw action with his tank regiment on 11th June 1918; on the first day of the action, de Beyssac's tank was hit by three shells and destroyed when taking part in a counter-attack near Mery-sur-Oise, north of Paris. De Beyssac was seriously wounded and died from his wounds two days later in a military hospital at St Remy. He was 28 at the time and buried at Saint-Remy-en-l'Eau in the Oise region in northern France.

INTERNATIONAL APPEARANCES

1st January 1912 France v. Ireland at Parc des Princes, Paris; Ireland won 11-6

20th January 1912 France v. Scotland at Inverleith; Scotland won 31-3

1st January 1914 France v. Ireland at Parc des Princes, Paris; Ireland won 8-6

2nd March 1914 France v. Wales at Swansea; Wales won 31-0

13th April 1914 France v. England at Colombes; England won 39-13

16.7 Paul Decamps (1884-1915)

born in Paris

Decamps played as a lock in one international for France, in 1911 against Scotland. The match against Scotland, which France won 16-15, was France's first win in the Five Nations and Decamps scored four of France's points by converting two of the four tries scored by France.

In the War, Decamps served as a corporal in the 246th Infantry Regiment. Decamps was killed in action on 27th June

1915 at Souchez, in the Pas-de-Calais region of France; he was 31 when he died.

16.8 Julien Dufau (1888-1916)
born in Biarritz

Dufau was picked to play in all four of France's Five Nations games in 1912, playing on the wing in three of them and as centre in the match against Scotland. All four matches were lost by France but Dufau did manage to score a try on his debut in the game against Wales and in the game against England. Dufau played in France's first game the following year, again on the wing, but after losing this match to Scotland, Dufau did not play again for France.

In the War, Dufau joined the 7th Regiment of the Colonial Infantry and posted to Niger in January 1916. After being involved in fighting at Zurrika, Amazalla and Tarbardak, Dufau's column was ambushed in December 1916 on its return from a mission in Bilma; over half the column were killed in the ambush but Dufau was one of five taken as prisoner and later beheaded on the orders of the Tegama Sultan of Agadez. With the ambush taking place on 28th December 1916, Dufau died either then or soon afterwards; his body was not recovered until March 1917 and he was subsequently buried at the Agadez French Cemetery. Dufau would have been 28 years old when he died.

1st January 1912 France v. Ireland at Parc des Princes, Paris; Ireland won 11-6

20th January 1912 France v. Scotland at Inverleith; Scotland won 31-3

25th March 1912 France v. Wales at Newport; Wales won 14-8

8th April 1912 France v. England at Parc des Princes, Paris; England won 18-8

1st January 1913 France v. Scotland at Parc des Princes, Paris; Scotland won 21-3

MILITARY HONOURS

Legion d'Honneur

16.9 Paul Dupre (1888-1916)

born in Gagny, an eastern suburb of Paris

Dupre played as a forward for Racing Club de Paris and was selected to play in France's game against Wales in February 1909, a game Wales won convincingly 47-5.

In the War, Dupre served with a light infantry regiment in the French Army. He was captured by the Germans and died from his wounds on 31st May 1916 in a prisoner-of-war camp in Altengrabow in Germany. Dupree was 27 when he died.

INTERNATIONAL APPEARANCE

23rd February 1909 France v. Wales at Colombes; Wales won 47-5

16.10 Albert Eutropius (1888-1915)

born in Cayenne, French Guyana

Eutropius moved to Paris in 1910 and played rugby for Sporting Club Universitaire de France as a flanker; he was picked for one international for France, against Ireland in 1913; Ireland won the game 24-0.

At the outbreak of war, Eutropius was working as a colonial administrator in Africa. After being commissioned as a second lieutenant, he was posted to fight in the Cameroon. Eutropius was killed when he was shot in the head at Masseng in the Cameroon on 26th May 1915 at the age of 27.

INTERNATIONAL APPEARANCE

24th March 1913 France v. Ireland at Cork; Ireland won 24-0

16.11 Marc Giacardy (1881-1917)

born in Bordeaux

Giacardy played for Stade Bordelais, winning the French championships with them six times, in 1899, four years in a row from 1904 and in 1909 when he was captain. He played in various positions, mostly as a prop or fly-half but also as a hooker or in the second row.

Giacardy played only one game for France, playing as a flanker against England in 1907; despite holding England to 13-13 at half time, France lost the match 13-41 with England's Danny Lambert (see Chapter 8.14) scoring five tries.

Giacardy was a journalist by profession. In the War, he served as a captain with the 6ᵗʰ Infantry Regiment; he was killed in action at the front at la Ferne-de-Mormont near Verdun on 20ᵗʰ August 1917 at the age of 36.

16.12 Pierre Guillemin (1887-1915)
born in Bonnevaux, Languedoc-Roussillon region

Guillemin played as a prop for Racing Club de France from 1906 to 1912. He was first picked to play for France in 1908; after playing two games for France in both 1908 and 1909, Guillemin played in all four of France's Five Nations matches in 1910 and the first three of their Five Nations matches in 1911 before losing his place for the final match of the season.

An architect by profession, Guillemin served as a lieutenant with the 23ʳᵈ Infantry Regiment in the War; he was killed on the front on 18ᵗʰ August 1915 at the age of 27 after taking part in a photographic reconnaissance mission in the Bois de Pretre in Belleville-sur-Meuse.

22nd January 1910 France v. Scotland at Inverleith; Scotland won 27-0

3rd March 1910 France v. England at Parc des Princes, Paris; England won 11-3

28th March 1910 France v. Ireland at Parc des Princes, Paris; Ireland won 8-3

2nd January 1911 France v. Scotland at Colombes; France won 16-15

28th January 1911 France v. England at Twickenham; England won 37-0

28th February 1911 France v. Wales at Parc des Princes, Paris; Wales won 15-0

16.13 Maurice Hedembaigt (1891-1918)
born in Anglet, near Biarritz

Hedembaigt played scrum-half for Aviron Bayonnais, winning the French championship with them in the 1912/13 season. He played three times for France, his first game being against Scotland in 1913; less than a fortnight after making his debut, he played in France's first game against South Africa. Hedembaigt's third and final game for France was in 1914 against Wales.

As well as being a rugby international, Hedembaigt was also a champion athlete, being the Basque Coast long jump champion.

Hedembaigt worked as a house painter; in the War he served as a sergeant with the 89th Infantry Regiment. He was killed in action on 5th August 1918 at the age of 27, at Jonchery, on the Marne.

INTERNATIONAL APPEARANCES

1st January 1913 France v. Scotland at Parc des Princes, Paris; Scotland won 21-3

11th January 1913 France v. South Africa at Bordeaux; South Africa won 38-5

2nd March 1914 France v. Wales at Swansea; Wales won 31-0

16.14 Emmanuel Iguiniz (1889-1914)

born in Bayonne

Iguiniz played number 8 for Aviron Bayonnais, with whom he won the French first division title in the 1912/13 season but made his debut for France as a hooker. His debut, which was the Five Nations fixture against England in April 1914, was his one and only game for France as it was in their last match before the War.

Iguiniz was a jeweller and, in the War, served as a corporal with the 49th Infantry Regiment. He was killed in action on 20th September 1914 at the age of 24, at Craonne on the Aisne.

INTERNATIONAL APPEARANCE

13th April 1914 France v. England at Colombes; England won 39-13

16.15 Daniel Ihingoue (1889-1917)

born in Iharre, the Pyrenees-Atlantiques region

Ihingoue played for a number of clubs, including Biarritz Stade, Biarritz Olympique and Stade Rochelais. His two games for France were in 1912, when he played as a centre alongside Julien Dufau (see Chapter 16.8).

During the War, Ihingoue worked on the medical staff with the Sengalese Infantry Regiment. He was awarded the Croix de Guerre with Vermeil Star but was killed in action on 16th April 1917 at the age of 28, at Craonne on the Aisne.

1st January 1912 France v. Ireland at Parc des Princes, Paris; Ireland won 11-6

20th January 1912 France v. Scotland at Inverleith; Scotland won 31-3

MILITARY HONOURS

Croix de Guerre with Vermeil Star

16.16 Henri Isaac (1883-1917)

born in Basse-Terre, Guadeloupe

Isaac played for Racing Club de France and was selected for two games for France, as full-back, the first game being against England in 1907 and the second being a year later, also against England.

In the War, Isaac served with the French Flying Corps. He died on 29th June 1917 at the age of 34; his death was reported as an accident, but may have resulted as a result of his parachute failing to open during a jump.

INTERNATIONAL APPEARANCES

5th January 1907 France v. England at Richmond, London; England won 41-13

1st January 1908 France v. England at Colombes; England won 19-0

16.17 Henri Lacassagne (1883-1918)

born in Viella, the Midi-Pyrenees region

Lacassagne played scrum-half for Stade Bordelais, winning the French club championships with them from 1904 to 1907.

On 1st January 1906, Lacassagne played in France's first international rugby match, the game at Parc des Princes in Paris against New Zealand. Lacassagne played his second and final game for France a year later, against England.

During the War, Lacassagne first served with the 59th Infantry Regiment and, after recovering from wounds he sustained in 1915, became a gunner with the 46th Squadron of the 2nd Aviation Group. He received his first citation for bravery for his courage and coolness when he overcame pain, after being seriously injured in a fight against 15 enemy aircraft.

On 14th September 1918, Lacassagne was involved in a major dogfight with seven planes from a German squadron above Saint Benedict in the Haute-Marne region. After shooting down one of the German planes, Lacassagne was first shot in the chest and then received a fatal shot to the head. Lacassagne received a second citation for bravery for his courage on the day he died.

Lacassagne was 34 when he was killed and was buried at the Misericoude Cemetery in Nantes.

INTERNATIONAL APPEARANCES

1st January 1906 France v. New Zealand at Parc des Princes, Paris; New Zealand won 38-8

5th January 1907 France v. England at Richmond, London; England won 41-13

MILITARY HONOURS

Two citations for bravery

16.18 Gaston Lane (1883-1914)

born in Paris

Lane first played for AS Bois-Colombes before joining the Paris Cosmopolitan Club and then moving to the Racing Club de France. Lane played in France's first international, against New Zealand in 1906, a game in which he scored his only try for France; in his second international, in the same year, Lane captained the French team against England.

Lane continued playing for France up until 1913. Lane played a total of 16 games for France and played nine of his games on the wing and seven as centre; he also captained France on five occasions. Included in his 16 games was France's solitary win before the War, over Scotland in 1911.

Lane was an engineer by profession and, in the War, joined the 346th Infantry Regiment; he was killed in action on the front at Lironville in the Moselle region on 23rd September 1914 at the age of 31.

INTERNATIONAL APPEARANCES

1st January 1906 France v. New Zealand at Parc des Princes, Paris; New Zealand won 38-8

22nd March 1906 France v. England at Parc des Princes, Paris; England won 35-8

5th January 1907 France v. England at Richmond, London; England won 41-13

1st January 1908 France v. England at Colombes; England won 19-0

2nd March 1908 France v. Wales at the National Stadium, Cardiff; Wales won 36-4

30th January 1909 France v. England at Leicester; England won 22-0

23rd February 1909 France v. Wales at Colombes; Wales won 47-5

20th March 1909 France v. Ireland at Lansdowne Road, Dublin; Ireland won 19-8

1st January 1910 France v. Wales at Swansea; Wales won 49-14

3rd March 1910 France v. England at Parc des Princes, Paris; England won 11-3

2nd January 1911 France v. Scotland at Colombes; France won 16-15

28th February 1911 France v. Wales at Parc des Princes, Paris; Wales won 15-0

1st January 1912 France v. Ireland at Parc des Princes, Paris; Ireland won 11-6

25th March 1912 France v. Wales at Newport; Wales won 14-8

8th April 1912 France v. England at Parc des Princes, Paris; England won 18-8

1st January 1913 France v. Scotland at Parc des Princes, Paris; Scotland won 21-3

16.19 Leon Larribau (1889-1916)

born in Anglet, near Biarritz

Larribau was a scrum-half who played his club rugby for Perigueux until 1912 and then for Biarritz Olympique.

Larribau played in all France's Five Nations matches in 1912 and, after not playing in 1913, in two more matches for France in 1914.

In the War, Larribau served as a sergeant in the 12th Infantry Regiment; he was killed in action on 31st December 1916 at the age of 27, at Louvremont near Verdun and is buried at Verdun National Necropolis Glorieux.

INTERNATIONAL APPEARANCES

1st January 1912 France v. Ireland at Parc des Princes, Paris; Ireland won 11-6

20th January 1912 France v. Scotland at Inverleith; Scotland won 31-3

25th March 1912 France v. Wales at Newport; Wales won 14-8

8th April 1912 France v. England at Parc des Princes, Paris; England won 18-8

1st January 1914 France v. Ireland at Parc des Princes, Paris; Ireland won 8-6

13th April 1914 France v. England at Colombes; England won 39-13

16.20 Marcel Legrain (1890-1915)

born in Paris

Legrain played as a lock for Stade Francais rugby club and made his debut for France against Ireland in 1909 at the age of 18. Over a five year period, Legrain played a total of 12 games for France, including all four of their Five Nations matches in 1911 and in their first fixture against South Africa, in 1913.

Legrain served as a sergeant with the 154th Infantry Regiment in the War; he was killed on 10th June 1915 at Neuville-Saint-Vaast, at the age of 24.

INTERNATIONAL APPEARANCES

20th March 1909 France v. Ireland at Lansdowne Road, Dublin; Ireland won 19-8

28th March 1910 France v. Ireland at Parc des Princes, Paris; Ireland won 8-3

2nd January 1911 France v. Scotland at Colombes; France won 16-15

28th January 1911 France v. England at Twickenham; England won 37-0

28th February 1911 France v. Wales at Parc des Princes, Paris; Wales won 15-0

25th March 1911 France v. Ireland at Cork; Ireland won 25-5

1st January 1913 France v. Scotland at Parc des Princes, Paris; Scotland won 21-3

11th January 1913 France v. South Africa at Bordeaux; South Africa won 38-5

25th January 1913 France v. England at Twickenham; England won 20-0

24th March 1913 France v. Ireland at Cork; Ireland won 24-0

1st January 1914 France v. Ireland at Parc des Princes, Paris; Ireland won 8-6

2nd March 1914 France v. Wales at Swansea; Wales won 31-0

16.21 Albert Mayssonnie (1884-1914)

born in Lavernose, near Toulouse

Mayssonnie was a scrum-half who played his club rugby for Toulouse, winning the French championships with them in 1912. When he was picked to play for France in 1908, Mayssonnie became Toulouse's first player to represent France – Auguste Pujol, who subsequently joined Toulouse had played for France before Mayssonnie did but not as a Toulouse player.

Mayssonnie played a total of three games for France, two in 1908 and one in 1910.

Once war broke out, Maysonnie volunteered for service, joining the 259th Infantry Regiment. Within three weeks, he had been cited for bravery in an action at d'Amel-Eton near Verdun. On 6th September 1914, at Osches during the early stages of the Battle of the Marne, he was reported missing and it was believed that he died later that day. His body was found by his Toulouse and French teammate Pierre Mounicq, who buried him while under enemy fire.

Mayssonnie was the first rugby international to be killed in the War; he was 30 years old when he died.

INTERNATIONAL APPEARANCES

1st January 1908 France v. England at Colombes; England won 19-0

2nd March 1908 France v. Wales at the National Stadium, Cardiff; Wales won 36-4

1st January 1910 France v. Wales at Swansea; Wales won 49-14

MILITARY HONOURS

Citation for bravery

16.22 Francois Poeydebasque (1891-1914)

born in Bayonne

Poeydebasque played for Bayonne and was selected for two games for France in 1914; in his first match, against Ireland, Poeydebasque played as a centre and, in his second, against Wales, as fly-half.

In the War, Poeydebasque served as a sergeant with the 249th Infantry Regiment; he was killed on 21st September 1914 at Crannelle on the Aisne at the age of 23.

INTERNATIONAL APPEARANCES

1st January 1914 France v. Ireland at Parc des Princes, Paris; Ireland won 8-6

2nd March 1914 France v. Wales at Swansea; Wales won 31-0

Some reports state that **Theodore Varvier,** who played six matches for France between 1906 and 1912, was killed in the War; however, official reports record that he died on 23rd August 1913, before the outbreak of war.

CHAPTER 17
USA RUGBY PLAYER

The USA played two international rugby matches before the Great War, the first against Australia in 1912 and the second against New Zealand in 1913; of the 27 Americans to represent the USA at rugby before the War, Frank Gard was the only one to be killed in the War.

17.1 Frank Gard (1892-1918)
born in Tremont City, Ohio

Gard attended Stanford University from 1910 to 1914 and, in his last year there, captained the university team at American football and at rugby.

Prior to captaining his university team, playing as flanker Gard had captained the American rugby team in its first two internationals, the first against the touring Australian team in 1912 and the second against the touring New Zealand team in 1913. The game against Australia was a close one with the US team leading 8-6 five minutes before the final whistle before finally losing the match 12-8; the game against New Zealand was more one-sided with the tourists winning 51-3 and the New York Tribune describing the game as easy for the New Zealanders.

Gard enlisted in the US Army in June 1917 and became a first lieutenant with the 362nd Infantry Regiment, 91st Division.

Gard's regiment was sent to Europe in July 1918 and, after several weeks training, arrived in September 1918 at the front as part of the Meuse-Argonne offensive.

As his regiment was moving towards Gesnes, Gard was given the task of identifying German positions. Whilst observing machine gun fire during the advance through Gesnes on 27th September 1918, Gard was killed either by machine gun fire or rifle fire. He was 26 years old and was buried at the Meuse-Argonne American Cemetery in Romagne in France.

INTERNATIONAL APPEARANCES

16th November 1912 USA v. Australia at Berkeley; Australia won 12-8

15th November 1913 USA v. New Zealand at Berkeley; New Zealand won 51-3

CHAPTER 18
British Olympians

18.1 Gordon Alexander (1885-1917)
born in London

After attending Harrow School, Alexander worked in the family business as a stockbroker. Alexander was an excellent sailor and golfer but it was as a fencer that he represented Great Britain at the 1912 Olympics in Stockholm.

Alexander was British champion at the foil and competed in both the foil and epee events in 1912. However he had little success at the Games and was not in the running to win any of the medals.

At the outbreak of the War, Alexander joined the British Army and served in France throughout 1915 and 1916; it was whilst serving as a private with the 13th East Surrey Regiment on 24th April 1917 that Alexander was involved in an attack on Villers-Plouich in France when one of the soldiers with him was wounded by an artillery shell, whilst digging a trench. As Alexander was bandaging his colleague, a further shell hit them, killing them both.

Alexander was 31 at the time and is commemorated at the Loos Memorial in France.

OLYMPIC APPEARANCE

1912 Stockholm – fencing

individual epee

individual foil

18.2 Gerard Rupert Lawrence "Laurie" Anderson (1889-1914)

born in Twickenham

After attending Eton College, Anderson went up to Oxford University, where he won a blue in athletics. By 1910, he was the AAA's champion hurdler over 120 yards and, in July 1910, set the first IAAF world record in the hurdles event over 440 yards, in a time of 56.8 seconds.

In 1912, Anderson was again the AAA champion in the 120 yards hurdles event and took part in the 110 yards hurdles event at the 1912 Olympics – the hurdles over 440 yards, in which Anderson had set the world record, was not one of the events at the 1912 Games. Anderson was amongst the favourites to win a medal but, after coming second in his first heat, failed to make the final after falling in the semi-final.

In the War, Anderson gained a commission as a second lieutenant and was posted with the 1st Battalion, the Cheshire Regiment, serving in France and Belgium in October 1914.

On 7th November 1914, Anderson was mortally wounded during the First Battle of Ypres at Hooge, near Ypres. His battalion's war diaries reported that the battalion was in the trenches that day and, after being heavily shelled in the morning, was attacked in the afternoon by the German infantry; although the enemy was repulsed, with 25 of their men captured, Anderson was one of four from his battalion who were killed, with 22 wounded and eight missing.

There is some doubt as to when Anderson died, with his battalion's war report stating that he died on 7th November 1914 and the Commonwealth War Graves Commission stating it was four days later. Whichever is correct, he was 25 at the time and is commemorated at the Ypres (Menin Gate) Memorial.

Anderson's brother, Arthur, also competed in the 1912 Olympics, in the 110 metres and 200 metres events.

OLYMPIC APPEARANCE

1912 Stockholm – athletics

110 yards hurdles

18.3 William Anderson (?-1915)

born in Ireland but moved with his family to Scotland before his first birthday.

Anderson was the Scottish 880 yards champion in 1905, the same year he represented Scotland against Ireland in a match over the same distance. In 1906, he retained his Scottish title and was selected to take part in the 1906 Intercalated Games in Athens, celebrating the 10th anniversary of the first Modern Games in 1896.

Anderson took part in the 400 metres and 800 metres events in Athens, reaching the final and coming seventh in the 400 metres event; in the 800 metres event, Anderson failed to progress beyond the round one heats.

After the 1906 Games, Anderson emigrated to Canada. At the outbreak of war, Anderson enlisted with the 5th Battalion, Canadian Infantry and was posted to France. He was killed in action on 26th April 1915 during the Second Battle of Ypres and was buried at the Boulogne Eastern Cemetery.

18.4 Henry Ashington (1891-1917)

born in Southport

After leaving Harrow School, Ashington went to Cambridge University, where he took part in four Varsity matches, in which he ran in the mile, the 880 yards and the 120 yards hurdles events and jumped in the high jump and long jump events.

Ashington represented Great Britain at the 1912 Olympics, competing in the long jump event and the standing long jump event, coming 10th in the long jump and 12th in the standing long jump.

During the War, Ashington served with the East Yorkshire Regiment; whilst serving in Belgium in the advance of July 1916, Ashington was wounded but, after recovering, was promoted to the rank of captain and returned to the front.

On 31st January 1917, Ashington was killed in action near Combles when he was hit by a sniper's bullet; he never regained consciousness and was buried, at the age of 25, at the Combles Communal Cemetery.

18.5 Isaac Bentham (1886-1917)

born in Wigan

Bentham was a member of the Great Britain water polo team which won the gold medal at the 1912 Olympics. Four of the team had already won the gold medal at the 1908 Games and three of the 1912 team, including Paulo Radmilovic and Charles Sydney Smith who had also been in the 1908 team, won the gold again at the 1920 Games in Antwerp.

At the 1912 Games, the Great Britain team beat Belgium 7-5 in the first round, the hosts Sweden 6-3 in the semi-final and Austria 8-0 in the final; Bentham was a forward and scored a goal in the games against Belgium and Sweden.

During the War, Bentham served as a sergeant with the Royal Field Artillery on the Western Front in France. In June 1916, he served with his battalion during the week long barrage before the commencement of the Battle of the Somme. Bentham was killed in action at the Battle of Arras on 15th May 1917 at the age of 30. He is commemorated at the Arras War Memorial.

OLYMPIC APPEARANCE

1912 Stockholm – water polo

gold medallist

18.6 Henry Brougham (1888-1923)

born at Wellington College, Berkshire

Brougham also attended Wellington College where he excelled at rackets; he reached the final of the public schools rackets championships three times in a row from 1907, winning the title at the third attempt, after having been runner-up in 1905 and 1906.

At the 1908 Olympics, Brougham represented Great Britain in the singles rackets event and, after receiving a walk-over in the first round, lost in the semi-final to the eventual winner, Evan Noel; by reaching the semi-final, Brougham won a bronze medal.

After leaving school, Brougham went to Oxford University and played rackets in the 1909 Varsity match against Cambridge. In the English amateur championships in 1909, Brougham was the runner-up but, in 1913, he went one better in the doubles event when he and his partner won the English amateur doubles title.

In the War, Brougham served as a major with the Royal Artillery; after being gassed in 1917, Brougham was invalided out of active service. In 1918, Brougham contracted tuberculosis whilst commanding a battery in Northern Ireland. Although he survived the War, Brougham never recovered from his war injuries and he died at the age of 34 at La Croix-Valmer in France on 18th February 1923.

Brougham also played county cricket for Berkshire and rugby for England and is covered in more detail in Chapter 8.3.

OLYMPIC APPEARANCE

1908 London – rackets

singles; bronze medallist

18.7 Edmond Bury (1884-1915)
born in Kensington, London

Bury played in the men's doubles rackets event at the 1908 Olympics in London. He and his partner, Cecil Browning, won the silver medal, losing in the final to the British pair, Vane Pennell and John Jacob Astor.

The 1908 Games are the only Olympics at which rackets has been played and, with the only participants in the rackets events at the 1908 Games being those representing Great Britain, Great Britain won all seven medals on offer.

During the War, Bury served as a captain with the King's Royal Rifle Corps. He was killed in action on 5th December 1915 near Fleurbaix in France, at the age of 31. He is buried at the Rue-Petillon Military Cemetery near Fleurbaix.

<u>*OLYMPIC APPEARANCE*</u>

1908 London – rackets

doubles; silver medallist

18.8 George Butterfield (1879-1917)
born in Stockton-on-Tees

Butterfield was a middle-distance runner affiliated with the Darlington Harriers and won the AAA mile title from 1904 to 1906; his winning time of 4 minutes 18.4 seconds in 1906 was the fastest time run that year and put him top of the world rankings. 1906 also saw him win the Northern title over 440 yards and one mile.

Butterfield competed in the 1908 Olympics in both the 800 metres and 1,500 metres events. In the 800 metres event, Butterfield came second in his heat and, in the 1,500 metres event, he came third in his heat, but neither was good enough to see him through to the next stage of the competition.

Before joining up with the Royal Field Artillery in 1916, Butterfield was the landlord of the Hole in the Wall pub in Darlington. A year later, whilst serving as a private with the Royal Garrison Artillery, he was killed when he had his legs blown off. He was 38 at the time and, although it was reported that he was killed in action in France on 24th September 1917, he was buried at the Birr Cross Roads Cemetery near Ypres in Belgium, making it likely that he was killed at the Third Battle of Ypres.

In his obituary, the Northern Despatch reported that Butterfield had once raced against a greyhound and beaten it.

OLYMPIC APPEARANCE

1908 London – athletics

800 metres

1,500 metres

18.9 Oswald Carver (1887-1915)

born in Manchester

After attending Charterhouse School, Carver went up to Cambridge University and, in 1908, rowed against Oxford in the Boat Race. Following Cambridge's success against Oxford, seven of the Cambridge eight which won the 1908 Boat Race, along with the cox, were selected to represent Great Britain in one of the two British boats taking part in the coxed eights rowing event at the 1908 Olympics; the eighth member of the boat, Henry Goldsmith (see Chapter 18.22) was a former Cambridge Boat Club President. Carver's boat won the bronze medal at the Games, the gold medal going to the other British boat.

In the War, Carver served as a captain with the East Lancashire Company of the Engineers. In May 1915, Carver went to Egypt en route to Gallipoli. The role of the Engineers in Gallipoli was to build trenches, strongpoints and dug-outs; on 4th June 1915, the Engineers took part in the Third Battle of Krithia, following behind the Territorial Battalion, Manchester Regiment, who were leading the attack on the Turkish positions; the Engineers were there to help secure captured Turkish trenches and to dig communication trenches back to the original British lines and build strongholds in case of counter-attacks. During the battle, Carver was wounded in the back and taken to one of the Casualty Clearing Stations on the landing beach.

Carver was not moved from the clearing station, probably because of the seriousness of his injuries and he died three days later, on 7th June 1915, at the age of 28. He is buried at the Lancashire Landing Cemetery at Gallipoli.

Carver's widow, Elizabeth, later married Field Marshall Montgomery.

OLYMPIC APPEARANCE

1908 London – rowing

coxed eights; bronze medallist

18.10 Ralph Chalmers (1891-1915)

born in Primrose Hill, London

Chalmers was one of 12 who represented Great Britain in the individual epee fencing event at the 1908 Olympics and, at 17 years and 185 days old, was the youngest competitor at the Games. Despite Great Britain having 12 of the 85 fencers taking part in the event, it was dominated by the French, who won all three medals.

Chalmers came third equal in his qualifying group but was eliminated when he lost in a play-off for the next round.

In the War, Chalmers served as a captain with the Suffolk Regiment. He was killed at the Second Battle of Ypres on 8th May 1915, at the age of 24. He is commemorated at the Ypres (Menin Gate) Memorial.

OLYMPIC APPEARANCE

1908 London – fencing

individual epee

18.11 Noel Chavasse (1884-1917)

born in Oxford in 1884, the younger of identical twins.

After attending Magdalen College School, Chavasse went up to Oxford University. After graduating, Chavasse qualified as a doctor, a number in his family having been prominent surgeons.

In 1908, Chavasse and his twin brother, Christopher, were both selected to run for Great Britain in the 400 metres event at the Olympics. Neither brother made it beyond the first heat.

In 1913, Chavasse joined the Royal Army Medical Corps. By the end of 1914, he had been posted to France and, in June 1915, was awarded the Military Cross for gallantry at Hooge in Belgium. Later that year, Chavasse was mentioned in despatches by his superior officer.

By 1916, Chavasse had been promoted to captain and, in August 1916, was at Guillemont in France. His actions on 9th August, when he was attending to the wounded whilst under heavy fire, led to him being awarded the Victoria Cross; his actions that day were cited as follows.

"Captain Chavasse attended to the wounded all day under heavy fire, frequently in view of the enemy, and during the night he searched for wounded in front of the enemy's lines. Next day he took a stretcher-bearer and under heavy shell-fire carried an urgent case 500 yards into safety, being wounded himself on the return journey. The same night, with 20 volunteers, he rescued three wounded men from a shell-hole 36 yards from the enemy's trenches, buried the bodies of two officers and collected many identity discs. Altogether he saved the lives of some 20 wounded men, besides the ordinary cases which passed through his hands."

Chavasse recovered from the shell splinters which had wounded him at Guillemont and was serving again with the Royal Army Medical Corps at the Battle of Passchendaele in July 1917. For his actions during this battle, Chavasse was awarded a second Victoria Cross, the following being cited for his actions on this occasion.

"During the period 31 July to 2 August 1917, at Wieltje, Belgium, Captain Chavasse, although severely wounded early in the action while carrying a wounded officer to the dressing station, refused to leave his post and not only continued to perform his duties, but in addition went out repeatedly under heavy fire and searched for and attended the wounded. During these searches, although practically without food, worn with fatigue and faint from his wound, he helped to carry in badly wounded men. He was instrumental in saving many wounded who would have undoubtedly died under the bad weather conditions."

Chavasse died of his wounds at Brandhoek on 4ᵗʰ August 1917, at the age of 32. He is buried at the Brandhoek New Military Cemetery at Vladmertinge in Belgium.

With his two Victoria Crosses, a Military Cross and a mention in despatches, Chavasse was the most highly decorated of all British officers in the First World War; he remains only one of three men who have been awarded two Victoria Crosses and the only one to be awarded two for his actions in the Great War.

Christopher Chavasse, his twin brother, was also decorated in the War, being awarded a Military Cross; after the War, Christopher followed in his father's footsteps by becoming a bishop.

OLYMPIC APPEARANCE

1908 London – athletics,

400 metres

MILITARY HONOURS

Military Cross

Victoria Cross (twice)

Mentioned in despatches

18.12 Geoffrey Coles (1871-1916)

born in Hastings, East Sussex

Coles went to Winchester College and, after leaving school, worked as an engineer.

Coles represented Great Britain in the team pistol event and the individual pistol event at the 1908 Olympics. In the team event, Coles picked up the bronze medal but only came 11th in the individual event.

During the War, Coles served as a private with the Royal Fusiliers. He was killed at Festubert in France on 27th January 1916, when an enemy grenade exploded near him whilst he was on outpost duty.

At the time of his death, Coles was 44; he is buried at the Brown's Road Military Cemetery at Festubert.

OLYMPIC APPEARANCE

1908 London – shooting

individual pistol shooting

team pistol; bronze medallist

18.13 Percy Courtman (1888-1917)

born in Chorlton-cum-Hardy, Lancashire

After attending William Hulme Grammar School, Courtman joined the Old Trafford Swimming Club and worked in his father's estate agency business. In 1907, Courtman was the Amateur Swimming Association's champion at the 200 yards breaststroke, a title he was to win another four times over the next six years.

In 1908, Courtfield swam in the 200 metres breaststroke event at the 1908 Olympics but, after coming second in his heat, did not progress to the next round. Four years later, Courtman was again representing Great Britain at the Olympics, this time in both the 200 metres and the 400 metres breaststroke events; also competing in the same events as Courtman were the German Wilhelm Lutzow (see Chapter 20.5.11) and the Hungarian Oszkar Demjan (see Chapter 20.7.2). Courtman came away from the 1912 Games with the bronze medal in the 400 metres breaststroke event and was placed fourth in the 200 metres breaststroke event.

Later in 1912, Courtman set world records for breaststroke over 400 metres and 500 metres and, on 28th July 1916 at the Garston Baths in Liverpool, the world record for breaststroke over 200 metres; his world record over 200 metres, in a time of 2 minutes 56.6 seconds, was the first sub- three minute time for the distance and lasted until 1922; it remained the British record for 59 years until broken by David Wilkie.

When war broke out, Courtman served as a private with the 6th Territorial Battalion, the Manchester Regiment. Courtman saw action in Gallipoli in August 1915 before being posted to France. On 2nd June 1917, Courtman was killed when his battalion, which was stationed at Neuville-Bourjonval in France, was heavily shelled, it being reported that he had been "blown to bits by one about breakfast". Courtman was 29 when he died and was buried at the Neuville-Bourjonval British Cemetery.

OLYMPIC APPEARANCES

1908 London – swimming,

200 metres breaststroke

1912 Stockholm – swimming,

200 metres breaststroke,

400 metres breaststroke; bronze medallist

18.14 Harry Crank (1889-1917)
born in Bolton, Lancashire

Crank was one of the 23 men who took part in the men's springboard diving event at the 1908 Olympics; he came fourth out of five in his group and therefore failed to make it through to the semi-finals. Two years later, Crank was photographed for a postcard performing a swan dive at Ramsey on the Isle of Man.

During the War, Crank served with the 17th Battalion, Lancashire Fusiliers, reaching the rank of second lieutenant. Crank was killed in action during a counter-attack by the Germans at Marechal Farm, near Ypres on 22nd October 1917 during the Third Battle of Ypres; Crank was 28 years old when he was killed and is commemorated at the Tyne Cot Memorial near Ypres.

OLYMPIC APPEARANCE

1908 London – diving

springboard

18.15 Robert Davies (1876-1916)

born in Paddington, London

After attending Marlborough College, Davies served as a major in the Second Boer War. After retiring as a regular in the British Army in 1908, Davies worked as a stockbroker before re-joining the Army at the outbreak of war in 1914.

In 1906, Davies won the National Rifle Association's King's Prize at Bisley. Two years later, Davies was competing in two of the rifle shooting events at the 1908 Olympics. One of the events was rifle shooting over 300 metres from three positions and the other was rifle shooting over 600 metres from any position; Davies came 39th out of a field of 91 in the shooting event over 300 metres and 37th out of a field of 85 in the shooting event over 600 metres.

In the War, Davies was a member of the 9th Battalion, London Regiment (Queen Victoria Rifles). In 1916, Davies was posted to France; on 9th September 1916, at the age of 39, he was killed in action "at the head of his men" whilst leading an attack at Bouleaux Wood during the Battle of Ginchy, one of the battles during the Battle of the Somme. Davies's body was never found and he is commemorated at the Thiepval Memorial in France.

OLYMPIC APPEARANCE

1908 London – shooting

rifle (300 metres)

rifle (600 metres)

18.16 Joseph Dines (1886-1918)

born in King's Lynn

Dines was a teacher who played amateur football. He made his debut as a half back for Lynn Town in 1904 and two years later appeared for them in their F. A. Cup match against Aston Villa. In 1910, Dines was a member of the Norfolk team which won the Southern Counties Championship.

By the time he moved to take up a teaching post in Ilford in 1910, Dines had already played the first of his 24 amateur internationals for England.

In 1912, Dines was selected as one of the 14 to represent Great Britain at football at the 1912 Olympics. Great Britain repeated their success at the 1908 Games, by taking the gold medal. In their first game, they overcame Hungary 7-0, with Harold Walden scoring six of their goals; in their second game, they beat Finland 4-0 and, in the final, Denmark 4-2. Dines played in all three games.

Dines retained his amateur status throughout his football career, but this did not stop him making appearances for a number of professional clubs including Norwich Reserves, Arsenal Reserves, Queens Park Rangers, Millwall and, on one occasion, Liverpool in an away game at Chelsea.

Dines volunteered for the British Army in November 1915, rising to the rank of second lieutenant with the King's Liverpool Regiment. Whilst serving on the Western Front in France, Dines was killed by machine gun fire on 27th September 1918, at the age of 32. He was buried at the Grande Ravine British Cemetery at Hagnicourt in France.

OLYMPIC APPEARANCE

1912 Stockholm – football

gold medallist

18.17 Hugh Durant (1877-1916)

born in Brixton, London

Durant competed in four events at the 1912 Olympics. Three of his events were shooting events and the fourth, which included as one of its disciplines shooting, was the first modern pentathlon to be staged at the Olympics.

Durant's three shooting events were the 30 metre team pistol event, the 50 metre team pistol event and the individual free pistol event over 50 metres; in both team events, Durant won the bronze medal and, in his individual event, he came 20th out of a field of 54.

In the modern pentathlon, Durant performed best in the shooting and fencing events and came 18th overall out of a field of 32.

In the War, Durant served as a second lieutenant with the 9th (Queen's Royal) Lancers and, as well as being mentioned in despatches, was awarded the Distinguished Conduct Medal. Durant was killed in action at Vermelles in France on 20th January 1916 at the age of 38 and was buried at the Vermelles British Cemetery.

OLYMPIC APPEARANCE

1912 Stockholm – shooting

individual pistol (50 metres)

team pistol (30 metres); bronze medallist

shooting, team pistol (50 metres); bronze medallist

modern pentathlon

MILITARY HONOURS

Distinguished Conduct Medal

Mentioned in despatches

18.18 George Fairbairn (1888-1915)

born in Melbourne, Australia

Fairbairn went up to Cambridge University in 1906, spending five years there. In 1908, Fairbairn took part in the Boat Race against Oxford, rowing immediately behind Oswald Carver (see Chapter 18.9). Although Cambridge won, their performance was considered lacklustre; as a consequence, Fairbairn, perhaps because he was an Australian, was the only member of the Cambridge team which won the Boat Race in 1908 to be replaced in the Cambridge boat picked to represent Great Britain in the coxed eights event at the 1908 Olympics, his replacement being Henry Goldsmith (see Chapter 18.22).

Although not picked for the coxed eights team, Fairbairn did however represent Great Britain at the 1908 Games in the men's coxless pairs, alongside Philip Verdon and, in winning the silver medal, went one better than the coxed eights boat he had been replaced in.

The following year Fairbairn missed the Boat Race through illness; Fairbairn also missed the Boat Race in 1910 but was selected to take part in his second Boat Race in 1911.

As well as being an Olympic rower, Fairbairn also played rugby and, although he did not win his blue at rugby as well as for rowing, he did play for Rosslyn Park.

In the War, Fairbairn served as a second lieutenant with the Durham Light Infantry. He was killed in action at Bailleul in the Somme region in France, on 20th June 1915. He was 26 years old when he died and was buried at the Bailleul Communal Cemetery Extension.

18.19 Alfred Flaxman (1879-1916)

born in Barnsley, Yorkshire

Flaxman competed in four events at the 1908 Olympics, the discus throw, the discus throw (Greek style), the standing high jump and the javelin throw. In the three throwing events, the distances Flaxman threw are recorded as "unknown", presumably because he was not challenging the medal positions; similarly in the standing high jump event, the height he jumped is recorded as "unknown" but, in this event, he was up against the American Ray Ewry who won the gold medal in the standing high jump event and in the standing long jump event at the 1900 Olympics, 1904 Olympics, the 1908 Olympics and the 1906 Intercalated Games.

As well as competing in the Olympics, Flaxman also competed in the AAA Championships, taking part in the hammer throwing event for 10 years from 1905 and winning it in 1910 and in discus and shot events; he also won the pole vault event at the AAA Championships in 1909, but was the only competitor taking part in this event.

In addition to being an athlete, Flaxman was a competent boxer and gymnast, as well as a musician and artist.

During the War, Flaxman served as a second lieutenant with the South Staffordshire Regiment. On the first day of the Battle of the Somme, on 1st July 1916, Flaxman was killed in an attack on enemy positions at Gommecourt in France; his remains were never found and he is commemorated at the Thiepval Memorial in France. He was 36 at the time of his death.

OLYMPIC APPEARANCE

1908 London – athletics

standing high jump

discus

discus (Greek style)

javelin

18.20 Herbert Henry "Bert" Gayler (1881-1917)
born in Christchurch, Dorset

Gaylor took part in the 1912 Olympics, competing in the road race individual event and coming 30th out of a field of 123. By virtue of competing in the individual event, Gayler was also a member of the England team competing in the team event, in which the times of the team's four fastest cyclists were added together to give the team time; Gayler's time was not one of the England team's four fastest times and therefore he was not one of the four in the British team who won the silver medal.

During the War, Gayler was posted to India as a soldier with the British Army's 25th County of London Cycle Battalion, as part of an expeditionary force sent to deal with a revolt by Mahsud tribesmen in Waziristan on the border with Afghanistan. Gayler was killed on 23rd June 1917 by rifle fire during an ambush in a valley near Kotkai Bozi Khel in the North West

Frontier region, in what is now a part of Pakistan. Gayler was 35 when he was killed and was buried at Waziristan; there is a memorial to him at the Anglican Church in Jullundur, in the Punjab State in India.

OLYMPIC APPEARANCE

1912 Stockholm – cycling

individual road race

18.21 Thomas Gillespie (1892-1914)
born in Alvington in Gloucestershire

Although he was Scottish, Gillespie lived and was educated in England, going up to Oxford University after leaving Winchester College. Whilst at university, Gillespie rowed for three years for his college, New College, twice being Head of the River; however, despite his success in his college boat, Gillespie did not row for Oxford in the Boat Race. Instead, the New College eight was one of two eights to represent Great Britain in the men's coxed eights at the 1912 Olympics, where they won the silver medal after losing in the final to the other British boat, from the Leander Club.

Gillespie enlisted at the outbreak of war and served as a lieutenant in the 2nd Battalion, the King's Own Scottish Borderers at the Battle of the Aisne in September 1914; a month later, on 18th October 1914, he was killed in action at La Bassee in France, at the age of 21. His body was never recovered and he is commemorated at the Le Touret Memorial in France.

18.22 Henry Goldsmith (1885-1915)
born in Plympton, Devon

After leaving school, Goldsmith went to Cambridge University and rowed in the Boat Race against Oxford in 1906, when he was President of the Cambridge University Boat Club and in 1907. Although he did not row in the 1908 Boat Race, Goldsmith was picked as a member of the Cambridge eight which represented Great Britain in the men's coxed eights at the 1908 Olympics, replacing George Fairbairn (see Chapter 18.18) who had rowed for Cambridge in the 1908 Boat Race. Goldsmith's boat, with Oswald Carver and Edward Williams (see Chapters 18.9 and 18.49) also in the boat, won the bronze medal.

During the War, Goldsmith served as a lieutenant with the Devonshire Regiment. Goldsmith was killed in action on 9th May 1915 at the age of 29, at the Battle of Aubers at Fromelles in Belgium, during the Second Battle of Ypres. His body was never recovered and he is commemorated at the Proegsteert Memorial in Belgium.

18.23 Wyndham Halswelle (1882-1915)

born in London in 1882, the son of Scottish parents.

After attending Charterhouse School and the Royal Military College at Sandhurst, Halswelle gained a commission with the Highland Light Infantry in 1901. A year later, he served with his regiment in South Africa in the Second Boer War.

Having been a successful athlete at school and Sandhurst, Halswelle took his athletics seriously on his return from South Africa in 1904. After winning the AAA title in the 440 yards event in 1905, Halswelle was selected to represent Great Britain in the Intercalated Games in 1906 in the 100 metres, 400 metres and 800 metres events. Although he did not get beyond the semi-final in the 100 metres event, Halswelle won the silver medal in the 400 metres event and the bronze medal in the 800 metres event.

Later that year, at the Scottish athletics championships, Halswelle won the 100 yards, 220 yards, 440 yards and 880 yards, all during the course of one afternoon.

Despite suffering an injury in 1907, in 1908 Halswelle set the world record over 300 yards in a time of 31.2 seconds and the British record over 400 yards in a time of 48.4 seconds, a record which was not broken until 1936.

At the 1908 Olympics, Halswelle represented Great Britain in the 400 metres event. Having reached the final in the fastest qualifying time, Halswelle found himself up against the three Americans, John Carpenter, William Robbins and John B. Taylor; in the final, before the race had been completed, it was declared void after Halswelle had been blocked by Carpenter, almost forcing Halswelle off the track – under U. S. rules at the time, blocking was permitted but it was not permitted under the Olympic rules. The final was re-run two days later, without Carpenter, who had been disqualified; in protest, Robbins and Taylor refused to take part in the re-run, leaving Halswelle to run the race all by himself. Halswelle was duly awarded the gold medal, making him the first Scot to win an Olympic gold; it remains the only occasion in Olympic history that a final has been won by a walkover.

During the War, Halswelle reached the rank of captain. On 12th March 1915, during the Battle of Neuve Chapelle in France, Halswelle was wounded by shrapnel or shell fragments, whilst leading his men over an area known as Layes Brook. Despite being wounded, he refused to be evacuated and continued at the front. Later that month, on 31st March 1915, Halswelle was killed when hit by a sniper during the course of the same battle in which he had been wounded earlier that month. His grave was marked with a wooden cross, with his name in charcoal; his body was later re-interred at the Royal Irish Graveyard at Laventie in France. Halswelle was 32 when he died.

In the regimental magazine announcing Halswelle's death appeared an article he had written a few days before his death about one of his experiences of trench warfare; Helswelle wrote "I called the men to get over the parapet. There is great difficulty in getting out of a trench, especially for small men laden with a pack, rifle and perhaps 50 rounds in the pack and a bandolier of 50 rounds hung around them, and perhaps four feet of slippery clay perpendicular wall with sandbags on the top. I got three men hit actually on the top of the parapet. I made a dash at the parapet and fell back. The Jocks then heaved me up and I jumped into a ditch – an old trench filled with liquid mud – which took me some time to get out of." In this encounter, 79 of Halswelle's fellow soldiers died in gaining only 15 yards;

after digging in for three hours, the survivors retreated to the position they had started from.

OLYMPIC APPEARANCES

1906 Athens – athletics

100 metres

400 metres; silver medallist

800 metres; bronze medallist

1908 London – athletics

400 metres; gold medallist

18.24 George Hawkins (1883-1917)

born in Tottenham, London

After failing to qualify for the final of the 220 yards event at the AAA Championships in 1908, Hawkins was a surprise winner in the 200 metres at the Olympics trials, which earned him a place in the British team at the 1908 Olympics.

Hawkins won his first heat in the 200 metres event and, with a time of 22.6 seconds, his semi-final heat; however, in the final, he was unable to match his time in the semi-finals, which would have been the winning time and instead finished fourth, to miss out on the medals.

During the War, Hawkins served as a gunner with the Royal Garrison Artillery. He was killed in action on 22nd September 1917 during the Third Battle of Ypres, when a shell exploded in the doorway of a dugout while he was on outpost duty. He was buried at Bard Cottage Cemetery in West-Vlanderen in

Belgium; at the time of his death Hawkins was 33, leaving a widow and five children.

18.25 Harold Hawkins (1886-1917)

born in Finchley, London

Hawkins represented Great Britain in four shooting events at the 1908 Olympics; one of the events was a team event and the other three individual events.

The team event was the free rifle event, involving six team members shooting from three positions over a distance of 300 yards; the individual events were all small-bore rifle events, the first shooting in a prone position over 50 and 100 yards, the second shooting at a disappearing target over 25 yards and the third shooting at a moving target over 25 yards.

Although Great Britain won all three medals in the moving target event, Hawkins was not one of the medal winners, finishing in joint 19th position. He fared better in the prone position event, coming 8th, but his best result was in the disappearing target event, in which Great Britain again won all three medals, with Hawkins taking the silver medal. In the team event in which Hawkins took part, the team was 6th.

In the War, Hawkins was reported missing between Bullecourt and Croisilles near Arras in France; he was last seen, having been wounded, lying in a very forward position, which had to be abandoned. It is recorded that he died, at the age of 30, in Arras on 16th June 1917.

OLYMPIC APPEARANCE

1908 London – shooting

team free rifle

small bore, prone position

small bore, disappearing target; silver medallist

small bore, moving target

18.26 George Hutson (1889-1914)
born in Lewes, Sussex

Hutson competed in two events at the 1912 Olympics, the 5,000 metres and the team 3,000 metres. In the 5,000 metres event, Hutson took the bronze medal, the gold medal being won by the Finn Hannes Kolehmainen in a new world record time; the silver medal was won by the Frenchman Jean Bouin, who was also killed in the War (see Chapter 20.4.4) and who also recorded a time quicker than the previous world record.

In the 3,000 metres team event, in which the times of the fastest three in the team were taken to produce the team score, Hutson picked up a second bronze medal, with team-mates Joe Cottrill and Cyril Porter.

Hutson was a regular soldier, having joined the Royal Sussex Regiment in 1908. By the start of the War, Hutson had reached the rank of sergeant; he was killed in action at the age of 24 on 14th September 1914, just five weeks after Britain entered the War, at the Battle of the Marne; his remains were never recovered and he is commemorated at the La Ferte-sous-Jouarre Memorial in France.

18.27 Frederick Kelly (1881-1916)
born in Sydney

After attending Sydney Grammar School, Kelly went to Eton College before winning a music scholarship to Oxford University. Whilst at university, Kelly took up sculling and won the Diamond Challenge Sculls at Henley in 1902. In 1903, Kelly rowed for Oxford in the Boat Race and, later that year, retained his Henley Diamond Challenge Sculls title.

After graduating, Kelly composed music and performed as a musician; he also continued rowing, joining the Leander Club and was in the Leander crews which won the Grand Challenge Cup at Henley in 1903, 1904 and 1905, as well as the Stewards' Challenge Cup in 1906.

Kelly won a third Diamond Challenge Sculls title in 1907 and, a year later, he was a member of the Leander eight picked to represent Great Britain in the coxed eights at the Olympics. Kelly, in the Leander boat, which also included Gilchrist Maclagan (see Chapter 18.35) and Ronald Sanderson (see Chapter 18.45) won the gold medal for Great Britain.

Kelly gave up rowing after the 1908 Olympics; in his book
A History of Rowing, published in 1956, Hylton Cleave
commented that, to many, Kelly as an oarsman was "the greatest
amateur stylist of all time".

When war broke out, Kelly volunteered for service with the
Royal Naval Volunteer Reserve. In February 1915, Kelly was
aboard the Grantully Castle, bound for Gallipoli; on board with
him was the poet Rupert Brooke. En route, Brooke became
seriously ill when a mosquito bite became infected and, whilst
Brooke was on his death bed, Kelly composed, as a tribute to
Brooke, "Elegy for String Orchestra: In Memoriam Rupert
Brooke"; Kelly was one of the six who buried Brooke on the
island of Skyros.

Kelly was wounded twice during the Gallipoli Campaign and
was awarded the Distinguished Services Cross for conspicuous
gallantry during the evacuation from Gallipoli in January 1916.
After spending time on leave in England, Kelly was sent to
France; as the Battle of the Somme was coming to an end, Kelly
was shot when leading the charge rushing against a German
machine gun post. He died on 16th November 1916 at the age
of 35, at Beaucourt-sur-Court and was buried at the Martinsart
British Cemetery in France.

OLYMPIC APPEARANCE

1908 London – rowing

coxed eights; gold medallist

18.28 Paul Kenna (1862-1915)

born in Liverpool in 1862.

After being educated at Stonyhurst College, Kenna had a distinguished military career, being decorated with the Victoria Cross and the Distinguished Service Order. He first served with the 2nd West India Regiment and, whilst in India, became a top-rated polo player. Kenna then transferred to the 21st Hussars.

During the Sudan Campaign in 1898, Kenna was a captain with the 21st Lancers (Empress of India's) Cavalry Regiment and was awarded the Victoria Cross; the account of the deed which earned him the VC reads as follows: "On 2nd September 1898 at the Battle of Khartoum Sudan, when a major of the 21st Lancers was in danger, as his horse had been shot in the charge, Captain Kenna took the major up on his own horse, to a place of safety. After the charge Captain Kenna returned to help a lieutenant who was trying to recover the body of an officer who had been killed."

After the Sudan Campaign, Kenna fought in the Second Boer War in 1899 and 1900 before commanding the Mounted Troops in the Somaliland Campaign in 1902. By 1905, Kenna had been appointed as ADC to the King.

Having proven himself an excellent horseman, both as a polo player and as a jockey winning over 300 National Hunt and Flat races, Kenna took up show-jumping later in life and led the British show-jumping team on tours to North America in 1910 and 1911. In 1912, Kenna was selected to represent Great Britain at the 1912 Olympics in three equestrian events, the individual jumping event, the individual three-day event and the team three-day event. In his view, poor preparation and training led to poor performances and, in each of the three-day events, Kenna did not finish; in the individual jumping event, Kenna fared little better, coming in 27th out of a field of 31. One of the other competitors in the three-day events was Prince Friedrich Carl of Prussia (see Chapter 20.5.23).

In August 1914, at the outbreak of war, Kenna was promoted to Brigadier-General, serving with the Nottinghamshire and Derbyshire Regiment. He was posted to Gallipoli and on 30th August 1915, whilst giving encouragement to his troops in the trenches, he was shot by a sniper and died shortly afterwards, at the age of 53, in the military hospital. He was buried at the Lala Baba Cemetery in the Gallipoli Peninsula.

OLYMPIC APPEARANCE

1912 Stockholm – equestrianism

show jumping

individual three-day eventing

team three-day eventing

MILITARY HONOURS

Victoria Cross

Distinguished Service Order

18.29 Alister Kirby (1886-1917)
born in London

After attending Eton College, Kirby went to Oxford University; whilst at Oxford, Kirby rowed in four Boat Races against Cambridge, but it was only in his final year, in 1909 when he was President of the Oxford University Boat Club, that he was in a winning crew. In his final year at Oxford, Kirby was also President of the university's Vincent's Club.

After graduating, Kirby rowed for the Leander Club and was in the Leander boat which represented Great Britain in the coxed eights and which won the gold medal at the 1912 Olympics.

On the outbreak of war, Kirby was commissioned with the London Rifle Brigade, serving as a captain. He died at the age of 30 on 29th March 1917 following an illness and was buried at the Mazargues War Cemetery in Marseilles.

OLYMPIC APPEARANCE

1912 Stockholm – rowing

coxed eights; gold medallist

18.30 Frederick Kitching (1886-1918)
born in Cockerton, County Durham

Kitching represented Great Britain in the standing long jump event at the 1908 Olympics; although local folklore has it that he won a medal, he was unplaced; the gold medal was won for the fourth time, including the Intercalated Games in 1906, by the American Ray Ewry.

Although initially an athlete who specialised in the standing jump events, Kitching also took up javelin throwing and became the first British athlete to throw the javelin distances of 120 feet, 130 feet and 140 feet.

Being a Quaker, Kitching was a conscientious objector and applied for exemption from military duties in the War;

exemption was granted on the condition that Kitching joined the Friends Ambulance Unit. After joining the Friends Ambulance Unit in April 1916, Kitching was sent to France in July 1916 where, in addition to carrying out farming duties, he spent most of his time as an orderly. On 11th August 1918, Kitching was killed when the headquarters of the Friends Ambulance Unit, located at the Hotel Pyl in Dunkirk, was hit by an enemy air raid. Kitching was 32 years old when he was killed.

OLYMPIC APPEARANCE

1908 London – athletics

standing long jump

18.31 Ivan Laing (1885-1917)
born in Hawick, Scotland

Laing was a member of one of the four British teams taking part in the hockey event at the 1908 Olympics. The four British teams consisted of an English team, a Welsh team, a Scottish team and an Irish team, Laing being a member of the Scottish team.

Two other teams also took part, a team from France and a team from Germany. In the first round, the Scottish team beat the German team 4-0 with Laing scoring two of the goals – the first of Laing's two goals was the first ever Olympic goal at hockey. In the semi-final, the Scottish team came up against the English team and lost 6-1, with Reggie Pridmore (see Chapter 18.41) scoring three of the England team's goals.

Despite refusing to play Wales, the other losing semi-finalists, in the third place play-off, Laing's team took the bronze medal for Great Britain, as did the Wales team; Great Britain also picked up the gold medal and the silver medal, with the England team beating the Ireland team in the final.

Laing's only two international games of hockey were the two he played for the Scotland team at the 1908 Olympics; after the Olympics, Laing went into partnership with his father in a hosiery business.

As well as being an international hockey player, Laing excelled at swimming and played rugby for Hawick RFC.

In the War, Laing joined the 28th Battalion, London Regiment and was gazetted to the Coldstream Guards, who he served as a lieutenant. Laing was awarded the Military Cross at the Battle of the Somme but was killed in action on 30th November 1917 at the age of 32 – he was hit by machine gun fire when his unit was taking Gouzeacourt. Laing was buried at the Metz-en-Couture Communal Cemetery.

OLYMPIC APPEARANCE

1908 London – hockey

bronze medallist

MILITARY HONOURS

Military Cross

18.32 Henry Leeke (1879-1915)
born in Stafford

Leeke was an all-round thrower in field events; whilst at Cambridge University, Leeke played in the athletics Varsity matches against Oxford in 1901, 1902 and 1903, competing in the hammer and shot events. Following in the footsteps of his father, who was also a Cambridge athletics blue and a former AAA hammer champion, Leeke was AAA hammer champion in 1906; on three occasions, he was also second in the shot event at the AAA Championships.

Leeke also tried his arm at the discus and, in 1908, set a new British record in the discus.

At the 1908 Olympics, Leeke competed in six different throwing events, the shot put, the discus, the discus (Greek style), the hammer, the javelin and the javelin (freestyle) but failed to reach the final in any of these events.

During the War, Leeke served as a lieutenant with the Royal Warwickshire Regiment. Leeke's battalion was due to depart to Gallipoli but, on the eve of their departure, Leeke was injured in action in France; instead of heading off for Gallipoli, Leeke was repatriated to England but died in the Thornhill Isolation Hospital in Aldershot from a fever on 29th May 1915, at the age of 35. He was buried at the Aldershot Military Cemetery.

OLYMPIC APPEARANCE

1908 London – athletics

discus

discus (Greek style)

hammer

18.33 Henry Macintosh (1892-1918)

born in Kelso

After attending Glenalmond College, Macintosh went to Cambridge University and, despite losing to his Oxford rival in the 100 yards event in the 1912 Varsity match, was selected for the British team in the 100 metres, 200 metres and 4 x 100 metres relay events at the 1912 Olympics.

Macintosh was eliminated in the heats for the 100 metres and 200 metres events but, in the relay event, running the second leg, won the gold medal; in the final, the German team, which had set a new world record in their semi-final heat, were disqualified when one of their sprinters failed to pass the baton within the permitted area, as had happened to the American team when racing against the British team in their semi-final heat.

In 1913, Macintosh was President of the Cambridge University Athletics Club and avenged his defeat at the hands of Oxford at that year's Varsity match. 1913 also saw Macintosh take the Scottish 100 yards title and equal the British 100 yards record in a time of 9.8 seconds.

After graduating in 1914, Macintosh served as an Assistant District Commissioner in South Africa but, once war broke out, he returned home where he was commissioned into the Argyll & Sutherland Highlanders. Whilst serving as a captain,

Macintosh died on 26th July 1918 at the age of 26, at Albert, in the Somme region, after sustaining wounds. He was buried at the Senlis French National Cemetery.

OLYMPIC APPEARANCE

1912 Stockholm – athletics

100 metres

200 metres

4 x 100 metres relay; gold medallist

18.34 Duncan Mackinnon (1887-1917)
born in London

After attending Rugby School, Mackinnon went up to Magdalen College, Oxford. Whilst at Oxford, he rowed for his college boat which won the Stewards' Challenge Cup and the Visitors' Challenge Cup at the Henley Royal Regatta in both 1907 and 1908, following which they were selected to row for Great Britain in the coxless fours event at the 1908 Olympics. After beating the Argonaut Rowing Club, representing Canada, in their first heat, the Magdalen College crew beat the Leander Club in the final to win the gold medal.

After the Olympics, Mackinnon returned to Oxford and rowed in the Boat Race against Cambridge in 1909, 1910 and 1911, winning all three races. Mackinnon also continued rowing at Henley and, with the Magdalen College boat, won the Grand Challenge Cup in 1910 and 1911.

After graduating, Mackinnon worked in his family's business in Calcutta, before returning to England at the outbreak of war, where he was commissioned into the Royal North Devon Hussars. He subsequently transferred to the Scots Guards and, whilst serving them as a lieutenant, was killed in action on 9th October 1917, at the age of 30, at the Battle of Passchendaele. His remains were never recovered and he is commemorated on the Tyne Cot Memorial near Ypres in Belgium.

OLYMPIC APPEARANCE

1908 London – rowing

coxless fours; gold medallist

18.35 Gilchrist Maclagan (1879-1915)
born in London

Gilchrist went to Eton College and Oxford University and whilst at Oxford, coxed the Oxford eight in four Boat Races against Cambridge, from 1899 to 1902. Whilst at Oxford, Maclagan was also a member of the Leander Club and coxed the Leander Boat at the Henley Royal Regatta from 1899 to 1908, winning the Grand Challenge Cup a record six times.

Maclagan was picked to cox the Leander Boat which was selected to represent Great Britain at the 1908 Olympics in the coxed eights event. The Leander boat, with Maclagan coxing, won the gold medal; alongside Maclagan in the boat were five other Old Etonians, including Frederick Kelly (see Chapter 18.27) and an Old Harrovian, Ronald Sanderson (see Chapter 18.45).

After graduating, Maclagan became a member of the London Stock Exchange; during the War, Maclagan served as a lieutenant with the Royal Warwickshire Regiment. He was killed in action on 25th April 1915, at the age of 35, at Pilckem Ridge, in Belgium, during the Second Battle of Ypres; he is commemorated at the Ypres (Menin Gate) Memorial in Belgium.

18.36 Edward Nash (1888-1915)

born in London

After attending Eton College, Nash went to the Royal Military College, Sandhurst, before joining the 16th Hussars in 1906. Nash was an all-round sportsman, who had excelled as an oarsman at school and as a middle distance runner at Sandhurst, where he was twice runner-up in the mile event at the Army Championships. After leaving Sandhurst, Nash devoted himself to riding and in 1912, he was picked to represent Great Britain at the Olympics in Stockholm. Nash competed in three equestrian events, the individual jumping event, the individual three-day event and the team three-day event. In the two three-day events, Nash did not finish in the individual event and the British team did not finish in the team event; Nash fared little better in the jumping event where he finished in 29th position.

As a regular soldier, Nash had been promoted to lieutenant in 1909. Once war had been declared, Nash was sent to France with the British Expeditionary Force and soon saw action, taking part in the retreat from Mons in August 1914, the Battles of Marne and Aisne in September 1914 and the first Battle of Ypres in October and November 1914. By October 1914, Nash had been promoted to captain, just days after being mentioned in despatches.

Nash was killed in action on 21st February 1915, at the age of 26, when the 16th Lancers suffered severe losses, including the loss of Nash, when a trench was blown up. Nash was buried at the Ypres Town Cemetery in Belgium.

Following his death, in the tribute to the fallen compiled by the Marquis de Ruvigny in his roll of honour, the following was written of Nash: "As conspicuous for dash, energy and endurance in war as in sport, he was the ideal cavalry officer and appeared to have a distinguished career ahead of him. His exuberant vitality found expression in all that he said or did, and one who knew him well observed on hearing that he had been killed "Of all the deaths in this war, his death is the hardest to realise"".

OLYMPIC APPEARANCE

1912 Stockholm – equestrianism

show jumping

individual three-day eventing

team three-day eventing

MILITARY HONOURS

Mentioned in despatches

18.37 Harcourt Ommundsen (1878-1915)

born in Alloa, Scotland in 1878, to a Norwegian father and Scottish mother.

After winning the King's Prize at Bisley, Ommundsen was selected as a member of the British team at the 1908 Olympics, taking part in the team military rifle event; the team, consisting entirely of soldiers, won the silver medal.

Four years later, Ommundsen was again selected to represent Great Britain in the team military rifle event at the 1912 Olympics, at which he also competed in the military rifle individual event, shooting from 600 metres. Ommundsen picked up his second silver medal in the team event and was placed 7th in the individual event.

During the War, Ommundsen was a lieutenant with the Honourable Artillery Company. In 1915, he co-wrote, with Ernest Robinson, the book "Rifles and Ammunition and Rifle Shooting", an authoritative book on the subject; later that year though, on 19th September, he was killed in action near Ypres at the age of 36. He was buried at the Brandhoek Military Cemetery in Belgium.

OLYMPIC APPEARANCES

1908 London – shooting

team military rifle; silver medallist

1912 Stockholm – shooting

individual military rifle

team military rifle; silver medallist

18.38 Alan Patterson (1886-1916)

born in Deal, Kent

Patterson was a middle-distance runner who was the AAA champion over 440 yards in 1909, when he won a run-off after the first race had ended in a dead heat. At the time, Patterson was already a regular soldier, having passed out from Woolwich; as a soldier, Patterson took part in the Army Championships, winning the 440 yards race in 1909 and 1911 and the 880 yards race in 1908, 1909 and 1912.

Patterson competed in the 400 metres event at the 1908 Olympics but, after coming second in his heat, failed to qualify for the semi-finals. Four years later, Patterson was again picked to represent Great Britain at the Olympics, this time in the 400 metres event and the 800 metres event; as had been the case four years earlier, Patterson failed to get beyond the first round of heats in the 400 metres event and the 800 metres event at the 1912 Olympics.

During the War, Patterson served as a captain with the Royal Artillery. Patterson was killed in action just two days after his 30th birthday on 14th March 1916 at Vermelles in France and buried at the Fosse 7 Military Cemetery nearby.

OLYMPIC APPEARANCES

1908 London – athletics

400 metres

1912 Stockholm – athletics

400 metres

800 metres

18.39 William Philo (1882-1916)

born in London

Philo represented Great Britain in the middleweight boxing event at the 1908 Olympics. After winning his first fight against his compatriot Arthur Murdoch, Philo had a bye in the second round before coming up against, and losing to, the Australian Snowy Baker in the semi-final; by reaching the semi-final, Philo won a bronze medal. Baker was a talented all-round sportsman; not only was he representing Australia at boxing at the 1908 Olympics, but he was also representing them in swimming and diving events; four years before the Olympics, he had played rugby for Australia against the touring Great Britain team. In the final, Baker lost to Britain's Johnny Douglas, another talented all-round sportsman, who not only won a gold medal at boxing at the Olympics but also played cricket for England in 23 Test matches, captaining them in 18 of them.

During the War, Philo served as a sergeant-major with the Royal Fusiliers. He was killed in action when leading his men over the top at Albert on 7th July 1916 during the Battle of the Somme. Philo was 34 years old when he was killed and his body was never recovered; he is commemorated on the Thiepval Memorial in France.

OLYMPIC APPEARANCE

1908 London – boxing

middleweight; bronze medallist

18.40 Kenneth Powell (1885-1915)

born in Hampstead

Powell went to Rugby School and Cambridge University. At school, Powell had captained the first XV at rugby and reached the final of the public school rackets championships but, at university, he concentrated on his tennis and athletics. Powell competed in four Varsity athletics matches against Oxford and three at tennis. In his first year in the tennis team, he partnered the captain Tony Wilding (see Chapter 19.3.2) and, in his second and third years, took over as captain.In 1905, at the end of his first year at university, Powell played at Wimbledon and continued competing there every year, until 1913, other than in 1912, when he was taking part in the Olympics. In the singles, Powell's best performances at Wimbledon came in 1913, when he reached the quarter-finals; in the doubles, his best years were with his Canadian partner Robert Powell (see Chapter 19.2.4) with whom he reached the semi-finals in 1909 and the final in 1910, losing out to his former university partner Tony Wilding and Major Ritchie. Powell also took part in the mixed doubles at Wimbledon in 1913 with Olive Manser, but they lost in the second round to Cecil Parke and Ethel Larcombe, who a year later went on to win the Wimbledon mixed title.

In 1908, the year in which he won the Queen's Club Championships and the Swedish Covered Court Championships, Powell represented Great Britain at the Olympics, both in the singles and doubles tennis events and in the 110 metres hurdles event. In the tennis events, Powell did not get beyond the first round in the singles but, in the doubles, just missed out on a bronze medal when he and his partner lost in the quarter-finals; in the hurdles event, Powell was eliminated in his first round heat.

Four years later, Powell was again selected to represent Great Britain at the Olympics in the 110 metres hurdles event; Powell made it through to the final and, after taking an early lead in the race, finished in 5th place.

After graduating, Powell joined the family business of leather factors in London. In the War, Powell served as a private with the Honourable Artillery Company. He was killed on 18th February 1915, at the age of 29, when he was hit by a bullet near Ypres; he was buried at Loker Churchyard in Belgium.

OLYMPIC APPEARANCES

1908 London – tennis

singles

doubles

athletics

110 metres hurdles

1912 Stockholm – athletics

110 metres hurdles

18.41 Reggie Pridmore (1886-1918)
born in Edgbaston, Birmingham

Pridmore played inside-left for Coventry at hockey and represented England on 19 occasions between 1908 and 1913. He was a member of the England team which was one of the four teams representing Great Britain at the 1908 Olympics and ended the tournament as a gold medallist and the leading goalscorer. In the first round, the England team representing Great Britain beat France 10-1, with Pridmore scoring three goals; in the semi-final, they beat the Scottish team representing Great Britain 6-1, with Pridmore scoring three more goals; and, in the final, they beat the Irish team representing Great Britain 8-1, with Pridmore scoring four of the goals.

Although he was still playing hockey for England in 1912 when the Olympics in Stockholm were held, Pridmore was not able to repeat his performances at those Games because hockey had been dropped as an Olympic event before being re-instated in 1920.

Pridmore was also an accomplished cricketer who played in the Minor Counties Championships for Hertfordshire in 1902 and 1903. He later played for Warwickshire as a middle-order batsman, playing in 10 County Championship matches for them in 1909, three in 1910 and one in 1912; in his 14 matches, he scored a total of 315 runs at an average of 12.60, with a top score of 49.

In the War, Pridmore served as a major with the Royal Horse and Field Artillery. Pridmore was awarded the Military Cross during the Battle of the Somme for providing vital intelligence on enemy activity; his citation read "he displayed great coolness under fire when his observation point was heavily shelled. Both he and his look-out man were partly buried, but he carried on and sent in valuable reports".

In 1918, Pridmore was serving in Italy when he was killed in action on 13th March 1918 as five British divisions helped Italian forces crush the Austro-Hungarian army at the Paive River near Treviso. Pridmore was 31 years old when he was killed and was buried at the Giavera British Cemetery, with the words "A most gallant sportsman and comrade" inscribed on his cross.

18.42 Thomas Raddall (1876-1918)

born in Farnborough, Hampshire

At the age of 15, Raddall joined the Royal Marines; life with the Royal Marines gave him the opportunity to become a leading shot. After competing at Bisley from 1905, Raddall was selected as a member of the British team taking part in the free rifle event, shooting from standing, kneeling and prone positions over 300 metres, at the 1908 Olympics. The Great Britain team came 6th out of the nine teams competing.

In 1913, Raddall emigrated to Canada. When war broke out, Raddall served with the 8th Battalion, Canadian Infantry, Manitoba Regiment. Raddall was wounded in 1915 at the Second Battle of Ypres but returned to the front later that year.

In 1918, Raddall was awarded the Distinguished Service Order for bravery and outstanding service. He was killed in action when hit by machine gun fire on 9th August 1918 at Meharicourt during the Battle of Amiens; Raddall was 41 years old when he was killed and was buried at the Manitoba Cemetery in Caix, France.

OLYMPIC APPEARANCE

1908 London – shooting

team free rifle

MILITARY HONOURS

Distinguished Service Order

18.43 John Robinson (1885-1916)

born in Malvern, Worcestershire

After attending Radley College, Robinson went to Oxford University and played in four hockey Varsity matches against Cambridge, from 1906 to 1909. In the first three of these matches, he played against his twin brother Laurence, who captained the Cambridge team in 1908; a year later, John was captain of the Oxford team and in 1912, a third brother, Hugh, captained the Cambridge team in the same fixture.

Whilst still at university, Robinson was picked as a member of the England hockey team representing Great Britain at the 1908 Olympics. The England team which included Reggie Pridmore (see Chapter 18.41) won the gold medal for Great Britain. In total, Robinson played nine times for England; his twin also played three times for England but not at the Olympics.

After graduating, Robinson became a teacher. By the start of the War, Robinson was a captain with the Prince of Wales's (North Staffordshire Regiment). After receiving a mention in despatches and being awarded the Military Cross and after having taken part in the

Gallipoli Campaign, Robinson was wounded in action at Al Hannah in Mesopotamia in 1916; he was transferred back to England but died from his wounds on 23rd August 1916 at Roehampton in London, at the age of 31. He was buried at the Great Malvern Cemetery.

OLYMPIC APPEARANCE

1908 London – hockey; gold medallist

MILITARY HONOURS

Mentioned in despatches

Military Cross

18.44 Patrick Roche (1886-1917)

born in Cork, Ireland

Roche was the 220 yards Gaelic AA Champion in 1906; a year later, he ran the 100 yards in 10.2 seconds, his fastest time over this distance and was the Irish AAA Champion over 100 yards and 200 yards. Roche retained his Irish AAA title over 100 yards in 1908 and 1909 and, on three occasions, won the 110 yards event for Ireland in its athletics fixture against Scotland.

Roche was picked as a member of the Great Britain team for the 1908 Olympics for both the 100 metres event and the 200 metres event. In both events, Roche won his first heat but lost out in the semi-finals; in the case of the 200 metres event, he lost in the semi-final to George Hawkins (see Chapter 18.24) despite recording the same time as him.

In the War, Roche served as a lieutenant with the Royal Engineers and was awarded the Military Cross. The exact circumstances and date of his death are uncertain; however, it is reported that he was killed in action in Mesopotamia and that he was killed either on 7th June 1917 or 25th August 1917. He would have been 30 years old when he died.

OLYMPIC APPEARANCE

1908 London – athletics

100 metres

200 metres

MILITARY HONOURS

Military Cross

18.45 Ronald Sanderson (1876-1918)
born in Uckfield, Sussex

After attending Harrow School, Sanderson went to Cambridge University; despite never having rowed before going up to university, Sanderson rowed for Cambridge against Oxford in the Boat Race in 1899 and 1900; Sanderson was in the winning boat on both occasions. Sanderson also rowed for the Leander Club and was a member of the coxed eights boat which won the gold medal for Great Britain at the 1908 Olympics; with him in the boat were Frederick Kelly (see Chapter 18.27) and, as cox, Gilchrist Maclagan (see Chapter 18.35).
After graduating, Sanderson joined the Royal Horse

Artillery and served with them in the Second Boer War, towards the end of which he was promoted to lieutenant. In the Great War, Sanderson achieved the rank of lieutenant-colonel, serving with the Royal Field Artillery and was mentioned in despatches, as well as awarded the Chevalier, Legion of Honour by France.

In the last week of June 1916, Sanderson saw action with the 148th Brigade as they provided part of the heavy barrage ahead of the Somme offensive at the beginning of July.

In 1917, Sanderson returned to England as commandant of the Royal Artillery depot at Ripon in North Yorkshire, before returning to the front in February 1918. Two months later, he was killed in action on 17th April 1918 at the age of 41, near Ypres and buried at the Lijssenthoek Military Cemetery nearby.

OLYMPIC APPEARANCE

1908 London – rowing

coxed eights; gold medallist

MILITARY HONOURS

Mentioned in despatches

Legion of Honour

18.46 Robert Somers-Smith (1887-1916)
born in Walton-on-Thames, Surrey

Following in his father's and his brother Richard's footsteps, Somers-Smith went to Eton College and Oxford University but unlike both his father, who won a blue at athletics and his brother, who won a blue at rowing, Robert did not win a blue; instead, he rowed for the Magdalen College coxless fours boat, which won at the Henley Regatta the Wyfold Challenge Cup in 1907, the Visitors' Challenge Cup in 1907 and 1908 and the Stewards' Challenge Cup in 1908.

Following their success at Henley, the Magdalen College boat, with Somers-Smith at stroke, was selected to represent Great Britain at the 1908 Olympics in the coxless fours; the Magdalen College crew, which included Duncan Mackinnon (see Chapter 18.34) beat the Leander boat in the final to win the gold medal for Great Britain.

After graduating, Somers-Smith qualified as a lawyer.

During the War, Somers-Smith served with the 5th London Regiment (London Rifle Brigade). During the Second Battle of Ypres in 1915, Somers-Smith was awarded the Military Cross for gallantry in action as a captain. A year later, Somers-Smith took part in the assault on Gommecourt on 1st July 1916, the first day of the Battle of the Somme but was killed when he fell in action; he died one year and one day after his brother had fallen at the front in Flanders. Somers-Smith was 28 when he died; his body was never found and he is commemorated at the Thiepval Memorial in France.

OLYMPIC APPEARANCE

1908 London – rowing

coxless fours; gold medallist

MILITARY HONOURS

Military Cross

18.47 Charles Vigurs (1888-1917)

born in Birmingham

Vigurs was a member of the British Olympic teams which competed in the Team All-Around gymnastics events at the 1908 and 1912 Olympics. At the 1908 Games, the event was dominated by the Scandinavian countries with Sweden, Norway and Finland taking the gold, silver and bronze medals respectively and Denmark finishing in fourth place; however, the success of these countries came as no surprise as the system of gymnastics which was the programme for the event was the Swedish system involving no apparatus. Great Britain came in last of the eight countries competing.

Somewhat ironically with Stockholm hosting the 1912 Games, the Swedish system which had been used four years earlier was changed and, in an event in which none of the Scandinavian countries took part, Great Britain came third to win the bronze medal.

In the War, Vigurs served as a private with the Royal Warwickshire Regiment. He was killed in action on 22nd February 1917 at the age of 28 and buried at the Maroc British Cemetery at Grenay in France.

OLYMPIC APPEARANCES

1908 London – gymnastics

team all-around

1912 Stockholm – gymnastics

team all-around; bronze medallist

18.48 Arthur Wilde (1883-1916)
born in Paris

After serving in the Second Boer War, Wilde first worked as a commercial traveller before working as a fine art dealer. He was also an accomplished shot and competed in three shooting events at the 1908 Olympics; all three events were shooting with a small-bore rifle, the first shooting from a prone position over 50 and 100 yards, the second shooting at a disappearing target from 25 yards and the third shooting at a moving target from 25 yards. In the event shooting from a prone position, Wilde finished in joint 10th position in a field of 20, with other British competitors taking the top nine positions; in the event shooting at a disappearing target, Wilde finished in 6th position out of the 22 competitors, with other Britons taking the first five positions; and, in the event shooting at a moving target, Wilde also came in in joint 10th position out of a field of 21, with Great Britain again dominating this event by taking the top five positions.

At the beginning of the War, Wilde enlisted with the London Regiment (Queen Victoria's Rifles) and was posted to France in November 1914. In April 1915, Wilde was commissioned into the 1st Battalion, Hampshire Regiment, although some of the official records suggest he served with the North Staffordshire Regiment. He was killed in action on 21st January 1916 at the age of 33 and buried at the Arras Memorial in France.

OLYMPIC APPEARANCE

1908 London – shooting

small bore, prone position

small bore, disappearing target

small bore, moving target

18.49 Edward Williams (1888-1915)

born in Honiton, Devon

After leaving Eton College, Williams went to Cambridge University and rowed for them against Oxford in the 1908, 1909 and 1910 Boat Races. At the end of his first year at university, Williams, along with six others of the Cambridge crew, including Oswald Carver (see Chapter 18.8) and the cox which won the 1908 Boat Race were selected to represent Great Britain at the 1908 Olympics in the coxed eights event; the last member of the crew was the 1907 President of the Cambridge University Boat Club, Henry Goldsmith (see Chapter 18.22). The Cambridge boat came third to win the bronze medal for Great Britain.

As well as rowing for Cambridge, Williams also rowed for the Leander Club and, in 1909 with Banner Johnstone, won the Silver Goblets & Nickalls' Challenge Cup for coxless pairs at the Henley Regatta.

After graduating, Williams was appointed as a colonial administrator in North-Western Rhodesia before returning to fight in the War, in which he served as a lieutenant with the Grenadier Guards. Williams was killed in action on 12th August 1915 at the age of 27 near Bethune, in France; he was buried at the St. Venant Communal Cemetery near to where he died.

OLYMPIC APPEARANCE

1908 London – rowing

coxed eights; bronze medallist

18.50 Arthur Wilson (1886-1917)

Arthur Wilson was a member of the rugby team representing Great Britain at the 1908 Olympics; the British team was represented by Cornwall, the 1908 county champions. After the withdrawal of France who were the defending Olympic champions, there were only two teams left in the competition, a team from Australasia and the Cornish team representing Great Britain. With only two teams taking part, the British team were guaranteed the gold or silver medal but had to be content with the silver medal after losing the final 32-3.

Wilson was also played rugby for England and is covered in Chapter 8.27.

OLYMPIC APPEARANCE

1908 London – rugby

silver medallist

18.51 Harold Wilson (1885-1916)

born in Horncastle, Lincolnshire

Wilson was a Hallamshire Harrier and, in 1908, was the first man to run the 1,500 metres in under four minutes. That same year he was the AAA mile champion, which led him to being selected to represent Great Britain at the 1908 Olympics, running in the 1,500 metres event and the three mile team event.

In the 1,500 metres event, Wilson was unable to match his world record-breaking title of 3 minutes 59.8 seconds but his time of 4 minutes 3.6 seconds was good enough to win him the silver medal for Great Britain. In the team three mile event, Wilson finished in fifth place, but his contribution was enough to secure the gold medal for the British team.

A year after the Olympics, Wilson turned professional, which saw him competing in races across North America, South Africa and Australia.

Little is known about Wilson's experiences in the War beyond the fact that he was killed in action in France on 7th July 1916, at the age of 31.

OLYMPIC APPEARANCE

1908 London – athletics

1,500 metres; silver medallist

team three mile; gold medallist

18.52 Herbert Wilson (1875-1917)

born in St Kilda, Victoria, Australia

Wilson was educated at Eton and Oxford University; soon after graduating, he joined the Sherwood Rangers (Nottinghamshire Yeomanry). At the outbreak of the Second Boer War in 1899, Wilson volunteered to serve in South Africa and, whilst serving there, was twice mentioned in despatches and awarded the DSO for gallantry whilst defending posts during the Boer attack on Lichtenburg.

Wilson was a member of the Hurlingham Committee, the governing body of polo. He played polo at the nearby Roehampton club and was a member of the Roehampton polo team which represented Great Britain at the 1908 Olympics; Wilson's Roehampton team beat the Hurlingham team also representing Great Britain in the first round 4-2 and an Ireland team, also representing Great Britain, in the final round 8-3, to win the gold medal.

During the War, Wilson served as a captain with the Royal Horse Guards. He was killed in action on 11th April 1917 at the age of 42 when attempting to capture Monchy-le-Preux during the Battle of Arras; he was buried at the Faubourg d'Amiens Cemetery in Arras.

OLYMPIC APPEARANCE

1908 London – polo

gold medallist

MILITARY HONOURS

Distinguished Service Order

Mentioned in despatches (twice)

18.53 Richard Yorke (1885-1914)
born in Kensington, London

Yorke represented Great Britain at both the 1908 Olympics and the 1912 Olympics. At the 1908 Games, he ran in the 3,200 metres steeplechase event but was disqualified in the first round heat, which was won by his compatriot

Arthur Russell, who went on the win the gold medal for Great Britain.

Four years later, Yorke was running in flat, rather than jumping, events, representing Great Britain in the 800 and 1,500 metres events; in neither event did Yorke get beyond the first heats.

In the War, Yorke served as a sergeant with the London Regiment (London Scottish). Following a request from the French for urgent help to put the German line further back in Arras, Yorke's regiment was transferred to France but Yorke was killed in action at the culmination of the Battle of Givenchy on 22nd December 1914, at the age of 29. He was buried at the Arras Road Cemetery in Roclincourt, in France.

OLYMPIC APPEARANCES

1908 London – athletics

3,200 metres steeplechase

1912 Stockholm – athletics

800 metres

1,500 metres

CHAPTER 19
COMMONWEALTH OLYMPIANS

19.1 Australia

19.1.1 Cecil Healy (1881-1918)
born in Sydney

Healy won his first Australian swimming title in 1905, when he won the 110 yards freestyle in a time of 58.2 seconds, to equal the world record. Healy went on to win the title a second time a year later, a third time in 1908 when he broke the world record with a time of 57.2 seconds, and again in 1909 and in 1910.

In 1906, Healy was one of the five athletes chosen to represent Australia at the Intercalated Games in Athens; at the Games, Healy took part in the 100 metres freestyle event, the 400 metres freestyle event and the one mile freestyle event. Healy did not finish in the one mile event and only came 6th in the 400 metres event but won the bronze medal in the 100 metres event.

After the 1906 Games, Healy toured Europe, winning the 220 yards English Amateur Swimming Association title.

A lack of available funding prevented Healy competing at the 1908 Olympics but, for the 1912 Games in Stockholm, Australia and New Zealand combined forces to send a team representing Australasia; the team included Healy who competed in the 100 metres freestyle event, the 400 metres freestyle event and the 4 x 200 metres freestyle relay event.

Although Healy set a new world record in his heat in the 400 metres event, his world record was subsequently beaten and he finished in 4th place. In the 100 metres event, Healy won the silver medal but the fact that he only won the silver, and not the gold, was in part down to his own intervention when the US competitors missed their semi-final heats; Healy argued in their favour and, as a result, the Americans were allowed to run an additional qualification race, thereby allowing Duke Kahanamoku the opportunity to go on and win the gold medal for the USA.

In the 4 x 200 metres relay event, Healy and his Australasian team mates broke a new world record in winning the gold medal.

As had been the case in 1906, competing at the 1912 Games allowed Healy to tour Europe once the Games were over and whilst touring, he broke another world record, over 220 yards, by more than three seconds.

Healy was a pioneer of the Australian crawl swimming stroke and, as well as being a champion swimmer, was also an accomplished surfer and water polo player; he was a founder member of Manly Surf Club and, for his role in saving many lives from the waters around Manly, was awarded a silver medal from the Royal Humane Society.

In 1915, Healy volunteered for service with the Australian Defence Force. He served as a quartermaster sergeant in Egypt and France before being sent to England for officer training; after training, Healy became a second lieutenant in the 19th Sportsman's Regiment.

Leading his men into battle for the first time on 29th August 1918, Healy was killed by machine gun fire attempting to storm a German stronghold at Mont St Quentin at the Somme battlefield in France; he was 36 when he died and was buried at the Assevillers New British Cemetery in France.

19.1.2 Keith Heritage (1882-1916)

born in Launceston, Tasmania

Heritage was a member of the Sydney Rowing Club and was picked as one of the squad of 12 to represent Australasia in the coxed eights at the 1912 Olympics. The squad included an eight from the Sydney Rowing Club and, before arriving in Stockholm, the Sydney Rowing Club, with Heritage on board, had rowed at the Henley Regatta, winning the Grand Challenge Cup.

At the Olympics though, Heritage was controversially dropped from the boat in favour of Hugh Ward, who was not a member of the Sydney Rowing Club but based at Oxford in England on a Rhodes Scholarship; Heritage therefore found himself only being a reserve for the boat. The change did not bring any success to the Australasian eight as they lost their quarter-final heat to the Leander boat representing Great Britain, the boat they had beaten only weeks earlier in the final at Henley. Ironically, as a member of his Oxford College boat, Ward had rowed against Heritage at Henley, but lost in the semi-final; in winning the silver medal for Great Britain, Ward's College boat, without him on board, also enjoyed more success at the 1912 Olympics than the Australasian boat with Ward on board.

Heritage is credited as being the first Australian volunteer to enlist when war broke out in August 1914. After serving in Papua New Guinea in 1914, Heritage was sent to Gallipoli in August 1915 and was one of the last to be evacuated from the Gallipoli peninsula in December 1915.

In June 1916, Heritage was awarded the Military Cross for leading a successful raid on enemy trenches. A month later, on 26th July 1916, he was killed in action at the Battle of Pozieres, one of the battles fought during the Battle of the Somme. Heritage was just one of 23,000 Australians to lose their lives between 23rd July and 3rd September 1916 at the Battle of Pozieres; the Australian casualties are commemorated at the Australian War Memorial at the Windmill site at Pozieres, a place described by the historian Charles Bean as being "more densely sown with Australian sacrifice than any other place on earth."

Heritage would have been 33 or 34 when he died.

OLYMPIC APPEARANCE

1912 Stockholm – rowing

coxed eights

19.1.3 Claude Ross (1893-1917)

born in Caulfield, Victoria

Ross worked as a travelling engineer who paid his own way to represent Australasia at the 1912 Olympics. Competing in the 400 metres event, he did not get beyond the round one heats.

In August 1914, Ross enlisted in the Australian Field Artillery and was amongst the first contingent from Australia to be sent to war. After being involved in the landings at and evacuation of Gallipoli, he was selected for a commission with the British Royal Flying Corps, with whom he served in France as a second lieutenant after his discharge from the Australian Imperial Force.

Ross was killed in action in the skies over France on 17th August 1917, at the age of 24; he is commemorated at the Arras Flying Services Memorial in France.

OLYMPIC APPEARANCE

1912 Stockholm – athletics

400 metres

19.2 Canada

19.2.1 Alex Decoteau (1887-1917)
(sometimes spelt Decouteau)
born on the Red Pheasant Indian Reserve in Saskatchewan.

Although Decoteau excelled at boxing, cricket and football at school, it was as a middle-distance and long-distance runner that he excelled most, winning numerous races in Canada. After leaving school, Decoteau joined the police force in 1909 and became the first native Indian police officer in Edmonton; by 1914, he had become Edmonton's first motorcycle cop.

Decoteau was given leave to represent Canada at the 1912 Olympics, at which he competed in the 5,000 metres event; after recording the fourth fastest time in the round one heats, Decoteau finished in sixth place in the final.

Decoteau enlisted with the Canadian Army in 1916, serving first with the 202nd Edmonton Battalion and later with the 49th Battalion. He was shipped to France in May 1917, serving in France and Flanders before being posted to Passchendaele in Belgium.

Decoteau was one of the many Canadian troops involved in the battles to take the Passchendaele Ridge, which they successfully secured on 10th November 1917. However, in doing so, 16,000 Canadian troops were killed or wounded or went missing, including Decoteau who was shot by a sniper and died on 30th October 1917; a gold watch, which had been presented to Decoteau by King George V for winning a five mile race in England, was taken from Decoteau by the sniper but recovered by Decoteau's comrades when they shot the sniper.

Decoteau was 29 when he died; his body was one of the few which was recovered and he was buried at the Passchendaele New British Cemetery.

OLYMPIC APPEARANCE

1912 Stockholm – athletics

5,000 metres

19.2.2 Jimmy Duffy (1890-1915)
born in County Sligo, Ireland

After growing up in Edinburgh, Duffy emigrated to Canada in 1911, where he worked as a tinsmith and a stonecutter.

After coming second in the 1912 Spectator Marathon, which served as a Canadian Olympic trial, Duffy was selected to represent Canada at the 1912 Olympics in the marathon. In unusually hot conditions, only 34 of the 68 starters finished the race, with Duffy finishing in fifth place; the Portuguese runner, Francisco Lazaro, was unable to cope with the conditions and died shortly after the race. Others running in the marathon at the 1912 Olympics included France's Renon Boissiere (see Chapter 20.4.2) and the Serbian Dragutin Tomasevic (see Chapter 20.9).

After the Olympics, Duffy continued running marathons, winning seven in a row, including the Boston Marathon in 1914; his first request after winning the Boston Marathon was for a cigarette and his first request after the post-race weigh-in was for a bottle of beer.

After winning the Boston Marathon, Duffy turned professional but, at the outbreak of war, he enlisted with the

Canadian Army; after joining the 91st Argyle Regiment, he transferred to the 16th Battalion of the Canadian Expeditionary Force. After a poison gas attack by the Germans on 22nd April 1915 during the Second Battle of Ypres, the 16th Battalion received orders to counter-attack under cover of night and retake a small wood which the Germans had captured earlier in the day. The faint sound of bayonet scabbards on a wire hedge alerted the Germans, who sent up a flare which exposed the Canadians' advance. Although the Canadians managed to rout the Germans from the wood, it was at a terrible cost, with only 27 out of 300 soldiers and five officers surviving. Duffy was fatally wounded and died on 23rd April 1915, within hours after being taken to a field hospital. He was 24 years old and was buried at the Vlamertinghe Cemetery in Belgium.

OLYMPIC APPEARANCE

1912 Stockholm – athletics

marathon

19.2.3 Percival Molson (1880-1917)
born in Cacouna, Quebec

One of the great-grandsons of John Molson, the founder of the Molson Brewery, Percival Molson studied at McGill University where, for three years in succession, he was named the university's best all -round athlete. He excelled in track and field events and captained the ice hockey team; as well as playing for the university ice hockey team, Molson also played for the Montreal Victorias and was a member of their 1897 Stanley Cup winning team.

In 1900, Molson set a new world record in the long jump but four years later, he was chosen to run for Canada in the 400 metres event at the 1904 Olympics in St Louis. With 10 of the 12 runners in the 400 metres event being American, the event was dominated by the Americans but, in finishing in 8th place, Molson had the satisfaction of being the highest placed of those not representing the host nation.

In the War, Molson formed an infantry company of former McGill graduates to help re-inforce the Princess Patricia's Canadian Light Infantry. On 2nd June 1916, in the Battle of Mount Sorrel, the Princess Patricia's occupied Sanctuary Wood and Molson, serving as a lieutenant, was noted to have led "a desperate and successful resistance to German attacks"; the German attacks claimed 8,430 Canadian casualties and, although he was wounded, Molson survived the attacks and was awarded the Military Cross for his efforts.

Returning to active service only weeks later, Molson was killed on 5th July 1917 when he took a direct hit from a mortar shell whilst his company was providing support on the western outskirts of Avion in France. He was 36 years old at the time and was buried at the Villers Station Cemetery in Villers-au-Bois, in France. In his will, Molson left $75,000 to pay for the costs of the football stadium named after him at McGill University.

OLYMPIC APPEARANCE

1904 St Louis – athletics

400 metres

MILITARY HONOURS

Military Cross

19.2.4 Robert "Bobby" Powell (1881-1917)

born in Victoria, British Columbia

From 1900 to 1904, Powell worked as the private secretary to the Lieutenant Governor of British Columbia. In 1904, he was a founding member of the North Pacific International Lawn Tennis Association and was elected its first secretary/treasurer. Later in 1904, he was posted to carry out government service work in Fiji.

Powell competed at Wimbledon from 1907 to 1913, in the men's singles and men's doubles events. In 1908, Powell enjoyed his most successful year in the singles, reaching the semi-finals before losing to the eventual winner Arthur Gore; a year later, he lost in the singles to his doubles partner Kenneth Powell (see Chapter 18.40) but, in the doubles, they reached the semi-final that year and the final the following year, where they lost to Major Ritchie and Tony Wilding (see Chapter 19.3.2).

Whilst in England in 1908, Powell also took part in the singles and doubles events at the 1908 Olympics. In the singles, Powell lost to Britain's George Caridia to claim joint ninth position and, in the doubles, lost to his Wimbledon partner, Kenneth Powell, to finish in joint seventh position.

Powell also represented Canada in the Davis Cup in 1913 and 1914. In 1913, he was a member of the Canadian team which reached the final which they lost to the USA; a year later, when he captained the team, the Canadian team lost to Australasia in the quarter-finals.

In the War, Powell enlisted with the 48th Battalion of the Canadian Infantry. Leading a platoon of 50 men across no-man's land during the Battle of Vemy Ridge on 28th April 1917, Powell was killed in action, at the age of 36. Only weeks before his death, Powell had written the following to his mother: "Please don't worry or be anxious about me. If I fall, I should like you to feel pride in the fact that I am trying to do my highest duty and never to mourn me. But I am confident that God will help me to come through it. But the whole thing is hell."

19.2.5 Geoffrey Taylor (1890-1915)

born in Toronto

Rowing for the Argonaut Rowing Club, Taylor was selected to represent Canada at both the 1908 Olympics and the 1912 Olympics.

At the 1908 Olympics, Taylor took part in two events, the coxed eights and the coxless fours. In the coxed eights event, the Canadian boat lost out to the Leander boat representing Great Britain in the semi-finals, which earned the Canadians the bronze medal whilst, in the coxless fours, the Canadian boat again lost to a Leander boat, in the first round; however, as only four boats were taking part in this event, losing in the first round was enough to win Taylor and the Canadians a second bronze medal.

Four years later in Stockholm, Taylor rowed in the coxed eights event; he and his Canadian colleagues were again up against a Leander boat, which beat them in a first round heat; the Leander boat went on to win the gold medal for Great Britain.

After graduating from Toronto University in 1913, Taylor went to Oxford University on a Rhodes Scholarship. However, when war broke out, he joined the 15th Battalion of the Canadian Infantry and served at the Second Battle of Ypres. On 25th April 1915, Taylor was last seen making his way to a deserted farmhouse a short distance back from the trenches; his body was never found and it is believed that he died from gas poisoning. He was 25 at the time and is commemorated at Ypres (Menin Gate) Memorial in Belgium.

OLYMPIC APPEARANCES

1908 London – rowing

coxed eights; bronze medallist

coxless fours; bronze medallist

1912 Stockholm – rowing

coxed eights

19.3 New Zealand

19.3.1 Albert Rowland (1885-1918)
born in Christchurch, New Zealand

After winning the one mile and three mile walking events at the New Zealand track and field championships in 1907,

Rowland was one of three New Zealanders to be selected as part of the team representing Australasia at the 1908 Olympics.

At the time of the Games, Rowland was working in London as a jeweller and optician. At the Games, Rowland took part in the 3,500 metres event and the ten mile event; in the 3,500 metres event, he came fifth overall but, in the ten mile event, did not get beyond the heats.

During the War, Rowland served as a second lieutenant with the New Zealand Rifle Brigade. In 1918, he was on temporary attachment to the New Zealand Cyclist Corps and, on 23rd July 1918 whilst with them, was killed by machine gun fire during an assault on the village of Marfaux, near Reims, during the Second Battle of the Marne.

Rowland was 32 when he died and was buried at the Marfaux British Cemetery in France.

OLYMPIC APPEARANCE

1908 London – athletics

3,500 metres

10 miles

19.3.2 Anthony "Tony" Wilding (1883-1915)
born in Christchurch, New Zealand

Wilding played two games of first class cricket for Canterbury, the first in 1901 and the second a year later; in his two games, he scored 60 runs at an average of 20, with a top score of 28 and took three wickets for 52 runs.

But it was at tennis that Wilding excelled; whilst at Cambridge University, he captained the tennis team and, in

1906, he won his first major titles, the Australian men's singles and men's doubles titles. A year later Wilding was a member of the Australasian team which won the Davis Cup, a competition Wilding was to win again with the Australasian team in 1908, 1909 and 1914.

The same year in which Wilding first won the Davis Cup also saw him win his first men's doubles title at Wimbledon; Wilding went on the win the Wimbledon men's doubles title three more times.

In 1910, Wilding won his first Wimbledon singles title; he retained the title in 1911, 1912 and 1913, but lost in the final in 1914 to the Australian Norman Brookes, with whom he won the men's doubles title that year.

As well as winning the Wimbledon title in 1913, Wilding also won in the same year the World Hard Court Championship title in Paris and the World Covered Court Championship title in Stockholm.

A year earlier, Wilding had taken part in the Olympics in Stockholm representing Australasia, playing in the indoors singles tennis event. After losing in his semi-final against Britain's Charlie Dixon, Wilding won the bronze medal after beating the other losing semi-finalist, Britain's Francis Lowe.

Shortly after the outbreak of war, Wilding joined the Royal Marines. In October 1914, Wilding joined the Royal Naval Armoured Car Division. After a week's leave in February 1915, Wilding returned to France in March 1915, being promoted to captain in May 1915.

On 8th May 1915, Wilding wrote what proved to be his last letter; in it he wrote, "for the first time in seven and a half months I have a job which is likely to end in my gun, myself and the whole outfit being blown to hell at any moment.

However there is a sporting chance. If we succeed, it will help our infantry no end."

The following day, Wilding was taking part in the Battle of Aubers Ridge at Neuve-Chapelle. He was in charge of a three-pounder gun; he directed the firing from early in the morning until the middle of the afternoon when he entered a dug-out for a rest. An hour later a heavy howitzer shell struck his dug-out and he was buried alive under the debris.

Wilding died that day, at the age of 31; he was initially buried at the front before he was re-interred at the Rue-du-Berceaux Military Cemetery in Richebourg-l'Avoue in France.

Wilding is considered by many to have been the greatest sportsman to have been killed in the Great War.

OLYMPIC APPEARANCE

1912 Stockholm – tennis

indoor singles; bronze medallist

19.4 South Africa

19.4.1 Ernest Keeley (1890-1918)

born in Pretoria

Keeley took part in four shooting events at the 1912 Olympics; two of his events were the individual and team free rifle events, shooting from three positions over 300 metres and the other two were the individual military rifle event shooting from three positions over 300 metres and the team military event shooting over 200, 400, 500 and 600 metres.

Keeley's best results were in the team events, his team coming fourth in the military rifle event and sixth in the free rifle event. In the individual military rifle event, he came 13th in a field of 91 and, in the individual free rifle event, 56th in a field of 84.

During the War, Keeley served as a second lieutenant with the 4th Regiment of the South African Infantry Unit. He was wounded on 19th July 1918 during an attack on Meteren in Belgium and died four days later. He was 28 years old at the time and is commemorated at the Ploegsteert Memorial to the Missing in Belgium.

OLYMPIC APPEARANCE

1912 Stockholm – shooting

individual free rifle

team free rifle

individual military rifle

team military rifle

CHAPTER 20
OTHER OLYMPIANS

20.1 Austria

20.1.1 Karl Braunsteiner (1891-1916)
born in Vienna

Braunsteiner played football as a defender for the Wiener Sportclub and was selected to represent Austria at football at the 1912 Olympics.

After beating Germany in the first round 5-1, the Austrian team lost 3-1 in the quarter-finals to The Netherlands. Because they lost in the quarter-finals, the Austrian team were allowed to compete in the Consolation competition, for teams that lost in the first round or the quarter-finals; in the Consolation competition, Austria beat Norway and Italy before losing in the final to Hungary.

Braunsteiner played in all of Austria's five matches at the Olympics and, in total, played eight times for Austria.

In the War, Braunsteiner served as a gunner in Poland, where he was captured and sent as a prisoner of war to Tashkent in Uzbekistan. Braunsteiner died on 19th April 1916 at the age of 24 whilst he was a prisoner of war, from typhoid.

OLYMPIC APPEARANCE

1912 Stockholm – football

20.1.2 Adolf Kofler (1892-1915)

born in Graz, Austria

Kofler represented Austria at the 1912 Olympics in the men's individual and team road race cycling events over a distance of 196 miles. In the individual event, Kofler finished 31st out of a field of 123 and in the team event, came 7th.

Also competing in the same events as Kofler were Britain's Bert Gayler (see Chapter 18.20) France's Joseph Racine (see Chapter 20.4.21) and Germany's Josef Rieder (see Chapter 20.5.15).

Kofler was killed in action on 13th April 1915 at the age of 23, whilst fighting on Monte Piano in the Bolzano region in Italy.

OLYMPİC APPEARANCE

1912 Stockholm – cycling

individual road race

team road race

20.1.3 Leopold Mayer (?-1914)

Little is known about Leopold Mayer, other than he represented Austria at the Intercalated Games in Athens in 1906.

Mayer was chosen for two swimming events, the first the mile freestyle event and the second the 4 x 250 metres freestyle relay. In the mile event, Mayer came 8th out of 28 starters; in the relay event, the Austrian team was one of only eight to take part and the only one not to finish.

Mayer was one of the early casualties of the War, when he was killed in action on 21st September 1914.

20.1.4 Robert Merz (1887-1914)

born in Vienna

Merz was a footballer who played as a striker for Wiener SV from 1904 to 1907 and for the Czech team DFC Prag from 1907 until 1914. He was chosen to represent Austria at the 1912 Olympics and played alongside Karl Braunsteiner (see Chapter 20.1.1) in the win over Germany in round 1 and the loss to The Netherlands in the quarter-finals; in the 5-1 win over Germany, Merz scored two of the goals. Merz also played in two of Austria's matches in the consolation tournament at the Games, the win over Norway and the loss to Hungary. Merz played a total of 13 games for Austria and scored five goals for them.

Merz was a very early casualty of the War, when he was killed in action at the age of 26 on 30th August 1914, at Poturzyn in Poland.

20.1.5 Rudolf Watzl (1882-1915)

born in Vienna

Waltz represented Austria at the 1906 Intercalated Games, as a Greco-Roman lightweight wrestler. With 12 competitors taking part in the lightweight division, the final was a three-way round-robin event between Watzl, Denmark's Carl Carlsen and Hungary's Ferenc Holuban; after Carlsen and Watzl had both defeated Holuban, they fought it out for the gold medal, with Watzl victorious after a 40 minute match.

By winning the gold medal in the lightweight division, Watzl qualified for the All-Round Greco-Roman wrestling competition, along with the winners of the heavyweight and middleweight divisions. The All-Round competition was fought out between the winners of the heavyweight and middleweight divisions, who took the gold and silver medals, with Watzl winning the bronze medal by virtue of winning the lightweight division.

In the War, Watzl was serving in Poland when he died on 15th August 1915 at the age of 33 from an illness whilst at Podkarpackie.

OLYMPÍC APPEARANCE

1906 Athens – wrestling,

Greco-Roman lightweight; gold medallist

All-round Greco-Roman; bronze medallist

20.2 Belgium

20.2.1 Herman Donners (1888-1915)
born in Antwerp

Donners was a member of the Belgian water polo team which competed at the 1908 Olympics and the 1912 Olympics.

At the 1908 Games, the Belgian team beat The Netherlands 8-1, with Donners scoring one of the goals and Sweden 8-4 before losing 9-2 to Great Britain in the final. Four years later, Donners added a bronze medal to the silver medal he had won in 1908; although the Belgian team lost 7-5 to Great Britain in the first round, they won their play-off matches to finish third. Donners played in all Belgium's matches at the 1908 Games but only in the defeat to the British team in 1912.

During the War, Donners was killed in action on 14th May 1915, at the age of 26.

OLYMPIC APPEARANCES

1908 London – water polo

silver medallist

1912 Stockholm – water polo

bronze medallist

20.2.2 Victor Willems (1877-1917 or 1918)

Willems competed in fencing events at both the 1908 Olympics and the 1912 Olympics. At the 1908 Games, he took part in the men's epee team event, winning the bronze medal as Belgium finished in third place.

At the 1912 Games, Willems took part in the individual foil and epee events and the team epee. In the individual epee event, Willems was eliminated in the first round; also competing in the individual foil and epee events were Germany's Hermann Plaskuda (see Chapter 20.5.14) and Hungary's Bela Bekassy (see Chapter 20.7.1); Plaskuda was also competing in the team epee event. In the foil event, Willems reached the semi-final but missed out on the bronze medal. However, in the team epee event, the Belgian team improved on their performance four years earlier and won the gold medal.

In the War, Willems was killed in action; some records state he was killed on 30th November 1917 and others that he was killed in 1918; depending on which record is correct, he would have been 40 or 41 when at the time.

OLYMPIC APPEARANCES

1908 London – fencing

team epee; bronze medallist

1912 Stockholm – fencing

individual epee

team epee; gold medallist

individual foil

20.3 Finland

20.3.1 Juho Halme (1888-1918)

born in Helsinki

Halme took part in the 1908 and 1912 Olympics, competing in field events. In 1908, he competed in four events, the javelin throwing event, the freestyle javelin throwing event, the shot put and the triple jump. He was unplaced in the shot put and triple jump but came sixth in the javelin throwing event and ninth in the freestyle javelin throwing event.

Four years later, in Stockholm, Halme competed in the javelin throwing event, the two-handed javelin throwing event and the triple jump; as had been the case at the 1908 Games, his best performance came in the javelin throwing event, in which he finished in fourth place; in the two-handed javelin throwing event, he came ninth and, in the triple jump, 11th.

During the War, Halme was caught up in the Finnish Civil War, which had been caused by the unrest caused on the Eastern Front following Finland's declaration of independence on 6th December 1917. Halme was killed in action in Helsinki on 1st February 1918, the sixth day of the Finnish Civil War; he was 29 when he died.

OLYMPIC APPEARANCES

1908 London – athletics

javelin

javelin (freestyle)

shot

triple jump

1912 Stockholm – athletics

javelin

javelin (two-handed)

triple jump

20.4 France

20.4.1 Louis Bach (1883-1914)
born in Paris

Bach played football for the Union des Societes Francaises de Sports Athletiques, the club which represented France at football at the 1900 Olympics in Paris. Only two other clubs competed at the Games, Upton Park FC representing Great Britain and the University of Brussels representing Belgium. The French team won the silver medal after beating the Belgian team 6-2 and losing to the British team 4-0.

In the War, Bach was killed in action on 16th September 1914 at the age of 31, at Servon-Melzicourt in the Marne region in France.

OLYMPIC APPEARANCE

1900 Paris – football; silver medallist

20.4.2 Renon Boissiere (1882-1915)

born in Amfreville-sous-les Monts in the Eure region of France

Boissiere ran in the marathon event at the 1912 Olympics; others also taking part were the Canadian Jimmy Duffy (see Chapter 19.2.2) and the Serbian Dragutin Tomasevic (see Chapter 20.9).

In unusually warm weather, Boissiere was one of the 34 finishers out of 68 starters; he finished in 13th position in a time of 2 hours 51 minutes 6.6 seconds, just over 14 minutes behind the winner.

In the War, Boissiere was killed in action on 25th September 1915 at the age of 33, at Ville-sur-Tourbe in France.

OLYMPIC APPEARANCE

1912 Stockholm – athletics

marathon

20.4.3 Henri Bonnefoy (1887-1914)

born in Le Tremblois, in the Haute-Saone region in East France

Bonnefoy took part in the 1908 Olympics, competing in the small-bore rifle individual and team events, shooting from a prone position over 50 and 100 metres.

In the individual event, Bonnefoy came 19th, in second last place but, in the team event, with only three countries competing, Bonnefoy and the French team were guaranteed a medal and duly won the bronze.

Bonnefoy was killed in action in Thann in the Haut-Rhin region in Alsace-Lorraine on 9th August 1914, less than two weeks after the outbreak of war. He was the first Olympian to be killed in the War and was 26 years old when he died.

OLYMPIC APPEARANCE

1908 London – shooting

small bore, prone position

team small bore; bronze medallist

20.4.4 Jean Bouin (1888-1914)

born in Marseilles

Bouin was a middle-distance runner who competed in the 1908 and 1912 Olympics and broke a number of world records.

At the 1908 Games, Bouin took part in the 1,500 metres event and the three mile team event. In the 1,500 metres event, Bouin failed to get beyond the first heat, coming second to Britain's Harold Wilson (see Chapter 18.51). In the three mile team event, Bouin did not finish the final after getting drunk the night before to celebrate his win in the heats but he still won the bronze medal when France came third.

Bouin broke the world record over 3,000 metres and 10,000 metres in 1911 and, in 1912, just before the Olympics, became the international cross-country champion.

At the 1912 Games, Bouin competed in the 5,000 metres event and the cross-country. The 5,000 metres final was one of the highlights of the Games with Bouin just losing out to the Finn Hannes Kolehmainen; Bouin was winning with 20 metres to go but was finally overtaken by Kolehmainen who finished a tenth of a second ahead of Bouin. The final saw both Kolehmainen and Bouin run the distance in times of under 15 minutes for the first time and, in doing so, Kohelhmainen set a new world record for the distance. Britain's George Hutson (see Chapter 18.25) won the bronze medal.

In the cross-country race, Kolehmainen won a second gold medal, adding to the one he won in the 5,000 metres but, by not finishing, Bouin was not able to add to the silver medal he won in the 5,000 metres.

A year after the 1912 Olympics, Bouin broke another world record when he ran a distance of 19.021 kilometres in a one-hour race.

In the War, Bouin served with the 163rd Infantry. He was killed in action on 29th September 1914 at Xivray-et-Marvoisin in the Mesne region in Lorraine. One account records that he was killed by enemy fire, whilst another records that it was a result of friendly fire. He was 25 at the time.

The Stade Jean Bouin in Paris, which is the home of the French rugby club Stade Francaise, is named after Bouin.

OLYMPIC APPEARANCES

1908 London – athletics

1,500 metres

three mile team; bronze medallist

1912 Stockholm – athletics

5,000 metres; silver medallist

cross-country

20.4.5 Joseph Caulle (1885-1915)

born in Bosc-le-Hard, near Rouen

Caulle was the French champion at 800 metres in 1909 and three years later represented France at the 1912 Olympics in the 800 metres event. At the Games, Caulle came last in his round one heat and therefore did not qualify for the semi-finals.

In the War, Caulle served as a sergeant-major with the 41st Infantry Regiment; he was killed in action on 1st October 1915 at Souchez, near Arras, just five days after Souchez had been taken from the Germans by French troops.

Caulle was 30 when he died and was buried at Vimy.

OLYMPIC APPEARANCE

1912 Stockholm – athletics, 800 metres

20.4.6 Louis de Champsavin (1867-1916)

born in Asserac, near St Nazaire in the Loire-Atlantique region

De Champsavin competed in two equestrian events at the 1900 Olympics in Paris, the mixed jumping event and the mixed hacks and hunter combined event.

In the mixed jumping event, there were 16 participants, 14 from France and two from Belgium; the two Belgians won the gold and silver medals but de Champsavin had the satisfaction of being the leading Frenchman, thereby taking the bronze medal.

In the mixed hacks and hunter combined event, which involved the riders performing on the flat at a walk, a trot, a canter and a gallop and jumping over two low fences, de

Champsavin finished in 8ᵗʰ place; the gold medal was won by Napoleon Bonaparte's great-nephew Louis Napoleon Murat.

In the War, de Champsavin was the commandant of the Regiment of Chasseurs and was awarded the Chevalier of the Legion d'Honneur. Following injuries suffered in the War, de Champsavin died on 20ᵗʰ December 1916 at the age of 49 in a hospital in Nantes.

OLYMPIC APPEARANCE

1900 Paris – equestrianism

mixed jumping; bronze medallist

mixed hacks and hunters combined

MILITARY HONOURS

Legion d'Honneur

20.4.7 Georges de la Neziere (1878-1914)
born in Paris

De la Neziere took part in the first modern Olympics, in Athens in 1896. He competed in the 800 metres event but, after coming third in his heat, did not qualify for the finals.

De la Neziere was killed in action near Arras on 9ᵗʰ October 1914, at the age of 36.

OLYMPIC APPEARANCE

1896 Athens – athletics

800 metres

20.4.8 Bertrand, Count de Lesseps (1875-1918)

born in Paris

Count de Lesseps competed in the sabre individual and team fencing events at the 1908 Olympics; also competing in the individual sabre event were his brother Ismael (see Chapter 20.4.9), his compatriot Jean de Mas Latrie (see Chapter 20.4.10) and the Hungarians Jeno Szantay and Bela Zulawszky (see Chapters 20.7.6 and 20.7.9).

In the individual sabre event, Count de Lesseps qualified for the semi-finals after getting through his round 1 and round 2 pools – in his round 2 pool, he qualified with Zulawszky – but he failed to qualify for the final. In the team event, Count de Lesseps just missed out on a medal with the French team finishing in fourth place.

Count de Lesseps died in action at Cauvigny in France on 28th August 1918 at the age of 43.

Count de Lesseps had another brother, Matthieu, who competed in equestrian events at the 1900 Olympics and who survived the War.

OLYMPIC APPEARANCE

1908 London – fencing

individual sabre

team sabre

20.4.9 Ismael de Lesseps (1871-1915)

born in Paris, the older brother of Bertrand, Count de Lesseps

(see Chapter 20.4.8).

Like his brother Bertrand, de Lesseps competed at the 1908 Olympics, in the individual sabre fencing event; however, unlike his brother, he failed to get beyond his round 1 pool.

De Lesseps was killed in action during the War, at Vigny in the Val d'Oise on 30th September 1915, at the age of 43.

OLYMPIC APPEARANCE

1908 London – fencing

individual sabre

20.4.10 Jean de Mas Latrie (1879-1914)

born in Paris

Latrie competed in two Olympic Games, the 1908 Games in London and the 1912 Games in Stockholm. At the 1908 Games, he took part in the individual sabre fencing event but failed to qualify beyond his round 1 pool.

At the 1912 Games, Latrie took part in the modern pentathlon event, coming 16th out of a field of 32; not surprisingly having competed as a fencer at the 1908 Games, Latrie's most successful discipline in the modern pentathlon was the fencing, in which he came 2nd.

Latrie was killed in action in the War at Rebais in France, on 5th September 1914 at the age of 30.

1908 London – fencing

individual sabre

1912 Stockholm

modern pentathlon

20.4.11 Felix Debax (1864-1914)

born in Toulouse

Debax joined the French army in 1882 and spent his army career in various infantry regiments, often on secondment to the army's gymnastics school. He received a number of appointments during his time with the army, including becoming a knight of the Swedish Order of the Sword, a knight of the Spanish Order of Isabella the Catholic, a member of the Order of Military Medal and a chevalier of the Legion d'Honneur.

Debax took time out from his military career to take part in the 1900 Olympics in Paris, competing in the individual sabre fencing event; after progressing through the first round heats and the quarter-finals, Debax came 4th in the final, with Frenchmen taking the first seven places.

In 1913, Debax wrote a book about bayonet fighting and, by the outbreak of war, was the chef de bataillon of the 240th Infantry Regiment.

Debax was killed in action on 25th August 1914 at Saint-Maurice-sous-les-Cotes in the Meuse region of France. He was 49 when he died.

OLYMPIC APPEARANCE

1900 Paris – fencing

individual sabre

MILITARY HONOURS

Legion d'Honneur

20.4.12 Charles Devendeville (1882-1914)

born in Lesquin, the Nord region of France, close to the Belgian border

Devendeville took part in two events at the 1900 Olympics, water polo and underwater swimming. In the water polo, Devendeville was a member of the Triton Lillois team representing France; in the first round, they came up against and lost to the eventual gold medallists, the team from the Osborne Swimming Club in Manchester representing Great Britain.

The only time the underwater swimming event has been an event at the Olympics was in 1900 and contestants were judged according to the distance they swam and time they spent under water; with two points being awarded for each metre swum and one point for each second under water, the winner was the one who could cover the distance and stay under water longest in doing so.

Devendeville won the gold medal, swimming 60 metres under water in one minute 8.4 seconds, lasting three seconds longer under water than the silver medallist, Andre Six (see Chapter 20.4.24).

Devendeville died on 19th September 1914 in Reims at the age of 32, from injuries he had received in the War.

20.4.13 Rene Fenouilliere (1882-1916)

born in Portbail, Lower Normandy

After playing football for the French team US Avranches, Fenouilliere spent time in England where he played rugby but, by 1903, he was back playing football again, with Espanyol in Spain. After playing for Espanyol against Barcelona in 1903 in the Barcelona Club, Fenouilliere was loaned by Espanyol to Barcelona; he was the first Frenchman to play for Barcelona and played a total of three games for them.

After his time in Spain, Fenouilliere returned to France and played for the Parisian clubs Racing Club and Red Star.

In 1908, whilst with Red Star, Fenouilliere was selected to play as a forward for one of the two French teams which competed in the football event at the 1908 Olympics. Neither French team had any success, with Fenouilliere's team losing to Denmark 17-1 in the only game they played.

In the War, Fenouilliere fought with the French army but was killed at the front, north of Reims, on 4th November 1916; he was 34 when he died.

20.4.14 Leon Flameng (1877-1917)

born in Paris

Flameng took part in the first Modern Olympics, in 1896, representing France in four cycling events; the events were over different distances and the longer the distance the better Flameng performed.

In the shortest race, a time trial over 333 metres, Flameng finished in tied fifth place, out of eight competitors, the race being won by Flameng's compatriot Paul Masson. In the 2KM sprint race, Masson won his second gold medal but Flameng came third of the four competitors, to clinch the bronze medal.

In the 10KM race, there were six taking part and again Flameng lost out to Masson, with Masson claiming his third gold medal and Flameng finishing less than a second behind him to win the silver medal. Flameng's fourth event was over 100KM and involved the nine taking part lapping the 333.33 metre track 300 times. Assisted by pacemakers, including Masson, Flameng was the first of only two finishers and won the gold medal. The silver medal was won by Greece's Georgios Koletis who finished 11 laps behind Flameng; during the race, Koletis's bicycle had mechanical problems and Flameng sportingly got off his bike until Koletis's bike had been repaired.

In the War, Flameng served as a sergeant-pilot with the 2nd Aviation Group. He was killed on 2nd January 1917 at the age of 39 when his parachute failed to open near Eve in the Oise region to the north of Paris.

OLYMPIC APPEARANCE

1896 Athens – cycling

333 metres time trial

2KM sprint; bronze medallist

10 KM; silver medallist

100 KM; gold medallist

20.4.15 Albert Jenicot (1885-1916)

born in Lille

Jenicot played football as a forward for the French club Roubaix and played in two friendlies for France, just months before the 1908 Olympics; one of the games was a 2-1 victory over Switzerland and the other a 2-1 defeat at the hands of the Belgians.

Jenicot was picked to represent one of the two French teams playing in the 1908 Olympics but his team went out after the first round after suffering a 9-0 defeat against Denmark; in the same French team as Jenicot were Pierre Six and Justin Vialaret (see Chapters 20.4.25 and 20.4.27).

In the War, Jenicot served as an under-lieutenant with the Regiment D Infantry; he was killed in action at Vacherauville in the Meuse region of France on 22nd February 1916 at the age of 31.

OLYMPIC APPEARANCE

1908 London – football

20.4.16 Octave Lapize (1887-1917)

born in Paris

Before turning professional, Lapize competed in three cycling events at the 1908 Olympics, the tandem sprint over 2,000 metres, the 20KM event and the 100KM event. In the tandem event, Lapize won his first heat but did not progress beyond the semi-finals; in the 20KM event, Lapize made it to the final but missed out on the medals; and, in the 100KM event, of the 17 finalists, Lapize was one of the nine finishers, finishing in third place to win the bronze medal. Included amongst the finalists was Georges Lutz (see Chapter 20.4.17) who also competed in the 20KM event.

After turning professional, Lapize took part in the Tour de France each year from 1909 to 1914; although he had a stage win in 1912 and 1914, the only year he completed the Tour de France was in 1910, when he had four stage wins and was the overall winner.

Lapize also won the Paris to Roubaix race in 1909, 1910 and 1911, the Paris to Tours race in 1911 and the Paris to Brussels race in 1911, 1912 and 1913; he was also the French national cycling champion in 1911, 1912 and 1913.

In the War, Lapize served as a sergeant in the artillery and as a fighter pilot. During an aerial fight on 14th July 1917 near Flirey in the Meurthe-et-Moselle region, he was shot down and died from his injuries later that day in a hospital in Toul. He was 29 when he died.

OLYMPIC APPEARANCE

1908 London – cycling

tandem 2,000 metres

20 KM

100 KM; bronze medallist

20.4.17 Georges Lutz (1884-1915)

born in Paris

Lutz took part in the 1908 Olympics, competing in the 20KM and 100KM cycling events.

In the 20KM event, Lutz did not qualify beyond his round one heat but, in the 100KM event, he made it to the final; however, he was one of the eight finalists who did not finish the race.

Lutz was killed in action in the War, on 31st January 1915 at Bar-le-Duc in the Meuse region in France. He was 30 when he died.

OLYMPIC APPEARANCE

1908 London – cycling

20 KM

100 KM

20.4.18 Alphonse Meignant (1882-1914)

born in Paris

Meignant was a member of the French in-rigger coxed fours boat which competed at the 1912 Olympics; in-rigger coxed fours has only featured at the Stockholm Olympics in 1912, in-rigger rowing being a popular form of rowing in the Scandinavian countries. Of the six teams taking part, the French four were the only ones not from a Scandinavian country and they were heavily beaten in the first round by one of the Norwegian boats.

In the War, Meignant lost his life on 4th November 1914 at the age of 32 at Sint-Elooi in Belgium during the First Battle of Ypres.

20.4.19 Alfred Motte (1887-1918)
born in Roubaix in the Nord region of France.

Motte took part in the 1908 and 1912 Olympics, competing in the standing high jump and standing long jump events at the 1908 Games and in the standing long jump event at the 1912 Games. In the standing high jump event in 1908, Motte was competing against Alfred Flaxman (see Chapter 18.19) and finished in tied fifth place in the final; in the standing long jump event, Motte was not placed amongst the 25 athletes taking part.

At the 1912 Games, Motte made it to the final in the standing long jump event and finished in tenth place; as has been the case in the standing high jump and standing long jump events in 1908, the American Ray Ewry won the gold medal in the standing long jump event in 1912.

In the War, Motte was killed in action at Sezanne in the Marne region on 31st October 1918, just 11 days before the signing of the Armistice; he was 31 years old when he died.

OLYMPIC APPEARANCES

1908 London – athletics,

standing high jump

standing long jump

1912 Stockholm – athletics

standing long jump

20.4.20 Leon Ponscarme (1879-1916)

born in Paris

Ponscarme competed in the 1900 Olympics in Paris, in the cycling sprint event over 1,000 metres. In an event dominated by the French, with six Frenchmen in the top ten and two of them taking the gold and silver medals, Ponscarme finished in 16th place.

In the War, Ponscarme was killed in action on 24th November 1916 at the age of 37, at Verdun in the Meuse region of France.

OLYMPIC APPEARANCE

1900 Paris – cycling

1,000 metres

20.4.21 Joseph Racine (1891-1914)

born in Clichy in the Hauts-de-Seine region of France

Racine took part in two cycling events at the 1912 Olympics, the individual and team road race events over 196 miles.

In the individual event, in which 123 cyclists took part, Racine was the first Frenchman to finish, in 40th place out of the 94 finishers; in the team event, the French team came 10th out of the 15 countries competing. Three other Olympians who competed against Racine, Britain's Bert Gayler (see Chapter 18.20), Austria's Adolf Kofler (see Chapter 20.1.2) and Germany's Josef Rieder (see Chapter 20.5.15), also lost their lives in the War.

In the War, Racine was with the 113th Infantry Regiment; he was killed in action on 28th October 1914 at the age of 23, at Foret d'Argonne in the Meuse region.

OLYMPIC APPEARANCE

1912 Stockholm – cycling

individual road race

team road race

20.4.22 Maurice Raoul-Duval (1866-1916)

born in Le Pecq in the Yveslines region just to the west of Paris.

Raoul-Duval was from a wealthy Parisian family and a graduate of Cambridge University.

Raoul-Duval took part in the Paris Olympics in 1900 in the polo tournament. In his first match, he played for the Compiegne Polo Club, losing 10-0 to the Foxhunters Hurlingham team made up of British and American polo players. With the Compiegne Polo team out of the tournament, Raoul-Duval then joined the Bagatelle Polo Club, which was made up of British and French polo players, but they lost 6-4 in the semi-final, also to the Foxhunters Hurlingham team. With only five teams competing, the Bagatelle team's bye to the semi-final was enough to earn their players the bronze medal.

In the War, Raoul-Duval was killed in action on 5th May 1916 at Verdun in the Meuse region, at the age of 50.

OLYMPIC APPEARANCE

1900 Paris – polo; bronze medallist

20.4.23 Maurice Salomez (1880-1916)

born in Paris

Salomez competed at the 1900 Olympics in the 800 metres event. In his round 1 heat, he finished in fourth place and therefore failed to qualify for the final. A year later, Salomez came second in the 800 metres event at the French championships.

In the War, Salomez was killed in action on 7th August 1916 at the age of 36, at Ville-sur-Cousances in the Meuse region.

OLYMPIC APPEARANCE

1900 Paris – athletics

800 metres

20.4.24 Andre Six (?-1914)

Very little is known about Andre Six other than that he took part in the underwater swimming event at the 1900 Olympics.

Six was affiliated with the swimming club Tritons Lillois, which suggests that he probably lived in or near Lille; it is not recorded whether he was related to Pierre Six (see Chapter 20.4.25) who played football for Olympique Lille but, if they were related, Andre might well have been born in the same town as Pierre, Le Havre.

At the 1900 Olympics, 11 of the 14 contestants in the underwater swimming event were French; the gold medal was won by Charles Devendeville (see Chapter 20.4.12) and the silver medal by Six, who swam the same distance as Devendeville under water but spent three seconds less time in doing so – with points being awarded on the basis of how far the swimmers swam and how long they stayed under water, the longer it took a swimmer to cover the distance he covered the better he scored.

As with his life, other than his performance at the 1900 Olympics, little is known about Six's death other than that he was killed in action in 1914. It has been reported that he was killed on 1st April 1915 at the age of 26 but this is unlikely to be correct as it would mean he would have been only 11 or 12 years old and younger than the youngest participant at the 1900 Games, when he won the Olympic silver medal.

OLYMPIC APPEARANCE

1900 Paris – swimming, underwater; silver medallist

20.4.25 Pierre Six (1888-1916)

born in Le Havre

Six played football as a forward for the French club Olympique Lille and was selected to play in one of the two French teams which competed at the 1908 Olympics; also in the same team as Six were Albert Jenicot (see Chapter 20.4.15) and Justin Vialaret (see Chapter 20.4.27). The two French teams were, by some distance, the weakest of the six teams taking part, with Six's team losing 9-0 to Denmark in the first round; the other French team fared no better, also losing to Denmark by the score of 17-1.

In the War, Six served as a first lieutenant with the 329th Infantry Regiment. He was killed in action on 7th July 1916 at the age of 28, at Estrees-Mons in the Battle of the Somme.

OLYMPIC APPEARANCE

1908 London – football

20.4.26 Michel Soalhat (1875-1915)

born in Clermont-Ferrand

Soalhat was French champion over 800 metres and 1,500 metres, as well as in the steeplechase and cross-country. He won his first title in 1894, in the 1,500 metres and a year later retained his title as well as becoming the 800 metres and steeplechase champion; in 1896, he retained his 800 metres and steeplechase titles and won the cross-country title. 1897 saw Soalhat retain his steeplechase title but it was not until

1904 that he won back his 800 metres and 1,500 metres titles, titles he retained in 1905.

Soalhat set French records over 800 metres, 1,000 metres and 1,500 metres and, in 1906, he recorded his fastest time over 800 metres, a time of 1 minute 59 seconds. In 1906, he represented France at the Intercalated Games in Athens in the 800 metres and 1,500 metres events. At the Games, he failed to qualify beyond his first round heat in the 800 metres and, in the 1,500 metres, came fifth in his heat, thereby failing by one place to qualify for the final.

Soalhat was killed in action in the War on 25th September 1915 at the age of 39, at Saint-Hilaire-le-Grand in the Marne region.

OLYMPIC APPEARANCE

1906 Athens – athletics

800 metres

1,500 metres

20.4.27 Justin Vialaret (1883-1916)

born in Millau in the Aveyron region in the south of France

Vialaret played football as a midfielder for Club Athletique de 14eme Arondissement in Paris and was selected to play for one of the two French teams which competed at the 1908 Olympics; two others who also died in the War, Albert Jenicot and Pierre Six (see Chapters 20.4.15 and 20.4.25) were also in the same team and another Frenchman who died in the War, Rene Fenouilliere (see Chapter 20.4.13) in the other French team.

Vialaret's team lost 9-0 to Denmark in the only match they played at the Olympics.

Vialaret was killed in action on 30th September 1916 at Marcelcave in the Somme; he was 32 when he was killed.

20.4.28 Edmond Wallace (1876-1915)

born in Saint-Maur-de-Dosses on the outskirts of Paris.

Wallace took part in the individual epee fencing event at the 1900 Olympics in Paris. There were a total of 102 participants in the event, 89 of whom were French and one of whom was Wallace's brother, Richard.

Despite the heavy presence of Frenchmen in the event, the gold medal was won by the Cuban Ramon Fonst. Wallace came second in his round 1 heat to qualify for the quarter-finals, first in his quarter-final heat to qualify for the semi-finals and second in his semi-final heat to qualify for the final; in the final though, he could only manage to finish sixth out of the nine finalists and so missed out on a medal.

In the War, Wallace was wounded in action and died in Paris on 18th August 1915; he was 38 years old when he died.

20.5 Germany

20.5.1 Fritz Bartholomae (1886-1915)
born in Krefeld in the Nordrhein-Westfalen region of Germany

Bartholomae rowed in the coxed eights event at the 1912 Olympics, in the Berliner Ruderverein von 1876 boat representing Germany. After beating the Hungarian boat in the first round and the Sport Borussia Berlin boat, also representing Germany, in the quarter-final, Bartholomae's boat, with his brother Willi also in the boat, took the bronze medal after losing in the semi-final to the eventual winners, the Leander Club boat representing Great Britain.

In the War, Bartholomae was killed in action on 12th September 1915 at the age of 28.

OLYMPIC APPEARANCE

1912 Stockholm – rowing

coxed eights; bronze medallist

20.5.2 Hermann Bosch (1891-1916)
born in Ohningen am Bodensee

Bosch played football for the Karlsruhe Club and was selected to represent the German team competing at the 1912 Olympics. Bosch played in the first round match against Austria, which the German team lost 5-1. In the consolation tournament for first round losers and losing quarter-finalists, Bosch missed the game against Russia which Germany won 16-0 and in which Gottfried Fuchs scored 10 goals to equal the record scored in one game, but he did play in the game against Hungary which Germany lost 3-1; despite their win over Russia, Germany were placed in equal last place, along with Italy and Sweden, of the 11 teams taking part.

Although one report suggests Bosch died in July 1916, the official records state that he was killed in action in Brasov in Romania on 15th November 1916, at the age of 25.

20.5.3 Johannes "Hanns" Braun (1886-1918)
born in Wernfels, Spalt in Bavaria

After studying art and architecture, Braun became a sculptor who competed in the 1908 and 1912 Olympics. At the 1908 Games, he took part in the 800 metres event, the 1,500 metres event and the 1,600 metres medley relay event.

In the 800 metres event, Braun won the bronze medal but, in the 1,500 metres event, failed to qualify for the final after coming third in his heat. The 1,600 metres relay event involved the first two runners running 200 metres, the third runner running 400 metres and the final runner running 800 metres; Braun ran the final leg and made up a five metre deficit to claim the silver medal just ahead of the Hungarians.

Before the 1912 Games, Braun won a number of championships; in 1909, 1910 and 1912, he was the German champion over 400 metres and, in 1909, 1911 and 1912, he was the British AAA champion over 880 yards. He also set the world indoor record over 1,000 metres.

At the 1912 Games, Braun ran in the 400 metres, 800 metres and 4 x 400 metres relay events. In the 400 metres, Braun won the silver medal after winning his round 1 and semi-final heats; in the 800 metres event, Braun made it to the final but finished in sixth place.

At the 1912 Olympics, the format for the relay over 1,600 metres had been changed so that each of the runners ran 400 metres; however, the German team, which consisted of Braun, Heinrich Burkowitz, Max Hermann and Erich Lehmann (see Chapters 20.5.6, 20.5.8 and 20.5.10) failed to qualify for the final after losing out in their round 1 heat to the eventual winners, the team from the USA.

In the War, Braun was a fighter pilot; he lost his life in an airplane crash near Saint-Quentin in the Aisne region in France on 9th October 1918 at the age of 31. He was buried at the Vladslo War Cemetery in Belgium.

OLYMPIC APPEARANCES

1908 London – athletics

800 metres; bronze medallist

1,500 metres

1,600 metres relay, silver medallist

1912 Stockholm – athletics

400 metres; silver medallist

800 metres

4 x 400 metres relay

20.5.4 Kurt Bretting (1892-1918)

born in Magdeburg

On 6th April 1912, Bretting broke the world swimming freestyle record over 100 metres in a time of 1 minute 2.4 seconds; his record only lasted a little over three months when it was broken by the American Duke Kahanamoku.

Bretting took part in the 1912 Olympics, competing in the 100 metres freestyle and the 4 x 200 metres freestyle relay. In the 100 metres event, Bretting won his round one, quarter-final and semi-final heats but, in the final, was unable to produce his best time and finished in fourth place, the gold medal going to Kahanamoku. In the 4 x 200 metres relay, Bretting again just missed out on a medal with the German swimmers finishing in fourth place in the final.

Bretting was killed in action in the War on 30th May 1918 at the age of 25, at Merville in the Nord region of France.

OLYMPİC APPEARANCE

1912 Stockholm – swimming

100 metres freestyle

4 x 200 metres freestyle relay

20.5.5 Wilhelm Brulle (1891-1917)

born in Lippstadt

Brulle was a member of the German gymnastics team which competed at the 1912 Olympics, in the all-around gymnastics event and in the all-around gymnastics freestyle event. Only five teams competed in each event and the German team came fourth in the freestyle event and last in the other event. With Brulle in the German team were Eberhard Sorge and Alfred Staats (see Chapters 20.5.17 and 20.5.18).

Brulle was killed in action in the War on 5th August 1917, at Westende, Middelkerke in West-Vlaanderen in Belgium; he was 26 years old when he died.

OLYMPİC APPEARANCE

1912 Stockholm – gymnastics

team all-around

team all-around freestyle

20.5.6 Heinrich Burkowitz (1892-1918)
born in Berlin

Burkowitz was the German champion over 400 metres in 1911 and 1913. In between, he was selected to represent Germany at the 1912 Olympics, in the 400 metres event and the 4 x 400 metres event. In the 400 metres relay event, Burkowitz came third in his heat, so failed to qualify for the final; in the 4 x 400 metres relay, only three teams qualified for the final and, with the German team coming second in their heat and recording the second slowest time, they did not make it to the final; all four members of the relay team, the other three members being Hanns Braun, Max Hermann and Erich Lehmann (see Chapters 20.5.3, 20.5.8 and 20.5.10), were killed in the War.

Burkowitz was reported missing in action "somewhere in Belgium" in November 1918, the last month of the War. He would have been 26 years old at the time.

OLYMPIC APPEARANCE

1912 Stockholm – athletics

400 metres

4 x 400 metres relay

20.5.7 Carl Heinrich Gossler (1885-1914)
born in Hamburg

Gossler was the cox in the coxed fours boat from the Germania Ruder Club from Hamburg which represented Germany in the coxed fours rowing event at the 1900 Olympics; two of the rowers in the boat were his brothers Gustav and Oskar and a third was Waldemar Tietgens (see Chapter 20.5.19).

Following a controversy as to which boats should compete against each other in the final due to the officials changing the qualifying criteria for the final, the International Olympic Committee took the unusual decision that there should be two finals; Gossler's boat won one of the finals and the German crew each received a gold medal for the event, as did the French team which won the other final.

Gossler was only 15 when he took part in the 1900 Olympics; it was recognised that having a cox as light as possible was an advantage and it was rumoured that some of the boats recruited local Parisian boys as young as 10 years old as their coxswains.

Gossler was killed in action in the War on 9th September 1914 at the age of 29; the exact location where he was killed is unknown other than that it was in France.

20.5.8 Max Hermann (1885-1915)
born in Gdansk in Poland

Hermann was the German 400 metres champion in 1911 and 1913 and, in between, represented Germany at the 1912 Olympics in five athletics events, the 100 metres, the 200 metres, the 400 metres, the 4 x 100 metres relay and the 4 x 400 metres relay.

In the 100 metres and 400 metres events, Hermann failed to qualify beyond his first round heat and, in the 200 metres, failed to qualify beyond his semi-final heat.

The four runners in the German team in the 4 x 400 metres relay event were Hanns Braun, Heinrich Burkowitz and Erich Lehmann (see Chapter 20.5.3, 20.5.6 and 20.5.10) but they failed to qualify for the final.

The 4 x 100 metres relay event was run for the first time at the 1912 Olympics and, after winning their round one heat, the German team set the Olympic record; they followed this up with a new world record in the semi-finals to qualify for the final but, in the final, were disqualified when one of their runners failed to pass on the baton within the permitted area.

It is reported that Hermann died on 29th January 1915 at the age of 29, when he did not return from a snowshoe patrol whilst on the Eastern Front; it was also rumoured that he was killed whilst in Russian captivity.

OLYMPIC APPEARANCE

1912 Stockholm – athletics

100 metres

200 metres

400 metres

4 x 100 metres relay

4 x 400 metres relay

20.5.9 Walther Jesinghaus (1887-1918)

born in Dusseldorf

Jesinghaus was one the German gymnasts competing at the 1912 Olympics. Along with Wilhelm Brulle (see Chapter 20.5.5) he competed in the all-around gymnastics event and the all-around gymnastics freestyle event, coming fourth out of the five teams competing in the freestyle event and last out of five in the other event.

In the War, Jesinghaus was killed in action in 1918 but the circumstances of his death are unknown; he would have been 30 or 31 when he died.

OLYMPIC APPEARANCE

1912 Stockholm – gymnastics

team all-around

team all-around freestyle

20.5.10 Erich Lehmann (1890-1918)

born in Treppendorf, Thuringen in Germany

Lehmann competed at the 1912 Olympics, running in the 400 metres, the 800 metres and the 4 x 400 metres relay event. In none of his events did Lehmann qualify beyond his first round heats. In the 4 x 400 metres relay, running in the same team as Lehmann were Hanns Braun, Heinrich Burkowitz and Max Hermann (see Chapters 20.5.3, 20.5.6 and 20.5.8) all of whom also died in the War.

Although one report states that Lehmann died on 9th July 1917 after being reported as missing in action, other reports state that he was killed in action on 9th July 1918 when he would have been 27 years old. It is likely that he was killed near Berlin as he is buried at the Berlin-Neukolin war cemetery.

OLYMPIC APPEARANCE

1912 Stockholm – athletics

400 metres

800 metres

4 x 400 metres relay

20.5.11 Wilhelm Lutzow (1892-1916)

born in Esslingen am Neckar, Baden-Wurttemberg in Germany,

Lutzow swam in the 200 metres breaststroke and 400 metres breaststroke events at the 1912 Olympics; also swimming in both events were Britain's Percy Courtman (see Chapter 18.13) and Hungary's Oszkar Demjan (see Chapter 20.7.2). In the 200 metres event, Lutzow won his round one heat and came second in his semi-final heat to qualify for the final, in which he finished in second place, behind his compatriot Walther Bathe, to win the silver medal.

In the 400 metres event, Lutzow won both his round one heat and semi-final heat to find himself in the final, swimming against the same other four finalists who had been in the 200 metres breaststroke final, including Britain's Percy Courtman. However, unlike Walther Bathe who also won the gold medal in the 400 metres event, Lutzow was unable to match his performance in the 200 metres event and ended the 400 metres event in last place not having finished the race.

Little is known about Lutzow in the War other than that he was killed in action in 1916, when he would have been 23 or 24.

OLYMPİC APPEARANCE

1912 Stockholm – swimming

200 metres breaststroke; silver medallist

400 metres breaststroke

20.5.12 Georg Mickler (1892-1915)
born in Berlin

Having been runner-up at the German championships at 1,500 metres in 1911 and 1912, Mickler was chosen to represent Germany at the 1912 Olympics in the 1,500 metres event and the 3,000 metres team event. In the 1,500 metres event, Mickler failed to qualify beyond his round one heat and, in the team event, Germany came second in their round one heat and therefore failed to qualify as one of the three finalists.

In 1913, Mickler was the German champion over 800 metres and 1,500 metres and set a new world record over 1,000 metres.

In the War, Mickler was killed in action on 15ᵗʰ June 1915 at Tarnow, Malopolski in Poland; he was 22 when he died.

20.5.13 Jakob "Jacques" Person (1889-1915)

born in Saverne in the Alsace region of France

Person was born at a time when the Alsace was part of the German Empire following the defeat, in 1871, of the French in the Franco-Prussian War.

At the 1912 Olympics, Person represented Germany in the 400 metres and 800 metres events. In the 400 metres event, Person won his first round heat but did not finish his semi-final heat and therefore failed to qualify for the final; in the 800 metres event, Person failed to progress beyond his round one heat.

In the War, Person was a member of the 7ᵗʰ Thuringia Infantry Regiment; he was killed in action on 15ᵗʰ July 1915 at Vlaanderen in Belgium, at the age of 26.

20.5.14 Hermann Plaskuda (1879-1918)

Plaskuda's place of birth is not recorded but, as he was a member of the German-Italian fencing club in Berlin, it is possible he was born in or near to Berlin.

Plaskuda represented Germany in four fencing events at the 1912 Olympics, the individual epee and foil events and the team epee and sabre events; also competing in the individual epee and foil events were the Belgian Victor Willems (see Chapter 20.2.2) and the Hungarian Bela Bekassy (see Chapter 20.7.1); Plaskuda also competed against Willem in the team epee event.

In the individual epee event, Plaskuda did not progress beyond his round one heat whereas, in the individual foil event, he progressed beyond the round one heats but not beyond the quarter-finals; in the team events, Plaskuda and his team members were eliminated in the semi-finals.

In the War, Plaskuda was killed in action on 21st March 1918 at the age of 38; he was buried at the war cemetery at St Quentin in France.

OLYMPIC APPEARANCE

1912 Stockholm – fencing,

ndividual epee

team epee

individual foil

team sabre

20.5.15 Josef Rieder (1893-1916)

born in Munich

Rieder was a cyclist who represented Germany at the 1912 Olympics in the individual and team road race events over 196 miles. In the individual event, Rieder finished in 57th place out of the 94 finishers – another 29 cyclists did not finish the race; in the team event, Germany came sixth but, as Rieder's time was not one of the four fastest German times, it was not taken into account. Racing against Rieder in both events were Britain's Bert Gayler (see Chapter 18.20), Austria's Adolf Kofler (see Chapter 20.1.2) and France's Joseph Racine (see Chapter 20.4.21).

In the War, Rieder died at the Battle of Verdun on 13th July 1916, at the age of 22.

OLYMPIC APPEARANCE

1912 Stockholm – cycling

individual road race

team road race

20.5.16 Heinrich Schneidereit (1884-1915)

born in Cologne

Schneidereit attended the 1906 Intercalated Games, competing in two weightlifting events and in the tug-of-war event. In the tug-of-war event, Schneidereit and the German team beat the Austrian team in their first match and the Greek team in the final to win the gold medal.

The two weightlifting events Schneidereit competed in at the Games were the one-handed weightlifting of a dumbbell and the two-handed weightlifting of a barbell weighing 142.4 kilograms. In the two-handed event, Schneidereit was tied in third place which won him a bronze medal and, in the one-handed event, he finished in third place on his own, to add a second bronze medal to the gold he had won in the tug-of-war. Schneidereit also competed in the world weightlifting championships from 1903 to 1911, winning a total of four medals, including a gold medal in 1906.

In the War, Schneidereit served as an artillery officer; he was killed in action on 30th September 1915 at the age of 30, at Thionville in the Moselle region of France.

20.5.17 Eberhard Sorge (1892-1918)
born in Braulange, Niedersachsen in Germany

Sorge was a member of the German gymnastics team which competed in the 1912 Olympics in the all-around event and in the all-around freestyle event. Included in the same team were Wilhelm Brulle and Alfred Staats (see Chapters 20.5.5 and 20.5.18).

In the all-around event, the German team finished in fourth place out of the five countries taking part and, in the other freestyle event, last of the five competitors.

In the War, Sorge was killed in action on 6th August 1918 at Bray-sur-Somme in the Somme region of France; he was 26 years old when he died.

20.5.18 Alfred Staats (1891-1915)

born in Hondelage, Niedersachsen in Germany

Staats was a member of the German gymnastics team competing at the 1912 Olympics, in the all-around event and the all-around freestyle event. Staats was one of three members of the team to be killed in the War, the other two being Wilhelm Brulle and Eberhard Solge (see Chapters 20.5.5 and 20.5.17).

In the two gymnastics events in which Staats was taking part at the Games, only five countries were taking part and Germany were last in the all-around freestyle event and fourth in the all-around event.

In the War, Staats was stationed on the Eastern Front and killed in action on 22nd October 1915 at the age of 23, at Kolky in Ukraine.

20.5.19 Waldemar Tietgens (1879-1917)

It is possible that he was born in or near Hamburg as he rowed for Hamburg's Germania Ruder Club.

Tietgens was selected to represent Germany at the 1900 Olympics in the coxed fours and coxed eights events. In the coxed eights event, Tietgens and the German boat were one of the four finalists but finished in fourth place to miss out on the medals.

In the coxed fours event, in the boat with Tietgens were Carl Heinrich Gossler (see Chapter 20.5.7) as cox and two of Gossler's brothers. Because of the controversy about the qualifying criteria for the final, there were two separate races for the coxed fours boats, with each competing for medals and, in one of the finals, Tietgens' boat won the race to win one of the gold medals for the event.

In the War, Tietgens was killed in action on 28th July 1917, fighting at Flanders in Belgium; he was 38 years old when he died.

OLYMPIC APPEARANCE

1900 Paris – rowing

coxed fours; gold medallist

coxed eights

20.5.20 Hermann von Bonninghausen (1888-1919)

born in Bocholt in the Nordrhein-Westfalen region of Germany

Von Bonninghausen competed at the 1908 Olympics and the 1912 Olympics. At the 1908 Games, he competed in the 100 metres event and the long jump but in neither event did he progress beyond the first round heats. Four years later, at the 1912 Games, von Bonninghausen took part in the 110 metres hurdles event and, after coming through his first qualifying round, failed to progress beyond the second qualifying round to the final.

Von Bonninghausen died after the War, on 26th January 1919 in Dusseldorf at the age of 31; he died as a result of wounds he had received when he was shot in the face during the War.

20.5.21 Bernhard von Gaza (1881-1917)

born in Usedom, Mecklenburg-Vorpommern in Germany

Von Gaza competed in the 1908 Olympics, rowing in the single sculls event. After winning his first round heat and his quarter-final, von Gaza lost in the semi-final to Britain's Alexander McCulloch but, by reaching the semi-final, won a bronze medal.

In the War, von Gaza was killed in action on 25th September 1917 at the age of 36, at Langemark, West-Vlaanderen in Belgium.

20.5.22 Eduard von Lutcken (1882-1914)
born in Syke, Niedersachsen in Germany

Von Lutcken competed in the individual and team three-day equestrian events at the 1912 Olympics; the events though were not the same format as current day three-day eventing and, with participation in the events being limited to commissioned officers, the events were more a military riding event involving five disciplines, consisting of a long distance ride over 55 KM, a cross-country ride over 5 KM, a steeplechase over 3,500 metres, jumping and dressage. In the individual event, von Lutcken came 8th out of the 27 taking part. The results of the best three from each country were calculated to determine the outcome of the team event and, with Germany's three best riders being in the top eight of the individual event, they won the silver medal behind the hosts Sweden.

In the War, von Lutcken was killed in action on 15th September 1914, at the age of 31. It is not recorded where he was killed.

OLYMPIC APPEARANCE

1912 Stockholm – equestrianism

individual 3 day eventing

team 3 day eventing; silver medallist

20.5.23 Friedrich Carl, Prince of Prussia (1893-1917)
born in Berlin

Prince Friedrich Carl was a nephew of Kaiser Wilhelm I.

Prince Friedrich Carl was the first member of the Hohenzollem royal family to take part in the Olympics when he competed in the individual and team show-jumping events at the 1912 Olympics. In the individual show-jumping event, Prince Friedrich Carl finished in tied 18th place out of 31. In the team event, the results were not based upon performances in the individual event but based on a separate show-jumping event and, although Prince Friedrich Carl's performance in the team event was not taken into account as his was not one of the best three performances by members of the German team, the German team won the bronze medal. Also competing in the same show-jumping events as the Prince was Britain's Paul Kenna (see Chapter 18.28).

Prince Friedrich Carl was also an accomplished footballer who played for the SCC Berlin club.

In the War, Prince Friedrich Carl fought as an aviator between 1914 and 1917, commanding an artillery spotting unit. During a patrol on 21st March 1917, his Albatros airplane was hit in the engine by a bullet fired by Australian troops. The damage to the engine and a slight wound to his foot forced Prince Friedrich Carl to land; after landing in no man's land, Prince Friedrich Carl was severely wounded in the back when running from his airplane to the German lines; he was taken into captivity by the Australians and died from his injuries on 6th April 1917, on his 24th birthday, in the Australian hospital at Saint-Atienne in the Seine-Maritime region in France.

OLYMPIC APPEARANCE

1912 Stockholm – equestrianism

show jumping

team show jumping; bronze medallist

20.6 Haiti

20.6.1 Andre Corvington (1877-1918)

born in Les Cayes, Haiti

Corvington competed at the 1900 Olympics in the individual foil fencing event; amongst the 54 taking part in the event were 39 Frenchmen, including Felix Debax (see Chapter 20.4.11). Corvington failed to qualify beyond round one to the quarter-finals.

In the War, Corvington fought for the French. It has been recorded that he was killed in action at Reims on 13th December 1918 at the age of 41; however, as this was a little over a month after the War had ended, it is likely that he died on this date but as a result of injuries sustained before the Armistice was signed on 11th November 1918.

20.7 Hungary

20.7.1 Bela Bekassy (1875-1916)
born in Debrecan, Hungary

Bekassy competed at the 1912 Olympics in the three individual fencing events, the foil, the epee and the sabre. Also taking part in the individual epee and foil events were Belgium's Victor Willems (see Chapter 20.2.2) and Germany's Hermann Plaskuda (see Chapter 20.5.14) and, in the sabre event, his compatriot Bela Zulawszky (see Chapter 20.7.9).

In the individual epee event, Bekassy did not progress beyond round one to qualify for the quarter-finals but in both the individual foil and the individual sabre events, he made it to the final pool. In the foil event, he only won one of his bouts in the final to finish in 7th place but, in the sabre event, Hungary won all three medals and, by winning five of his seven bouts in the final pool, Bekassy took the silver medal.

In the War, Bekassy was killed in action on 6th July 1916 at the age of 40, at Volyn-Podilsk in Ukraine.

OLYMPIC APPEARANCE

1912 Stockholm – fencing

individual epee

individual foil

individual sabre; silver medallist

20.7.2 Oszkar Demjan (1891-1914)

born in Budapest

Demjan swam at the 1912 Olympics in the 200 metres breaststroke and 400 metres breaststroke events; also swimming in these events were Percy Courtman for Great Britain (see Chapter 18.13) and Wilhelm Lutzow for Germany (see Chapter 20.5.11).

In the 200 metres event, Demjan won his first round heat but did not make it beyond the semi-finals heats; in the 400 metres event, Demjan was disqualified in his first round heat for failing to touch the wall with both hands at one of the turns.

Demjan was killed in action during the War, on 4th September 1914 at the age of 22, at Sianky in Ukraine.

OLYMPIC APPEARANCE

1912 Stockholm – swimming

200 metres breaststroke

400 metres breaststroke

20.7.3 Lajos Gonczy (1881-1915)

born in Szeged, Hungary

Gonczy competed in high jump events at the 1900, 1904 and 1906 Games, competing in the high jump at all three Games and in the standing high jump at the 1904 and 1906 Games.

In the high jump events, Gonczy won the bronze medal at the 1900 Games; four years later in St Louis, Gonczy finished in fourth place to miss out on the medals but, in Athens in

1906, achieved his best result in winning the silver medal. In the standing high jump events, he finished in fifth place in both St Louis and Athens.

Gonczy was killed in action on 4th December 1915 at the age of 34, fighting in the area around Doberdo del Lago in Gorizia in Italy.

<u>*OLYMPİC APPEARANCES*</u>

1900 Paris – athletics

high jump; bronze medallist

1904 St Louis – athletics

high jump

standing high jump

1906 Athens – athletics

high jump; silver medallist

standing high jump

20.7.4 Istvan Mudin (1881-1918)
born in Bekes, Hungary

Mudin competed at the 1906 Intercalated Games in Athens and the 1908 Games in London. At the 1906 Games, he took part in the standing long jump, the shot put, the discus throw, the discus throw (Greek style), the javelin and the pentathlon. His best results were in the discus throw (Greek style) in which he won the bronze medal and the pentathlon in which he won the silver medal.

Two years later, Mudin competed in the shot put, the discus throw (Greek style), the hammer and the javelin, his best result being in the discus throw (Greek style) in which he finished in seventh place.

Mudin was killed in action in the War on 22ⁿᵈ July 1918 at the age of 36, at Dosodelfine in Italy.

OLYMPİC APPEARANCES

1906 Athens – athletics

standing high jump

discus

discus (Greek style); bronze medallist

javelin

shot

pentathlon; silver medallist

1908 London – athletics

shot

discus (Greek style)

hammer

javelin

20.7.5 Arpad Pedery (1891-1914)

born in Budapest

Pedery was a member of the Hungarian team which competed at the 1912 Olympics in the team all-around gymnastics event; also competing in the same event for the German team were Wilhelm Brulle, Eberhard Sorge and Alfred Staats (see

Chapters 20.5.5, 20.5.17 and 20.5.18) Only five teams took part and the Hungarian team came second to win the silver medal.

In the War, Pedery joined the Austro-Hungarian army; he was killed in action on 21st November 1914 at the age of 23, at Luzsek in Galicia, in what is now a part of Ukraine.

OLYMPIC APPEARANCE

1912 Stockholm – gymnastics

team all-around; silver medallist

20.7.6 Jeno Szantay (1881-1914)

born in Limanowa, Poland

Szantay competed in the 1908 Olympics in the individual sabre fencing event; others who competed in this event were his compatriot Bela Zulawszky (see Chapter 20.7.9) and the Frenchmen Bertrand, Count of Lesseps, Ismael de Lesseps and Jean de Mas Latrie (see Chapters 20.4.8, 20.4.9 and 20.4.10).

In an event dominated by the Hungarians, Szantay came fourth out of 76 taking part, to just miss out on a medal.

In the War, Szantay was killed in action at the Battle of Limanowa on 11th December 1914, at the age of 33.

OLYMPIC APPEARANCE

1908 London – fencing

individual sabre

20.7.7 Amon Ritter von Gregurich (1867-1915)

born in Vienna

Von Gregurich competed in the 1900 Olympics in the individual sabre event, just missing out on a medal when finishing fourth out of the 23 competitors.

During the War, von Gregurich fought on the Eastern Front and was killed in action on 28ᵗʰ June 1915 at the age of 48, at Mukachevo in Ukraine.

OLYMPIC APPEARANCE

1900 Paris – fencing

individual sabre

20.7.8 Bela von Las-Torres (1890-1915)

born in Budapest

Von Las-Torres competed in freestyle swimming events at the 1908 and 1912 Olympics. At the 1908 Games, he reached the semi-finals in the 400 metres freestyle event but failed to qualify for the final and, in the 4 x 200 metres freestyle relay event, he and his Hungarian teammates won the silver medal.

Four years later, von Las-Torres competed in the same two events as he had competed in at the 1908 Games and also in the 1,500 metres freestyle event. In the 400 metres event, von Las-Torres arrived at the Games as the new world record holder, having broken the record on 5ᵗʰ June 1912 but, at the Games, his world record was beaten and he was only able to finish in fifth place in the final. In the 1,500 metres event, von Las-Torres did not finish and, in the 4 x 200 metres relay event, the Hungarian team were one of the five teams to qualify for the final but they failed to show up for the final.

Von Las-Torres was killed in action during the War, fighting in Italy. He was killed on 12th October 1915 at the age of 25.

OLYMPİC APPEARANCES

1908 London – swimming

400 metres freestyle

4 x 200 metres freestyle relay; silver medallist

1912 Stockholm – swimming

400 metres freestyle

1,500 metres freestyle

4 x 200 metres freestyle relay

20.7.9 Bela Zulawszky (1869-1914)
born in Tokaj, Hungary

Zulawszky competed in the individual epee and sabre fencing events at the 1908 Olympics and in the individual foil and sabre fencing events at the 1912 Olympics.

At the 1908 Games, Zulawszky did not get beyond the first round heats in the epee event but won the silver medal in the sabre event. At the 1912 Games, Zulawszky reached the semi-finals in both his events but failed to qualify for the finals; in the sabre event, he lost out to his compatriot Bela Bekassy (see Chapter 20.7.1)

Zulawszky was killed in action in the War on 24th October 1914 at the age of 44, fighting in the Balkans.

OLYMPÍC APPEARANCES

1908 London – fencing

individual epee

individual sabre; silver medallist

1912 Stockholm – fencing

individual foil

individual sabre

20.8 Russia

20.8.1 Andrey Akimov (1888-1916)

born in Nikolskoye in the Russian Empire

Akimov was a midfielder who played his football for OKS Orekhevo-Zuyevo from 1907 to 1908 and for Klub Sporta Orekhevo, Orekhevo-Zuyevo from 1909 to 1914.

In 1912, Akimov was selected as a member of the Russian team taking part in the Olympics that year and made his debut for Russia in the quarter-final match against Finland. Akimov scored Russia's only goal in their 2-1 defeat. Akimov did not play in their consolation round match against Germany, a match which resulted in Russia losing 16-0. However, he did make three more appearances for them after the Olympics.

Little is known about where and when Akimov died in the War other than that he was killed in action in 1916, when he would have been 27 or 28.

20.8.2 Georg Baumann (1892-1915?)

born in St Petersburg, to Estonian parents.

In 1912, Baumann represented the Russian Empire at the 1912 Olympics, wrestling in the Greco-Roman lightweight wrestling event; after losing his first two bouts, the first to the eventual gold medallist, Finland's Emil Ware, Baumann was eliminated.

Baumann enjoyed more success a year later when he won the World Championships in the lightweight class to win the gold medal. In the same year, he won a gold medal at the Russian Olympiad and was awarded the title for the best amateur wrestler in the Baltic States.

At the beginning of the War, Baumann was sent to the front, never to return. The date and place of his death are not known but it is believed he may have died in 1915, when he would have been 22 or 23.

20.8.3 Nikolay Kynin (1890-1916)

born in Nikolskoye

Kynin's football career almost mirrored that of Andrey Akimov (see Chapter 20.8.1); as well as having been born in the same town, they both played midfield for the same club, were both selected to represent the Russian Empire at the 1912 Olympics and both made their debuts against Finland in the quarter-final, which they lost 2-1. They were also both not selected to play in the consolation round match against Germany which ended in a humiliating 16-0 defeat.

Kynin also played for Russia after the Olympics but only made one more appearance for them.

In the War, Kynin was killed in action in 1916; he would have been 25 or 26 at the time.

OLYMPIC APPEARANCE

1912 Stockholm – football

20.8.4 Feliks Leparsky (1875-1917)

Leparsky represented the Russian Empire at the 1912 Olympics.

Leparsky took part in the individual foil fencing event at the 1912 Games but failed to qualify beyond his round 1 heat. Of the 94 fencers taking part in the individual foil event at the 1912 Games, Leparsky was one of five to lose their lives in the War.

In the War, Leparsky served as a captain in the Russian Army and was posted to the Eastern Front. He was killed in action on 10th January 1917 at Dobruja in Bulgaria; he would have been 41 or 42 when he died.

20.8.5 Grigory Nikitin (1890-1917)
born in St Petersburg

Nikitin played his club football as a forward for Sport St Petersburg and was picked as a member of the team representing the Russian Empire at the 1912 Olympics.

Unlike Andrey Akimov and Nikolay Kynin (see Chapters 20.8.1 and 20.8.3) who also represented Russia in the football competition at the 1912 Games, Nikitin missed the opening game against Finland which Russia lost 2-1 but played in the game against Germany in the consolation round, a game which Russia lost 16-0; Nikitin was never selected again to play for Russia.

Although little is known about his war experiences, it is reported that Nikitin was killed fighting in the War in 1917, when he would have been 27.

20.9 Serbia

20.9.1 Dragutin Tomasevic (1891-1915)

Although some reports state Dragutin Tomasevic was born in 1890, more reliable sources state he was born in Bistrica in Serbia in 1891.

Tomasevic ran in the marathon at the 1912 Olympics; also running in the marathon were the Canadian Jimmy Duffy (see Chapter 19.2.2) and the Frenchman Renon Boissiere (see Chapter 20.4.2). In conditions which resulted in the death of one of the runners, Portugal's Francisco Lazaro, from the effects of the hot weather, Tomasevic was one of the 34 starters, out of a total of 68 starters, who did not finish the race.

In the War, Tomasevic was killed in action fighting at Rasanec in Serbia. As with the year of his birth, reports differ as to the month in 1915 in which he died, with some reports stating it was May 1915 and others saying it was October 1915; either way he would have been 24 at the time.

OLYMPIC APPEARANCE

1912 Stockholm – athletics

marathon

20.10 United States of America

20.10.1 William Lyshon (1887-1918)
born in Philadelphia

Lyshon was working as a service operator for the Philadelphia Bell Telephone Corporation when he decided he wanted to compete at the 1912 Olympics in Stockholm. However, due to insufficient funding, he was not originally selected, so decided to pay his own way, following which funds were raised to enable him to go.

Lyshon took part in the featherweight Greco-Roman wrestling event but, after losing his first two bouts, was eliminated.

Being an American, Lyshon would not have fought in the War until after 6th April 1917 when the USA declared war on Germany but, on 13th October 1918, less than a month before the end of the War, Lyshon was killed in action in France. He was 30 years old when he died.

OLYMPIC APPEARANCE

1912 Stockholm – wrestling

Greco-Roman featherweight

20.10.2 Arthur Wear (1880-1918)

born in St Louis, Missouri

After attending Yale University, for which he played baseball, Wear took part in the 1904 Olympics in his home town, competing in the men's doubles tennis event. In the first round and quarter-finals, Wear and his partner, Clarence Gamble, beat other American pairs to reach the semi-final where they were beaten by the eventual winners; by reaching the semi-finals, Wear and his partner won bronze medals, as did Wear's older brother Joseph, who lost in the other semi-final in the same event.

After America entered the War, Wear commanded an infantry battalion at the Battle of St Mihiel, in the Meuse region of France, in September 1918; although Wear was not wounded, his health was suffering but he refused to have proper treatment for what was probably a perforated ulcer. Instead, Wear continued to command his battalion and died during fighting in the Meuse-Argonne offensive. Wear's death came on 6th November 1918, less than a week before the Armistice was signed; he was 38 years old when he died.

OLYMPIC APPEARANCE

1904 St Louis – tennis

doubles; bronze medallist

CHAPTER 21
OTHER NOTABLE SPORTSMEN

21.1 Donald Bell (1890-1916)

born in Harrogate, Yorkshire

Bell attended Harrogate Grammar School where he excelled in sport, representing his school at athletics, football, cricket, rugby, hockey and swimming. After leaving school, he went to Westminster College in Oxford to train as a teacher. Whilst at college, he signed amateur forms with Crystal Place but did not play any first team games for them. Bell returned to Harrogate in 1911 to teach and played a few games, as an amateur, for Newcastle United's reserve team.

In 1913, Bell signed as a professional with Bradford Park Avenue; he made his debut for the first team in 1913 and went on to make five more appearances for them as they secured promotion to the first division.

Soon after the outbreak of war, Bell asked to be released by Bradford Park Avenue, allowing him to enlist in November 1914 as a private in the 9th Battalion, West Yorkshire Regiment; he was the first professional footballer to enlist.

Not long after, Bell was commissioned as a second lieutenant into the 9th Battalion, Green Howards (Alexandra, Princess of Wales's Own Yorkshire Regiment). Bell arrived in France with his battalion in August 1915; Bell spent the first few months at Armentierre but, by July 1916, had moved to prepare for involvement in the Somme offensive. On the opening day of the Battle of the Somme, 1st July 1916, Bell's battalion was placed in reserve at Saint-Saveur but it was not long before they were on the front line. On 5th July 1915, Bell was running across no man's land under heavy fire, to destroy a German machine gun nest that was holding up the British advance; Bell threw a Mills bomb that knocked the gun out and then shot the gunner dead before throwing more bombs into the trench, killing 50 Germans. This resulted in the Germans offering no further resistance and the trench was taken. In a letter to his mother two days later, Bell wrote "I must confess it was the biggest fluke alive and I did nothing. I just chucked one bomb but it did the trick"; he finished his letter with the words "please don't worry about me, I believe God is watching over me and it rests with him whether I pull through or not".

For his actions on 5th July, Bell was awarded the Victoria Cross for conspicuous bravery. The account given of his action in winning the Victoria Cross is as follows.

"On 5 July 1916 at Horseshoe Trench, Somme, France, a very heavy enfilade fire was opened on the attacking company by an enemy gun, Second Lieutenant Bell immediately, on his own initiative, crept up a communication trench, and then, followed by a corporal and a private, rushed across the open under heavy fire and attacked the machine gun, shooting the firer and destroying the gun and personnel with bombs."

Five days later, Bell carried out a similar attack, when leading his troops across open ground near the village of Contalmaison; Contalmaison had been captured from the Germans but was under counter-attack; in the words of one of his fellow officers,

Bell "dashed forward with an armful of bombs, and started to clear out a hornet's nest of Huns who were ready to take toll of our advancing troops. He advanced with great courage right up to where the enemy were posted. He took careful aim and bowled out several Germans. Unfortunately he was hit; for a while he fought on, but was hit again. He got weaker and weaker, and had to relax his efforts. He collapsed suddenly and when we reached him he was dead"; he had been cut down by machine gun fire. He was 25 when he died and was buried at the Gordon Dump Cemetery at Ovillers-La Boissell near Albert in France.

Bell was the only English professional footballer to be awarded the Victoria Cross in the First World War; his Victoria Cross was bought by the Professional Footballers Association in 2010 for £210,000 and is on display at the National Football Museum in Manchester.

MILITARY HONOURS

Victoria Cross

21.2 Norman Callaway (1896-1917)
born in Hay, New South Wales

After playing grade cricket in Sydney, Callaway was picked to play for New South Wales against Queensland in February 1915. After Queensland had been bowled out for 137, Callaway came in to bat with New South Wales having lost their first three wickets for only 17 runs. By lunchtime on the second day, Callaway had scored 200 in only 206 minutes, having put on 256 runs for the fifth wicket with his captain Charles Macartney. Callaway was out soon after lunch on the second day, having scored 207 runs, making him only the second cricketer to score a double century on his first-class debut. With Queensland only scoring 100 in their second innings, New South Wales were not required to bat again, having won the match by an innings and 231 runs.

In 1916, without having played another first-class game of cricket, Callaway enlisted in the Australian Imperial Army and was posted as a private to the 19th Battalion. He left Sydney in October 1916, arriving in France in December 1916.

On 3rd May 1917, Callaway was reported missing in action during an attack on the Hindenberg Line in the Second Battle of Bullecourt; it was not until three months later though that it was confirmed that he had died the day he had been reported missing. Callaway was only 21 at the time and is commemorated at the Villers-Bretonneux Memorial in France.

With a first-class batting average of 207, Callaway holds the highest average of any first-class cricketer.

21.3 A. E. J. "James" Collins (1885-1914)
born in India

In 1899, whilst playing in a junior house match whilst at Clifton College, Collins scored, over four days, 628 runs not out, his innings coming to an end when he ran out of partners; he also took 11 wickets in the match. His innings remained the highest-ever recorded innings in cricket until overtaken by the Mumbai schoolboy Pranav Dhanawade when he scored 1,009 runs not out in January 2016.

Collins went to the Royal Military Academy in Woolwich in 1901, representing the Academy at football and rugby, as well as cricket. He joined the British Army in 1904, being commissioned as a second lieutenant with the Royal Engineers.

Collins was posted to France when the War broke out and was mentioned in despatches. He was killed in action on 11th November 1914 at the First Battle of Ypres while serving as a captain with the 5th Field Company of the Royal Engineers; he was wounded when signalling for more men to protect the flank of his trench but died within an hour of being dragged back into a trench.

Collins was 29 years old when he died; although burials were carried out the day after he died, Collins' grave and remains were never found and he was commemorated at the Ypres (Menin Gate) Memorial in Belgium.

MILITARY HONOURS

Mentioned in despatches

21.4 Francois Faber (1887-1915)

born in Aulnay-sur-Iton in the Haute-Normandie region of France

The son of a Luxembourger, Faber took the same nationality as his father.

As an amateur cyclist, Faber worked as a furniture removal man and as a docker before turning professional in 1906. Faber took part in his first Tour de France in 1906 but did not finish; a year later he finished in 7th place and, in 1908, came second after winning four of the stages.

In 1909, Faber won six of the stages in the Tour de France, including a record five in a row, on his way to becoming the first non-Frenchman to win the Tour. A year later, Faber was the overall leader up until stage 7 when he was seriously injured after colliding with a dog; although he was able to finish the Tour, he was only able to manage second place behind Octave Lapize (see Chapter 20.4.16).

Faber continued cycling professionally up until the outbreak of war, by which time, in addition to winning the Tour de France and a total of 19 stages of the Tour, he had won the Giro di Lombardia in 1908, the Paris-Tours race in 1909 and 1910, the Paris-Brussels race in 1909 and the Bordeaux-Paris race in 1911.

When war broke out, Faber joined the French Foreign Legion and was assigned to the 2nd Marching Regiment of the 1st Foreign Regiment. On 9th May 1915, the same day he received a telegram informing him that his wife had given birth to a daughter, Faber was killed when he was shot while carrying a colleague back from no man's land between Carency and Mount-Eloi. Faber was 28 years old when he died and is commemorated by a plaque at the Notre Dame de Lorette church near Arras. After his death, Faber was awarded the Medaille Militaire.

MILITARY HONOURS

Medaille Militaire

21.5 John "Jack" Harrison (1890-1917)
born in Hull

Whilst studying at St John's College York, Harrison played five games for York rugby league club, scoring three tries for them. In September 1912, Harrison returned to live in Hull and joined the Hull rugby league club. In the 1913/14 season, he scored a record 52 tries for them, including one in the final against Wakefield Trinity when Hull won the Challenge Cup.

In 1914, Harrison was selected for the England tour to Australia but it was cancelled because of the outbreak of war. Harrison continued playing for Hull though and, in his four seasons with them, played 116 games for them, scoring 106 tries.

Towards the end of 1915, Harrison volunteered for military service and, after his officer training, was commissioned as a second lieutenant with the East Yorkshire Regiment. By February 1917, Harrison was on the front line and, for his actions on 25th March, when leading a patrol into no man's land, was awarded the Military Cross; the citation for his Military Cross reads "for conspicuous gallantry and devotion to duty. He handled his platoon with great courage and skill, reached his objective under the most trying conditions, and captured a prisoner. He set a splendid example throughout."

On 3rd May 1917, Harrison received orders to attack, along with the rest of his brigade, a wood near Oppy in France. The account of his actions that day, which led him to receiving a Victoria Cross for most conspicuous bravery and self-sacrifice in an attack, reads as follows.

"Owing to darkness, to smoke from the enemy barrage and our own, and to the fact that the objective was in a dark wood, it was impossible to see when the barrage had lifted off the enemy front line. Nevertheless, Second Lieutenant Harrison twice led his company against the enemy trench under terrific rifle and machine-gun fire, but was repulsed. Then finally he made a dash at the machine-gun, hoping to knock it out of action and so save the lives of many of his company."

Armed with a pistol and hand grenades, Harrison fell whilst tossing a hand grenade in the general direction of a German machine gun post.

Harrison was 26 years old at the time. His body was never found and he is commemorated at the Arras Memorial in France.

MILITARY HONOURS

Military Cross

Victoria Cross

21.6 Frank McGee (1882-1916)

born in Ottawa

McGee played lacrosse and rugby, winning the Canadian rugby club championship with Ottawa City in 1898, but it was at ice hockey that he excelled most.

Playing for a local Canada Railway Pacific Railway team, McGee lost the use of an eye when he was hit in the face by the puck but, despite the use of only one eye, McGee joined the Ottawa Hockey Club and played for them from 1902 until 1906.

During his time playing for Ottawa, the Stanley Cup was played for by the holders of the Cup and the league champions and, after winning the Cup in 1903, Ottawa, with McGee playing for them, retained the Stanley Cup until 1906. On 16th January 1905, McGee scored a record 14 goals in the 23-2 win over Dawson City, eight of his goals coming in less than nine minutes.

McGee retired from ice hockey after Ottawa lost the Stanley Cup in 1906 to Montreal Wanderers.

In the War, McGee served as a lieutenant with the 21st Infantry Battalion of the 43rd Regiment (Duke of Cornwall's Own Rifles); he departed for England in May 1915. In December 1915, McGee was wounded in the knee but returned to the front in August 1916, after turning down the offer of a position in Le Havre, away from the fighting.

On 16th September 1916, McGee was killed in action near Courcelette in France during the Battle of the Somme; his body was never recovered. McGee was 33 years old when he died and is commemorated at the Canadian National Vimy Memorial in Pas-de-Calais.

21.7 Walter Tull (1888-1918)

born in Folkestone, Kent

The son of a Barbadian father and English mother and orphaned at the age of nine, Tull was then brought up in an orphanage in London.

In 1908, Tull signed for the top amateur football club, Clacton and, by the end of his first season with them, had won the F. A. Amateur Cup. In the summer of 1909, he joined Tottenham Hotspur, touring Uruguay and Argentine with them before the start of the 1909/10 season; by signing for Spurs, Tull became only the second black footballer to play professional football in England. After 10 league appearances for Spurs, in which he scored two goals, Tull was dropped from the first team, although it may have been as much due to the racial abuse he received from opposing fans rather than because of his form.

In October 1911, Tull joined Northampton Town and, in his three seasons with them, he played 111 games for them and scored nine goals.

During the War, Tull served with the Footballers Battalion, Middlesex Regiment. After seeing action at the Battle of the Somme in 1916, Tull attended officer training and, in May 1917, was commissioned as a second lieutenant, making him the first black infantry officer in the British Army, something he achieved despite the 1914 Manual of Military Law prohibiting soldiers whom were not of pure European descent from becoming commissioned officers. In June 1917, Tull took part in the Battle of Messines and, later that year, in the Third Battle of Ypres.

In November 1917, Tull was posted to Italy where he was mentioned in despatches for "gallantry and coolness" when leading his company of 26 men on a raiding party into enemy territory during the Battle of Piave. Tull was the first to cross the Piave River prior to the raid on 1st and 2nd January 1918; during the raid, Tull took the covering party of the main body across and brought them back without a casualty, in spite of heavy fire.

By March 1918, Tull had returned to action in France. On 25th March 1918, during the Spring Offensive near the village of Favreuil in France, Tull was leading an attack when he was hit by a German bullet in the head soon after entering no man's land; valiant efforts were made to bring him back to British trenches but his body was never recovered. Tull died at the age of 29 and is commemorated at the Arras Memorial in France.

21.8 Sandy Turnbull (1884-1917)

born in Hurlford, Ayrshire

In 1902, Turnbull signed for Manchester City and, by the end of the 1903/04 season, Turnbull was an F. A. Cup winner with them, with Turnbull scoring five goals for them en route to the final where they beat Bolton Wanderers 1-0.

The following season Turnbull was the league's top scorer with 20 goals and in his four seasons with Manchester City, made 110 league appearances for them and scored 53 goals. Following allegations that a number of players, including Turnbull, were being paid more than the maximum £4 per week, Turnbull was suspended from football until January 1907; during his suspension, he and three other suspended Manchester City players signed for their neighbours Manchester United. In his first season with Manchester United, Turnbull scored 25 goals in 30 matches as the team secured its first championship title. In the 1908/09 season, the team won the F. A. Cup with Turnbull scoring the only goal in the final in a 1-0 victory over Bristol City; included in the Manchester United team was Billy Meredith, who had also been in Manchester City's Cup-winning team back in 1904, alongside Turnbull. After their Cup success, Manchester United moved to their new home, Old Trafford, where Turnbull scored the first ever goal at that ground.

Turnbull enjoyed more success with Manchester United when they won the league for a second time in the 1910/11 season. Turnbull's football career came to a premature end in 1915 when he was suspended for a second time, this time for his involvement in a match-fixing scandal.

After enlisting with the 23rd Battalion, Middlesex Regiment, Turnbull was transferred to the 8th Battalion, East Surrey Regiment and posted to France where he was initially located between Hazebrouck and Bailleul in preparation for the upcoming offensive north of the River Somme. After his battalion was involved in an attack on Boom Ravine near the Somme, Turnbull was moved north to take part in the Arras offensive.

By May 1917, Turnbull was preparing to take part in the Spring Offensive east of Arras, which had started in April 1917; on 3rd May 1917, by which time he had been promoted to lance-sergeant, Turnbull took part in an attempt to capture the village of Cherisy. During the assault, Turnbull's battalion did make it to the village and it was reported that Turnbull had used a Lewis gun to great effect against enemy machine guns and had carried on fighting despite being hit twice, the second time whilst rushing an enemy gun; a third bullet smashed his knee and brought him down. The injury to his knee was too much for him to continue fighting but he refused to leave the battlefield for treatment so that he could, with the map he was carrying, help his comrades.

Although it was initially thought that he might have been captured by the Germans, this was not the case; one report suggests that he made it to the village of Cherisy and found shelter in a house, only to be shot by a sniper lying low in one of the houses, whilst another report suggests he died from the wound to his knee.

Turnbull was 32 when he died and is commemorated at the Arras Memorial to the Missing in France.

21.9 Bernard Vann (1887-1918)

born in Rushden, Northamptonshire

At school, Vann proved himself to be an all-round sportsman, captaining his school team at football, cricket and hockey. Not long after leaving school, he played two games of football for Northampton Town in the Southern League before moving, in 1906, to Burton United. After playing four league games for Burton, Vann moved to Derby County, playing three league games for them; the following season, he moved to Leicester Fosse, but did not make any league appearances for them.

In 1908, Vann put his football days behind him and went to Cambridge University, winning a blue in hockey in 1910. After graduating, Vann was ordained as a priest and became chaplain of Wellingborough School.

When war broke out, Vann volunteered as an army chaplain but the application process was too slow for his liking, resulting in him enlisting in the infantry with the 28th (County of London) Battalion, London Regiment (Artists' Rifles). In September 1915, he was commissioned in the 1/8th Battalion, Sherwood Foresters (the Nottinghamshire and Derbyshire Regiment).

In 1915, Vann was awarded his first Military Cross for his actions at Kemmel, in Belgium, in April and at Ypres in July. The citation reads:

"At Kemmel on 24th April 1915 when a small advance trench which he occupied was blown up, and he himself was wounded and half buried, he showed the greatest determination in organising the defence and rescuing buried men under heavy fire, although wounded and severely bruised he refused to leave his post until directly ordered to do so. At Ypres on 31st July 1915, and subsequent days, he ably assisted another officer to hold the left trench of the line, setting a fine example to those around him. On various occasions he has led patrols up to the enemy's trenches and obtained valuable information."

The fighting at Kemmel saw 14 of Vann's colleagues killed and 16 wounded.

In October 1915, Vann was injured during the Battle of Hohenzokern Retreat when a bullet went through his left arm whilst leading an assault on a German position; after recovering from the bullet wound, Vann was back on the front line by March 1916.

A second Military Cross was awarded to Vann for conspicuous gallantry in action when, on 21st September 1916, he led his men on a raid against enemy trenches at Bellacourt, near Arras; after firing the enemy trenches with mortars in order to create gaps in the wire, he went through the gaps attacking the enemy lines; after shooting and killing one of the Germans and wounding another, the other five German soldiers surrendered.

The withdrawal of Russia from the War in 1918 increased the threat from German forces and, between March and September 1918, Vann and his men moved between those sections of the Allied front line which were weakened. By September 1918, Vann had moved to the St Quentin canal region; it was for his deeds on 29th September 1918 at Bellinglise and Lehaucourt that he was awarded the Victoria Cross. The citation for his Victoria Cross reads that, on that day, Vann "led his battalion with great skill across the Canal de St Quentin through a very thick fog and under heavy fire from field and machine guns. On reaching the high ground above Bellenglise the whole attack was held up by fire of all descriptions from the front and right flank. Realising the importance of the advance going forward with the barrage, Colonel Vann rushed up to the firing line with the greatest gallantry and led the line forward. By his prompt action and absolute contempt for danger the whole situation was changed, the men encouraged and the line swept forward. Later he rushed a field gun single-handed and knocked out three of the detachment. The success of the day was in no small degree due to the splendid gallantry and the leadership displayed by this officer."

Only four days later, on 3rd October 1918, Vann was shot and killed by a German sniper while his battalion was waiting to attack the Fonsomme-Beaurevoir line. Vann was 31 when he died and was buried at the Bellicourt British Cemetery in France.

Vann was the only clergymen ordained in the Church of England to win the Victoria Cross in the Great War and, with his Victoria Cross, two Military Crosses and the Croix de Guerre awarded to him by the French in early 1917, the most decorated of those who had played in the first division of English football. Almost nine months after his death, Vann's widow gave birth to a son, conceived whilst Vann had been on leave only weeks before his death.

MILITARY HONOURS

Military Cross (twice)

Victoria Cross

Croix de Guerre

APPENDIX 1

A Summary of the Battles and Campaigns at which the Casualties Occurred

The Battle of the Marne
(7th September 1914 to 12th September 1914)

The Battle of the Marne took place to the east of Paris, between 7th and 12th September 1914.

The battle followed the advance by German forces into France; a counter-attack by six French field armies and the British Expeditionary Force along the River Marne brought to a halt the advance by the Germans and forced them to retreat, leading to the First Battle of the Aisne.

The battle, which saw the start of trench warfare which was to continue until the end of War, was a decisive victory for the French and British forces but casualties on both sides were high, with the French and German armies each having in excess of 250,000 casualties and the British 13,000, 1,700 of whom were killed. Amongst those who were killed was George Hutson, the British Olympic athlete.

First Battle of the Aisne
(12ᵗʰ September 1914 to 15ᵗʰ September 1914)

The First Battle of the Aisne took place in Picardy in northern France, between 12ᵗʰ and 15ᵗʰ September 1914.

In August 1914, the British and French had been defeated by the Germans at the Battle of Charleroi and the Battle of Mons; following these defeats, the retreat by the Allied forces continued beyond the River Marne but, following the Battle of the Marne in early September, the Germans were forced to retreat towards the River Aisne.

The First Battle of the Aisne took place when the French and British armies realised the German army was not going to retreat beyond the north side of the river, where they were able to entrench themselves in well-protected positions.

Although small advances were made by the French and British, these could not be consolidated and fighting was eventually abandoned on 28ᵗʰ September as both sides realised they were unable to mount frontal attacks against the enemy.

13,541 British troops were killed or wounded in the battle; included amongst the dead were James Huggan and Ronald Simson, the Scottish rugby internationals and Charles Wilson, the English rugby international.

First Battle of Ypres
(19ᵗʰ October 1914 to 22ⁿᵈ November 1914)

The First Battle of Ypres took place on the Western Front around the town of Ypres in Belgium, close to the English Channel, between 19ᵗʰ October 1914 and 22ⁿᵈ November 1914.

After the Germans had been defeated at the Battle of the Marne in September 1914, the opposing armies headed northwards, constructing trenches in the "race to the sea", the race ending at Ypres.

The First Battle of Ypres was between the allied Belgian, French and British forces and the German forces. A number of separate battles took place within the First Battle of Ypres, including the Battle of Langemarck, battles at La Bassee and Armentieres, the Battle of Messines, the Battle of Gheluvelt and the Battle of Nonne Bosschen.

Fighting continued until 22nd November 1914 but, with neither side having moved forces quickly enough to win a decisive victory, the fighting was brought a halt with the arrival of winter weather.

Nearly 50,000 Germans were killed or wounded or went missing during the First Battle of Ypres; Belgian casualties exceeded 20,000 and French casualties exceeded 50,000. British casualties consisted of 7,960 killed, 29,563 wounded and 17,873 missing. Included amongst the dead were the Scottish rugby internationals Lewis Robertson and James Ross, the British Olympic athlete Laurie Anderson, the British Olympic rower Thomas Gillespie, the French Olympic rower Alphonse Meignant and the record-breaking schoolboy cricketer A. E. J. Collins.

The Mesopotamia Campaign
(6th November 1914 to 30th October 1918)

When Turkey entered the War on 29th October 1914, Britain opened a new military front in the Ottoman province of Mesopotamia (now Iraq).

Within the first month of the campaign, British and Indian troops had captured the towns of Basra and Kurna. Further advances were made up the River Tigris with little resistance until November 1915 when the British and Indian forces suffered their first major setback at the Battle of Ctestipha. Following the siege of Kut-al-Amara where 11,800 troops were garrisoned, the Allied forces were to suffer their second major setback of the campaign when attempts to relieve the siege failed and the British surrendered.

By early 1917, with reinforcements, the British and Indian troops were able to continue their advance up the River Tigris and, by May 1917, British troops had entered Baghdad.

When Turkey signed the Armistice of Mudros on 30th October 1918, it brought to an end the fighting in Mesopotamia, although it was not until a few days later that the British forces seized control of Mosul.

The campaign, which lasted four years, was carried out in an area with extreme weather conditions and a high risk of disease. 15,000 of the Allied forces were killed or died from wounds and 12,500 died from sickness; another 50,000 were wounded. Amongst those to die was the British Olympic athlete Patrick Roche.

Battle of Limanowa
(1st December 1914 to 13th December 1914)

The Battle of Limanowa took place around the town of Limanowa, close to Cracow in Poland. The battle was between the Russian Army and the Austro-Hungarian Army. With the Russians being forced to retreat from the positions from which they threatened Cracow, the Austro-Hungarian Empire claimed victory in the battle.

Included amongst the dead from the battle was the Hungarian Olympic fencer Jeno Szantay.

Battle of Givenchy
(18th December 1914 to 22nd December 1914)

The Battle of Givenchy took place around the town of Givenchy in northern France, from 18th to 22nd December 1914. It took place following orders that the British forces provide relief for the French, who were under heavy pressure at Arras, by attacking the Germans around Givenchy, thereby preventing the Germans from providing reinforcements at Arras.

Indian troops from the Lahore division were successful in capturing two German trenches but were then pushed back by a counter-attack. After the Germans were able to break through, two British reserve battalions were brought into the action and, by the end of 20th December 1914, the village of Givenchy was back in British hands.

Fighting stopped on 22nd December 1914 with neither side having made any gains but, with 4,000 casualties, the British forces suffered twice as many casualties as the Germans. Included amongst those killed in the battle was Richard Yorke, the British Olympic athlete.

Battle of Dogger Bank
(24ᵗʰ January 1915)

The Battle of Dogger Bank took place in the North Sea on 24ᵗʰ January 1915.

The battle, which was a naval engagement between the British Grand Fleet and the German High Seas Fleet, took place after the British were on notice, after having intercepted and decoded German wireless transmissions, that a German raiding squadron was heading for Dogger Bank in the North Sea.

After the German squadron was intercepted by the British fleet, the Germans headed for home but the British caught up with them and fired on them with their long-range gunfire.

With a German armoured cruiser being sunk and the loss of 954 German lives, the battle was a decisive victory for the British fleet, which only lost 15 lives. Included amongst the 15 British servicemen to lose their lives was the Welsh rugby international Charles Taylor.

The Sinai and Palestine Campaign
(28ᵗʰ January 1915 to 30ᵗʰ October 1918)

The Sinai and Palestine Campaign was fought between the British Empire forces and those of the Ottoman Empire, supported by the Germans. The campaign was that part of the Great War that was fought in the Middle East.

Before war broke out, much of the Middle East was part of the Turkish Ottoman Empire but the Sinai Peninsula and to its west the Suez Canal were part of the British Protectorate of Egypt. Fighting in the campaign began when, in January 1915, the Ottoman forces, led by Germans, invaded the Sinai Peninsula with the aim of raiding the Suez Canal.

After the Battles of Romani and Magdhaba in 1916 and the Battle of Rafa in January 1917, the Sinai had been re-captured from the Ottomans; further victories followed at the First Battle of Gaza in March 1917 and the Second Battle of Gaza in April 1917 in South Palestine.

After these victories, there followed stalemate for six months up until the end of October 1917, when the Egyptian Expeditionary Force made up of troops from the British Empire, under General Allenby, captured Beersheba; the Third Battle of Gaza at the beginning of November 1917 resulted in more Ottoman territory being captured. The Battle of Jerusalem commenced on 17th November 1917 and the City of Jerusalem was surrendered to the Egyptian Expeditionary Force in early December 1917.

Attempts to capture Amman in the First Transjordan attack in March 1918 and to capture Shunet Nimrin and Es Salt in the Second Transjordan attack in April 1917 were unsuccessful, but General Allenby's forces resumed the offensive at the Battle of Megiddo in Syria in September 1918.

Following the capture of Damascus and Aleppo in October 1918, the Ottoman Empire agreed to the Armistice of Mudros on 30th October 1918, bringing to an end the Sinai and Palestine Campaign.

It is estimated that 1,200,000 Allied troops took part in the campaign and that there were more than 600,000 casualties. Included amongst those who died in the campaign are the Scottish rugby international Walter Forrest at the Second Battle of Gaza, the Australian Test cricketer Tibby Cotter at the Battle of Beersheba, the Scottish rugby international Stephen Steyn and the Irish rugby international William Edwards at the Battle of Jerusalem, the New Zealand rugby international Eric Harper during the Second Transjordan attack at Shunet Nimrin and the South African Test cricketer Gordon White at the Battle of Megiddo.

Battle of Neuve Chapelle
(13ᵗʰ March 1915 to 15ᵗʰ March 1915)

The battle took place around the village of Neuve Chapelle in the Artois region of France, with Allied forces consisting of British and Indian troops attempting to break the German lines.

A 35 minute artillery bombardment was followed by infantry advances and Neuve Chapelle was secured within four hours. German reserves were called up but the Allied forces were able to hold on to the ground they had gained; however they were not able to make further progress towards Aubers, which had not been bombarded and the attacks were halted after three days.

British casualties were 7,000 and Indian casualties 4,200; the Germans casualties were much the same as for the Allied forces.Amongst those to be killed in the battle was the British Olympic athlete Wyndham Halswelle.

Second Battle of Ypres
(22nd April 1915 to 25th May 1915)

The Second Battle of Ypres took place in and around Ypres, from 22nd April 1915 until 25th May 1915. The battle comprised the only major attack launched by the German forces on the Western Front in 1915.

The Germans were keen to gain control of the town of Ypres and, for the first time on the Western Front, used chlorine gas in their attacks. The Belgian forces defending their town were joined by French forces supported by Moroccans and Algerians and the British forces were supported by troops from India, South Africa, Canada, Newfoundland, Australia and New Zealand.

A lack of supplies and manpower resulted in the Germans calling off the offensive after a little over a month and instead bombarded the town until it was demolished.

Due to the use of poison gas, the casualties suffered by the Allied forces were far greater than those suffered by the Germans, with British losses totalling 59,000 and French losses 10,000, compared to the 35,000 losses suffered by the Germans. The Canadian forces also bore significant losses with 5,975 casualties, 1,000 of whom were killed. Amongst those to be killed at the Second Battle of Ypres were the Irish rugby international Basil Maclear, the Scottish rugby international James Pearson, the Welsh rugby international Billy Geen, the British Olympic athlete William Anderson, the British Olympic rowers Henry Goldsmith and Gilchrist Maclagan, the British Olympic fencer Ralph Chalmers, the Canadian Olympic athlete Jimmy Duffy and the Canadian Olympic rower Geoffrey Taylor.

The Gallipoli Campaign
(25th April 1915 to 9th January 1916)

The Gallipoli Campaign took place on the Gallipoli Peninsula in Turkey, from 25th April 1915 until 9th January 1916. The campaign was fought between Turkey (which was then a part of the Ottoman Empire) and Allied forces from Britain, France, Australia, New Zealand, Newfoundland and India.

The objective of the campaign was to open up the sea route to the Black Sea and thereby allow a link up with the Russian Empire. After the British and French had launched an unsuccessful naval attack in February and March 1915, a major land invasion on the Gallipoli Peninsula commenced on 25th April 1915. Landings, involving significant numbers of troops from not only Britain and France but also from the Australian and New Zealand Army Corps, continued up until September 1915.

The Turkish opposition was underrated and, with little headway being made by the Allied troops, evacuation from the peninsula commenced in December 1915 and was complete in January 1916.

It is estimated that 250,000 casualties were suffered on each side, with 46,000 Allied troops being killed and 65,000 Turkish troops being killed. Amongst those that died in the Gallipoli Campaign were Ron Rogers (who played rugby for Great Britain), the English rugby internationals Arthur Dingle and Billy Nanson, the Irish rugby international Vincent McNamara, the Scottish rugby internationals David Bedell-Sivright, William Church and Eric Young, the Australian rugby internationals Harold George, Edward Larkin, Blair Swannell and Frederick Thompson, the New Zealand rugby internationals

Henry Dewar and Albert Downing, the South African Test cricketer Frederick Cook, the British Olympic rower Oswald Carver and the British Olympic equestrian Paul Kenna.

Battle of Aubers Ridge
(9th May 1915)

The Battle of Aubers Ridge took place on 9th May 1915. The battle was a British offensive forming part of the Second Battle of Artois.

With the British underestimating the strength of the German positions, the bombardment by the British forces was unable to break the German defences. With the British artillery equipment and ammunition being in poor condition, no ground or tactical advantage was gained and, with British casualties exceeding 10,000, many of whom were killed within yards of their own trenches and the Germans suffering less than 1,000 casualties, the battle was a disaster for the British.

Amongst those to die were the English rugby international Henry Berry and New Zealand's Olympic tennis player and Wimbledon champion Tony Wilding.

Battle of Loos
(25th September 1915 to 13th October 1915)

The Battle of Loos was a British offensive which was part of the Third Battle of Artois and took place between 25th

September and 13th October 1915. During the battle, the British used poison gas for the first time but not to great effect due to adverse wind conditions.

The battle commenced after four days of heavy artillery bombardment and the British enjoyed initial success when they captured Loos on the first day but their advance was then brought to a halt due to supply problems and the need for reserves.

On the second day of the battle, British attacks were launched without adequate cover and the British suffered heavy losses as the German machine guns tore them apart. After several days of fighting, the British were forced to retreat but the attacks were renewed on 13th October. After further heavy losses and with poor weather conditions, the offensive was called off on 13th October. British casualties were estimated to be 50,000, approximately twice the German casualties. Those who died in the battle include the English rugby internationals Harry Alexander and Danny Lambert, the Irish rugby international Ernest Deane, the Welsh rugby international Richard Williams and the Scottish rugby international Mike Dickson.

The Macedonian Front
(21st October 1915 to 30th September 1918)

The Macedonian Front was part of the Balkan Theatre of the First World War, in Eastern Europe. The Front was formed by Allied forces in an attempt to assist Serbia but, following the retreat by the Serbian army to Greece after Serbia had been overthrown by German, Austrian and Bulgarian troops, a front was formed along the Greek border to Salonika.

The front remained stable until September 1918 when attacks by a combined French, Serbian, Greek and British army forced the Bulgarian government to seek peace; following the recapturing of Serbia in October 1918, the Allied offensive came to an end when the Hungarian leaders offered to surrender in November 1918.

Amongst those to be killed during the fighting on the Macedonian Front were the Welsh international footballer William Jones and the British rugby international Charles Adamson.

The Battle of Verdun
(21st February 1916 to 18th December 1916)

The Battle of Verdun took place on the hills north of Verdun-sur-Meuse in north-eastern France between 21st February and 18th December 1916 between the French army and the German army.

The battle was instigated by the Germans whose aim was to weaken the French armies to such an extent that it would change the course of the War. The Germans believed that, by attacking the forts around Verdun, the French would do everything in their power to protect Verdun falling to the Germans and, in doing so, make themselves easier targets for the German artillery bombardments.

The will of the French led by Marshal Petain to win at all costs was underestimated by the Germans and, with German divisions being diverted from the battle to fight the Battle of the Somme in July 1916 and to fight on the Eastern Front, the French claimed victory in the battle as the Germans brought to an end their attacks in December 1916. The battle was the longest single battle of the War, lasting 303 days. As with the Battle of the Somme, casualties were high on both sides, with over 300,000 men killed and the French suffering an estimated 377,000 casualties and the Germans 340,000; and although neither side gained much in the way of territory, the Germans failed to achieve their objective of causing so much damage to the French army to make it no longer a force to be reckoned with in the War.

Included amongst those killed in the battle were the French rugby internationals Marc Giacardy and Leon Larribau, the French Olympic cyclist Leon Ponscarme, the French Olympic polo player Maurice Raoul-Duval and the German Olympic cyclist Josef Rieder; although it is not recorded as such, it is likely that, of the other French international sportsmen who died between 21ˢᵗ February 1916 and 18ᵗʰ December 1916, a number of them also died at the Battle of Verdun.

Battle of Jutland
(31ˢᵗ May 1916 to 1ˢᵗ June 1916)

The Battle of Jutland took place on 31ˢᵗ May and 1ˢᵗ June 1916, between the Royal Navy's Grand Fleet and Germany's High Seas Fleet, in the North Sea off the west coast of the Jutland Peninsula in Denmark.

Before the battle, the British Navy had blocked sea routes from Germany to the Atlantic; with Germany keen to break the blockade and Britain wanting to protect its merchant fleet and shipping lanes, the battle took place after Britain had intercepted messages that Germany had put to sea 40 ships.

With Britain engaging 151 combat ships to Germany's 99, the battle was the largest sea battle of the War and not since the Battle of Jutland has one been fought primarily by battleships. With its smaller fleet, the Germans were unable to break the blockade; however, Britain's Navy suffered greater losses than the German Fleet during the battle, with the loss of 14 battleships and over 6,000 lives, compared to the nine ships and 2,500 lives lost by the Germans. Amongst those who died in the battle were the Scottish rugby internationals Cecil Abercrombie and John Wilson.

Although both sides claimed victory, the outcome of the battle had a greater adverse impact on the effectiveness of the German Fleet as it ceased to be a powerful fighting force for the remainder of the War.

The Battle of the Somme
(1st July 1916 to 18th November 1916)

The Battle of the Somme was fought following the decision by the Allied High Command to attack the Germans north of Verdun, where the French had been taking heavy losses, with the aim of forcing the Germans to move troops away from Verdun and thereby providing relief for the French.

The battle took place on the upper reaches of the River Somme in France and began on 1st July 1916. The battle lasted until 18th November 1916 when the snowy conditions brought the fighting to an end. The battle started after a week-long artillery bombardment by the Allied forces but the Germans had dug themselves into deep trenches and, when the British went over the top, they were all too easy targets for the German machine guns; on the first day of the battle, the British suffered 57,540 casualties, of which 19,240 were killed. Records differ as to what the exact numbers of casualties were by the end of the battle but it is estimated that there were 420,000 British casualties of which 95,675 were killed; the French suffered nearly 200,000 casualties of which more than 50,000 were killed and the Germans suffered more than 500,000 casualties of which 164,000 were killed.

The Battle of the Somme is viewed by many as the one which most epitomised the horrors of the Great War, with so many casualties suffered and lives lost and so little to show for it – by the end of the battle, the Allied forces had advanced no more than six miles on a front stretching no more than 16 miles.

In terms of international sportsmen, the Battle of the Somme claimed many more lives than any other battle of the War; those who were killed include the English international footballer Evelyn Lintott, the Welsh international footballer Leigh Roose, the Irish international footballer Barney Donaghy, the English Test cricketers Major Booth and Kenneth Hutchings, the South African Test cricketer Claude Newberry, the English rugby internationals Rupert Inglis, John King, Alfred Maynard, Robert Pillman and Andrew Slocock, the Scottish rugby internationals Rowland Fraser and Eric Milroy, the Welsh rugby internationals Dick Thomas, Horace Thomas, David Watts and Johnnie Williams, the Australian rugby international Hubert Jones, the New Zealand rugby international Bobby Black, the South African rugby international Toby Moll, the British Olympic shot Robert Davies, the British Olympic rowers Frederick

Kelly and Robert Somers-Smith, the British Olympic athlete Alfred Flaxman, the British Olympic boxer William Philo, the Australian Olympic rower Keith Heritage, the French Olympic footballers Pierre Six and Justin Vialaret, the English footballer Donald Bell and the Canadian ice hockey player Frank McGee.

Battle of Arras
(9th April 1917 to 16th May 1917)

The Battle of Arras took place between 9th April and 16th May 1917 and involved a British offensive against the Germans around the city of Arras in northern France.

With the Germans deciding on a defensive strategy on the Western Front in 1917, the Allied Forces decided that, to end the stalemate, a breakthrough was needed; it was therefore agreed that British Empire forces would launch an offensive around Arras, in the hope that it would draw German forces away from the Aisne region where the French were launching an offensive at the same time.

Although large gains were made by the British forces on the first day of the battle, it soon fell into a stalemate and, with the British unable to achieve a breakthrough, the battle came to an end on 16th May 1917.

Although the Allied forces claimed victory, their casualty figures of 160,000 were higher than those of the Germans, who suffered 125,000 casualties. Included amongst those that died in the battle were the Scottish rugby international Albert Wade, the British Olympic water polo player Isaac Bentham and the British Olympic polo player Herbert Wilson.

Battle of Vemy Ridge
(9th April 1917 to 12th April 1917)

The Battle of Vemy Ridge was part of the Battle of Arras and took place between 9th and 12th April 1917, between all four divisions of the Canadian Expeditionary force and a British division against three divisions of the German army.

The objective was for the Canadians to take control of the high ground along an escarpment at the most northern end of the Arras offensive, which was held by the Germans. After capturing most of the ridge on the first day of the battle, the Canadians achieved their final objective on 12th April 1917 when they took the village of Givenchy-en-Gohelle, causing the German troops to retreat to the Oppy-Mericourt line.

Although the Canadian and British forces, with 170,000 men, vastly out-numbered their enemy, 3,598 were killed and over 7,000 wounded. One of those who took part in the battle and was killed shortly afterwards whilst still in the battlefield area was the Canadian Olympic tennis player Bobby Powell.

Second Battle of Bullecourt
(3rd May 1917 to 17th May 1917)

The Second Battle of Bullecourt took place between 3rd and 17th May 1917 and was part of the Battle of Arras.

The battle involved Australian troops launching an attack to the east of the village of Bullecourt with the intention of piercing the Hindenburg Line whilst British troops attacked the village. The attacks were launched early in the morning of 3rd May 1917 and renewed efforts to take the village were made on 7th May following strong resistance from the Germans.

It was not until 15th May 1917 that the German counter-attacks were finally repulsed and, with the Germans withdrawing from what was left of the village, the battle ended on 17th May 1917.

The Australian Imperial Force suffered over 7,400 casualties during the battle and one of those who lost his life in the battle was the Australian cricketer Norman Callaway.

Battle of Messines
(7th June 1917 to 14th June 1917)

The Battle of Messines was the Allied offensive to capture Messines Ridge and land to the south-east of Ypres with the intention of gaining control of the higher ground in the Messines salient.

During the week before the battle, artillery guns had pounded the German lines and destroyed 90% of the German artillery guns. In the early hours of 7th June 1917, mines that had been laid in tunnels built under the German lines were detonated, the 19 explosions killing 10,000 Germans; immediately after the explosions, infantry attacks, covered by a continuous artillery barrage, were launched and by midday on 7th June, the Allied forces had achieved all their initial objectives for the battle.

Although the Germans kept counter-attacking up until 14th June, the Allied forces were able to continue their advance and, by 14th June, had gained control of the entire Messines salient.

Despite the devastating effect on the Germans of the explosions from the mines in the tunnels under their lines, the Allied forces suffered 17,000 casualties but this compared favourably to the 25,000 suffered by the Germans. Those that died in the battle include the English rugby international John Raphael and the New Zealand rugby internationals Jim Baird, Jim McNeece, George Sellars and Reg Taylor.

The Third Battle of Ypres
(31st July 1917 to 10th November 1917)

The Third Battle of Ypres, which is also known as the Battle of Passchendaele, was a British offensive launched on 31st July 1917 which lasted until 10th November 1917.

The battle was fought for control of the ridges to the south and east of Ypres in Belgium with the aim of allowing the Allied forces to be able to destroy the threat posed by German submarines based on the Belgian coast. General Haig was intent on launching an offensive at a time when French morale was low following its unsuccessful Nivelle offensive in May 1917 and when there was uncertainty about Russia's continued involvement in the War, with any withdrawal from hostilities by the Russians allowing the Germans to reinforce the Western Front with troops engaged on the Eastern Front.

Early gains were rendered impossible by terrible weather conditions but, by the end of September, the Allied forces had taken possession of the ridge to the east of Ypres. The offensive continued towards Passchendaele Ridge and, despite the use of mustard gas by the Germans in defending the ridge,

Passchendaele village was captured by British and Canadian troops on 6th November 1917, following which Haig called off the offensive claiming victory.

The strategy employed by Haig in the battle was heavily criticised and came at a huge cost, with the Allied forces sustaining 310,000 casualties, 50,000 more than the Germans. Amongst those who died in the battle were the England football international Edwin Latheron, the Scottish international footballers Donald McLeod and James Speirs, the Welsh international footballer Frederick Griffiths, the England Test cricketer Colin Blythe, the South Africa Test cricketer Bill Lundie, the England rugby internationals Edgar Mobbs and Arthur Wilson, the Ireland rugby internationals Albert Stewart and Alfred Taylor, the Scotland rugby international James Henderson, the Wales rugby international Dai Westacott, the New Zealand rugby international David Gallaher, the British Olympic athletes Noel Chavasse and George Hawkins, the British Olympic diver Harry Crank, the British Olympic rower Duncan Mackinnon and the Canadian Olympic athlete Alex Decoteau.

The Ludendorff Offensive
(21st March 1918 to 18th July 1918)

The Ludendorff Offensive, also called the German Spring Offensive, involved a series of attacks by the Germans along the Western Front, which began on 21st March 1918 and continued until 18th July 1918.

With Russia's withdrawal from the War on 3rd March 1918, Germany had 500,000 additional troops available for active service on the Western Front and was keen to use this numerical advantage to try and win the War before American troops would be available to support the Allied forces.

A German artillery bombardment followed by attacks by elite storm troops saw the Germans make huge initial advances but their supply lines were not able to keep up with the advances made, thereby hindering further progress. By the end of March 1918, more than 250,000 American forces had joined the conflict.

As the number of casualties grew, Germany was not able to hold on to the gains it had made early on during the offensive, many of which the Allied forces had sacrificed to allow them to hold on to more strategic positions. When the last attack of the offensive launched on 15th July 1918 proved to be a disaster for the Germans, the offensive came to an end, without the Germans having achieved a decisive breakthrough.

Casualties were high on both sides, with the Germans suffering 688,000 and the French and British more than 850,000. Included amongst the dead were the South African Test cricketer Arthur Ochse, the South African Test cricketer and England rugby international Reginald Hands, the England rugby international Harold Hodges, the Scottish rugby international William Hutchison and the Australian rugby international Clarrie Wallach.

The Second Battle of the Marne
(15ᵗʰ July 1918 to 6ᵗʰ August 1918)

The Second Battle of the Marne was the last major German offensive launched on the Western Front.

The initial advances made by the Germans in crossing the river Marne were halted by the French troops on 17ᵗʰ July 1918 and with the counter-attacks by the Allied forces gaining ground, General Ludendorff ordered the Germans to retreat on 20ᵗʰ July.

The offensive by the Germans failed when a counter-attack by French and American forces overwhelmed the Germans on their right hand flank and, by 6ᵗʰ August, the Germans had fallen back to the line they occupied at the start of the Ludendorff Offensive back in March 1918. With the Allied forces digging in, the battle ended on 6ᵗʰ August 1918, as the Allied forces prepared for their next offensive, which was to start two days later with the Battle of Amiens.

Casualties in the battle were high with the French suffering 95,165 dead or wounded, the British 16,552 and the Americans 12,000; the Germans suffered worse with 139,000 dead or wounded, over 29,000 being taken prisoner and the loss of 793 guns and 3,000 machine guns. Included amongst those to die in the battle were the New Zealand Olympic athlete Albert Rowland and the French rugby international Maurice Hedemhaigt.

Battle of Amiens
(8th August 1918 to 12th August 1918)

The Battle of Amiens, also known as the Third Battle of Picardy, was the opening phase of the Allied offensive known as the Hundred Day Offensive, which ultimately led to the end of the War.

The battle started on 8th August 1918 near the city of Amiens and, by the end of the first day, with the Allied forces advancing more than seven miles, the Germans had lost more ground on the Western Front than on any other day in the War.

The battle only lasted five days as, against the wishes of the French commander-in-chief, General Haig brought it to an end in order to launch a fresh offensive near the river Ancre.

Casualties were on the high side for what appeared to be such a decisive victory for the Allied forces; however the Allied forces fared better than the Germans, with the Allied forces suffering 44,000 casualties compared to the 75,000 suffered by the Germans. Amongst those to die in the battle were the Australian rugby international William Tasker and the British Olympic shot Thomas Raddall.

The Second Battle of the Somme
(21st August 1918 to 2nd September 1918)

The Second Battle of the Somme was part of the Hundred Days Offensive undertaken by Allied forces following the failure of the Ludendorff Offensive on the part of the German forces. The purpose of the battle, which started on 21st August

1918, was to push parts of the German lines behind their supply lines, thereby cutting off supplies required to maintain the German forces on the front line.

By 2nd September 1918, the Germans had been forced back to the Hindenburg Line from which they had launched the Ludendorff offensive five months earlier and, by noon on 2nd September 1918, General Ludendorff had ordered the German forces to fall back to the Canal du Nord.

Although the Canadian Corps suffered 5,600 casualties in the battle, overall casualties were much lower than in other battles but the Australian Olympic swimmer Cecil Healy lost his life in the battle.

APPENDIX 2

The Olympic Events Competed in by the Olympians who died in the Great War

The 1896 Olympics, Athens

Sport	Event	Olympians who died	Medals
Athletics			
	800 metres	Georges de la Neziere (France)	
Cycling			
	333 metres time trial	Leon Flameng (France)	
	2 KM sprint	Leon Flameng (France)	Bronze
	10 KM	Leon Flameng (France)	Silver
	100 KM	Leon Flameng (France)	Gold

The 1900 Olympics, Paris

Sport	Event	Olympians who died	Medals
Athletics			
	800 metres	Maurice Salomez (France)	
	High jump	Lajos Gonczy (Hungary)	Bronze
Cycling			
	1,000 metres	Leon Ponscarme (France)	
Equestrianism			
	Mixed jumping	Louis de Champsavin (France)	Bronze
	Mixed hacks and hunters combined	Louis de Champsavin (France)	
Fencing			
	Individual epee	Edmond Wallace (France)	
	Individual foil	Andre Corvington (Haiti)	
	Individual sabre	Felix Debax (France)	
		Amon, Ritter von Gregurich (Hungary)	
Football			
		Louis Bach (France)	Silver
Polo			
		Maurice Raoul-Duval (France)	Bronze

Sport	Event	Olympians who died	Medals
Rowing			
	Coxed 4s	Carl Heinrich Gossler (Germany)	Gold
		Waldemar Tietgens (Germany)	Gold
	Coxed 8s	Waldemar Tietgens (Germany)	
Swimming			
	Underwater	Charles Devendeville (France)	Gold
		Andre Six (France)	Silver
Water polo			
		Charles Devendeville (France)	

The 1904 Olympics, St Louis

Sport	Event	Olympians who died	Medals
Athletics			
	400 metres	Percival Molson (Canada)	
	High jump	Lajos Gonczy (Hungary)	
	Standing high jump	Lajos Gonczy (Hungary)	
Tennis			
	Doubles	Arthur Wear (USA)	Bronze

The 1906 Intercalated Games, Athens

Sport	Event	Olympians who died	Medals
Athletics			
	100 metres	Wyndham Halswelle (GB)	
	400 metres	William Anderson (GB)	
		William Halswelle (GB)	Silver
	800 metres	William Anderson (GB)	
		William Halswelle (GB)	Bronze
		Michel Soalhat (France)	
	1,500 metres	Michel Soalhat (France)	
	High jump	Lajos Gonczy (Hungary)	Silver
	Standing high jump	Lajos Gonczy (Hungary)	
		Istvan Mudin (Hungary)	
	Discus	Istvan Mudin (Hungary)	
	Discus (Greek style)	Istvan Mudin (Hungary)	Bronze
	Javelin	Istvan Mudin (Hungary)	
	Shot	Istvan Mudin (Hungary)	
	Pentathlon	Istvan Mudin (Hungary)	Silver
Swimming			
	100 metres freestyle	Cecil Healy (Australia)	Bronze
	400 metres freestyle	Cecil Healy (Australia)	
	1 mile freestyle	Cecil Healy (Australia)	
		Leopold Mayer (Austria)	
	4 x 250 metres relay	Leopold Mayer (Austria)	
Tug-of-War			
		Heinrich Schneidereit (Germany)	Gold

Sport	Event	Olympians who died	Medals
Weightlifting			
	One-handed	Heinrich Schneidereit (Germany)	Bronze
	Two-handed	Heinrich Schneidereit (Germany)	Bronze
Wrestling			
	Greco-Roman lightweight	Rudolf Watzl (Austria)	Gold
	All-round Greco-Roman	Rudolf Watzl (Austria)	Bronze

The 1908 Olympics, London

Sport	Event	Olympians who died	Medals
Athletics			
	100 metres	Patrick Roche (GB)	
		Hermann von Bonninghausen (Germany)	
	200 metres	George Hawkins (GB)	
		Patrick Roche (GB)	
	400 metres	Noel Chavasse (GB)	
		Wyndham Halswelle (GB)	Gold
		Alan Patterson (GB)	
	800 metres	George Butterfield (GB)	
		Hanns Braun (Germany)	Bronze
	1,500 metres	George Butterfield (GB)	
		Harold Wilson (GB)	Silver
		Jean Bouin (France)	
		Hanns Braun (Germany)	
	3,500 metres	Albert Rowland (New Zealand)	

Sport	Event	Olympians who died	Medals
	10 miles	Albert Rowland (New Zealand)	
	1,600 metres relay	Hanns Braun (Germany)	Silver
	Team 3 mile	Harold Wilson (GB)	Gold
		Jean Bouin (France)	Bronze
	110 metres hurdles	Kenneth Powell (GB)	
	3,200 metres steeplechase	Richard Yorke (GB)	
	Long jump	Hermann von Bonninghausen (Germany)	
	Standing high jump	Alfred Flaxman (GB)	
		Alfred Motte (France)	
	Standing long jump	Frederick Kitching (GB)	
		Alfred Motte (France)	
	Triple jump	Juho Halme (Finland)	
	Discus	Alfred Flaxman (GB)	
		Henry Leeke (GB)	
	Discus (Greek style)	Alfred Flaxman (GB)	
		Henry Leeke (GB)	
		Istvan Mudin (Hungary)	
	Hammer	Henry Leeke (GB)	
		Istvan Mudin (Hungary)	
	Javelin	Alfred Flaxman (GB)	
		Henry Leeke (GB)	
		Istvan Mudin (Hungary)	
		Juho Halme (Finland)	
	Javelin (free style)	Henry Leeke (GB)	
		Juho Halme (Finland)	
	Shot	Henry Leeke (GB)	
		Juho Halme (Finland)	
		Istvan Mudin (Hungary)	

Sport	Event	Olympians who died	Medals
Boxing			
	Middleweight	William Philo (GB)	Bronze
Cycling			
	Tandem 2,000 metres	Octave Lapize (France)	
	20 KM	Octave Lapize (France)	
		Georges Lutz (France)	
	100 KM	Octave Lapize (France)	Bronze
		Georges Lutz (France)	
Diving			
		Harry Crank (GB)	
Fencing			
	Individual epee	Ralph Chalmers (GB)	
		Bela Zulawszky (Hungary)	
	Team epee	Victor Willems (Belgium)	Bronze
	Individual sabre	Bertrand, Count de Lesseps (France)	
		Ismael de Lesseps (France)	
		Jean de Mas Latrie (France)	
		Jeno Szantay (Hungary)	
		Bela Zulawszky (Hungary)	Silver
	Team sabre	Bertrand, Count de Lesseps (France)	
Football			
		Rene Fenouilliere (France)	
		Albert Jenicot (France)	
		Pierre Six (France)	
		Justin Vialaret (France)	

Sport	Event	Olympians who died	Medals
Gymnastics			
	Team all-around	Charles Vigurs (GB)	
Hockey			
		Ivan Laing (GB)	Bronze
		Reggie Pridmore (GB)	Gold
		John Robinson (GB)	Gold
Polo			
		Herbert Wilson (GB)	Gold
Rackets			
	Doubles	Edmond Bury (GB)	Silver
	Singles	Henry Brougham (GB)	Bronze
Rowing			
	Coxed 8s	Oswald Carver (GB)	Bronze
		Henry Goldsmith (GB)	Bronze
		Frederick Kelly (GB)	Gold
		Gilchrist Maclagan (GB)	Gold
		Ronald Sanderson (GB)	Gold
		Edward Williams (GB)	Bronze
		Geoffrey Taylor (Canada)	Bronze
	Coxless pairs	George Fairbairn (GB)	Silver
	Coxless 4s	Duncan Mackinnon (GB)	Gold
		Robert Somers-Smith (GB)	Gold
		Geoffrey Taylor (Canada)	Bronze
	Single sculls	Bernhard von Gaza (Germany)	Bronze
Rugby			
		Arthur Wilson (GB)	Silver

Sport	Event	Olympians who died	Medals
Shooting			
	Individual pistol	Geoffrey Coles (GB)	
	Team pistol	Geoffrey Coles (GB)	Bronze
	Rifle (300 metres)	Robert Davies (GB)	
	Rifle (600 metres)	Robert Davies (GB)	
	Team military rifle	Harcourt Ommundsen (GB)	Silver
	Team free rifle	Harold Hawkins (GB)	
		Thomas Raddall (GB)	
	Small bore, prone position	Harold Hawkins (GB)	
		Arthur Wilde (GB)	
		Henri Bonnefoy (France)	
	Small bore, disappearing target	Harold Hawkins (GB)	Silver
		Arthur Wilde (GB)	
	Small bore, moving target	Harold Hawkins (GB)	
		Arthur Wilde (GB)	
	Team small bore	Henri Bonnefoy (France)	Bronze
Swimming			
	200 metres breaststroke	Percy Courtman (GB)	
	400 metres freestyle	Bela von Las-Torres (Hungary)	
	4 x 200 metres freestyle relay	Bela von Las-Torres (Hungary)	Silver
Tennis			
	Singles	Kenneth Powell (GB)	
		Bobby Powell (Canada)	
	Doubles	Kenneth Powell (GB)	
		Bobby Powell (Canada)	

Sport	Event	Olympians who died	Medals

Water polo

		Herman Donners (Belgium)	Silver

The 1912 Olympics, Stockholm

Sport	Event	Olympians who died	Medals

Athletics

	100 metres	Henry Macintosh (GB)	
		Max Hermann (Germany)	
	200 metres	Henry Macintosh (GB)	
		Max Hermann (Germany)	
	400 metres	Alan Patterson (GB)	
		Claude Ross (Australia)	
		Hanns Braun (Germany)	Silver
		Heinrich Burkowitz (Germany)	
		Max Hermann (Germany)	
		Erich Lehmann (Germany)	
		Jacques Person (Germany)	
	800 metres	Alan Patterson (GB)	
		Richard Yorke (GB)	
		Joseph Caulle (France)	
		Hanns Braun (Germany)	
		Erich Lehmann (Germany)	
		Jacques Person (Germany)	

Sport	Event	Olympians who died	Medals
	1,500 metres	Richard Yorke (GB)	
		Georg Mickler (Germany)	
	5,000 metres	George Hutson (GB)	
		Alex Decoteau (Canada)	
		Jean Bouin (France)	Silver
	Marathon	Jimmy Duffy (Canada)	
		Renon Boissiere (France)	
		Dragutin Tomasevic (Serbia)	
	4 x 100 metres relay	Henry Macintosh (GB)	Gold
		Max Hermann (Germany)	
	4 x 400 metres relay	Hanns Braun (Germany)	
		Heinrich Burkowitz (Germany)	
		Max Hermann (Germany)	
		Erich Lehmann (Germany)	
	Team 3,000 metres	George Hutson (GB)	Bronze
		Georg Mickler (Germany)	
	110 metres hurdles	Laurie Anderson (GB)	
		Kenneth Powell (GB)	
		Hermann von Bonninghausen (Germany)	
	Cross-country	Jean Bouin (France)	
	Long jump	Henry Ashington (GB)	
	Standing long jump	Henry Ashington (GB)	
		Alfred Motte (France)	
	Triple jump	Juho Halme (Finland)	
	Javelin	Juho Halme (Finland)	
	Javelin (two-handed)	Juho Halme (Finland)	

Sport	Event	Olympians who died	Medals
Cycling			
	Individual road race	Bert Gayler (GB)	
		Adolf Kofler (Austria)	
		Joseph Racine (France)	
		Joseph Rieder (Germany)	
	Team road race	Adolf Kofler (Austria)	
		Joseph Racine (France)	
		Joseph Rieder (Germany)	
Diving			
		Harry Crank (GB)	
Equestrianism			
	Show jumping	Paul Kenna (GB)	
		Edward Nash (GB)	
		Friedrich Carl, Prince of Prussia (Germany)	
	Team show jumping	Friedrich Carl, Price of Prussia (Germany)	Bronze
	Individual 3-day eventing	Paul Kenna (GB)	
		Edward Nash (GB)	
		Eduard von Lutcken (Germany)	
	Team 3-day eventing	Paul Kenna (GB)	
		Edward Nash (GB)	
		Eduard von Lutcken (Germany)	Silver
Fencing			
	Individual epee	Gordon Alexander (GB)	
		Victor Willems (Belgium)	
		Hermann Plaskuda (Germany)	
		Bela Bekassy (Hungary)	

Sport	Event	Olympians who died	Medals
	Team epee	Victor Willems (Belgium)	Gold
		Hermann Plaskuda (Germany)	
	Individual foil	Gordon Alexander (GB)	
		Victor Willems (Belgium)	
		Hermann Plaskuda (Germany)	
		Bela Bekassy (Hungary)	
		Bela Zulawszky (Hungary)	
		Feliks Leparsky (Russia)	
	Individual sabre	Bela Bekassy (Hungary)	Silver
		Bela Zulawszky (Hungary)	
	Team sabre	Hermann Plaskuda (Germany)	

Football

Sport	Event	Olympians who died	Medals
		Joseph Dines (GB)	Gold
		Karl Braunsteiner (Austria)	
		Robert Merz (Austria)	
		Hermann Bosch (Germany)	
		Andrey Akimov (Russia)	
		Nikolay Kynin (Russia)	
		Grigory Nikitin (Russia)	

Gymnastics

Sport	Event	Olympians who died	Medals
	Team All-around	Charles Vigurs (GB)	Bronze
		Wilhelm Brulle (Germany)	
		Walther Jesinghaus (Germany)	
		Eberhard Sorge (Germany)	
		Alfred Staats (Germany)	
		Arpad Pedery (Hungary)	Silver

Sport	Event	Olympians who died	Medals
	Team All-around freestyle	Wilhelm Brulle (Germany)	
		Walther Jesinghaus (Germany)	
		Eberhard Sorge (Germany)	
		Alfred Staats (Germany)	
Modern Pentathlon			
		Hugh Durant (GB)	
		Jean de Mas Latrie (France)	
Rowing			
	Coxed 8s	Thomas Gillespie (GB)	Silver
		Alister Kirby (GB)	Gold
		Keith Heritage (Australia)	
		Geoffrey Taylor (Canada)	
		Fritz Bartholomae (Germany)	Bronze
	Coxed 4s	Alphonse Meignant (France)	
Shooting			
	Individual pistol (50 metres)	Hugh Durant (GB)	
	Team pistol (30 metres)	Hugh Durant (GB)	Bronze
	Team pistol (50 metres)	Hugh Durant (GB)	Bronze
	Individual free rifle	Ernest Keeley (South Africa)	
	Team free rifle	Ernest Keeley (South Africa)	
	Individual military rifle	Harcourt Ommundsen (GB)	
		Ernest Keeley (South Africa)	
	Team military rifle	Harcourt Ommundsen (GB)	Silver
		Ernest Keeley (South Africa)	

Sport	Event	Olympians who died	Medals
Swimming			
	200 metres breaststroke	Percy Courtman (GB)	
		Wilhelm Lutzow (Germany)	Silver
		Oszkar Demjan (Hungary)	
	400 metres breaststroke	Percy Courtman (GB)	Bronze
		Wilhelm Lutzow (Germany)	
		Oszkar Demjan (Hungary)	
	100 metres freestyle	Cecil Healy (Australia)	Silver
		Kurt Bretting (Germany)	
	400 metres freestyle	Cecil Healy (Australia)	
		Bela von Las-Torres (Hungary)	
	4 x 200 metres freestyle relay	Cecil Healy (Australia)	Gold
		Kurt Bretting (Germany)	
Tennis			
	Indoor singles	Tony Wilding (New Zealand)	Bronze
Water polo			
		Isaac Bentham (GB)	Gold
		Herman Donners (Belgium)	Bronze
Wrestling			
	Greco-Roman lightweight	Georg Baumann (Russia)	
	Greco-Roman featherweight	William Lyshon (USA)	

APPENDIX 3

THE FOOTBALL INTERNATIONALS PLAYED IN BY BRITISH AND IRISH FOOTBALLERS WHO DIED IN THE GREAT WAR

Date	Fixture	Score	Venue	Footballers Who Died
1884				
15th Mar	Scotland v. England	1-0	Glasgow	Robert Christie (Scotland)
1891				
7th Feb	Ireland v. Wales	7-2	Belfast	Richard Moore (Ireland)
7th Mar	England v. Ireland	6-1	Wolverhampton	Richard Moore (Ireland)
28th Mar	Scotland v. Ireland	2-1	Glasgow	Richard Moore (Ireland)
1896				
7th Mar	Ireland v. England	0-2	Belfast	Edward Turner (Ireland)
1898				
19th Feb	Wales v. Ireland	0-1	Llandudno	Bobby Atherton (Wales)
28th Mar	Wales v. England	0-3	Wrexham	Bobby Atherton (Wales)
1900				
3rd Feb	Scotland v. Wales	5-2	Aberdeen	Frederick Griffiths (Wales)
24th Feb	Wales v. Ireland	2-0	Llandudno	Leigh Roose (Wales)
26th Mar	Wales v. England	1-1	Cardiff	Frederick Griffiths (Wales)

Date	Fixture	Score	Venue	Footballers Who Died
1901				
2nd Mar	Wales v. Scotland	1-1	Wrexham	Leigh Roose (Wales)
				William Jones (Wales)
18th Mar	England v. Wales	6-0	Newcastle	Leigh Roose (Wales)
				William Jones (Wales)
23rd Mar	Ireland v. Wales	0-1	Belfast	Leigh Roose (Wales)
1902				
3rd Mar	Wales v. England	0-0	Wrexham	Leigh Roose (Wales)
				William Jones (Wales)
15th Mar	Scotland v. Wales	5-1	Greenock	Leigh Roose (Wales)
				William Jones (Wales)
9th Aug	Ireland v. Scotland	0-3	Belfast	Barney Donaghy (Ireland)
1903				
14th Feb	England v. Ireland	4-0	Wolverhampton	Harold Sloan (Ireland)
2nd Mar	England v. Wales	2-1	Portsmouth	Bobby Atherton (Wales)
9th Mar	Wales v. Scotland	0-1	Cardiff	Bobby Atherton (Wales)
28th Mar	Ireland v. Wales	2-0	Belfast	Bobby Atherton (Wales)
1904				
29th Feb	Wales v. England	2-2	Wrexham	Bobby Atherton (Wales)
				Leigh Roose (Wales)
12th Mar	Scotland v. Wales	1-1	Dundee	Bobby Atherton (Wales)
21st Mar	Wales v. Ireland	0-1	Bangor	Bobby Atherton (Wales)
9th Apr	Ireland v. Scotland	1-1	Dublin	Harold Sloan (Ireland)
1905				
25th Feb	England v. Ireland	1-1	Middlesbrough	Harold Sloan (Ireland)
6th Mar	Wales v. Scotland	3-1	Wrexham	Leigh Roose (Wales)
18th Mar	Scotland v. Ireland	4-0	Glasgow	Donald McLeod (Scotland)
27th Mar	England v. Wales	3-1	Liverpool	Leigh Roose (Wales)

Date	Fixture	Score	Venue	Footballers Who Died
8th Apr	Ireland v. Wales	2-2	Belfast	Bobby Atherton (Wales)
				Leigh Roose (Wales)
1906				
3rd Mar	Scotland v. Wales	0-2	Edinburgh	Donald McLeod (Scotland) Leigh Roose (Wales)
17th Mar	Ireland v. Scotland	0-1	Dublin	Donald McLeod (Scotland)
19th Mar	Wales v. England	0-1	Cardiff	Leigh Roose (Wales)
2nd Apr	Wales v. Ireland	4-4	Wrexham	Leigh Roose (Wales)
				Harold Sloan (Ireland)
7th Apr	Scotland v. England	2-1	Glasgow	Donald McLeod (Scotland)
				James Conlin (England)
1907				
16th Feb	England v. Ireland	1-0	Liverpool	Harold Sloan (Ireland)
23rd Feb	Ireland v. Wales	2-3	Belfast	Harold Sloan (Ireland)
				Leigh Roose (Wales)
4th Mar	Wales v. Scotland	1-0	Wrexham	Leigh Roose (Wales)
18th Mar	England v. Wales	1-1	London	Leigh Roose (Wales)
1908				
15th Feb	Ireland v. England	1-3	Belfast	Evelyn Lintott (England)
7th Mar	Scotland v. Wales	2-1	Dundee	James Speirs (Scotland)
				Leigh Roose (Wales)
14th Mar	Ireland v. Scotland	0-5	Dublin	Harold Sloan (Ireland)
16th Mar	Wales v. England	1-7	Wrexham	Leigh Roose (Wales)
				Evelyn Lintott (England)
4th Apr	Scotland v. England	1-1	Glasgow	Evelyn Lintott (England)
11th Apr	Wales v. Ireland	0-1	Aberdare	Harold Sloan (Ireland)

Date	Fixture	Score	Venue	Footballers Who Died
1909				
13th Feb	England v. Ireland	4-0	Bradford	Evelyn Lintott (England)
1st Mar	Wales v. Scotland	3-2	Wrexham	Leigh Roose (Wales)
3rd Mar	England v. Scotland	2-0	London	Evelyn Lintott (England)
15th Mar	England v. Wales	2-0	Nottingham	Leigh Roose (Wales)
20th Mar	Ireland v. Wales	2-3	Belfast	Leigh Roose (Wales)
1909				
29th May	Hungary v. England	2-4	Budapest	Evelyn Lintott (England)
31st May	Hungary v. England	2-8	Budapest	Evelyn Lintott (England)
				5th March 1910
1910				
14th Mar	Wales v. England	0-1	Cardiff	Leigh Roose (Wales)
11th Apr	Wales v. Ireland	4-1	Wrexham	Leigh Roose (Wales)
1911				
6th Mar	Wales v. Scotland	2-2	Cardiff	Leigh Roose (Wales)
1913				
17th Mar	England v. Wales	4-3	Bristol	Edwin Latheron (England)
1914				
14th Feb	England v. Ireland	0-3	Middlesbrough	Edwin Latheron (England)

APPENDIX 4

The Cricket Test Matches played

in by the Test Cricketers who died

in the Great War

Date	Test – Result	Venue	Test Cricketer Who Died
1888/89	South Africa v. England (1st Test) England won	Port Elizabeth	Arthur Edward Ochse (South Africa)
	South Africa v. England (2nd Test) England won	Cape Town	Arthur Edward Ochse (South Africa)
1895/96	South Africa v. England (1st Test) England won	Port Elizabeth	Frederick Cook
1901/02	Australia v. England (1st Test) England won	Sydney	Colin Blythe (England)
	Australia v. England (2nd Test) Australia won	Melbourne	Colin Blythe (England)
	Australia v. England (3rd Test) Australia won	Adelaide	Colin Blythe (England)

Date	Test – Result	Venue	Test Cricketer Who Died
1901/02	Australia v. England (4th Test) Australia won	Sydney	Colin Blythe (England)
	Australia v. England (5th Test) Australia won	Melbourne	Colin Blythe (England)
1903/04	Australia v. England (4th Test) England won	Sydney	Tippy Cotter (Australia)
	Australia v. England (5th Test) Australia won	Melbourne	Tippy Cotter (Australia)
1905	England v. Australia (1st Test) England won	Nottingham	Tippy Cotter (Australia)
	England v. Australia (3rd Test) Draw	Leeds	Colin Blythe (England)
	England v. Australia (4th Test) England won	Manchester	Tippy Cotter (Australia)
	England v. Australia (5th Test) Draw	Oval	Tippy Cotter (Australia)
1905/06	South Africa v. England (1st Test) South Africa won	Johannesburg	Colin Blythe (England) Reggie Schwarz (South Africa) Gordon White (South Africa)

Date	Test – Result	Venue	Test Cricketer Who Died
	South Africa v. England (2nd Test) South Africa won	Johannesburg	Reggie Schwarz (South Africa) Gordon White (South Africa) Colin Blythe (England) Leonard Moon (England)
	South Africa v. England (3rd Test) South Africa won	Johannesburg	Reggie Schwarz (South Africa) Gordon White (South Africa) Colin Blythe (England) Leonard Moon (England)
	South Africa v. England (4th Test) England won	Cape Town	Reggie Schwarz (South Africa) Gordon White (South Africa) Colin Blythe (England) Leonard Moon (England)
	South Africa v. England (5th Test) South Africa won	Cape Town	Reggie Schwarz (South Africa) Gordon White (South Africa) Colin Blythe (England) Leonard Moon (England)
1907	England v. South Africa (1st Test) Draw	Lord's	Colin Blythe (England) Reggie Schwarz (South Africa) Gordon White (South Africa)
	England v. South Africa (2nd Test) England won	Leeds	Colin Blythe (England) Reggie Schwarz (South Africa) Gordon White (South Africa)
	England v. South Africa (3rd Test) Draw	Oval	Colin Blythe (England) Reggie Schwarz (South Africa) Gordon White (South Africa)
1907/08	Australia v. England (1st Test) Australia won	Sydney	Tippy Cotter (Australia) Colin Blythe (England) Kenneth Hutchings (England)

Date	Test – Result	Venue	Test Cricketer Who Died
	Australia v. England	Melbourne	Tippy Cotter (Australia)
	(2nd Test)		Kenneth Hutchings (England)
	England won		
	Australia v. England	Adelaide	Kenneth Hutchings (England)
	(3rd Test)		
	Australia won		
	Australia v. England	Melbourne	Kenneth Hutchings (England)
	(4th Test)		
	Australia won		
	Australia v. England	Sydney	Kenneth Hutchings (England)
	(5th Test)		
	Australia won		
1909	England v. Australia	Birmingham	Tippy Cotter (Australia)
	(1st Test)		Colin Blythe (England)
	England won		
	England v. Australia	Lord's	Tippy Cotter (Australia)
	(2nd Test)		
	Australia won		
	England v. Australia	Leeds	Tippy Cotter (Australia)
	(3rd Test)		
	Australia won		
	England v. Australia	Manchester	Colin Blythe (England),
	(4th Test)		Tippy Cotter (Australia)
	Draw		Kenneth Hutchings (England)
	England v. Australia	Oval	Tippy Cotter (Australia)
	(5th Test)		Kenneth Hutchings (England)
	Draw		

Date	Test – Result	Venue	Test Cricketer Who Died
1909/10	South Africa v. England (1st Test) South Africa won	Johannesburg	Reggie Schwarz (South Africa) Gordon White (South Africa)
	South Africa v. England (2nd Test) South Africa won	Durban	Reggie Schwarz (South Africa) Gordon White (South Africa)
	South Africa v. England (3rd Test) England won	Johannesburg	Gordon White (South Africa)
	South Africa v. England (4th Test) South Africa won	Cape Town	Reggie Schwarz (South Africa) Gordon White (South Africa) Colin Blythe (England)
	South Africa v. England (5th Test) England won	Cape Town	Reggie Schwarz (South Africa) Colin Blythe (England)
1910/11	Australia v. South Africa (1st Test) Australia won	Sydney	Tippy Cotter (Australia) Reggie Schwarz (South Africa)
	Australia v. South Africa (2nd Test) Australia won	Melbourne	Tippy Cotter (Australia) Reggie Schwarz (South Africa)
	Australia v. South Africa (3rd Test) South Africa won	Adelaide	Tippy Cotter (Australia) Reggie Schwarz (South Africa)
	Australia v. South Africa (4th Test) Australia won	Melbourne	Tippy Cotter (Australia) Reggie Schwarz (South Africa)

Date	Test – Result	Venue	Test Cricketer Who Died
	Australia v. South Africa	Sydney	Tippy Cotter (Australia)
	(5th Test)		Reggie Schwarz (South Africa)
	Australia won		
1911/12	Australia v. England	Sydney	Tippy Cotter (Australia)
	(1st Test)		
	Australia won		
	Australia v. England	Melbourne	Tippy Cotter (Australia)
	(2nd Test)		
	England won		
	Australia v. England	Adelaide	Tippy Cotter (Australia)
	(3rd Test)		
	England won		
	Australia v. England	Melbourne	Tippy Cotter (Australia)
	(4th Test)		
	England won		
1912	Australia v. South Africa	Manchester	Reggie Schwarz (South Africa)
	(1st Test)		Gordon White (South Africa)
	Australia won		
	England v. South Africa	Leeds	Reggie Schwarz (South Africa)
	(1st Test)		Gordon White (South Africa)
	England won		
	Australia v. South Africa	Lord's	Reggie Schwarz (South Africa)
	(2nd Test)		Gordon White (South Africa)
	Australia won		
	Australia v. South Africa	Nottingham	Gordon White (South Africa)
	(3rd Test)		
	Draw		

Date	Test – Result	Venue	Test Cricketer Who Died
	England v. South Africa (2nd Test) England won	Oval	Gordon White (South Africa)
1913/14	South Africa v. England (1st Test) England won	Durban	Major Booth (England)
	South Africa v. England (2nd Test) England won	Johannesburg	Claude Newberry (South Africa)
	South Africa v. England (3rd Test) England won	Johannesburg	Claude Newberry (South Africa)
	South Africa v. England (4th Test) Draw	Durban	Claude Newberry (South Africa)
	South Africa v. England (5th Test) England won	Port Elizabeth	Bill Lundie (South Africa) Claude Newberry (South Africa) Reginald Hands Major Booth (England)

APPENDIX 5

THE RUGBY INTERNATIONALS PLAYED

IN BY THOSE WHO DIED IN THE GREAT

WAR

Date	Fixture	Score	Venue	Players who died
1881				
19th Feb	England v. Wales	8G-0G	Blackheath	Richard Williams (Wales)
1884				
5th Jan	England v. Wales	1G-1G	Leeds	Charles Taylor (Wales)
12th Jan	Wales v. Scotland	0G-1G	Newport	Charles Taylor (Wales)
12th Apr	Wales v. Ireland	1G-0	Cardiff	Charles Taylor (Wales)
				William Hallaran (Ireland)
1885				
3rd Jan	Wales v. England	1G-1G	Swansea	Charles Taylor (Wales)
10th Jan	Scotland v. Wales	0G-0G	Glasgow	Charles Taylor (Wales)
1886				
2nd Jan	England v. Wales	1G,2T-1G,0T	Blackheath	Rupert Inglis (England)
				Charles Taylor (Wales)
9th Jan	Wales v. Scotland	0G-2G	Cardiff	Charles Taylor (Wales)
6th Feb	Ireland v. England	0-0	Dublin	Rupert Inglis (England)
13th Mar	Scotland v. England	0-0	Edinburgh	Rupert Inglis (England)

Date	Fixture	Score	Venue	Players who died
1887				
8th Jan	Wales v. England	0G-0G	Llanelli	Charles Taylor (Wales)
12th Mar	Ireland v. Wales	0G-1G	Birkenhead	Charles Taylor (Wales)
1895				
26th Jan	Scotland v. Wales	5-4	Edinburgh	Harry Dods (Scotland)
2nd Mar	Scotland v. Ireland	6-0	Edinburgh	Harry Dods (Scotland)
9th Mar	England v. Scotland	3-6	Richmond	Harry Dods (Scotland)
1896				
25th Jan	Wales v. Scotland	6-0	Cardiff	Harry Dods (Scotland)
15th Feb	Ireland v. Scotland	0-0	Dublin	George Macallan (Ireland)
				Harry Dods (Scotland)
14th Mar	Scotland v. England	11-0	Glasgow	Harry Dods (Scotland)
14th Mar	Ireland v. Wales	8-4	Dublin	George Macallan (Ireland)
30th July	South Africa v. Great Britain	0-8	Port Elizabeth	Alexander Todd (GB)
22nd Aug	South Africa v. Great Britain	8-17	Johannesburg	Alexander Todd (GB)
29th Aug	South Africa v. Great Britain	3-9	Kimberley	Alexander Todd (GB)
5th Sept	South Africa v. Great Britain	5-0	Cape Town	Alexander Todd (GB)
1897				
20th Feb	Scotland v. Ireland	8-3	Edinburgh	Harry Dods (Scotland)
13th Mar	England v. Scotland	12-3	Manchester	Harry Dods (Scotland)
1898				
5th Feb	England v. Ireland	6-9	Richmond	Edward Wilson (England)
12th Mar	Scotland v. England	3-3	Edinburgh	Thomas Nelson (Scotland)

Date	Fixture	Score	Venue	Players who died
1899				
4th Mar	Scotland v. Wales	21-10	Inverleith	George Lamond (Scotland)
11th Mar	England v. Scotland	0-5	Blackheath	Reggie Schwarz (England)
				George Lamond (Scotland)
24th June	Australia v. Great Britain	13-3	Sydney	Charles Adamson (GB)
22nd July	Australia v. Great Britain	0-11	Brisbane	Charles Adamson (GB)
				Blair Swannell (GB)
5th Aug	Australia v. Great Britain	10-11	Sydney	Charles Adamson (GB)
				Blair Swannell (GB)
12th Aug	Australia v. Great Britain	0-13	Sydney	Charles Adamson (GB)
				Blair Swannell (GB)
1900				
6th Jan	England v. Wales	3-13	Gloucester	Lou Phillips (Wales)
27th Jan	Wales v. Scotland	12-3	Swansea	Lou Phillips (Wales)
				David Bedell-Sivright (Scotland)
3rd Feb	England v. Ireland	15-4	Richmond	Harry Alexander (England)
				Alexander Todd (England)
24th Feb	Ireland v. Scotland	0-0	Dublin	John Campbell (Scotland)
10th Mar	Scotland v. England	0-0	Inverleith	Harry Alexander (England)
				Alexander Todd (England)
17th Mar	Ireland v. Wales	0-3	Belfast	Lou Phillips (Wales)
1901				
5th Jan	Wales v. England	13-0	Cardiff	Harry Alexander (England)
				Reggie Schwarz (England)
9th Feb	Ireland v. England	10-6	Dublin	Harry Alexander (England)
				Reggie Schwarz (England)

Date	Fixture	Score	Venue	Players who died
9th Feb	Scotland v. Wales	18-8	Inverleith	David Bedell-Sivright (Scotland)
				James Ross (Scotland)
				Lou Phillips (Wales)
23rd Feb	Scotland v. Ireland	9-5	Inverleith	David Bedell-Sivright (Scotland)
				James Ross (Scotland)
9th Mar	England v. Scotland	3-18	Blackheath	Harry Alexander (England)
				Percy Kendall (England)
				David Bedell-Sivright (Scotland)
				James Ross (Scotland)

1902

Date	Fixture	Score	Venue	Players who died
11th Jan	England v. Wales	8-9	Blackheath	Harry Alexander (England)
				Percy Kendall (England)
				John Raphael (England)
1st Feb	Wales v. Scotland	14-5	Cardiff	David Bedell-Sivright (Scotland)
				James Ross (Scotland)
8th Feb	England v. Ireland	6-3	Leicester	Harry Alexander (England)
				John Raphael (England)
22nd Feb	Ireland v. Scotland	5-0	Belfast	David Bedell-Sivright (Scotland)
15th Mar	Scotland v. England	3-6	Inverleith	David Bedell-Sivright (Scotland)
				John Raphael (England)

1903

Date	Fixture	Score	Venue	Players who died
7th Feb	Scotland v. Wales	6-0	Inverleith	David Bedell-Sivright (Scotland)
				Walter Forrest (Scotland)
14th Feb	Ireland v. England	6-0	Dublin	Robertson Smyth (Ireland)
28th Feb	Scotland v. Ireland	3-0	Inverleith	David Bedell-Sivright (Scotland)
				Walter Forrest (Scotland)
				Robertson Smyth (Ireland)

Date	Fixture	Score	Venue	Players who died
21st Mar	England v. Scotland	6-10	Richmond	Percy Kendall (England)
				Walter Forrest (Scotland)
				James Ross (Scotland)
15th Aug	Australia v. New Zealand	3-22	Sydney	Edward Larkin (Australia)
				David Gallaher (New Zealand)
26th Aug	South Africa v. Great Britain 1	0-10	Johannesburg	Robertson Smyth (GB)
5th Sept	South Africa v. Great Britain	0-0	Kimberley	Robertson Smyth (GB)
12th Sept	South Africa v. Great Britain	8-0	Cape Town	Robertson Smyth (GB)

1904

Date	Fixture	Score	Venue	Players who died
6th Feb	Wales v. Scotland	21-3	Swansea	David Bedell-Sivright (Scotland)
				Walter Forrest (Scotland)
13th Feb	England v. Ireland	19-0	Blackheath	Robertson Smyth (Ireland)
27th Feb	Ireland v. Scotland	3-19	Dublin	David Bedell-Sivright (Scotland)
				Walter Forrest (Scotland)
12th Mar	Ireland v. Wales	14-12	Belfast	Charles Pritchard (Wales)
19th Mar	Scotland v. England	6-3	Inverleith	David Bedell-Sivright (Scotland)
				Walter Forrest (Scotland)
2nd July	Australia v. Great Britain	0-17	Sydney	Jack Verge (Australia)
				David Bedell-Sivright (GB)
				Sidney Crowther (GB)
				Blair Swannell (GB)
23rd July	Australia v. Great Britain	3-17	Brisbane	Jack Verge (Australia)
				Sidney Crowther (GB)
				Blair Swannell (GB)
30th July	Australia v. Great Britain	0-16	Sydney	Sidney Crowther (GB)
				Blair Swannell (GB)

Date	Fixture	Score	Venue	Players who died
13th Aug	New Zealand v. Great Britain	9-3	Wellington	David Gallaher (New Zealand)
				Eric Harper (New Zealand)
				Sidney Crowther (GB)
				Ron Rogers (GB)
				Blair Swannell (GB)

1905

Date	Fixture	Score	Venue	Players who died
14th Jan	Wales v. England	25-0	Cardiff	Charles Pritchard (Wales)
				John Raphael (England)
4th Feb	Scotland v. Wales	3-6	Inverleith	Walter Forrest (Scotland)
				Andrew Ross (Scotland)
				Charles Pritchard (Wales)
11th Feb	Ireland v. England	17-3	Cork	Basil Maclear (Ireland)
25th Feb	Scotland v. Ireland	5-11	Inverleith	Walter Forrest (Scotland)
				Andrew Ross (Scotland)
				Basil Maclear (Ireland)
1st Mar	Wales v. Ireland	10-3	Swansea	Basil Maclear (Ireland)
18th Mar	England v. Scotland	0-8	Richmond	John Raphael (England)
				George Lamond (Scotland)
				Andrew Ross (Scotland)
2nd Sept	New Zealand v. Australia	14-3	Dunedin	Ernie Dodd (New Zealand)
				Hubert Turtill (New Zealand)
				Blair Swannell (Australia)
18th Nov	Scotland v. New Zealand	7-12	Inverleith	David Bedell-Sivright (Scotland)
				David Gallaher (New Zealand)
25th Nov	Ireland v. New Zealand	0-15	Dublin	Basil Maclear (Ireland)
2nd Dec	England v. New Zealand	0-15	London	John Raphael (England)
				David Gallaher (New Zealand)
16th Dec	Wales v. New Zealand	3-0	Cardiff	Charles Pritchard (Wales)
				David Gallaher (New Zealand)

Date	Fixture	Score	Venue	Players who died
1906				
1st Jan	France v. New Zealand	8-38	Paris	Henri Lacassagne (France)
				Gaston Lane (France)
				David Gallaher (New Zealand)
				Eric Harper (New Zealand)
13th Jan	England v. Wales	3-16	Richmond	George Dobbs (England)
				Harold Hodges (England)
				John Raphael (England)
				Hopkin Maddock (Wales)
				Charles Pritchard (Wales)
3rd Feb	Wales v. Scotland	9-3	Cardiff	Hopkin Maddock (Wales)
				David Bedell-Sivright (Scotland)
				William Church (Scotland)
10th Feb	England v. Ireland	6-16	Leicester	George Dobbs (England)
				Harold Hodges (England)
				Basil Maclear (Ireland)
24th Feb	Ireland v. Scotland	6-13	Dublin	Basil Maclear (Ireland)
				David Bedell-Sivright (Scotland)
10th Mar	Ireland v. Wales	11-6	Belfast	Basil Maclear (Ireland)
				Hopkin Maddock (Wales)
				Charles Pritchard (Wales)
				Dai Westacott (Wales)
17th Mar	Scotland v. England	3-9	Inverleith	David Bedell-Sivright (Scotland)
				John Raphael (England)
22nd Mar	France v. England	8-35	Paris	Gaston Lane (France)
				John Raphael (England)
17th Nov	Scotland v. South Africa	6-0	Glasgow	David Bedell-Sivright (Scotland)
				Adam Burdett (South Africa)
24th Nov	Ireland v. South Africa	12-15	Belfast	Basil Maclear (Ireland)
				Adam Burdett (South Africa)

Date	Fixture	Score	Venue	Players who died
1st Dec	Wales v. South Africa	0-11	Swansea	Charles Pritchard (Wales)
				Dick Thomas (Wales)
				Johnnie Williams (Wales)

1907

Date	Fixture	Score	Venue	Players who died
5th Jan	England v. France	41-13	Richmond	Danny Lambert (England)
				Billy Nanson (England)
				Lance Slocock (England)
				Marc Giacardy (France)
				Henri Isaac (France)
				Henri Lacassagne (France)
				Gaston Lane (France)
12th Jan	Wales v. England	22-0	Swansea	Hopkin Maddock (Wales)
				Charles Pritchard (Wales)
				Johnnie Williams (Wales)
				Billy Nanson (England)
				Lance Slocock (England)
2nd Feb	Scotland v. Wales	6-3	Inverleith	David Bedell-Sivright (Scotland)
				Hopkin Maddock (Wales)
				Charles Pritchard (Wales)
				Johnnie Williams (Wales)
9th Feb	Ireland v. England	17-9	Dublin	Basil Maclear (Ireland)
				Lance Slocock (England)
23rd Feb	Scotland v. Ireland	15-3	Inverleith	David Bedell-Sivright (Scotland)
				Basil Maclear (Ireland)
9th Mar	Wales v. Ireland	29-0	Cardiff	Charles Pritchard (Wales)
				Johnnie Williams (Wales)
				Basil Maclear (Ireland)
16th Mar	England v. Scotland	3-8	Blackheath	Lance Slocock (England)
				David Bedell-Sivright (Scotland)

Date	Fixture	Score	Venue	Players who died
1908				
1st Jan	France v. England	0-19	Colombes	Pierre Guillemin (France)
				Henri Isaac (France)
				Gaston Lane (France)
				Alfred Mayssonnie (France)
				Danny Lambert (England)
				Lance Slocock (England)
18th Jan	England v. Wales	18-28	Bristol	Danny Lambert (England)
				Lance Slocock (England)
				Charles Pritchard (Wales)
				Johnnie Williams (Wales)
1st Feb	Wales v. Scotland	6-5	Swansea	Johnnie Williams (Wales)
				David Bedell-Sivright (Scotland)
8th Feb	England v. Ireland	13-3	Richmond	Lance Slocock (England)
29th Feb	Ireland v. Scotland	16-11	Dublin	David Bedell-Sivright (Scotland)
				John Wilson (Scotland)
2nd Mar	Wales v. France	36-4	Cardiff	Dick Thomas (Wales)
				Pierre Guillemin (France)
				Gaston Lane (France)
				Alfred Mayssonnie (France)
14th Mar	Ireland v. Wales	5-11	Belfast	Dick Thomas (Wales)
				Johnnie Williams (Wales)
21st Mar	Scotland v. England	16-10	Inverleith	Lewis Robertson (Scotland)
				Albert Wade (Scotland)
				Danny Lambert (England)
				Lance Slocock (England)
6th June	New Zealand v. Anglo-Welsh	32-5	Dunedin	Johnnie Williams (Anglo-Welsh)
27th June	New Zealand v. Anglo-Welsh	3-3	Wellington	Johnnie Williams (Anglo-Welsh)
12th Dec	Wales v. Australia	9-6	Cardiff	Phil Waller (Wales)
				Johnnie Williams (Wales)

Date	Fixture	Score	Venue	Players who died
1909				
9th Jan	England v. Australia	3-9	Blackheath	Alfred Maynard (England)
				Francis Tarr (England)
16th Jan	Wales v. England	8-0	Cardiff	Phil Waller (Wales)
				Johnnie Williams (Wales)
				Alfred Maynard (England)
				Francis Tarr (England)
1909				
30th Jan	England v. France	22-0	Leicester	Alfred Maynard (England)
				Ronnie Poulton-Palmer (England)
				Francis Tarr (England)
				Pierre Guillemin (France)
				Gaston Lane (France)
6th Feb	Scotland v. Wales	3-5	Inverleith	Andrew Ross (Scotland)
				John Wilson (Scotland)
				Dick Thomas (Wales)
				Phil Waller (Wales)
				Johnnie Williams (Wales)
13th Feb	Ireland v. England	5-11	Dublin	Ernest Deane (Ireland)
				Alfred Maynard (England)
				Ronnie Poulton-Palmer (England)
				Arthur Wilson (England)
23rd Feb	France v. Wales	5-47	Colombes	Paul Dupre (France)
				Gaston Lane (France)
				Phil Waller (Wales)
				Johnnie Williams (Wales)
27th Feb	Scotland v. Ireland	9-3	Inverleith	James Pearson (Scotland)
				Andrew Ross (Scotland)
13th Mar	Wales v. Ireland	18-5	Swansea	Phil Waller (Wales)
				Johnnie Williams (Wales)

Date	Fixture	Score	Venue	Players who died
20th Mar	England v. Scotland	8-18	Richmond	Alfred Maynard (England)
				Ronnie Poulton-Palmer (England)
				James Pearson (Scotland)
20th Mar	Ireland v. France	19-8	Dublin	Marcel Burgun (France) Pierre
				Guillemin (France)
				Gaston Lane (France)
				Marcel Legrain (France)

1910

Date	Fixture	Score	Venue	Players who died
1st Jan	Wales v. France	49-14	Swansea	Hopkin Maddock (Wales)
				Charles Pritchard (Wales)
				Phil Waller (Wales)
				Joe Andurin (France)
				Marcel Burgun (France)
				Pierre Guillemin (France)
				Gaston Lane (France)
				Alfred Mayssonnie (France)
15th Jan	England v. Wales	11-6	Twickenham	Henry Berry (England)
				Leonard Haigh (England)
				Ronnie Poulton-Palmer (England)
				Charles Pritchard (Wales)
22nd Jan	Scotland v. France	27-0	Inverleith	James Pearson (Scotland)
				Rene Boudreaux (France)
				Marcel Burgun (France)
				Pierre Guillemin (France)
5th Feb	Wales v. Scotland	14-0	Cardiff	Eric Milroy (Scotland)
				James Pearson (Scotland)
				Walter Sutherland (Scotland)

Date	Fixture	Score	Venue	Players who died
12th Feb	England v. Ireland	0-0	Twickenham	Henry Berry (England)
				Leonard Haigh (England)
				Alfred Maynard (England)
				Alfred Taylor (Ireland)
26th Feb	Ireland v. Scotland	0-14	Belfast	Alfred Taylor (Ireland)
				Cecil Abercrombie (Scotland)
				James Pearson (Scotland)
3rd Mar	France v. England	3-11	Paris	Pierre Guillemin (France)
				Gaston Lane (France)
				Henry Berry (England)
				Reginald Hands (England)
				Alfred Maynard (England)
12th Mar	Ireland v. Wales	3-19	Dublin	Alfred Taylor (Ireland)
				Johnnie Williams (Wales)
19th Mar	Scotland v. England	5-14	Inverleith	Cecil Abercrombie (Scotland)
				James Pearson (Scotland)
				Walter Sutherland (Scotland)
				Henry Berry (England)
				Leonard Haigh (England)
				Reginald Hands (England)
28th Mar	France v. Ireland	3-8	Paris	Marcel Burgun (France)
				Pierre Guillemin (France)
				Marcel Legrain (France)
25th June	Australia v. New Zealand	0-6	Sydney	Harold George (Australia)
				Jimmy Ridland (New Zealand)
27th June	Australia v. New Zealand	11-0	Sydney	Harold George (Australia)
				Jimmy Ridland (New Zealand)
2nd July	Australia v. New Zealand	13-28	Sydney	Harold George (Australia)
				Jimmy Ridland (New Zealand)
6th Aug	South Africa v. Great Britain	14-10	Johannesburg	Phil Waller (GB)

Date	Fixture	Score	Venue	Players who died
27th Aug	South Africa v. Great Britain	3-8	Port Elizabeth	Toby Moll (South Africa)
				Phil Waller (GB)
3rd Sept	South Africa v. Great Britain	21-5	Cape Town	Phil Waller (GB)

1911

Date	Fixture	Score	Venue	Players who died
2nd Jan	France v. Scotland	16-15	Colombes	Marcel Burgun (France)
				Paul Decamps (France)
				Pierre Guillemin (France)
				Gaston Lane (France)
				Marcel Legrain (France)
				Cecil Abercrombie (Scotland)
				Rowland Fraser (Scotland)
				James Pearson (Scotland)
				Walter Sutherland (Scotland)
				Frederick Turner (Scotland)
21st Jan	Wales v. England	15-11	Swansea	Johnnie Williams (Wales)
				Leonard Haigh (England)
				John King (England)
				Danny Lambert (England)
28th Jan	England v. France	37-0	Twickenham	Leonard Haigh (England)
				John King (England)
				Danny Lambert (England)
				Marcel Burgun (France)
				Pierre Guillemin (France)
				Marcel Legrain (France)
4th Feb	Scotland v. Wales	10-32	Inverleith	Cecil Abercrombie (Scotland)
				Rowland Fraser (Scotland)
				Lewis Robertson (Scotland)
				Frederick Turner (Scotland)
				Johnnie Williams (Wales)

Date	Fixture	Score	Venue	Players who died
11th Feb	Ireland v. England	3-0	Dublin	Leonard Haigh (England)
				John King (England)
				Danny Lambert (England)
25th Feb	Scotland v. Ireland	10-16	Inverleith	Rowland Fraser (Scotland)
				Frederick Turner (Scotland)
28th Feb	France v. Wales	0-15	Paris	Pierre Guillemin (France)
				Gaston Lane (France)
				Marcel Legrain (France)
				Johnnie Williams (Wales)
11th Mar	Wales v. Ireland	16-0	Cardiff	Johnnie Williams (Wales)
18th Mar	England v. Scotland	13-8	Twickenham	Leonard Haigh (England)
				John King (England)
				Ronald Lagden (England)
				Ronnie Poulton-Palmer (England)
				Bavid Bain (Scotland)
				Rowland Fraser (Scotland)
				James Henderson (Scotland)
				William Hutchison (Scotland)
				Eric Milroy (Scotland)
				Ronald Simson (Scotland)
				Stephen Steyn (Scotland)
				Walter Sutherland (Scotland)
				Frederick Turner (Scotland)
25th Mar	Ireland v. France	25-5	Cork	Marcel Legrain (France)

Date	Fixture	Score	Venue	Players who died
1912				
1st Jan	France v. Ireland	6-11	Paris	Maurice Boyau (France)
				Marcel Burgun (France)
				Jean-Jacques Conilh de Beyssac (France)
				Julien Dufau (France)
				Daniel Ihingoue (France)
				Gaston Lane (France)
				Leon Larribau (France)
				William Edwards (Ireland)
				Alfred Taylor (Ireland)
20th Jan	England v. Wales	8-0	Twickenham	Henry Brougham (England)
				John King (England)
				Ronnie Poulton-Palmer (England)
20th Jan	Scotland v. France	31-3	Inverleith	David Bain (Scotland)
				Mike Dickson (Scotland)
				David Howie (Scotland)
				James Pearson (Scotland)
				Walter Sutherland (Scotland)
				Frederick Turner (Scotland)
				John Will (Scotland)
				Maurice Boyau (France)
				Marcel Burgun (France)
				Jean-Jacques Conilh de Beyssac (France)
				Julien Dufau (France)
				Daniel Ihingoue (France)
				Leon Larribau (France)

Date	Fixture	Score	Venue	Players who died
3rd Feb	Wales v. Scotland	21-6	Swansea	David Bain (Scotland)
				Mike Dickson (Scotland)
				David Howie (Scotland)
				Eric Milroy (Scotland)
				James Pearson (Scotland)
				Lewis Robertson (Scotland)
				Walter Sutherland (Scotland)
				Frederick Turner (Scotland)
				John Will (Scotland)
10th Feb	England v. Ireland	15-0	Twickenham	Henry Brougham (England)
				John King (England)
				Ronnie Poulton-Palmer (England)
				William Edwards (Ireland)
24th Feb	Ireland v. Scotland	10-8	Dublin	David Howie (Scotland)
				Eric Milroy (Scotland)
				Lewis Robertson (Scotland)
				Stephen Steyn (Scotland)
				Frederick Turner (Scotland)
				John Will (Scotland)
9th Mar	Ireland v. Wales	12-5	Belfast	Bryn Lewis (Wales)

Date	Fixture	Score	Venue	Players who died
16th Mar	Scotland v. England	8-3	Inverleith	David Bain (Scotland)
				Mike Dickson (Scotland)
				David Howie (Scotland)
				Eric Milroy (Scotland)
				Lewis Robertson (Scotland)
				Walter Sutherland (Scotland)
				Frederick Turner (Scotland)
				John Will (Scotland)
				Henry Brougham (England)
				John King (England)
				Ronnie Poulton-Palmer (England)
25th Mar	Wales v. France	14-8	Newport	Maurice Boyau (France)
				Julien Dufau (France)
				Gaston Lane (France)
				Leon Larribau (France)
8th Apr	France v. England	8-18	Paris	Maurice Boyau (France)
				Julien Dufau (France)
				Gaston Lane (France)
				Leon Larribau (France)
				Henry Brougham (England)
16th Nov	USA v. Australia	8-12	Berkeley	Frank Gard (USA)
				Harold George (Australia)
				George Pugh (Australia)

Date	Fixture	Score	Venue	Players who died
23rd Nov	Scotland v. South Africa	0-16	Inverleith	David Bain (Scotland)
				Patrick Blair (Scotland)
				Mike Dickson (Scotland)
				David Howie (Scotland)
				Eric Milroy (Scotland)
				James Pearson (Scotland)
				Lewis Robertson (Scotland)
				Walter Sutherland (Scotland)
				Frederick Turner (Scotland)
				Sep Ledger (South Africa)
				Jacky Morkel (South Africa)
				Gerald Thompson (South Africa)
30th Nov	Ireland v. South Africa	0-38	Dublin	Robert Burgess (Ireland)
				Sep Ledger (South Africa)
				Jacky Morkel (South Africa)
				Gerald Thompson (South Africa)
14th Dec	Wales v. South Africa	0-3	Cardiff	Billy Geen (Wales)
				Fred Perrett (Wales)
				Horace Thomas (Wales)
				Jacky Morkel (South Africa)
				Gerald Thompson (South Africa)

Date	Fixture	Score	Venue	Players who died
1913				
1st Jan	France v. Scotland	3-21	Paris	Marcel Burgun (France)
				Julien Dufau (France)
				Maurice Hedembaigt (France)
				Gaston Lane (France)
				Marcel Legrain (France)
				Cecil Abercrombie (Scotland)
				David Bain (Scotland)
				Patrick Blair (Scotland)
				Mike Dickson (Scotland)
				Roland Gordon (Scotland)
				David Howie (Scotland)
				Eric Milroy (Scotland)
				Walter Sutherland (Scotland)
				Frederick Turner (Scotland)
4th Jan	England v. South Africa	3-9	Twickenham	John King (England)
				Ronnie Poulton-Palmer (England)
				Sep Ledger (South Africa)
				Jacky Morkel (South Africa)
11th Jan	France v. South Africa	5-38	Bordeaux	Albert Chatau (France)
				Maurice Hedembaigt (France)
				Marcel Legrain (France)
				Sep Ledger (South Africa)
				Jacky Morkel (South Africa)
18th Jan	Wales v. England	0-12	Cardiff	Billy Geen (Wales)
				Fred Perrett (Wales)
				Horace Thomas (Wales)
				John King (England)
				Ronnie Poulton-Palmer (England)

Date	Fixture	Score	Venue	Players who died
25th Jan	England v. France	20-0	Twickenham	John King (England)
				Ronnie Poulton-Palmer (England)
				Marcel Burgun (France)
				Marcel Legrain (France)
1st Feb	Scotland v. Wales	0-8	Inverleith	Cecil Abercrombie (Scotland)
				David Bain (Scotland)
				Patrick Blair (Scotland)
				Mike Dickson (Scotland)
				Roland Fraser (Scotland)
				David Howie (Scotland)
				Eric Milroy (Scotland)
				Lewis Robertson (Scotland)
				Walter Sutherland (Scotland)
				Frederick Turner (Scotland)
				Fred Perrett (Wales)
8th Feb	Ireland v. England	4-15	Dublin	Arthur Dingle (England)
				John King (England)
				Ronnie Poulton-Palmer (England)
22nd Feb	Scotland v. Ireland	29-14	Inverleith	David Bain (Scotland)
				Patrick Blair (Scotland)
				Mike Dickson (Scotland)
				Roland Fraser (Scotland)
				Eric Milroy (Scotland)
				James Pearson (Scotland)
				Lewis Robertson (Scotland)
				Walter Sutherland (Scotland)
				Frederick Turner (Scotland)
27th Feb	France v. Wales	8-11	Paris	Maurice Boyau (France)
				Fred Perrett (Wales)

Date	Fixture	Score	Venue	Players who died
8th Mar	Wales v. Ireland	16-13	Swansea	Billy Geen (Wales)
				Bryn Lewis (Wales)
				Fred Perrett (Wales)
				Albert Stewart (Ireland)
15th Mar	England v. Scotland	3-0	Twickenham	John King (England)
				Francis Oakeley (England)
				Ronnie Poulton-Palmer (England)
				Francis Tarr (England)
				David Bain (Scotland)
				Patrick Blair (Scotland)
				Eric Milroy (Scotland)
				James Pearson (Scotland)
				Lewis Robertson (Scotland)
				Walter Sutherland (Scotland)
				Frederick Turner (Scotland)
				William Wallace (Scotland)
24th Mar	Ireland v. France	24-0	Cork	Albert Stewart (Ireland)
				Maurice Boyau (France)
				Albert Eutropius (France)
				Marcel Legrain (France)
6th Sept	New Zealand v. Australia	30-5	Wellington	Henry Dewar (New Zealand)
				Albert Joseph (New Zealand)
				George Sellars (New Zealand)
				Harold George (Australia)
				Bryan Hughes (Australia)
				Hubert Jones (Australia)
				William Tasker (Australia)
				Fred Thompson (Australia)
				Clarrie Wallach (Australia)

Date	Fixture	Score	Venue	Players who died
13th Sept	New Zealand v. Australia	25-13	Dunedin	Jim Baird (New Zealand)
				Jim McNeece (New Zealand)
				Reg Taylor (New Zealand)
				Bryan Hughes (Australia)
				Hubert Jones (Australia)
				William Tasker (Australia)
				Fred Thompson (Australia)
20th Sept	New Zealand v. Australia	5-16	Christchurch	Jim McNeece (New Zealand)
				Reg Taylor (New Zealand)
				Harold George (Australia)
				Bryan Hughes (Australia)
				Hubert Jones (Australia)
				William Tasker (Australia)
				Fred Thompson (Australia)
				Clarrie Wallach (Australia)
15th Nov	USA v. New Zealand	3-51	Berkeley	Frank Gard (USA)
				Henry Dewar (New Zealand)
				Albert Joseph (New Zealand)
				George Sellars (New Zealand)

Date	Fixture	Score	Venue	Players who died
1914				
1st Jan	France v. Ireland	6-8	Paris	Leon Larribau (France)
				Jean-Jacques Conilh de Beyssac (France)
				Marcel Legrain (France)
				Francois Poeydebasque (France)
				Albert Stewart (Ireland)
17th Jan	England v. Wales	10-9	Twickenham	Alfred Maynard (England)
				Ronnie Poulton-Palmer (England)
				James Watson (England)
				David Watts (Wales)
7th Feb	Wales v. Scotland	24-5	Cardiff	David Watts (Wales)
				David Bain (Scotland)
				Walter Sutherland (Scotland)
				John Will (Scotland)
				William Wallace (Scotland)
14th Feb	England v. Ireland	17-12	Twickenham	Arthur Harrison (England)
				Alfred Maynard (England)
				Francis Oakeley (England)
				Ronnie Poulton-Palmer (England)
				Vincent Macnamara (Ireland)
28th Feb	Ireland v. Scotland	6-0	Dublin	Vincent Macnamara (Ireland)
				David Bain (Scotland)
				Eric Milroy (Scotland)
				Frederick Turner (Scotland)
				John Will (Scotland)
				William Wallace (Scotland)

Date	Fixture	Score	Venue	Players who died
2nd Mar	Wales v. France	31-0	Swansea	David Watts (Wales)
				Jean-Jacques Conilh de Beyssac (France)
				Maurice Hedembaigt (France)
				Marcel Legrain (France)
				Francois Poeydebasque (France)
14th Mar	Ireland v. Wales	3-11	Belfast	Jasper Brett (Ireland)
				Vincent Macnamama (Ireland)
				David Watts (Wales)
21st Mar	Scotland v. England	15-16	Inverleith	James Huggan (Scotland)
				Eric Milroy (Scotland)
				Frederick Turner (Scotland)
				John Will (Scotland)
				William Wallace (Scotland)
				Eric Young (Scotland)
				Arthur Dingle (England)
				Alfred Maynard (England)
				Francis Oakeley (England)
				Ronnie Poulton-Palmer (England)
				James Watson (England)

Date	Fixture	Score	Venue	Players who died
13th Apr	France v. England	13-39	Colombes	Marcel Burgun (France)
				Jean-Jacques Conilh de Beyssac (France)
				Emmanuel Iguiniz (France)
				Leon Larribau (France)
				Arthur Dingle (England)
				Arthur Harrison (England)
				Francis Oakeley (England)
				Robert Pillman (England)
				Ronnie Poulton-Palmer (England)
				James Watson (England)
18th July	Australia v. New Zealand	0-5	Sydney	Harold George (Australia)
				William Tasker (Australia)
				Fred Thompson (Australia)
				Clarrie Wallach (Australia)
				Bobby Black (New Zealand)
				Albert Joseph (New Zealand)
				Jim McNeece (New Zealand)
1st Aug	Australia v. New Zealand	0-17	Brisbane	William Tasker (Australia)
				Fred Thompson (Australia)
				Clarrie Wallach (Australia)
				Albert Joseph (New Zealand)
				Jim McNeece (New Zealand)
15th Aug	Australia v. New Zealand	7-22	Sydney	Harold George (Australia)
				William Tasker (Australia)
				Fred Thompson (Australia)
				Clarrie Wallach (Australia)
				Albert Joseph (New Zealand)
				Jim McNeece (New Zealand)

APPENDIX 6

The dates on which the casualties occurred (where known)

1914

July

28th OUTBREAK OF WAR

August

4th BRITAIN DECLARES WAR ON
   GERMANY

9th Henri Bonnefoy

25th Felix Debax

30th Robert Merz

September

4th Oszkar Demjan

5th Jean de Mas Latrie

6th Alfred Mayssonnie

9th Carl Heinrich Gossler

14th Ronald Simson, George Hutson

15th Eduard von Lutcken

16th James Huggan, Louis Bach

17th Charles Wilson

19th Charles Devendeville

20th Emmanuel Iguniz

21st Leopold Mayer, Francois Poeydebasque

23rd Gaston Lane

29th Jean Bouin

October

2nd Joe Anduran

9th Georges de la Neziere

15th James Watson

18th Sidney Crowther, Thomas Gillespie

24th Bela Zulawszky

28th Joseph Racine

31st James Ross

November

Laurie Anderson

3rd Lewis Robertson

4th Alphonse Meignant

11th A. E. J. Collins

21st Arpad Pedery

December

1st Francis Oakeley

11th Jeno Szantay

22nd Richard Yorke

1915

January

10th Fred Turner

24th Charles Taylor

25th Percy Kendall

29th Max Hermann

31st Georges Lutz

February

18th Kenneth Powell

21st Edward Nash

March

3rd Ronald Lagden

21st Wyndham Halswelle

April

13th Adolf Kofler

21st Alexander Todd

23rd Jimmy Duffy

25th Edward Larkin, Blair Swannell, Gilchrist
　　Maclagan, Geoffrey Taylor

26th William Anderson

May

5th Ronald Poulton-Palmer

8th Ralph Chalmers

9th Henry Berry, Henry Goldsmith, Tony Wilding,
　　Francois Faber

10th Harold George

14th Herman Donners

22nd James Pearson

25th Basil Maclear

26th Albert Eutropius

29th Fred Thompson, Henry Leeke

June

3rd David Bain

4th Billy Nanson

7th Oswald Carver

10th Marcel Legrain

15th Georg Mickler

20th George Fairbairn

27th Paul Decamps

28th Bill Church, Eric Young, Ron Rogers, Amon
　　Ritter von Gregurich

July

6th Patrick Blair

15th Jacques Person

18th Francis Tarr

31st Billy Geen

August

8th Doolan Downing

9th Henry Dewar

12th Edward Williams

15th Rudolf Watzl

18th Pierre Guillemin, Edmond Wallace

22nd Arthur Dingle, William Wallace

30th Paul Kenna

September

5th David Bedell-Sivright

8th Jack Verge, Rene Boudreaux

12th Fritz Bartholomae

19th Harcourt Ommundsen

25th Ernest Deane, Renon Boissiere, Michel Soalhat

26th Mike Dickson

27th Richard Williams

30th Ismael de Lesseps, Heinrich Schneidereit

October

1st Joseph Caulle

12th Bela von Las-Torres

13th Danny Lambert

17th Harry Alexander, Charlie Adamson

22nd Alfred Staats

November

29th Vincent McNamara

30th Frederick Cook

December

4th Lajos Gonczy

5th Edmond Bury

9th Robert Burgess

30th John Dods

1916

January

19th Dave Howie

20th Hugh Durant

21st Arthur Wilde

February

22nd Albert Jenicot

March

14th Lou Phillips, Alan Patterson

April

5th Robertson Smyth

6th Andrew Ross

19th Karl Braunsteiner

May

5th Maurice Raoul-Duval

15th Jackie Morkell

31st Cecil Abercrombie, John Wilson, Paul Dupre

June

20th Gerald Thompson

July

1st Evelyn Lintott, Barney Donaghy, Major Booth, Rowland Fraser, Alfred Flaxman, Robert Somers-Smith

6th Bela Bekassy

7th Dick Thomas, William Philo, Harold Wilson, Pierre Six

9th Ronald Pillman

10th Donald Bell

12th Johnnie Williams

13th Josef Rieder

14th David Watts

15th Toby Moll

18th Eric Milroy

26th Keith Heritage

August

1st Claude Newberry

6th Leonard Haigh

7th Maurice Salomez

9th John King, Andrew Slocock

14th Charles Pritchard

20th Marc Giacardy

23rd John Robinson

September

2nd Marcel Burgun

3rd Kenneth Hutchings, Horace Thomas

5th George Pugh

9th Robert Davies

16th Frank McGee

18th Rupert Inglis

19th Frank Wilson

21st Bobby Black

30th Justin Vialaret

November

4th Hubert Jones, Rene Fenouilliere

13th Alfred Maynard

15th Hermann Bosch

16th Frederick Kelly

23rd Leonard Moon

24th Leon Ponscarme

December

20th Louis de Champsavin

28th Julien Dufau

31st Leon Larribau

1917

January

2nd Leon Flameng

10th Feliks Leparsky

21st Harold Sloan

23rd William Hallaran

27th Geoffrey Coles

31st Henry Ashington

February

4th Jasper Brett

22nd Charles Vigurs

March

25th George Will

29th Alister Kirby

April

2nd Bryn Lewis

6th AMERICA DECLARES WAR ON GERMANY

6th Friedrich Carl, Prince of Prussia

9th Tommy Nelson

11th Herbert Wilson

12th Sep Ledger

16th Daniel Ihingoue

19th Walter Forrest

24th Gordon Alexander

28th Albert Wade, Bobby Powell

May

3rd Norman Callaway, Jack Harrison, Sandy Turnbull

15th Isaac Bentham

June

2nd Percy Courtman

7th Jim Baird, George Sellars, Patrick Roche

11th John Raphael

16th Harold Hawkins

17th George Dobbs

20th Reg Taylor

21st Jim McNeece

23rd James Conlin, Bert Gayler

29th Henri Isaac

July

1st Arthur Wilson

5th Percival Molson

14th Octave Lapize

28th Waldemar Tietgens

31st Edgar Mobbs, Alfred Taylor, James Henderson

August

4th Noel Chavasse

5th Wilhelm Brulle

17th Claude Ross

20th James Speirs

28th Dai Westacott

September

2nd Edward Turner

11th Bill Lundie

22nd George Hawkins

24th George Butterfield

25th Bernhard von Gaza

October

4th Albert Stewart, David Gallaher

6th Donald McLeod

7th Leigh Roose

9th Duncan Mackinnon

14th Edwin Latheron

19th Bobby Atherton

22nd Harry Crank

30th Frederick Griffiths, Alex Decoteau

31st Tibby Cotter

November

8th Colin Blythe

30th Ivan Laing

December

1st John Campbell

8th Stephen Steyn

14th Phil Waller

29th William Edwards

1918

February

1st Juho Halme

25th George Lamond

March

13th Reggie Pridmore

21st Hermann Plaskuda

22nd William Hutchison

24th Harold Hodges

25th Walter Tull

27th Noel Humphries

April

9th Hubert Turtill

11th Arthur Edward Ochse

17th Ronald Sanderson

20th Reginald Hands

22nd Clarrie Wallach

23rd Arthur Harrison

30th Eric Harper

May

William Jones

15th Robert Christie

30th Kurt Bretting

June

13th Jean-Jacques Conilh de Beyssac

July

9th Erich Lehmann

22nd Istvan Mudin

23rd Albert Rowland, Ernest Keeley

26th Henry Macintosh

August

5th Maurice Hedembaigt

6th Bryan Hughes, Eberherd Sorge

9th William Tasker, Thomas Raddall

11th Frederick Kitching

28th Bertrand, Count de Lesseps

29th Cecil Healy

30th Roland Gordon

September

11th Ernie Dodd

14th Henri Lacassagne

16th Maurice Boyau

17th Charles Adamson

27th Joseph Dines, Frank Gard

October

3rd Bernard Vann

4th Walter Sutherland

9th Hanns Braun

13th William Lyshon

17th Gordon White

29th Richard Moore

31st Alfred Motte

November

Heinrich Burkowitz

4th Adam Burdett

5th Jimmy Ridland

6th Arthur Wear

11th ARMISTICE SIGNED

After the Armistice was signed

18th November 1918 Reggie Schwarz

1st December 1918 Fred Perrett

4th December 1918 George McAllan

13th December 1918 Andre Corvington

26th January 1919 Hermann von Bonninghausen

10th February 1919 William Beatty

15th December 1921 Hopkin Maddock

18th February 1923 Henry Brougham

15th July 1924 Albert Chatau

Bibliography

Archives and Databases

A Cambridge Alumni Database

Corpus Christie College Oxford Roll of Honour World War I : Biographies

Radley College archives

Welsh Football Data archive

Articles and Newspapers

Harold Sloan : A Forgotten Ranger by Ciaran Priestley

Supplement to *The London Gazette*, 17th March 1919

The British Medical Journal, 28th October 1916

The Irish Examiner, 26th February 2015

The Irish Times, 19th August 1916

The London Gazette, 19th October 1914

The London Gazette, 30th July 1915

The Scotsman, 25th March 2006

The Scotsman, 6th November 2009

Books

A Century of Welsh Rugby Players by Wayne Thomas

After The Final Whistle by Stephen Cooper

Anthony Wilding, A Sporting Life by Len and Shelley Richardson

A Portrait of Scottish Rugby by Allan Massie

A Social History of English Rugby Union by Tony Collins

Born to Lead – Wallaby Test Captains by Max Howell

Boston : The Canadian Story – Jimmy Duffy 1914 by David Blaikie

British Lions by John Griffiths

Canadian Expeditionary Force 1914-1919 by Gerald Nicholson

Captain Anthony Wilding by A. Wallis Mayers

Cardiff Rugby Club, History and Statistics 1876-1975 by D. E. Davies

Case Study : Rosslyn Park's Unknown Soldiers by Richard Cable

Catastrophe by Max Hastings

Chavasse : Double VC by Ann Clayton

Dave Gallaher – The Original All Black Captain by Matt Elliott

Dictionary of Australian Biography

Dragon in Exile, the Centenary History of London Welsh R. F. C. by Stephen
Jones and Paul Beken

Encyclopedia Judaica

Fields of Praise : The Official History of The Welsh Rugby Union by David
Smith and Gareth Williams

Final Wicket Test and First Class Cricketers Killed in the Great War by Nigel
McCrery

Football League Players Records 1888-1939 by Michael Joyce

For Poulton and England : the Life and Times of an Edwardian rugby hero
by James Corsan

Haka! The All Blacks Story by Winston McCarthy

Into Touch Rugby Internationals Killed in the Great War by Nigel McCrery

John Buchan and his Friends by Janet Adam Smith

Merton College register 1900-1964 by R. G. C. Levens

Oxford Dictionary of National Biography

Plymouth Argyll : Miscellany by Rick Cowdery and Mike Curno

Princess Patricia's Canadian Light Infantry by Ralph Hodder-Williams

Reminiscences of the First World War by H. L. Silberbauer

Scottish Rugby Internationals Who Fell by Alistair McEwen

Sport's Great All-Rounders by James Holder

Springboks in Wales by John Billot

The Barbarians by Nigel Starmer-Smith

The Bond of Sacrific : A Biographical Record of All British Officers who fell in the Great War by L. A. Clutterbuck

The Chavasse Twins : A biography of Christopher M. Chavasse, Bishop of Rochester and Noel G. Chavasse by Selwyn Gummer

The Complete Who's Who of Rugby Union Internationals by Raymond Maude

The Final Over : The Cricketers of Summer 1914 by Christopher Sandford

The Final Season The Footballers Who Fought and Died in the Great War by Nigel McCrery

The Final Whistle The Great War In Fifteen Players by Stephen Cooper

The Fourth Olympiad, Being the Official Report by Theodora Andrea Cook

The Life of Ronald Poulton by Sir Edward Bagnall Poulton

The Official History of the Olympic Games and the IOC Athens to London 1894-2012

The Phoenix Book of International Rugby Records by John Griffiths

The Register of the Victoria Cross

The Rugby Football Internationals Roll of Honour by E. H. D. Sewell

The Scottish Rugby Miscellany by Richard Bath

The Wisden Book of Test Cricketers Volume I (1877-1977)

Walter Sutherland Scotland's Rugby Legend 1890-1918 by Kenneth Bogle

Who's Who of Welsh International Rugby Players by John M. Jenkins

Who's Who of Welsh International Soccer Players by Gareth Davies

Wisden Cricketers' Almanack 1917

Wisden on the Great War

Websites

www.20thcenturylondon.co.uk

adb.anu.edu.au

www.allblacks.com

www.awm.gov.au

barbarians.co.uk

www.bathrugbyheritage.org

www.britishlegion.org.uk

www.coldstreamhistorysociety.org

www.cricbuzz.com

Cricket Archive.com

www.cricketcountry.com

www.cricketweb.net

www.cwgc.org

databaseOlympics.com

www.dungannonwardead.com

www.durhamatwar.org.uk

www.edinburghaccies.com

www.edinburghs-war.ed.co.uk

www.englandfc.com

www.englandfootballonline.com

www.englandrugby.com

EnglandStats.com

en.wikipedia.org

www.espncricinfo.com

eu-football.info

eyewitnesstours.com

www.fifa.com

www.findagrave.com

www.firstworldwar.com

www.fitbastats.com

www.footballandthefirstworldwar.org

www.gloucesterrugbyheritage.org.uk

www.gloucestershirelive.co.uk

greatwarlondon.wordpress.com

www.hambo/kingscanterbury

www.historyofnewport.co.uk

www.howstat.com

invisionzone.com

www.irishtimes.com

www.kentcricket.co.uk

www.lemsfordww1.co.uk

www.lionsrugby.com

www.londonhearts.com

www.longlongtrail.co.uk

www.keble.ox.ac.uk

www.kelsoconnections.co.uk

kirkcaldyrugby.co.uk

www.militarian.com

www.millhillatwar.org.uk

www.mkheritage.org.uk

www.nationalarchives.gov.uk

www.newbattleatwar.com

nifootball.blogspot.com

www.nixonpuictures.co.nz

www.northamptonsaints.co.uk

www.nzherald.co.nz

www.ourfc.org

www.pitchero.com

www.prescot-rollofhonour.info

remembered.co.za

www.rbwm.gov.uk

www.roll-of-honour.com

www.rowinghistory.net

www.rugbyfootballhistory.com

www.rugby-memorabilia.co.uk

www.scotlandswar.ed.ac.uk

www.scottishfa.com

www.scottishrugby.org

www.scottishsporthistory .com

www.soccer-ireland.com

www.spartacus-educational.com

www.sports-reference.com

www.teamgb.com

www.thehawickpaper.co.uk

www.the peerage.com

www.therugby historysociety.co.uk

www.therugbypaper.co.uk

trackfield.brinkster.net

unequipped-benchpress.de

www.victoriacrossonline.co.uk

www.visitdarlington.com

www.westbriton.co.uk

www.wimbledon.com

www.worldrugbymuseumblog.wordpress.com

www.wru.co.uk